Romances of the Archive
in
Contemporary British Fiction

D0707292

Romances of the Archive in Contemporary British Fiction is a lively discussion of the debates about the uses of the past contained in British fiction since the Falklands crisis. Drawing on a diverse and original body of work, Suzanne Keen provides a detailed examination of the range of contemporary 'romances of the archive,' a genre in which British novelists both deal with the loss of Empire and a nostalgia for the past, and react to the postimperial condition of Great Britain. Keen identifies the genre and explains its literary sources from Edmund Spenser to H.P. Lovecraft and John LeCarre. She also accounts for the rise in popularity of the archival romance and provides a context for understanding the British postimperial preoccupation with history and heritage.

Avoiding a narrow focus on postmodernist fiction alone, Keen treats archival romances from A.S. Byatt's Booker Prize–winning *Possession* to the paperback thrillers of popular novelists. Using the work of Peter Ackroyd, Julian Barnes, Lindsay Clarke, Stevie Davies, Peter Dickinson, Alan Hollinghurst, P.D. James, Graham Swift, and others, Keen shows how archival romances insist that there is a truth and that it can be found. By characterizing the researcher who investigates, then learns the joys, costs, and consequences of discovery, *Romances of the Archive* persistently questions the purposes of historical knowledge and the kind of reading that directs the imagination to conceive the past.

SUZANNE KEEN is a professor of English at Washington and Lee University in Lexington, Virginia.

Romances of the Archive
in
Contemporary British Fiction

SUZANNE KEEN

UNIVERSITY OF TORONTO PRESS
Toronto Buffalo London

© University of Toronto Press Incorporated 2001
Toronto Buffalo London
Printed in Canada

Reprinted in paperback 2003

ISBN 0-8020-3589-2 (cloth)
ISBN 0-8020-8684-5 (paper)

∞

Printed on acid-free paper

National Library of Canada Cataloguing in Publication Data

Keen, Suzanne
Romances of the archive in contemporary British fiction

Includes bibliographical references and index.
ISBN 0-8020-3589-2 (bound). – ISBN 0-8020-8684-5 (pbk.)

1. English fiction – 20th century – History and criticism.
2. Libraries in literature.   3. Archives in literature.   4. Research in
literature.   I. Title.

PR881.K38 2001   823'.91409   C2001-901695-6

University of Toronto Press acknowledges the financial assistance to its
publishing program of the Canada Council for the Arts and the
Ontario Arts Council.

University of Toronto Press acknowledges the financial support for its
publishing activities of the Government of Canada through the
Book Publishing Industry Development Program (BPIDP).

for
Fran and Edward,
my interlocutors

Contents

Acknowledgments

Folk wisdom says that having a child adds two years to the time it takes to finish a book. It surely would have been even longer had it not been for the aid of babysitters and caregivers. Heartfelt thanks to Alyssa Sellers, Lizzie Perkins, Barbara Dickens, Maya Ujie, Lesley Hawkins, Hayes and Celeste Larsen, Courtney Miller, Taylor Horner, Miller Wild, and Stephanie Wolfe for the care they provided. Glenn Grants from Washington and Lee University paid for vital hours of babysitting during the summers of 1998 and 1999. Marai Wise, Diane Mason, Lisa D'Amelio, Catherine Bodnar, Maryam Broomall, Theresa Rhodes, and Suzanne Friedrichs of the Montessori Center for Children have my eternal gratitude, as do Stephanie Wilkinson, Duane Zobrist, Beth Belmont, and Laura Brodie. Finally, my son Jacob reminded me every day that I should be 'all done reading now.'

I am indebted to the National Endowment for the Humanities for a fellowship year and to the Beinecke Rare Book and Manuscript Library at Yale University for the John D. and Rose H. Jackson Fellowship, which supported my study of the Peter Ackroyd papers. A sabbatical leave from Washington and Lee University enabled me to complete my work; Dean Laurent Boetsch of Washington and Lee found the money to supplement subvention from the Glenn Grant fund. I am grateful to all these sources for their material support. Sandy O'Connell made life in the English Department easy and pleasant. Especial thanks to Claude Rawson, Ian Duncan, Vincent Giroud, Pat Willis, and Harry Stout, Master of Berkeley College. My colleagues Edward Adams, Marc Conner, Kary Smout, Jim Warren, and Lesley Wheeler helped me hone grant applications. Though they had never met me, David Leon Higdon and Michael Gorra generously criticized early drafts of my grant proposal. Countless people talked to me about romances of the archive, supplying titles of novels and significantly broadening the range of my reading. I am indebted to Anna Brodsky, Barbara Brown, Edwin Craun, Ian Duncan, John Elrod, Elizabeth Fowler, Michael Gorra, Louise Halper, John Hollander, Jim Hutchisson, William P. Keen, Tim Lubin, Larry Manley, Ellen Mayock, Michael O'Driscoll, Claude Rawson, Katherine Rowe, Taylor Sanders, Adam Storch, Dabney Stuart, Grant Williams, Patrick Williamson, and Bob Youngblood. Lewis John, Yolanda Merrill, Nancy Castaldo, and A.L. Chua helped me with research problems. Jim Warren kept me going. Paul Baumann of *Commonweal Magazine* has helped me develop an appropriate prose style. Fran MacDonnell listened to every word of every chapter, often more than once. For tireless processing of interlibrary loans and steady acquisition of many volumes, I am grateful to Betsy Brittigan and Annette John, respectively. Unlike the obstructing guardians of so many romances of the archive, the librarians at the Leyburn Library, Washington and Lee University, are the epitome of generosity and indefatigible resourcefulness. In the last stages, I have benefited from the advice of editors and readers at the University of Toronto Press. Thanks are due to Kristen Pederson, Barbara Porter, and John St James. Needless to say, the inevitable errors within these pages belong to me alone.

Romances of the Archive
in
Contemporary British Fiction

1

Contemporary Fiction, Postimperial Conditions

The past few decades of British fiction have witnessed a proliferation of representations of archives in which scholarly and amateur characters seek information in collections of documents. Copious examples can be enumerated from serious and popular British fiction. These stories of archival research occur not only in postmodern novels and literary fiction, but also in popular sub-genres of the contemporary novel such as detective fiction, fantasies, gothics, and thrillers. Each of these sub-genres provides in its turn multiple examples of stories meeting my criteria to be called romances of the archive. They have scenes taking place in libraries or in other structures housing collections of papers and books; they feature the plot action of 'doing research' in documents. They designate a character or characters at least temporarily as archival researchers, as questers in the archive. They unabashedly interpret the past through its material traces; they build on a foundation of 'documentarism,' answering the postmodern critique of history with invented records full of hard facts.[1] Despite the prevailing view that postmodernism has scuttled old-fashioned notions of Truth, by far the majority of romances of the archive seek and find solid facts, incontrovertible evidence, and well-preserved memories of times past. In the face of postmodern scepticism, this kind of contemporary fiction claims that its world-making can answer questions about what really happened, though it does so without surrendering its licence to invent. Some romances of the archive win the approval of professional historians; others revel in the counterfactual freedoms of make-believe. Thus, a lively debate about the uses of the past can be discovered in romances of the archive, where British writers conjure up earlier time periods not only in the disciplined mode of historical fiction, but as fictional contributions to a shared and defended heritage.[2]

Written in a period often characterized as one of postimperial decline and shrinking global status, contemporary British romances of the archive characteristically invoke historical periods in which the British (often English) national story is central and influential. This means neither that romances of the archive celebrate the national past uncritically nor that they adopt a single philosophy of history. Written by a wide array of novelists, including Peter Ackroyd, Kingsley Amis, Julian Barnes, A.S. Byatt, Lindsay Clarke, Stevie Davies, Peter Dickinson, Margaret Drabble, Patricia Duncker, Robert Goddard, Robert Harris, Alan Hollinghurst, P.D. James, Penelope Lively, Adam Mars-Jones, Lawrence Norfolk, Charles Palliser, Vikram Seth, Graham Swift, Barry Unsworth, Alan Wall, Nigel Williams, and A.N. Wilson, romances of the archive employ the research quest to connect separate time periods, deeper and nearer pasts. By characterizing the researcher who investigates, and then learns the joys, costs, and consequences of discovery, romances of the archive persistently question the purposes of historical knowledge and the kind of reading that directs the imagination to conceive the past. Perhaps the central romance of these fictions lies in their contention that research into the past does anything at all; rarely do we find a romancer of the archive who ceaselessly reads and searches for documents just for the fun of it – simply learning for the sake of adding to the store of human understanding. Instead, the fun of research quests lies in their adventure formulae and their exceptionally consequential effects. In romances of the archive, characters are transformed, wrongs righted, disasters averted, villains exposed, crimes solved.

Perhaps the most readily recognizable version of a fictional researcher is the detective who pores over scraps of paper for clues, finds the hidden or overlooked significance in documentary evidence, and uses brainpower to reveal the truth and solve the mystery of what really happened. Indeed, as Patricia Merivale and Susan Elizabeth Sweeney observe, 'The research novel is by far the most flourishing branch of the metaphysical detective story, at least in economic (bestseller) terms, perhaps because it is the least flamboyantly postmodernist' ('Game's Afoot' 20). In the 'tentative genealogy' proffered by Merivale and Sweeney, the research novel from Henry James to Paul Auster is a 'textualized, gentrified, palimpsestic/antiphonal' treatment of 'missing persons.' It bequeaths key characteristics to Merivale and Sweeney's object of study, the metaphysical detective story ('Game's Afoot' 18). As will be seen in chapter 3, 'Wellsprings,' I emphasize the research narrative's debt to classic detective fiction, extending Merivale's and Sweeney's perceptive work back a generation or two. Though the legacy of detective fiction makes up an important component of romances of the archive, this book comments on a diverse array of novels from all over the literary map.

Collecting a variety of fiction under the umbrella of the term romances of the archive points up the problem of why so many different kinds of fiction share these settings, plot actions, characters, and questions about the past. Romances of the archive often present a past inflected less by academic history than by British heritage. In Jonathan Raban's words, this heritage (so often substituted for history by Margaret Thatcher and her followers) means 'something we have possession of after the death of the original owners' that we are 'free to use ... as we choose' (Mrs. Thatcher 24). The history invoked by romances of the archive is predominantly a usable past, so this book also confronts fictional representations of the past that, from a postmodern perspective, seem conservative, nostalgic, defensive, or insufficiently sceptical about finding the truth. Thus, I make the case for a broader view of contemporary British fiction than one focused solely on postmodernist novels – by which I mean those contradictory, discontinuous, sceptical, ontological, border-violating, anachronism-loving, game-playing, fabulating fictions that have understandably fascinated critics and theorists of contemporary literature. I concur with Brian McHale, one of the most important of these critics, when he comments that 'postmodernism should not be defined so liberally that it covers all modes of contemporary writing, for then it would be of no use in drawing distinctions' (Postmodernist 4).

Seeing how contemporary British fiction deploys the romance of the archive to argue about the uses of the past depends upon a wider range than just the narrow canon of postmodern novels so often singled out by literary critics.[3] This means not dismissing postmodern fiction, but comparing the ideas in what Linda Hutcheon calls 'historiographic metafictions' with the attitudes of a variety of contemporary novels often left out of critics' discussions.[4] Postmodernist fiction's debunking treatment of history, facts, events, evidence, objectivity, disinterestedness, and truth represents only one of many points of view. I believe that we can understand postmodern fiction better if we also account for the other channels of the main stream, which, as I hope to show, also respond to the postimperial condition of Great Britain in the 1980s and 1990s. Martin Green observes that 'in 1900 Englishmen ruled a great empire, and their minds thrilled with power; now in the 1980s they have lost it, and their minds sag with the sadness of loss.' Novelists, of course, often express attitudes at odds with the broader culture in which they work, and readers do not find in contemporary fiction a universal lament for the lost British Empire. The recent vogue for romances of the archive suggests instead that the postimperial condition stimulates interest in and reconsiderations of the national past that are not necessarily best served by postmodernist aesthetics. Writing in the early 1980s, Green points out that the literary significance of the 'doom of empire' has not been recognized (*English Novel* 1); from the vantage point of the end of the millennium we might agree that this 'obvious' and 'enormous' change has in fact been recorded in the burgeoning work on postcolonial writing of all kinds. The highly productive and much broader view of literature in English encouraged by postcolonial approaches has effectively replaced a British-centred view of literature in many quarters. In the small world of literary criticism, contemporary British fiction – though widely read, reviewed, and taught – often falls between the postcolonial and the postmodern stools. This study attempts to balance upon them in order to respond to what one postmodern theorist disparages as 'that large number of authors still writing traditional plot-and-character novels' (Ermarth *Sequel to History* 6).

The remaining pages of this introduction outline the stages of my argument, establish the aims, terms, and limits of my study, explain my approach to fiction, and situate the reader in respect to contemporary British literature – meaning not just recent books, but a distinct literary period dating from the 1950s through the turn of the millennium. Readers hoping to isolate the pages on a particular novel will find this introduction and the index their best starting points. Though my chapters are not organized exclusively by types of fiction, a glance at the chapter summaries (p. 24 ff.) will guide a reader to the sections focused on fantasies, detective stories, or other sub-genres of interest. Throughout this book I make every effort to write about fiction in terms that a novel-reader can understand without resorting to an encyclopedia of literary terms. However, good criticism, just like good car repair or cooking, requires the use of some specialized language. All literary-critical jargon has been defined right where it first appears, though in the interests of brevity, I have not redefined terms when I use them more than once. Matters of history and literary history I have woven into my main analysis under the assumption that context enriches a reader's understanding of the work under scrutiny. I occasionally refer to events and dates, with brief explanations and footnotes that lead a curious reader to some of the many reputable and accessible histories of the British Empire and the contemporary postcolonial world. Finally, the thread of my argument about British fiction's engagement with debates about the uses of the past confronts issues that arise out of the teaching of school history and from historiography (the techniques, theories, methods, and principles of historical research and writing). Though some recent historiographical writing has become as challenging to the lay reader as literary theory, I assume throughout that the contested topics of historiography can be presented in plain language.

I am a feminist literary critic who takes a mixed approach to studying fiction, blending cultural studies, narrative theory, and genre criticism. I began my work with the Victorian novel, where it is not considered odd to bring matters of form, context, politics, gender, and accounts of the material conditions of authorship together. Questions of form and content dovetail here, in a study analysing narrative strategies, themes, and contexts in a core sample of novels. A number of important theorists, critics, and teachers have helped me craft my hybrid approach. Without the work of Edward Said (*Orientalism* [1978]), current postcolonial theory and criticism is unimaginable, but his *Culture and Imperialism* (1993) has also dramatically revised the way critics think about the central texts of the English novelistic tradition, directing our attention to the traces of Britain's imperial past in British fiction. My work on contemporary British fiction carries an aspect of Said's project forward to the present day, though perhaps it should be acknowledged that in the views of some postcolonial critics, this would mean that it shares a weakness – in the form of a continuing interest in the English novel. So be it. My primary intellectual allegiance to Raymond Williams, the great English cultural materialist critic, shows in my assumption that the forms of writing (both popular and literary) express and embody in culture some of the most pressing contests among residual, emergent, and dominant political ideas.[5] Williams's terms describe the cultural forms existing in a specific time period – the old, the new, and the everyday overlapping. Williams suggests that whatever the dominant form of the day may be, 'a new structure of feeling will usually already have begun to form, in the social present' (*Marxism* 132). This emergent form can be discerned despite the familiarity of the dominant and residual forms. Because romances of the archive have what I call wellsprings in many different older source texts and literary kinds, they owe much to residual forms of imagining. Structurally, the romance of the archive embodies a still dominant form of narrative, the English novel, to reimagine the past and reactivate residual forms. By studying a genre that germinates and breaks into full flower during a definable period of years, however, I attend to an emergent response to the dominant postimperial context. Though I am not a Marxist critic, I am indebted to Williams's way of thinking about artistic forms as expressing cultural change.

It follows that my feminism is of the variety that cannot fail to notice how the operations of power in the world and in literature are often represented in gendered terms. I consider Rita Felski, Susan Stanford Friedman, Catherine Gallagher, and Mary Poovey important influences on my convictions that gendered forms of imagining intersect with specific historical circumstances. Feminist narratologists Robyn Warhol and Sally Robinson have provided me with useful models for studying the way narrative organizes perceptions of gender within culture (on behalf of dominant culture and also giving voice to strategies of resistance). Naturally, I am interested in women writers: contemporary fiction would be impoverished without them. However, *Romances of the Archive* is not a work of 'gynocriticism,' that sort of feminist criticism that focuses exclusively on the works of women writers. Rather, I treat both female and male authors and attend to the gendering of the central motifs in their romances of the archive, asking how gender and sexuality inflect contemporary quest romances, their 'delving' into archives, their character-researchers, and the uncovered results of their searches.

Narrative theory and genre criticism both provide rich descriptive vocabularies for critics of the novel, and specialized terms from these areas often appear in the pages that follow, with definitions and explanations of their usefulness. Narratology's interest in discovering the shared structures of seemingly dissimilar stories, and its willingness to consider humble examples as well as high-literary texts, certainly influences my comparative method and my desire to describe a class of texts. My argument with critics who see contemporary fiction through the limiting lens of postmodernism depends on looking at examples that are not always taken seriously; by now cultural studies has authorized the inclusion of a wide range of texts, not only those that have garnered critical praise and prizes. Even as he sceptically undermines the possibility of a contemporary genre criticism, Fredric Jameson admits that 'the older generic categories do not, for all that, die out, but persist in the half-life of the subliterary genres of mass culture, transformed into the drugstore and airport paperback lines of gothics, mysteries, romances, bestsellers, and popular biographies, where they await the resurrection of their immemorial, archetypal resonance' (*Political* 107). This project plumbs the depths of these subliterary categories, and my argument about the pervasiveness of romances of the archive depends in part on the evidence they provide. Departing from narratology's pure structuralist analysis for a contextualist approach to narrative and genre allows me to offer a more persuasive explanation for the popularity and cultural functions of the genre I describe. Not least, these texts show that ideas about history, heritage, and the uses of the past flourish in zones far from the rarified areas of serious literary fiction. Examining the conversation of history, historiography, and literature has been made possible by many theorists of history. Like many readers of my generation, I began with Hayden White, who is always a stimulating guide, but as will become plain, I am at least as indebted to the earlier historiographers (Carl Becker, Herbert Butterfield, R.G. Collingwood, J.H. Plumb, *et alia*), whose essays helped to shape several generations of novelists' ideas about the uses of the past.

As far as my main subject goes, this book comes out of decades of pleasure reading. My primary materials are the novels and short stories of contemporary British writers, so an interest in fiction is all that I require of my readers. My references to book reviews, interviews, magazine articles, and scholarly criticism acknowledge areas of indebtedness and alternative views. Like the theoretical discussions, these notes can be safely disregarded by the non-professional reader. In a few cases I footnote the URLs of scholarly websites or direct the reader's attention to materials available on the World Wide Web. I have tried to refer only to sites that pass muster as reputable sources and as relatively durable presences on the Internet, though no one can guarantee what will happen when we actually type addresses into our web browsers.

As this cautious step in the direction of the electronic 'e-book' indicates, more and more research is conducted and presented on computers. Nowadays, even the most erudite of the old-fashioned paper-and-notecard scholars must pay attention to listserv discussions, e-mail, and websites providing (or purporting to offer) fast and easy access to the key materials of their fields. The rare library still keeps its physical card catalogue up-to-date, so even the most resistant researcher must navigate electronic catalogues. In fact few scholars would readily return to the slower, harder ways when they have been replaced by efficient and reliable substitutes. Yet many scholars and teachers fear that the traditional and still essential methods of conducting research in books, printed periodicals, and papers will be neglected by students whose first impulse is to plug keywords into a search engine on the Internet. In the face of this information revolution, nostalgia for the old ways, inconvenient and expensive though they were, infuses fictional romances of the archive. Featuring as it always does hands-on work in actual papers, and requiring real travel on the part of questing characters, the romance of the archive invests scholarly research with glamour and excitement. No one in a romance of the archive gets carpal-tunnel syndrome from too much time at the computer keyboard. Yet as I will argue, the efflorescence of British romances of the archive cannot be explained merely as a reaction to the postmodern condition of the information age. Instead, a pervasive set of responses to the loss of Empire and a half-century of postimperial diminishment of status defines the contemporary period of English literature. A more extensive explanation of my argument follows, in a section that begins by defining the key terms that recur throughout this study.

'Romance of the archive' suggests both a kind of story and an attitude towards the past. For a reader attuned to poststructuralist literary theory, the phrase might also imply a relationship to Jacques Derrida's recent writings on Freud (in *Archive Fever* [1995]) and Michel Foucault's *Archaeology of Knowledge* (1971). Though in chapter 2 I will have a few words to say about both Derrida and Foucault's influential uses of the term 'archive,' I should make plain at the outset that I employ the term 'archive' most literally. Though in a few special cases novelists deliberately invoke deconstructive or Foucauldian associations of the archive, mainly they imagine archives as places containing books and papers, vital settings for adventure plots in which research questers seek the truth. Each of the contemporary British examples of the romance of the archive I discuss thus contains scenes taking place in libraries or in other structures housing collections of papers and books. Each employs the plot action of 'doing research.' I do not discuss the traditional kind of novel consisting entirely of a wholly imaginary archive or collection, such as Richardson's *Clarissa* (1748–9), Wilkie Collins's *The Moonstone* (1868), or Doris Lessing's sequence *Canopus in Argos: Archives* (1979–83). These fictions expect the reader to play the role of the researcher in the archive, whereas romances of the archive represent fictional characters questing in the archive, like the literary biographer Mark Lamming, who finds two trunks of his subject's papers in Penelope Lively's *According to Mark* (1984). All romances of the archives have something to say about the proper uses of the past, but they do not all agree with one another about what happened or what it meant. Clashing perspectives on the past are often an important part of the story, and disagreements about what to do with discoveries are no less contentious. Lively illustrates the challenge of relativism by depicting the same scene three times over, in the versions of each person present (*According to Mark* 94–100). The biographer's task thus seems impossibly elusive, especially when compulsive liars and interested parties add unverifiable tales to the mix. Yet by reading the gaps, Mark's 'Lies and Silences file' grows, and he discovers the truth about a concealed tragedy in the writer's life. Feeling for the first time true sympathy for his subject, Mark Lamming experiences a crisis – should he tell all, or collude with the dead man's desire for privacy? Lively's interest lies in the transformation of her 'living' characters, so she focuses on the reverberations of the research quest in the biographer, who puts together his best version of a life, not gospel truth, but the closest thing 'according to Mark.'

Though I deliberately draw my examples from a wide variety of kinds of fiction, not only from realistic novels like those of Lively, I discover in romances of the archive shared conventions of an ancient kind of storytelling. Romance in its many forms contains supernatural occurrences, exotic places and people, love stories, and adventure plots. Within the constraints of the domestic realism of her fictional world, Lively gives Mark Lamming three delightful adulterous days travelling through France with the granddaughter of the writer whose life he studies. She goes off with another man, however, and in the end Lamming puts his suffering in perspective by contrasting it with the tragedy he has discovered in the life of his subject. Thus, the archival work pays off in the form not only of a better-researched product, but an improved character – tested, rebuked, and strengthened in the style of the romance quest.

Romance descends to contemporary readers and moviegoers in thrillers, gothics, horror, fantasy, westerns, love stories, and action adventures. Throughout the history of the English novel, romance interpenetrates a form devoted to the representation of ordinary everyday life, allowing some flexibility in respect to verisimilitude. Even high-brow postmodern fiction is often imbued with romance (and romance has sometimes been considered postmodern before its time).[6] Often described as the opposite of realism, romance lends elements to be intermingled with realistic details in mimetic novels. Here is an excerpt from Nathaniel Hawthorne's classic definition of romance from his preface to *The House of the Seven Gables* (1851):

When a writer calls his work a Romance, it need hardly be observed that he wishes to claim a certain latitude, both as to its fashion and material, which he would not have felt himself entitled to assume, had he professed to be writing a Novel. The latter form of composition is presumed to aim at a very minute fidelity, not merely to the possible, but to the probable and ordinary course of man's experience. The former – while as a work of art, it must rigidly subject itself to laws, and while it sins unpardonably so far as it may swerve aside from the truth of the human heart – has fairly a right to present that truth under circumstances, to a great extent, of the writer's own choosing or creation ... The point of view in which this tale comes under the Romantic definition lies in the attempt to connect a bygone time with the very present that is flitting away from us.[7]

All the works discussed in this study share the traits of romance enumerated above, even when they belong first to some more obvious sub-grouping of the novel. The presence within their fictional worlds of an archive ensures, in Hawthorne's words, an 'attempt to connect a bygone time with the very present that is flitting away from us.' The papers themselves physically link present and past, and the experience of the researcher makes the import of the bygone time live again.

I construe archives literally, as collections of documents and the places housing, protecting, and concealing them. As Paul Voss and Marta Werner have recently demonstrated, even the most painstaking definition can be slippery. They write:

The archive is both a physical site – an institutional space enclosed by protective walls – and an imaginative site – a conceptual space whose boundaries are forever changing ... If the first archons originally conceived of the archive as a space of pure knowledge, then for those who came after, including ourselves, the archive has more often revealed itself as an ideologically-charged space. This space, inseparable from the ensemble of operations deployed within it, confers order on its contents and creates a system whereby an official record of the past may be preserved and transmitted intact. The archive may be, in effect, a political space, a gendered space, a memorial space. ('Toward a Poetics of the Archive' i)

The inherent complications in the definition of 'archive' have sometimes led to the extension of archives to include (by analogy) museum collections, puzzles, labyrinths, mapping, anatomies, and fictional representations of memory. I regard the textual archive as sufficiently rich an ideological site by itself; by excluding its analogues I approach with greater specificity the question of why recent British fiction so frequently represents characters searching for something in collections of papers.

So common a phenomenon has attracted the attention of other critics. For instance, novelist Tim Parks writes of Vikram Seth's recent novel *An Equal Music* (1999): [W]e are thus treated to one of those episodes, now so familiar in contemporary fiction, where someone searches for the crucial but elusive text in specialist libraries and secondhand shops' ('Sentimental

Education' 20). Many more critics (notably David Leon Higdon, Steven Connor, Margaret Scanlan, and Frederick Holmes) have commented on the historical impulse so evident in contemporary British fiction. Higdon observes what he considers a

> very significant development in post-war fiction ... the interest shown in a new group of protagonists – biographers, bibliographers, historians, geologists, anthropologists, archaeologists, and even paleontologists – whose lives are caught up with the past. These protagonists define the spirit of the age as did the artist protagonists in the fiction of the 1910s and 1920s. Their restorations, excavations, journeys, and research into a culture's past parallel their search for individual identities and utilize the culture's artifacts as complex metaphors for complex inner processes. (*Shadows* 11–12)

Though recent critics are less prone to admit to discerning the spirit of the age in the plots, characters, and themes of fiction, genre criticism still provides a sturdy methodology for tracking emergent forms. This task does not require retreating into arid bibliography. Steven Connor sees the novel as one of the tools by which history is made. He studies the ways that contemporary fiction seeks 'to consider and dramatise its own place in contemporary history,' in terms of the novel's role in articulating 'the sense of national belonging and unbelonging' and its negotiating the relationship of groups and individuals to 'the narrative of the past' (*English Novel* 43). The novel even brings the composition of that historical narrative into question. As Linda Hutcheon observes, postmodern novels scrutinize the process of 'event becoming fact' (*Poetics* 76); she argues that historiographic metafiction is the quintessential postmodernist genre. Hayden White allows for a greater variety of kinds that fictionalize history, agreeing that '*docudrama, faction, infotainment, the fiction of fact, historical metafiction*' represent the 'new genres of postmodern parahistorical representation' (*Figural Realism* 67).[8] A broader account would reach beyond the novel to include the new documentary films, such as *The Thin Blue Line* (1988), and the new journalism.

To offer the benefits of a generic description that attends to literary genealogy, extra-literary contexts, formal traits, and prominent themes requires sustained treatment of a discrete set of examples representing a larger group. The romances of the archive treated in the subsequent chapters have been chosen as much for their differences from one another as for their shared traits, but they do possess striking resemblances. Their romance plots and questing characters emphasize the search for historical evidence in a fashion that opens the contemporary story world to fictive versions of the past. Visiting the atmospheric locations of library, bookshop, and special collection, romances of the archive provide opportunities for detective work and intellectual adventure. They can serve as repositories of memory, as alternatives to history, as verifications of the core values of heritage, and as places stocked with infinite hidden stories. They are rich in descriptions of documents, images, and manuscripts, and with embedded samples of these representative archival materials. Thus, writing a romance of the archive can justify a writer's desire to try a pastiche, or imitation, of an earlier writing style, or to create a fictive past world without adhering to the conventions of traditional historical fiction.[9] The research quest itself permits movement between times and spaces and invites reflection on the intentions and consequences of delving into the past. The central romance of the archive shared by the variety of novels I treat lies in the recovery or discovery of the 'truth,' a quasi-historical truth that makes sense of confusion, resolves mystery, permits satisfying closure, and, most importantly, can be located. The truth, suggests the marvelously yielding imaginary archive, has not been irrevocably lost.

According to most accounts, postmodernism represents a serious assault on the idea of truth or fixed knowledge.[10] According to others, postmodern writing is that literature authored in the era following the Second World War.[11] Both points would appear to be relevant to a study of the uses of the past in contemporary British fiction, though they cannot both be true simultaneously. Very few critics would agree that *all* British literature since 1945 disavows attempts to represent truths in favour of language games and experimentation, though Fredric Jameson makes a bold case for considering postmodernism the 'cultural logic of late capitalism,' which is to say, the condition of all people in all parts of the globe since the Second World War.[12] Since I do not share Jameson's Marxist views, I avoid the totalizing use of the term, following instead Linda Hutcheon and Brian McHale in considering postmodernism an important *style* of fiction (and the other arts) that appears during the contemporary period, in reaction to modernism. This style radically questions and revises long-held views about history, knowledge, truth, and representation.[13] I never use postmodern to indicate the literary period to which a work belongs, since periodization is one of the most vulnerable targets of postmodernism's critique of metanarratives (the stories we employ, consciously or by long habit, to organize and simplify our thinking about complicated aspects of the past). Unlike some postmodern theorists, however, I find the labels we use to divide up periods of literary production useful fictions.

When it comes to labeling British writings of the second part of the twentieth-century century, however, no consensus has yet been reached. Other than the term 'postmodern,' three terms are often used: contemporary, postcolonial, and postimperial. George Landow's 'Contemporary Postcolonial and Postimperial Literature in English' website[14] covers all the bases. 'Contemporary' indicates the time period (the second half of the twentieth century). 'Postcolonial' refers to the writing of people from nations formerly colonized by, or still seeking freedom from, the British Empire.[15] That the writing is in English distinguishes anglophone literature from postcolonial writings in languages inherited from other imperial powers, a useful clarification for African, Canadian, and Caribbean writing. 'Postcolonial' replaces and extends the now discarded label 'Commonwealth literature.' Because Landow includes British writers and does not want to call the inhabitants of the former imperial center 'postcolonial,' he uses the less common term 'postimperial' for contemporary British writers. (To acknowledge a wrinkle, some writers from Scotland, Northern Ireland, and less frequently Wales would consider themselves postcolonial writers urgently engaged in distinguishing themselves from a Britain that seems to be defined by Englishness.) Like Landow, I find it useful to distinguish between British and postcolonial writing.[16] I use 'contemporary' to designate that period of British literature that overlaps with decolonization (in the 1950s, 1960s, and 1970s, when most of Britain's imperial possessions gained independence) and the postimperial 1980s and 1990s. For many contemporary British novelists, the experience of decolonization, the crisis of Suez, the spasms of patriotism stirred up by the Falklands War, the transition to a postimperial condition, and the concomitant rise of the postcolonial novel in English come together to make the archive an especially vivid emblem of what remains when the Empire is no more.

The loss of what was the British Empire and British reconsideration of the imperial past inflect the romance of the archive's adventures – its goals, the risks it entails, and the treasure, in the form of knowledge, that it yields. From the relinquishing of the Indian subcontinent in 1947 to the return of Hong Kong to mainland China in 1997, Britain has shed its role as an imperial power in the second half of the twentieth century. Victory in war was tempered by nearly a decade of postwar privation and adjustment to a loss of status in the world. During the contemporary period, the expansion of the previous century underwent a steady contraction. The Empire that was adding foreign dominions in the nineteenth and early twentieth centuries disappeared, to be replaced by the Commonwealth of Nations, a voluntary association of dependencies and sovereign states. (Since 1931 the

Empire that was so vividly represented as the 'pink bits' on the map, covering a quarter of the world's territory and population, has not officially existed.) After the Second World War, the pace of true independence and self-government accelerated, with India and the newly created Pakistan gaining independence (1947). Many of the new nations accepted membership in the Commonwealth of Nations, which permitted an illusion of continuing world status in an era of emergent Soviet and North American superpowers. Events in the 1950s, especially the 1956 Suez crisis, marked British consciousness by dramatizing to a world audience their nation's diminished position in global politics.[17]

During the Suez crisis of 1956, Egypt's President Nasser nationalized the canal, after eighty years of British control. American President Dwight Eisenhower chose not to support what appeared to be an imperial adventure. Some Britons felt betrayed by their ally; others were mortified by their leaders' attempt to cling to imperial possessions.[18] Because Suez represents the most shocking blow to British national pride or, alternatively, the most embarrassing recurrence of imperial adventuring, 1956 makes a useful date for pinpointing the start of the contemporary period. Like the range of responses to the Vietnam War, the reaction to Suez marks a generation, not through unanimity, but through the experience of dissent and violently felt differences of opinion. For younger writers, other social changes and historical events (such as the Falklands Islands war) loom larger, but they amplify, as in an echo chamber, the resonance of Suez. Because it transpires over decades, postwar decolonization effects all four generations of contemporary writers.

Particularly when studying attitudes towards the past, it is vital to keep in mind that contemporary writing is not the product of a single peer group. In a single year, a reader of new fiction may find side-by-side in the bookstore works by writers in their eighties, sixties, forties, and even their twenties. Penelope Fitzgerald's last publication shared shelf space with Zadie Smith's first book. These novels may have relatively little in common besides a publication date, but they are all examples of contemporary fiction. Writers contributing to contemporary British fiction belong to four distinct generations. Members of the eldest group, such as Graham Greene, Elizabeth Bowen, and Anthony Powell, were all born before the Great War (1914–18). As their early works were published before the conclusion of the Second World War, they can be considered either modern or contemporary writers. Greene, Bowen, and Powell, for instance, began as modern writers, but all published significant works into the late 1960s and early 1970s.[19] In the teens and twenties was born the first unambiguously 'contemporary' generation, including Anthony Burgess, Muriel Spark, Doris Lessing, Iris Murdoch, P.D. James, Kingsley Amis, Nadine Gordimer, Christine Brooke-Rose, Anita Brookner, and Alan Sillitoe. (Though older, William Golding belongs to this group, because his first novel was published in 1954.) These writers, with the exception of the late-blooming Anita Brookner, published their first fiction in the 1950s; many of them are still producing today. A third generation includes writers born in the 1930s and early 1940s: Fay Weldon, John Le Carré, Malcolm Bradbury, Penelope Lively, David Lodge, A.S. Byatt, Emma Tennant, Margaret Drabble, Michael Moorcock, and Angela Carter. The fourth generation of contemporary novelists, among them Julian Barnes, Graham Swift, Salman Rushdie, Ian McEwan, Hilary Mantel, Martin Amis, Peter Ackroyd, Kazuo Ishiguro, Sara Maitland, and Jeanette Winterson,[20] came into being after the war. (Zadie Smith, young enough to look up to Jeanette Winterson as a role model, may be regarded as the advance guard of the first twenty-first-century generation.) These young writers can be expected to continue publishing fiction well into the next millennium. Until it becomes clear to us what the commonly adopted end date of the current literary period will be (perhaps the year 2000 will be too strong a candidate to allow for alternatives), critics of contemporary British literature can expect that more and more of what they read and evaluate will be written by people whose experience of their nation has been conditioned by decolonization and a declining global status.

One advantage in emphasizing the postimperial nature of the contemporary period lies in its relationship to the already-established terminology of 'postcolonial' writing. Postcolonial and postimperial contemporary writers share some of the same historical background, though they naturally view that background from dramatically different perspectives. From the point of view of the postimperial centre, postcolonial writing permanently alters the meaning of 'English' literature. The period marked by the Suez crisis also witnesses the addition of anglophone postcolonial novelists such as V.S. Naipaul, Chinua Achebe, Nadine Gordimer, Patrick White, Doris Lessing, and others to the field of English novelists. With novels and volumes of stories such as Naipaul's *A House for Mr. Biswas* (1961), Achebe's *Things Fall Apart* (1958), Gordimer's *The Soft Voice of the Serpent* (1953), White's *Voss* (1957), and Lessing's *The Grass Is Singing* (1950), writers born and raised far from Great Britain made significant contributions to English fiction. The Booker Prize, founded in 1969, explicitly includes the English novels of writers from all Commonwealth nations and states formerly part of the British Empire, so long as the novels are published in Great Britain.[21] In the last two decades, the promise has been fulfilled, as nearly half the Booker Prizes have gone to postcolonial writers, including Salman Rushdie (1981), Thomas Keneally (1982), J.M. Coetzee (1983 and 1999), Keri Hulme (1985), Peter Carey (1988), Ben Okri (1991), Michael Ondaatje (1992), Roddy Doyle (1993), and Arundhati Roy (1997).

The enrichment of the English novel by postcolonial writers is justly celebrated, but jealousy, competition, and defensiveness show in the controversies surrounding the increasingly multicultural Booker Prize short lists. The same process that has enriched the English novel with works by anglophone writers from all over the globe also inflects British writers' sense of the century, as their representations of archives show. Even as the Empire writes back,[22] the contemporary British novel also turns towards the past, assesses the present, and imagines the future of the nation. Romances of the archive, whether leading to discoveries of crimes and shames of the past, or defending Britain's historical role in world affairs, evince a continuing fascination with imperial history. Remarkably, the contraction of the Empire in the contemporary period has enhanced rather than detracted from the status of the archive, since the libraries and collections leave a relatively positive legacy compared to many of the real-life situations of the postcolonial world.

The connection between the growth of the British Empire and establishment of real and imaginary archives in the nineteenth and twentieth centuries has been made by Thomas Richards. In his 1993 study *The Imperial Archive: Knowledge and the Fantasy of Empire* Richards argues that the expanding British Empire was held together by information (*Imperial* 1, 4). Yet for Richards, the imperial archive was 'neither a library [n]or a museum, though imperial fiction is full of little British libraries and museums scattered all over the globe. Rather the imperial archive was a fantasy of knowledge collected and united in the service of state and Empire' (6). No one person could ever master the contents of this imaginary body of knowledge. The 'archives' of Richards's account are projects rather than places, each portion, like the British Museum, a part of the 'collectively imagined junction of all that was known or knowable' (11). In the 1860s, for instance, imperial surveyors walked at a set pace over the terrain of Tibet, disguised as monks in order to foil the Tibetan government's ban on foreign geographers. Other Victorian systems of knowledge treated by Richards include morphology (the science of form) and the 'double' of the imperial archive, the imaginary body of knowledge belonging to the intelligence agencies of the enemy. Once the process of imperial expansion goes into reverse, these processes and projects fossilize into the boundary lines, maps, records, collections, and actual archives of the postimperial and postcolonial worlds.

In modern (early-twentieth-century) British fiction, the library's connection with the imperial past cannot escape notice. In her novel *Between the Acts* (1941), Virginia Woolf sets at odds the library, 'the heart of the house ... the nicest room in the house' (*Between* 16), and the dilapidated imperial fantasies of the old man who snoozes within: 'drowsily, seeing as in a glass, its lustre spotted, himself, a young man helmeted; and a cascade falling. But no water; and the hills like grey stuff pleated; and in the sand a hoop of ribs; a bullock maggot-eaten in the sun; and in the shadow of the rock savages; and in his hand a gun' (*Between* 17). Written during the early years of the Second World War, *Between the Acts* already suggests the contraction of Empire; Colonel Mayhew protests not the pageant's treatment of two centuries in a quarter of an hour, but the omission of the British Army: 'What's history without the Army, eh?' (157).

In the last several decades, the vestige grows slighter and slighter. In contrast to the imperial adventure, such as the British India Survey's covert mapping of Tibet, the postimperial walking tour either visits former possessions, as in Peter Hopkirk's *Quest for Kim* (1996), or can be confined to the well-tramped footpaths of Great Britain. Paul Theroux's 1983 travel book *The Kingdom by the Sea: A Journey around Great Britain* undertakes such a tour. As an American, Theroux may overstate the sad state of English energy, curiosity, and self-knowledge in the early 1980s, but he captures a late moment in the struggle for Empire. The repeated line, '*It's like this Falklands business,*' makes a refrain of the attitudes of English people. When the Argentines sink the *Sheffield*, and the British suffer their first casualities, Theroux reports from Littlestone-on-Sea: 'As long as the Falklands War has been without British deaths, it was an ingenious campaign, clever footwork, an adventure. That was admired here: a nimble reply, no blood, no deaths. But this was dreadful and incriminating and it had to be answered. It committed Britain to a struggle that no one really seemed to want' (*Kingdom* 39). The painful conjunction in the reaction to the Falklands crisis of national pride, disaffection from the government, and embarrassment at the petty stakes makes the contrast of the once-great imperial centre to its more confident past all too plain. Though Theroux cannot be taken as a neutral observer, similar utterances of his British contemporaries can be picked out from the general celebration and jingoistic din of the time. David Monaghan argues in *The Falklands War: Myth and Countermyth* (1998) that the two-month-long 1982 conflict 'lasted long enough for Margaret Thatcher to transform the struggle for the Falklands into a myth of national rebirth in which feats of arms would open up the way for a simultaneous retrieval of pre-Welfare State verities and radical change along monetarist economic lines' (*Falklands* xi). Working strenuously against Thatcher's version, 'countermythic works' recast the official story as 'a network of lies constructed by a self-interested politician willing to distort language and history in order to advance her own political agenda' (xiii).

Ian McEwan's screenplay for Richard Eyre's film *The Ploughman's Lunch* (1985) makes this point by setting the researches of the repellent revisionist historian James Penfield against Thatcher's response to the Falklands crisis.[23] 'The eruption of jingoism, the thunderous Churchillian rhetoric which was so readily available to politicians of all persuasions,' McEwan writes of this episode, 'showed that this was less a matter of real territorial ambition, or a desire to protect "our own"; but, like Suez, more an affair of the heart, of who we thought we were, who we wanted to be' (*Ploughman's* vi). James Penfield's project in the film is a revision of the meaning of Suez, 're-interpreted while the amateur historian unconsciously acted out in his private life a sequence of betrayals and deceits which ... parallel the events he was distorting in his history' (v). If history can be manipulated to suit the market (in the film, the Suez crisis must be presented in a fashion inoffensive to American college students [6]), heritage has already been manufactured for purchase by gullible consumers. The traditional English pub food of the film's title is revealed as 'the invention of an advertising campaign they ran in the early sixties to encourage people to eat in pubs. A completely successful fabrication of the past' (29–30). McEwan's layering of inauthenticity upon inauthenticity can be seen as a homage to his mentor Malcolm Bradbury's *The History Man* (1975), in which the relationship between theory and practice (and its catastrophic effects on the 'lifestyle' of the liberated sociology professor Dr Howard Kirk) is also represented in a heavily ironic fashion. Penfield's career-advancing, politically expedient, and fundamentally corrupt revision of recent history may be all that is possible for the post-Suez generations. This makes younger people especially vulnerable to being taken in by invented traditions and history, to take the grimmest view offered by McEwan's screenplay. As David Monaghan observes, the reshaped official myth of recent history functions 'as a metaphor for a neoconservative Britain utterly lacking in the integrity fundamental to the fulfillment of Thatcher's promises of national rebirth' (*Falklands* xiii). A depressing assessment of the meaning of British past, present, and future arises out of this self-critical understanding: 'Britain is no longer a country infused with a spirit of new hope but one where power and wealth are concentrated in the hands of a small corrupt elite, leaving the rest of the population to seek escape from their unsatisfactory lives in nostalgia or violence' (*Falklands* xiii).

In representing research, the authors of post-Falklands romances of the archive give their characters more complicated, more nuanced, and more self-conscious relationships with the past and with present contexts than Bradbury's and McEwan's protagonists possess. Penelope Lively's Mark Lamming reflects that his work on his literary biography 'would be inappropriately associated with the predatory profile of Mrs. Thatcher rearing from the front pages of newspapers. Your own doings were interwoven with the coarser and more indestructible fabric of history, to give the movement of time a grander name than it seems to deserve when one is part of it' (*According to Mark* 27). The disconnect between historical context and individual activities invoked by Lively in this 1984 novel depends upon an earlier dissevering of national and personal identity, a retraction from historical context that must still be acknowledged at least as backdrop or part of the flavour of the times. Ian McEwan describes the cause of this disconnection: 'To a generation the Suez crisis of 1956 appeared to speed the collapse of the idea – by that time an illusion anyway – of Britain as a world power. The government of the day had acted deceitfully while trying to appear virtuous. Our subservient role to the Americans was dramatised, and the crisis initiated a long period of national introspection' (*Ploughman's* v). The meaning for a writer of the 1980s of this event a generation earlier suggests that Suez emblematizes the powerful disillusionment following upon Britain's victory over the Axis.[24] McEwan writes:

> The Falklands War was not, of course, a re-run of the Suez crisis. The Egyptians had a legitimate claim on the canal that runs through their territory, while the Argentinians had little more than an emotional claim on the Falkland Islands. However, the connections between the two events were striking. A large task force was to be despatched and lives were to be risked to regain territory which successive British governments had been trying quietly to unload on the Argentinians. The Islanders themselves had consistently been denied full British citizenship. It was not clear, then, and it is even less clear now, that the Government conducted negotiations in good faith to avoid armed conflict. (*Ploughman's* vi)

For McEwan, Suez haunts the Falklands crisis for personal reasons, as well. As an eight-year-old living in Libya in 1956, he was put with other English children in an armed camp, where they were kept for weeks for their own protection. As a result of this experience, the child who becomes the writer understands 'for the first time that political events were real and affected people's lives – they were not just stories in the papers that grown-ups read' (*Ploughman's* v). In this simple form McEwan articulates one of the primary impulses driving romances of the archive and connecting them with the Victorian Condition-of-England novels they resemble and revise: the impulse to account for the effects of historical events on ordinary people's lives and to make the accomplishments and crimes of the past real again by recovering them for sympathetic reimagining. But to what uses can writers of fiction put a recovered past? If, as David Monaghan argues, the self-critical antidote to jingoism transforms Britain into 'a decaying place where the past serves not as a repository of the national essence but as a nostalgic bolt hole for a despairing petit bourgeoisie,' then the future 'is likely to be even more violent and repressive than the present' (*Falklands* xvi). Romances of the archive tend to resist despairing conclusions, even as they acknowledge and encounter episodes from earlier periods of British imperial history.

Readers of romances of the archive might not immediately identify these texts as political, or even as historical. Yet in this study I insistently refer to ostensibly escapist pleasure-reading in political and historical terms. In this I follow the lead of scholar and literary critic Martin Green, who has devoted his career to the study of adventure, empire, power, masculinity, and their vicissitudes in the later twentieth century.[25] His sense of the decline of the adventure genre reflects the historical changes described above:

> The respectable adventure genre as a whole has had a career, which now seems to be in decline. That career is comparable and related to the career of white empire; more exactly, that career corresponds to the self-respect and self-image of empire. In terms of power, and of secret pride in that power, the white empire has never been so great as today. (And we should always be skeptical also about the decline of adventure fiction when it is men of letters who give us that news.) But empire's self-consciousness is uneasy today – in part accepting censure, in part resenting it, and as a whole preferring not to invite attention. This corresponds to an uneasiness in the adventure tale, which nowadays shows itself in a crude, self-disfiguring violence, or in an attempt at self-satire, or in would-be blends of adventure with comedy. (*Seven Types* 30–1)

Green's description of a tapped-out genre bespeaks the late twentieth century's mixed feelings about the fundamental ingredients of adventure, 'killing, conquering, dominating other people and countries or about building up hierarchies and empires of power' (28). The link between the postimperial context and the undergirding adventure stories (transformed from imperial romances into contemporary romances of the archive) makes attention to the vestiges of Empire rewarding.

For instance, J.G. Farrell's Booker Prize–winning novel *The Seige of Krishnapur* (1974) fictionalizes the seige of Lucknow (an episode in the Indian Revolution, or Sepoy uprising, of 1857). In the novel, as in the historical event, British administrators and their families hole up in a fortress during a revolutionary uprising against British occupation of India.[26] Farrell's novel both mocks and celebrates British power, exposes foolishness, and celebrates the heroism of those who held out in the seige. Farrell explodes the imperial archive in a spectacular vindication of an emblem of power. The representation of the archive shows what it used to be (a locus of knowledge and power), what it becomes (a hiding place), and how it is destroyed (it explodes). Paradoxically, in its destruction, the archive asserts the British capacity to confuse and distract their Indian attackers. At first, Farrell's Collector watches over a 'vernacular record room ... the very centre of the British administration in Krishnapur' (*Seige* 105). More records than could ever be consulted collect here, for 'in India all official proceedings, even the most trivial, were conducted in writing, and so the rapidity with which the piles of paper grew was alarming and ludicrous' (106). Cut off from the imperial centre by the seige, the Collector finds the archive a cozy hiding place, in which he indulges a fantasy of safety from bombardment:

> There were salt reports bound in red tape under each elbow; a voluminous, but extraordinarily comfortable correspondence with a local landowner concerning the Permanent Settlement cradled his back at just the right angle ... From outside, a few yards away, came the regular discharge of cannons and mortars; but inside, such was the thickness of the paper padding, one felt very safe indeed. (170)

Unexpectedly, Farrell not only exposes the false sense of security gained from hiding out in the archive, but also revises the source of power inhering in the papers. Not their bullet-stopping quality, but their destruction, halts the climactic advance of the Sepoys on the garrison, when an unseasonable snowstorm of 'large white flakes' – the scattered documents – blinds and confuses those who would challenge British power (233–4).

In *The Imperial Archive*, Tom Richards makes the persuasive case that the Victorian expansion of imperial domination went hand in hand with the acquisition and storage of knowledge in a vast and virtually unknowable archive. The meaning of the archive shifts in the contemporary period, during and after decolonization, as adventures of imperial romance contract into romances of the archive. Not every romance of the archive so directly invokes the link to imperial domination as does Farrell's *The Seige of Krishnapur*, but in novel after novel, the recovery of lost, concealed, or undervalued texts through archival research validates both the quester and the original collector, rescuing for the now something left over from the national past. From condemning to exonerating, the variety of verdicts about the documents and literature discovered in archives suggests that the work of understanding the uses of Britain's past makes a compelling project for contemporary fiction at the end of the century. The increase in romances of the archive suggests both a defence and a celebration of the novel and English literature itself, against the backdrop of Empire. The library provides access to specific historical periods of that imperial history – the beginnings of the East India Company in Lawrence Norfolk's *Lemprière's Dictionary* (1991), the eighteenth-century Liverpool slave trade in Barry Unsworth's *Sugar and Rum* (1988), the early-twentieth-century erotic adventure in colonial territories in Alan Hollinghurst's *The Swimming-Pool Library* (1988), the war years in many novels.

This study is not organized in historical order. It follows neither the order of the novels' publication nor the chronology of pasts depicted within the novels. The demands of generic description impose a different procedure. In the following two chapters, 'Romances of the Archive: Identifying Characteristics,' and 'Wellsprings,' the identifying characteristics of the romance of the archive are laid out and contextualized. Using as its central exemplar the most well-known British romance of the archive, A.S. Byatt's *Possession* (1989), chapter 2 describes the romance of the archive's key traits: its character-researchers; its romance adventure stories, in which 'research' features as a kernel plot action; its strong closure, with climactic discoveries and rewards; its depiction of discomforts and inconveniences suffered in the service of knowledge; its suggestion that sex and physical pleasure can be gained as a result of questing; its use of settings (such as libraries and country houses) that contain archives of actual papers; its revelation of material traces of the past holding the truth; and its evocation of history, looking back from a postimperial context.

Chapter 3 acknowledges that the romance of the archive arises out of a rich tradition of precursors, and undertakes the genealogical work of identifying sources for the elements of romances of the archive. The sources and analogues I examine suggest some of the representative texts and literary sub-genres (ranging from sixteenth-century allegorical quest romances to novels in the high-realist mode) from which romances of the archive inherit a complex set of formal characteristics and themes. These it reworks, responding to an end-of-the-millennium impulse to scrutinize, defend, expose, and celebrate Great Britain's imperial past. I argue here that in the wake of patriotism stirred up by the 1982 Falkland Islands conflict, the phenomenal success of Umberto Eco's *The Name of the Rose* (1980, trans. 1983) stimulates the writing of many romances of the archive by British writers.

In the fourth chapter, 'History or Heritage?' I provide an account of the cultural context in which romances of the archive should be placed and understood. Politicized debates about the appropriate uses of the past have run through recent discussions of history, British heritage, and the new National Curriculum for the teaching of school history. One does not have to be attending to the latest developments in postmodern historiography to feel invested in the meaning and uses of the past. As Penelope Lively's realistic novel *The Road to Lichfield* (1977) reminds us, many ordinary people experience something like the discoveries of archival research when clearing out a dead or dying loved one's desk, in search of unpaid bills and instructions to executors. In this sense, the surprises and forced re-evaluation of the past of the romance of the archive are not alien experiences to most readers of a certain age. This chapter imagines a humble origin for romances of the archive – ordinary authorial experiences. To put it in the simplest terms, because some novelists conduct research in order to write, their work comes to reflect their experiences in the archives. Yet the act of delving into the past does not automatically translate into the production of history, particularly when the quest for knowledge begins and ends with more personal motives. Two authors' contrasting romances of the archive illustrate the alternatives of history and heritage. Close readings of *Sugar and Rum* (1988) and *Losing Nelson* (1999) show Barry Unsworth meditating on the difficult process of writing historical fiction in a society more interested in 'heritage' than history. In contrast to the blocked writers of Unsworth's imagining, perhaps no novelist has so fluently produced pastiche of so many periods as Peter Ackroyd. He resolutely links the past with the present in his fictions of sympathetic connection and he celebrates a specifically English tradition in many of his novels and biographies. Presenting the 'heritage' version of the past in its most seductive form, Ackroyd's fictions transmute the research experience in time-shifting novels such as *Chatterton* (1987) and *The House of Doctor Dee* (1993).

The following three chapters treat fantasy, detective fiction, and realistic novels in order to focus on the formal traits and historiographical issues emphasized by romances of the archive in these different modes. Chapter 5, 'Time Magic and the Counterfactual Imagination,' examines the origins, originals, conspiracies, and explanations of 'time magic' fantasy fiction for adults. The more fantastic romances of the archive flirt with the collapse of time and distance by making research a hazardous, magical activity that threatens to obliterate the self, as the object of research takes over the researching subject. In these hermetic fictions, the successful containment of the dangerous archive's contents emphasizes the necessary distance between *then* and *now*. In the mode of H.P. Lovecraft, secrecy buffers and protects the present from full knowledge of past crimes and ancient evil. In chapter 6, 'Custody of the Truth,' I look closely at the four main types of detective fiction to discuss debates about the uses of the past for purposes of praise and blame. Fault-finding motivates many romances of the archive, and few subjects elicit such agitated response as war. The epistemological genre of detective fiction provides answers to mysteries. Once the truth about the past has been uncovered, these novels ask, what should be done with it? I closely examine three romances of the archive in which research quests for missing persons lead back to the Second World War years, and one that transpires in the more recent history of Pol Pot's Cambodia. In contradistinction to metaphysical detective fiction, in which 'finding the missing person' leads to the discovery that the seeker *is* the sought (Merivale and Sweeney 'Game's Afoot' 20), these romances of the archive leave their questers with the dilemma of who should retain custody of the truth once it has been recovered. In chapter 7, 'Envisioning the Past,' I show how realistic romances of the archive bridge the gap between the late twentieth century and the historical periods they seek to reach. In a group of more traditionally verisimilar novels, passionate researchers attempt to make connections with the past through archival quests. They are aided in their quests by the existence of physical evidence and visual records, which enliven and correct the documentary evidence. Informed by liberal, feminist, and queer perspectives, these novels connect with people in the past by exercising the sympathetic imagination. They sustain the romance element through their overt eroticism, which imbues with desire the acts of envisioning and interpreting the extraordinarily yielding past.

That romances of the archive celebrate Great Britain's national past as often as they expose and excoriate villainy shows not that British writers are immune to political correctness and its attendant narratives of heroical reversal, breast-beating, and redressing of injury, but that even in hypercritical mode, they create fictions of textual and visual evidence exonerating present-day characters, even when revealing awful truths about their ancestors. While part of the power of the archive lies in its capacity to enable discoveries and to reveal hidden things to the present quester, it also conveniently serves as an automatic device of displacement that means 'not *us*, now, but *them*, back then.' Whether denying, exposing, or attempting to mitigate historical sin and guilt, the anxious project of romances of the archive coincides with the burgeoning of postcolonial literature, which has made the novel in English a key instrument by means of which 'the Empire writes back,' in Salman Rushdie's phrase. The epilogue, 'Postcolonial Rejoinders,' suggests that British responses to the successes of postcolonial writing in the past two decades have flavoured the postimperial romance of the archive. That these novels often create exonerating fictions has not escaped the notice of postcolonial writers, and the book concludes by examining critical responses to romances of the archive in versions of the genre selected from international English literature.

Although not all British romances of the archive present defensive and unrepentant rejoinders to the reproaches of former colonial subjects, they share more than a habit of revisiting the past. As narratives, romances of the archive reinvest in corporeality, strong characterization, action, and closure. They remake the idealized and metafictional labyrinth into a tangible site – the library or private collection – in which more conventionally drawn characters do research. They capture the playfulness of Borges and Calvino, but they domesticate the archive by placing it in the university, in the British Museum or London Library, in the country house – in short, at home. Romances of the archive repeatedly insist that there is a truth and that it can be found in a library or a hidden cache of documents. Romances of the archive create temporarily risky worlds in which the character – and by extension the reader – can seek and find that truth. In the broadest terms, this book investigates the sources and shapes of a fantasy about the capacities and purposes of fiction. A reader's pleasure in these romances depends upon the thematizing of a researcher's pleasure. Since that pleasure in turn depends upon the recovery of truth from a fictive archive, it is my intention to scrutinize what kinds of truths these enticing fictions beguile us to accept.

2

Romances of the Archive:
Identifying Characteristics

The recent British novel is saturated with representations of archival research. Though the postmodern romancer seems at home in a labyrinthine library, and the detective is traditionally allowed a certain amount of digging through papers, a startlingly large number of fictional characters of recent creation perform the intellectual questing scholars call research. A list of recent romances of the archive would include writers of four generations and jumble realistic and historical novels, fantasy, feminist fictions, social satires, tales of counterfactual future worlds, thrillers, postmodern historiographic metafictions, detective stories, and 'serious' literary fiction. No study of this length can hope to comment on every writer producing romances of the archive, nor to enumerate all the examples, but some generalizations about their diversity can be made. Distinguished prizewinners sit cheek by jowl with popular best-sellers. The generic label embraces authors male, female, Scottish, Irish, English, gay, straight, left-leaning, right-leaning, lauded, and all-but-forgotten. For all their diversity of theme, technique, genre, politics, and perspective, these fictions share a preoccupation with the secrets and hidden truths that can be ferreted out of archives.[1] Even the most experimental of them relies on a fictional character, cast temporarily or permanently in the role of a researcher. This is stranger than it may seem at first glance.

To be a literary scholar has been a deadly attribute for a fictional character since George Eliot's Casaubon wasted his life in futile research, blighting the existence of Dorothea Brooke, and failing to produce *A Key to All Mythologies*. In the mainstream English realist tradition, too close an acquaintance with mouldering books, indices, monographs, bibliographies, slips of paper, and footnotes denotes inflexibility, lack of imagination, petty-mindedness, infirmity, and impotence. Romancers depict antiquarians and researchers rather more favourably, but even Walter Scott rarely lingers on the archival frame he creates to surround his historical adventures. Spies, detectives, and the fugitives in romances of pursuit can pause to examine collections of papers only so long as more exciting and violent activities follow without delay. Oddly enough, then, a scholarly habit of mind and an aptitude for interpreting texts has become, in recent British fiction, an attractive trait of fictional characters. (As I explain in the subsequent chapter, we have Umberto Eco and Indiana Jones to thank for at least some of the revision of the scholar's fictional image.)

As gratifying as this turn of events may be to those academics among us who have grappled with our research projects with the 'clear head, stout heart and common sense' recommended by G. Kitson Clark (*Guide for Research Students* 20), it must be granted that the make-over of the archival researcher into an action hero comes as a surprise. Filling out call-slips, enduring the inquiries of suspicious librarians, waiting for one's request to arrive, wading through pages, files, boxes, and cartloads of irrelevant material, transcribing in ever-dulling pencil, or getting migraines from staring at the laptop screen – these activities hardly seem candidates for what Seymour Chatman calls 'kernel' plot events: those key actions without which a summary of a plot would be inaccurate and misleading (*Story* 53–6). Yet in romances of the archive, research and discovery become kernel components of adventure plots, key actions in plots of discovery. These plot actions derive much of their significance from the impact of research on the questing characters, whether they find what they started out looking for or not.

In real life, the tedium of scholarship is indeed alleviated by a discovery, even a small one: archival research *can* be thrilling. But among the potential actions of fictional characters, doing research surely ranks fairly low on the scale of excitement. Since it is not an activity covered by what E.M. Forster calls 'the main facts in human life ... birth, food, sleep, love, and death' (*Aspects of the Novel* 47), library research cannot be justified on the grounds that Everyman, or Everywoman, experiences it. As a form of labour, archival research lacks proletarian credentials and requires too much self-suppression to be dignified as art. One might object that the literary novel in the second part of the century cares little for action and less for thrills, so that in eschewing adventure, it might indeed hit upon scholarship as the perfect occasion for character-revealing daydreaming.[2] Indeed, the inward-looking meditative fiction of memory may take its cue from a document, such as Miss Kenton's letter, considered and reconsidered by the butler Stevens in Kazuo Ishiguro's *The Remains of the Day*

(1989), but the representation of the character's consciousness invariably takes precedence over the stimulating text.[3] Another kind of novel, a favourite of modernists, detective novelists, and parodists, makes the reader into a 'researcher,' by presenting a potted collection of documents for examination and interpretation. In itself depicting no research, but inviting the reader to mimic the activity of a scholar or an interpreter who puts together the big picture (or, in the postmodern variant, in deconstructing the very idea of a final answer), a novel of this sort eliminates the representation of active scholarship.

The romance of the archive dares to be different; it hazards the casting of characters in the unprepossessing roles of researchers, readers, and thinkers. It makes an adventure out of the intellectual quest. Who better to carry out that quest, one might assume, than characters officially qualified to do research, already insiders of the academic world – the professors?

UNIVERSITY NOVELS ≠ ROMANCES OF THE ARCHIVE

In fact, full-fledged academic professionals rarely appear as central questing characters in romances of the archive. As the subsequent discussion of A.S. Byatt's *Possession* suggests, earning academic job opportunities may be one of the rewards on offer for a successful quester such as Roland Michell, but his very marginality qualifies him for his role in the romance of the archive and allows him to carry on unnoticed long enough to get a good lead in the race against his rivals, the professional scholars. Romances of the archive typically validate the insights and abilities of popular writers, amateur researchers, graduate students, detectives, and (in general) those lacking professional certification in scholarship or permanent academic posts. An academic outsider makes a better truth-finder than a 'qualified' researcher in romances of the archive. More intuitive, more prone to risk-taking, more powerfully motivated to *know* than a mere academic, the quester in the archive is less bound by conventions, less hampered by respect for hierarchy, and less concerned about career and reputation. For these reasons, romances of the archive rarely overlap with 'university,' 'academic,' or 'campus' novels, interchangeable labels for those works satirizing the follies of professors and academic administrators on both sides of the Atlantic.

Novels by David Lodge, the best known author of works in this subgenre, illustrate the typical handling of academic life and labour in contemporary fiction.[4] In his hands, the British Museum serves not as a site of intellectual work, but only as a backdrop against which we view his tormented character Adam Appleby's attempt to manage married life before birth control (*The British Museum Is Falling Down* [1965]). *Small World: An Academic Romance* (1984) features paired academics, one English and one American, both assiduously avoiding actual work in favour of gathering goodies and enjoying the perks of position. In *Nice Work* (1988), Lodge's adjunct faculty member, Robyn Penrose, learns more about her subjects, the Condition of England and the industrial novel, by driving away from the library and the scholar's study to shadow an actual industrialist. A generation earlier, in one of the original academic satires, *Lucky Jim* (1953), Kingsley Amis's Jim Dixon demonstrates his aversion to archival research, indeed to any form of work, when he wonders how he will fill up his lecture:

> Some sort of pabulum for a further forty-eight and a half minutes was evidently required, with perhaps a minute off for being introduced to the audience, another minute for water-drinking, coughing, and page-turning, and nothing at all for applause or curtain-calls. Where was he going to find this supplementary pabulum? The only answer to this question seemed to be Yes that's right, where? Ah, wait a minute; he'd get Barclay to find him a book on medieval music. Twenty minutes at least on that, with an apology for 'having let my interest run away with me' … He blew bubbles for a moment with the milk in his spoon at the thought of being able to do himself so much good without having to think at all. (*Lucky Jim* 169–70)

In the English novel academics and scholars are usually represented away from their work. Instead of daily life and work presented realistically, the blended modes of social comedy and satire govern the campus novel. These kinds of writing require the observation of characters' behaviour when in groups; hence, the solitary locale of the archive or library is eschewed in favour of the department meeting, the disastrous seminar or tutorial, the excruciating office hours, the tea or sherry party, and the public lecture – all much more promising venues for the exposure and excoriation of academics in their natural habitats.[5]

Either academics do no work, shirking like Jim Dixon, or they fail to recognize the relationship between the lessons of the past and their own incompetently managed lives. When they do produce, as Lodge's Morris Zapp does (in *Small World*), fictional academics are more often theory-spouting flim-flam men, jetting from conference to conference rather than waiting for dusty volumes to emerge from the bowels of libraries. Even in the common contrast of theoretical American and scholarly Brit, the academics of English fiction are rarely caught actually carrying out research, but are celebrated instead for the accomplishment of previously published criticism or for a successful performance of a lecture, as in Anita Brookner's *Providence* (1982). Their expertise established as a part of characterization, their labours can be discreetly relegated to the implied back-story. Readers do not expect of these characters either deep engagement with or serious meditation on the uses of the past. This situation is radically revised in the most well-known romance of the archive, A.S. Byatt's *Possession*, which invigorates the academic satire with a celebration of intellectual questing.

POSSESSION: A ROMANCE

In *Possession*, A.S. Byatt places a Victorian love story within a contemporary plot about scholarly research. The race to complete a collection of long-lost papers reveals most of the truth about the relationship between two invented nineteenth-century poets, Christabel LaMotte and Randolph Henry Ash. The discovery of their love affair, which upsets scholars' assumptions about both poets, sets off a contest between passionate British scholarship and unscrupulous American acquisitiveness. Byatt celebrates the recovery of an important episode of an imaginary British literary history in a tour-de-force of manufactured evidence, complete with imitations of Victorian poems, stories, letters, and diaries. The present-day scholars, Roland Michell and Maud Bailey, who most deserve to possess the knowledge of Ash and LaMotte, race only a few steps ahead of representatives of the English and American literary establishments, recovering the thrill of scholarship for themselves and for Byatt's readers. Even if the scholars know slightly less than the readers, Byatt shows the intellectual quest to be a character-transforming process, with life-altering benefits not only for Maud and Roland, but also for many of the minor characters who alternatively aid and stand in the way of scholarly truth-seeking.

Byatt's affirmation of the ends of archival research has led some critics to describe the novel as redemptive, which immediately distinguishes it from most academic satires. This reading of the successful truth-seeking of *Possession* also calls into question the appropriateness of labelling it a postmodern novel, though many reviewers and critics have done so. The case for *Possession*'s postmodernism rests partly on matters of narrative technique. Byatt does employ several narrative strategies associated with the postmodern style, most notably pastiche, self-reflexivity, and ironic doubling. The imitation of period styles characterizes many postmodernist fictions with settings in the past. The works of John Fowles provide many examples of pastiche used to postmodernist ends, and Byatt can be seen as participating in this playful tradition. The stock-in-trade of metafictional writers such as Martin Amis, Julian Barnes, and Jeanette Winterson, theoretically aware, self-reflexive characters and narrators can be a significant ingredient of postmodernist style. Ironic doubling, and indeed all the forms of irony that destabilize readerly expectations of coherence, unity, and closure, can contribute to the disruptive effects of postmodernist fiction. Even the overtly knowing narrator of nineteenth-century realism can appear a postmodern trick; for instance, several key revelations Byatt makes known only to the reader, withholding final knowledge from her researchers.

In a postscript dated 1868, Byatt makes it clear that she reserves the whole truth only for her privileged readers: 'There are things that happen and leave no discernible trace, are not spoken or written of, though it would be very wrong to say that subsequent events go on indifferently, all the same, as though such things had never been' (*Possession* 508). Roland and Maud never know of the meeting of Ash and his daughter, though Byatt shows her readers this scene. Though this point has led some critics to emphasize the postmodernity of the novel, it surely reinforces the reader's certainty about 'what really happened,' in contradistinction to the usual aims of postmodern undecidability. Indeed, each of the techniques mentioned above Byatt uses playfully, in order to affirm more traditional representational aims.[6] Jackie Buxton and Ivana Djordjevic have persuasively argued that Byatt is no postmodernist, particularly when her ideas about history are taken into account. Djordjevic writes that if Byatt 'does deploy the entire paraphernalia of postmodernist techniques and devices, this is in order to hoist postmodernism with its own petard. A somewhat reluctant Leavisite and an admirer of Browning, George Eliot, and Iris Murdoch, she firmly believes that literature is, or should be, about something she refers to – deliberately unfashionably – as "truth"' ('Footsteps' 46).

Dana Shiller adjudicates the apparent clash between technique and content, arguing that neo-Victorian novels like *Possession* reveal a contest between 'writing as though there are no persisting truths' and 'writing as though there is indeed a recoverable past' ('Redemptive Past' 541). The latter strategy works against typically postmodern treatments of the past, since it shows the past as enriching and redeeming the present ('Redemptive Past' 558). While 'questioning the certitude of our historical knowledge,' in Shiller's view neo-Victorian novels also 'preserve and celebrate' the past. I agree with Shiller that this phenomenon cannot be explained away as mere period nostalgia, or as what Fredric Jameson regards as the vacuous, apolitical, and even personally damaging representation of an empty history (*Postmodernism* 19). Clearly the represented past is being called upon to perform some kind of important work for the contemporary novelists who invoke it so persistently. Not only redemptive, but escapist, defensive, nostalgic, and revisionist in both traditional historical and postmodern senses, *Possession* uses the past for the pleasure of evoking a vanished world and time, for articulating the significance of the humanities (particularly English literature and historical research), for the dress-up fun of imitating the Victorians, and for celebrating undervalued British national treasures.

As will already be clear, romances of the archive contain representations of other historical periods than Victorian times; however, Shiller's insight into the seemingly antithetical attitudes towards the Victorian past can be extended to include all the other times reached and reinterpreted in romances of the archive. A full understanding of these texts would require the scrutiny of the chosen historical period conjured up by research, an exploration of the novel's and characters' views about the recovered past, and an account of the consequences of doing research for the questing characters. This chapter acknowledges all three goals, but emphasizes the consequences for the researching characters of the framing present-day story. The transformation of characters through encounters with a previously unknown past reveals a highly romanticized, even mystical, vision of history that intersects with, but which cannot be fully accounted for, by postmodernism. This chapter thus initiates one of the projects of this study in considering the uses of the past in recent British fiction. Reading Byatt's witty novel helps to reveal how romances of the archive respond to the challenges of postmodern historiography and to the attitudes towards the past supposedly held by contemporary novelists. Romances of the archive show how novelists call into question many of the critical commonplaces about these matters.

Before delving into these entangling questions, I draw from Byatt's *Possession* a short list of the common traits, themes, and motifs of romances of the archive, to be used as a critical template for examining many of the generically diverse novels treated in this study. I undertake here, in the tradition of descriptive poetics, to assemble a group of 'the repertory of motifs and devices, and the system of relations and differences, shared by a particular class of texts' (McHale *Postmodernist* xi). *Possession* provides examples of the following:

- character-researchers, endowed with the corporeality and 'round' psychology of the realistic novel
- romance adventure stories, in which 'research' features as a kernel plot action, resulting in strong closure, with climactic discoveries and rewards
- discomforts and inconveniences suffered in the service of knowledge (actually part of the romance plot, but so played up as to deserve separate emphasis)
- sex and physical pleasure gained as a result of questing (these stories about 'brains' are always also stories about bodies)
- settings and locations (such as libraries and country houses) that contain archives of actual papers
- material traces of the past revealing the truth
- and evocation of history, looking back from a postimperial context

To be sure, not all romances of the archive emphasize each of these traits to the same degree, and some of the categories contain a diversity of clashing examples. If *Possession* emphasizes the revelation of hidden truths, for example, postmodern novels such as Julian Barnes's *Flaubert's Parrot* (1984) typify the undercutting and sceptical attitudes towards historical understanding associated with historiographic metafiction. My concern is not to rule out postmodern fiction from consideration, but to take care that the powerful ideas expressed in this relatively small number of literary fictions do not obscure the interesting contests about history contained in romances of the archive, a more widely dispersed kind of contemporary fiction.

Preoccupied though it may be by redefining and undermining history and historiography, postmodern fiction does not have a monopoly on novelistic representations of the past. I find that the views about the uses of the past expressed in romances of the archive often run counter to those associated with postmodernism. By casting a wider net, this study differs fundamentally from recent work such as Frederick M. Holmes's thoughtful monograph *The Historical Imagination: Postmodernism and the Treatment of the Past in Contemporary British Fiction* (1997). Limiting his study to postmodern fiction means that Holmes arrives at a rather different assessment of the uses of the past than I do, though we scrutinize some of the same works and authors and arrive at similar judgments about works such as *Possession*. The romance of the archive cuts across apparently antithetical categories, such as historiographic metafictions and traditional realistic historical novels, fantasy and detective fictions. When the examples from popular genres are read critically, their treatment of the past reveals strikingly different historical and historiographical impulses at work. Seen in this light, the postmodern historiographic metafiction retains the oppositional energy of the minority view, rather than demonstrating with tedious predictability a theoretical innovation already dulled by being diffused everywhere. The variety of sub-genres harnessed by the romance of the archive accounts for some of the deviations in its traits, but as we will see, romances of the archive have a great deal more in common with one another than their apparent differences would suggest. Let us begin with an influential example.

RESEARCHERS: CHARACTERS TRANSFORMED

The researchers of romances of the archive may be professional scholars, detectives, 'history buffs,' or ordinary citizens. In *Possession*, Byatt fills her cast with a variety of academics, more or less credentialed by rank and institutional affiliation. I have already suggested that the romance of the archive tends to empower the more marginal researchers and to show them beating the professionals at their own game (one of many inheritances from the classic British mystery novel). As we will see, many romances of the archive show how amateurs can be caught up by intellectual quests. Whether an uncredentialed temporary scholar or a professor, however, these characters conduct research in recognizable ways: they visit libraries or gain access to private collections of papers; they read, study, take notes, chase down references, and interpret evidence. They acquire expertise if they start without it. They show ingenuity, daring, and dedication. A romance of the archive can employ rival questers, racing against one another to seize the next clue. The unlikely alliance of the Ash expert, Roland Michell, old-fashioned underemployed textual critic, and LaMotte specialist Maud Bailey, feminist scholar, builds on a gendered contest expressed in terms of clashing areas of expertise and theoretical allegiances. Ordinarily, we are meant to feel, these critics wouldn't give one another the time of day. Shades of Hepburn and Tracy underlie the opposites who clash in order to attract one another. Before the characters' attitudes towards one another can change, they must unbend about their subjects, admitting the significance of what they have earlier dismissed as outlandish or out-of-field. The desire for narrative satisfaction, for knowing as fully as possible what happened between Ash and LaMotte, changes the scholars' interests, broadening and taking them far afield, always building on their impressive individual expertise.

The romance of the archive on offer from Byatt gives liberal educations and lessons in love to the highly educated but sterile pair Maud and Roland. The story they discover, of Ash and LaMotte's affair, is ready-made to celebrate making literary and corporeal connections. The basic transformation of characters and literary history wrought by Byatt depends upon replacing each individual poet's original context with a transgressive relationship that puts received knowledge into a fruitful state of disarray. The received wisdom of the late twentieth century poses a different problem, for it rests on profound suspicion about the possibility of coherent characters developing as a result of plots of discovery and self-discovery. Nonetheless, Byatt takes on the postmodern attitudes as she mirrors the transformation of her Victorians in her twentieth-century characters, who (isolated, in states of sexual dissatisfaction, taken over by their long-dead objects of study) markedly improve as a result of their intellectual questing together.

In both past and present fictional worlds, traditional realist notions of personality govern characterization, despite the knowing resistance of the theoretically minded characters to being caught in such plots. Roland worries, 'partly with precise postmodern pleasure, and partly with a real element of superstitious dread, that he and Maud were being driven by a plot or fate that seemed, at least possibly, to be not their plot or fate but that of those others ... Coherence and closure are deep human desires that are presently unfashionable. But they are both frightening and enchantingly desirable' (*Possession* 422). Byatt affirms the undiminished transforming power of romance (through love and questing) when her contemporary characters relinquish their cherished separateness. This aspect of the novel urges the reader to see the romance of the archive as 'good for character,' despite the theft and deceptions with which Roland and Maud begin their quest. By the end they fully measure up to Barzun and Graff's list of virtues required of the modern researcher: they are accurate, order-loving, logical, honest, imaginative, and self-aware (*The Modern Researcher* 47–50).

Self-awareness represents a formidable barrier to the most important transformation of character wrought by Byatt, for she creates late-twentieth-century characters mistrustful of 'love' and 'romance':

They were theoretically knowing: they knew about phallocracy and penisneid, punctuation, puncturing and penetration, about polymorphous and polysemous perversity, orality, good and bad breasts, clitoral tumescence, vesicle persecution, the fluids, the solids, the metaphors for these, the systems of desire and damage, infantile greed and oppression and transgression, the iconography of the cervix and the imagery of the expanding and contracting Body, desired, attacked, consumed, feared. (*Possession* 423)

This daunting set of obstacles is defeated by silent company-keeping, shared purpose, mutual respect, and equal careers when the expert on boundaries and the stumbler on thresholds meet in a scene of consummation reflected in the storm-deranged outside world, smelling of 'death and destruction,' smelling 'fresh and lively and hopeful' (507).

Not all researchers in romances of the archive benefit so dramatically from acting on a desire to know. These questers can be villains as easily as heroes, and they can go too far in their quest to possess the truth, particularly if they have bad instincts about their object of study. Passionate British scholarship must contend with two contrasting threats, poststructuralist theory and well-funded American collectors. Byatt invokes in her chief antagonist Mortimer Cropper the bad cowboy in the dark hat, the consumer of specialized pornography, the overzealous curator, the grave-robbing violator of privacy. The descendant of a spiritualist charlatan, Cropper's most menacing trait as a scholar is his desire to possess everything about Randolph Henry Ash. His hope is to control and annul the Victorian poet, to take him over, to annihilate him by retracing his every move. At once an obsessive collector of the sort who keeps a private treasure room full of illicitly gained souvenirs and a respected scholar and curator of an important American Ash archive, Cropper threatens British dominion over its own poets even as he offends academic propriety. Where Roland has all the lines of Ash's verse in his head, Cropper wears the Victorian poet's watch. Byatt's scathing portrait of the perversity of Cropper sets up a simple contrast between the aims of American and British academics. The recovery work undertaken by *Possession*, though entirely fictive, on one level 'corrects' literary history's misunderstanding of the lives of two poets, allowing British insight and perseverance to triumph. Byatt does not spare her countrymen, however: the keepers of the trust of literature are dilatory and out of touch. Blackadder and his team of researchers working in the Ash Factory in the urinous basement of the British Museum do not inspire confidence, nor do the theory-mongering younger generation, represented by Fergus Wolff. Yet in the end, Byatt celebrates the recovery of English literary history by English scholars, who win the contest with the avaricious American of the bottomless chequing account. Their rightness secures their rights over their own literature.

ROMANCE PLOTS AND THEIR REWARDS

The novel organizes a contemporary archival-quest-romance around an epistolary Victorian adulterous-love-romance. It contains within its omniscient third-person-narrative situation various characters' consciousnesses. Particularly in the contemporary frame, these 'minds' are represented traditionally, through the narrator's generalizations about states of mind and feelings (psycho-narration) and through the meshing of narrator's tense and person with characters' distinctive 'voices' (narrated monologue).[7] The Victorians' fictive minds open up to the reader through documents, especially letters and embedded examples of LaMotte's work (her verse, fairy tales, versions of Breton stories, selections from her epic poem about Melusina), Ash's work (his dramatic monologues, his Icelandic saga, and his debunking poem about spiritualism), and three journals by witnesses to one aspect or another of Ash and LaMotte's affair. For Maud and Roland, the romance of research holds off a love story, upon which the Victorian plot centres. Whether actual readers skip the verse, the researchers Roland Michell and Maud Bailey, present-day experts on Ash and LaMotte, read every scrap of text they can get their hands on for the evidence of a passionate affair that will change the face of both Ash and LaMotte scholarship.

Romance tropes permeate every level of the text, from the epigraph drawn from Nathaniel Hawthorne's foreword to *The House of the Seven Gables* to the embedded fairy tales authored by Byatt's invented poet, Christabel LaMotte. (The fairy tales present Byatt's superb pastiche of the brothers Grimm with shades of George MacDonald.) Mystery, quest, chase, race, and flight from pursuers all provide the justification for plots involving lots of travel through space (including libraries or collections) and imaginative engagement with times past. A sense of entering a world far from everyday experience accompanies the archival element of the story, but it must be emphasized that the novel everywhere respects the boundaries between Victorian and contemporary worlds. The only collapses in time occur as a result of *thinking*, in the specialized form of scholarly intuition, or in parallels and other patterns discernible only by the reader. Thus, as a romance, the novel respects realistic conventions for fictional world-making, while setting off ripples of coincidence and repetition in every action.

The quest begins with the presentation of a package, brought up from the stacks of the London Library: 'The book was thick and black and covered with dust. Its boards were bowed and creaking; it had been maltreated in its own time. Its spine was missing, or, rather, protruded from amongst the leaves like a bulky marker. It was bandaged about and about with dirty white tape, tied in a neat bow' (*Possession* 1). Though this copy of Vico has seen better days, it has been preserved because it once belonged to Randolph Henry Ash. Preserved but ignored, like so many of the items stowed in archives, the book embodies those multifarious objects no one else has bothered to look at. In it Roland Michell finds two drafts of a letter, just where Randoph Henry Ash left them. Thus, Byatt almost instantaneously rewards her protagonist for his good old-fashioned scholarly habits, for Roland is in the process of checking Ash's reading the better to understand and annotate the Victorian poet's allusions. Indeed, the discovery of the beginning of the correspondence with Christabel LaMotte (as yet unidentified) will demand reinterpretation of Ash's later work and its coded references, fuelling critical work for at least another generation. The discovery of that irony lies in the future at this early point in the novel: the reader merely observes Roland taking a strange swerve away from his already-rewarded proper behaviour. Though he is a trained scholar, well aware of the rules and regulations of legitimate academic research, Roland steals the letter, 'seized by a strange and uncharacteristic impulse of his own. It was suddenly impossible to put these living words back into page 300 of Vico and return them to Safe 5' (*Possession* 8). The chase this discovery and theft sets off runs through many variants of romance plots, as Roland himself muses, late in the action:

> He was in a Romance, a vulgar and a high romance simultaneously; a Romance was one of the systems that controlled him, as the expectations of Romance control almost everyone in the Western world, for better or worse, at one point or another.
>
> He supposed the Romance must give way to social realism, even if the aesthetic temper of the time was against it.
>
> In any case, since Blackadder and Leonora and Cropper had come, it had changed from Quest, a good romantic form, into Chase and Race, two other equally valid ones. (*Possession* 425)

Blackadder is Roland's adviser, erstwhile mentor, and lord of the underworld rooms of the British Museum dedicated to the study of Randolph Henry Ash – the Ash Factory. Leonora Stern is an American psychoanalytic feminist critic, one of the leading proponents of the view that Christabel LaMotte, who shared a home with a woman painter, should be read as a lesbian poet. Though Blackadder, Stern, and Cropper all have competing agendas, together they represent the intrusion of 'reality' on the escapist romance of wayward scholarship.[8] If they can, Blackadder, Stern, and Cropper will apprehend and discipline Roland and Maud, the rogue runaways who recover the excitement of literary scholarship by breaking its rules and defying the codes of proprietorship, hierarchy, and peer review. The reader has no trouble rooting for Roland and Maud.

Not only do they travel around Britain and France chasing down the scattered evidence of Ash and LaMotte's affair, but they bring encyclopedic knowledge of the body of work to the mystery, so the 'allusiveness' of texts created for the fiction can be recognized and interpreted within the scholarly frame-story. Where Byatt's earlier novels *The Virgin in the Garden* (1978) and *Still Life* (1985) rely upon straightforward allusions to art and literature, *Possession*'s manufactured intertextuality requires next to no knowledge on the part of a reader for the vicarious experience of the literary echoing to be enjoyed. The characters cue less scholarly readers to moments of allusive *frisson*. Reading *Possession* is not hard work. As Louise Yelin points out, it appeals both to 'middlebrow' and 'culturally literate' audiences: 'It entices us with its depiction of scholarship as a detective game ... and it flatters us by offering us the pleasures of recognizing the intertextual allusions and revisionary rewritings out of which it is made' ('Cultural Cartography' 38). Choked with literary allusions and in-jokes, *Possession*'s satire and social comedy rely upon some familiarity with literary history and academic types, but its main accomplishment is the presentation of the romance of learning and scholarship in a package as undemanding to the reader as any other romance plot. Just as one need know little about submarines or dinosaurs to enjoy *The Hunt for Red October* (1984) or *Jurassic Park* (1990), *Possession*'s literary material, like the techno-babble of Tom Clancy and Michael Crichton, requires only that the reader notes the attribution of expertise to specific characters. Naturally, palaeontologists may judge how well Crichton captures the current state of their science, and Victorianists will respond to Byatt's representation of their period and tacit recommendations about the direction of their scholarship and theorizing.[9] Yet readers propelled by the deftly deployed romance plots of the novel need only feel that the apparatus of scholarship not get too much in the way of the action. A reading motivated by the desire to see Roland and Maud win the race underlies more critical interpretations and analyses that run against the grain of the story's pleasures.

When they untangle the mystery, an abundance of rewards – enhanced prestige, multiple job offers, cash, career changes, even better sex – results from their newly acquired knowledge of Randolph Henry Ash and Christabel LaMotte. The truth about the Victorians has been pinned down. While only the reader is privy to all the details (about, for instance, Ellen Ash's frigidity, or Ash's meeting with his daughter by Christabel), the romance of the archive yields major discoveries, material for scholarly editions and articles, money for the down-at-the-heels aristocrats, and love for Roland and Maud. The past not only fascinates, but it yields tangible benefits. Byatt's contemporary Britain, a crippled nation that cannot afford to provide electric wheelchairs to its lovable elderly in their decayed stately homes, is a far cry from the vigorous, creative Victorian Britain whose recovered poets and poetry rejuvenate love lives, bank accounts, scholarship, and even academic careers. Questing in the archive turns up documents that are worth something. It is no accident that most of the beneficiaries are British, though some token sharing can be arranged in the information age.

The novel rewards both characters and readers with a strong finish to a page-turning chase. Added to the literary-historical connections, we find the corporeal or genetic tie that underlines the endogamous Britishness of *Possession*'s resolutions: Maud turns out to be a direct descendent of both Christabel and Ash, for their illegitimate child is her great-great-grand-mother. She is the inheritor of the letters and the genetic traces: Roland notes that she physically resembles Ash. The final act of taking possession that the novel details brings the contemporary characters into the body-contact without which a romance of the archive – not to mention a romance novel – would seem unfulfilled: 'And very slowly and with infinite gentle delays and delicate diversions and variations of indirect assault Roland finally, to use an outdated phrase, entered and took posses-sion of all her white coolness that grew warm against him, so that there seemed to be no boundaries' (*Possession* 507). This fantastic dissolution of boundaries brings Roland, Maud, and through Maud their Victorian coun-terparts together in bed. Having debunked fraudulent spiritualism, the book romantically celebrates a physical union of present and past, scholar and subject. Best of all, Roland will follow his true calling, becoming a poet, taken over no longer by Ash, but possessed by his own words.

The bang-up finish typifies the closure of romances of the archive.[10] Here I disagree with Frederick Holmes, who regards the end of *Possession* as 'parodically overdetermined,' so extreme as to deliberately undermine a sense of closure (*Historical* 21). Holmes quotes Anita Brookner's review, in which Brookner describes the novel's closure as 'impertinently uncon-vincing' (21).[11] Just because an ending is melodramatic and old-fashioned does not mean that it fails to provide readers their full measure of narrative satisfaction; confusion arises when the taste for a certain kind of realism obscures the generic demands of work drawing on detective fiction. Mysteries and thrillers demand strong finishes; indeed, as Frank Kermode has observed, the desire for closure in the detective novel is so intense that a critical taboo on revealing the ending has evolved, a taboo that I everywhere violate in this study (readers beware – spoilers abound).[12] Rather than avoiding romance plotting as hazardously fictive, romances of the archive foreground the imaginative storyline in order to frame unlikely encounters with the past. They are not designed to frustrate readers with balked inquiries. Unlike many real scholarly projects, these tales of research rarely trail off into blind alleys or lose themselves in a welter of unimportant details. Loose ends are common only in the romance vein of the sequel – 'to be continued.' Even in tales of forgery, the truth about the past can be attained, if only by correcting the false history created by fraud. Postmodern romances of the archive do not eschew the effects of strong closure, by the way; even their prolonged divagations come to strong finishes, revealing with a certainty rarely exposed to sceptical questioning *which* truths lie permanently inaccessible, beyond the reach of the fallible questioner. The proving of 'no answer' then becomes just as positive and final a truth as the dramatic disclosures of *Possession*. Whether it endorses, defies, revises, or magically extends historians' views about the past, the romance of the archive arrives at something labelled truth, recovers lost or concealed knowledge, and reassures the reader with the promise of answers that can be located, despite the intervening obstructions and obfuscation.

Romances of the archive do not have to be postmodern to introduce relativism, in which the facts look different from different subject positions, and versions of the past can be impermanent and subject to change. Like many mysteries, romances of the archive sometimes reveal an alternative story, attributed to an insignificant character, as containing the true answers. This trait arises from the canonical English realistic novel, not just from recent revisionist tales or from romance sub-genres. Within the great tradition of realist fiction, George Eliot's description of the power of ego to alter the perceived centre of the story provides one of many sources for a relativist historiography in the novel:

[P]lace now against [the polished mirror] a lighted candle as a centre of illumination, and lo! the scratches will seem to arrange themselves in a fine series of concentric circles round that little sun. It is demonstrable that the scratches are going everywhere impartially, and it is only your candle which produces the flattering illusion of a concentric arrangement ... The scratches are events, and the candle is the egoism of any person now absent ... (*Middlemarch* 264).

The romance of the archive endorses the procedure of shifting the candle in order to reveal a new set of facts and answers invisible until the questing researcher changes the centre around which events arrange themselves for interpretation.

DISCOMFORT AND INCONVENIENCE

The emphasis in the preceding section on the rewards of successful questing underplays an important element shared by romances of the archive, the depiction of strenuous effort, physical discomfort, and all sorts of obstacles to the achievement of the goal. No quest romance would be complete without its difficulties and barriers – impassable bridges, terrifying caves, unclimbable mountains, misty moors, mazes, darkness, obstructions of geography and magic. Add to this set-up the traditional character flaws that weaken romance protagonists: they are easily tricked or led astray despite their equally traditional strength, resourcefulness, and bravery. The contemporary romance of the archive works with a far more ordinary cast than the knights, princesses, and magicians of its antecedents, and its realism of situation demands that the obstacles and difficulties besetting its researching characters confirm a sense of extraordinary effort without tipping over into the superhuman or supernatural areas.

The positive image of heroic striving in the face of impediments comes not only from the romance models, however, but from the testimony of archival researchers. As the comments of historians Joyce Appleby, Lynn Hunt, and Margaret Jacob make clear, a willingness to make the effort of archival research betokens a 'practical realism' about truth-finding and a refreshing freedom from the solipsistic language games of postmodernism:

The archives in Lyon, France, are housed in an old convent on a hill overlooking the city. It is reached by walking up some three hundred stone steps. For the practical realist – even one equipped with a laptop computer – the climb is worth the effort; the relativist might not bother. Historians find more than dust in archives and libraries; the records there offer a glimpse of a world that has disappeared. Assuming a tolerance for a degree of indeterminacy, scholars in the practical realist camp are encouraged to get out of bed in the morning and head for the archives, because there they can uncover evidence, touch lives long passed, and 'see' patterns in events that otherwise might remain inexplicable. (*Telling the Truth* 251)

The muscular researcher of this description does not shirk the three-hundred-step climb; indeed, making it to the hilltop archive becomes a test of identity. Novels like *Possession* make a great deal of mundane difficulties to establish scholarly credentials and to heighten the sense of accomplishment in carrying out the quest. Roland is poor. Maud is lonely. Both suffer from inadequate love lives. The people who own the LaMotte/Ash correspondence distrust academics. When Roland and Maud finally get to read their first cache of letters, they work in bitter cold. Job insecurity, lack of time, tedium, social awkwardness, and the necessity of working in filthy places (Byatt especially emphasizes the smell of cat piss) all contribute to the sense that the questers strive, suffer, and selflessly endure privation for the sake of gaining knowledge. This distinguishes them from the undeserving, comfort-loving, modem-addicted softies who would claim authority without sweating or freezing for it.

PLEASURES

As we have seen, the romance genre also guarantees that research questers are amply reimbursed for their efforts, as the settings through which they travel provide equal measures of difficulty, discoveries, and pleasant diversions. Before the good sex with which Byatt ends the love romance of her contemporary plot, many other pleasures are doled out to Roland and Maud. Beds with clean white sheets, warm baths and sea-water showers, excellent meals at home and abroad, beautiful scenery, warm weather, and intriguing jewellery provide the sensual counterparts to the intellectual conversations that ostensibly embody the gratifying quest and the pleasures of the text. While it may in many cases be true, as Richard Marius effuses, that '[h]istorians who have worked in the archives ... experience a pleasure that can hardly be described,' more easily rendered and readily apprehended delights always accompany the scholarly thrills in romances of the archive (*Writing about History* 112). These material and physical gratifications not only buttress the novel with the rich descriptions that allow a reader to envision a mimetic fictional world, but they underline one of Byatt's important points about her characters, contemporary and Victorian: these are fleshly creatures. Elisabeth Bronfen has written well about how Byatt employs romance to enmesh the carnal and the textual in the stories of both sets of characters, fulfilling both intellectual and physical desires and addressing readers' desires to believe in a realistic fictional world furnished with three-dimensional characters, things, places, tastes, smells, emotions, and sensations ('Romancing Difference' 118, 121). Despite the 'postmodern belief in an incoherent, fragmentary and multiple self ... where each is in strife with the other,' Bronfen observes, 'the scholars possessed by the past in the last instance have recourse to the Real' (128). The tokens of sensual response scattered throughout the novel underwrite both the climactic discoveries and the physical consummation of the romance conclusion with the gold standard of realistic representation. The things that happen to bodies make certain that the romance is not all in the mind.

PLACES CONTAINING ARCHIVES

Common sense would dictate that the least debatable point about a collection of documents is that it must be located somewhere. *Possession* strongly endorses this view, as each hiding-place yields up its piece of the sought treasure. The archive may be lost, forgotten, overlooked, or deliberately hidden, like the collection of LaMotte and Ash love letters tucked into a doll's bed in the Bailey's ancestral home, but it can be found, especially when a qualified quester comes looking. Maud Bailey knows not only that Christabel LaMotte wrote a series of poems about dolls, but when she sees the 'three rigid figures, semi-recumbent under a dusty counterpane, in a substantial if miniature fourposter bed' (*Possession* 81), she recites from memory the poem containing the treasure-hunt clue:

Dolly keeps a Secret
Safer than a Friend
Dolly's Silent Sympathy
Lasts without end.

...

Dolly ever sleepless
Watches above
The Shreds and relics
Of our lost Love ...
(82–3)

Maud removes the dolls, the pillow, the counterpane, blankets, shawls, a feather mattress, and a straw palliasse: 'She reached in under this, into the wooden box beneath it, prised up a hinged board and brought out a package, wrapped in fine white linen, tied with tape, about and about and about, like a mummy' (*Possession* 84). Inside the bundle she and Roland find both sides of the correspondence between Christabel LaMotte and Randolph Henry Ash.

It is a spectacular find, worthy of the best literary discoveries celebrated in Richard Altick's 1950 *The Scholar Adventurers.*[13] Indeed, one of Byatt's accomplishments in *Possession* is to make available for general readers a version of the exciting textual discoveries that archivists, historians, collectors, and even some members of English Departments find thrilling enough to motivate long careers in scholarship. Though few can match Roland and Maud's find, in the last century or so assiduous scholars have discovered the papers of James Boswell, the poems of Thomas Traherne, countless letters, drafts, unpublished first novels, diaries, and what experts in the earlier periods of literature call 'life records.' Buried in official archives or stashed in unexpected places, as often as not hidden in plain view, these masses of documents have added immeasurably to our store of knowledge about writers and the contexts in which they worked. Perhaps because the discoverers are so often overshadowed by their discoveries, a compensatory myth about the special sort of person doing scholarship imbues Altick's extolling account. He lauds the kinds of scholars who labour to bring missing pieces of the literary record to light: brilliant, patient, brave, and optimistic,

> the literary researcher is confronted with a vast and tangled puzzle – the contradictions, the obscurities, the very silences which the passage of time leaves behind in the form of history. To repair the damage done by those who in past ages have falsified, distorted, or destroyed the written record, even in the dustiest corner of literary history or biography, requires detective talents – and staying power – of the highest order. The scholar's path may be barred at every turn by a result of one or another of the accidents of fate and human error. He must face the fact that a great deal more of the materials of literary history, including the very works of literature themselves, have been destroyed than have been preserved. He sustains the hope nevertheless that somehow the particular documents he needs have been spared from the bonfire of the moment and the damp of the centuries, and that somewhere ... they are safe and await his coming. (*Scholar Adventurers* 2–3)

The belief that the documents are out there, somewhere, sustains searches that take decades and even now leads scholars to compose wish lists: a copy of Byron's journal, perhaps, or what archivist Mark Samuels Lasner calls 'the "big ones" – the diaries of the poet William Allingham said to have been destroyed by "enemy action" during the Second World War, and the manuscript of George Gissing's lost novel; the papers of Ella D'Arcy; and ... the manuscript of Max Beerbohm's "The Happy Hypocrite."'[14] Documents like these and many more surprising have turned up in family homes, in law offices and publishers' files, in the seemingly inexhaustible holdings of the Public Record Office, or on the shelves of the local library. Literary scholars may not know where they are, but the possibility of locating them means believing in the box, the sack, the attic, the barn, the secret compartment, the family collection, and even the container in the grave.

Possession represents the archive as material objects in actual places, providing plausible contexts for the various texts it recovers and reprints. The documents that Roland and Maud bring together are located in libraries and special collections, in a country house, in the hands of scholars in other countries, and (with a touch of Dante Gabriel Rossetti) in Ash's grave. While many readers might doubt the felicitous chain of events that leads to the reconstitution of such a widely scattered corpus, few would question the idea that an archive can be located in a specific place. Most scholars only need to discover where the principal collections of materials are deposited, in university or national libraries, for their work to begin. In these days of on-line catalogues, many such questions can be answered simply by typing names or keywords into automated databases such as WorldCat. The reservations that researchers admit have to do with the likelihood of decay and destruction, or the possibility that an important piece of paper or box of documents has not made it into the comprehensive library catalogue. Sometimes researchers imagine that curators and librarians prevent them from getting at materials 'reserved' by a senior scholar, and everyone wonders what those cartons closed until some remote time in the future contain. Real cases of the selling off, breaking up, and dispersal into private hands of valuable collections legitimately dismay scholars, and no one would argue that the expense of travelling to far-off libraries may effectively prevent a scholar from consulting locatable materials. Nor is the Internet a viable solution: though many more descriptive catalogues, runs of journals, and unique collections have been placed on the World Wide Web, the utopian dream of universally accessible, fully digitized collections makes some archivists 'give a hollow laugh,'[15] as Byatt does at Cropper's hologram projections, which theatrically proffer the simulacrum as an improvement on the real thing (*Possession* 386–7). Scholars who need to read in far-away archives will still need to travel, for the forseeable future. This fact of the researcher's life undergirds the romance of the archive's quest plot: searching for the truth necessitates the traditional narrative delights of travel.

On the path of the archival quest lie those special locations – the libraries, special collections, offices, and stately homes in which documents reside. Alice Kaplan, a historian and literary scholar, writes movingly of the way the atmosphere of the research space stimulates the imagination of the researcher, feeds the archival passion, informs and fruitfully misinforms the personal stories of motivation that drive all archival quests. She writes that an archive 'can be anyplace, but for the archive to be, there should be too much of it, too many papers to sift through. And there must also be pieces missing, something left to find. The best finds in the archives are the result of association and accident: chance in the archives favours the prepared mind' ('Working' 103). Having done the hard slog of preparation, a researcher receives the rewards of insight and fortuitous discovery by actually traveling to the locations where the imaginary contents of one's subject's desk can be reconstituted ('Working' 110–11). Writing of one such library, the Center for Contemporary Jewish Documentation in Paris, Kaplan conjures up the atmosphere of the place, which is guarded by an iron gate, modern security technology, and cautious librarians wary of vandals, bombers, and Holocaust deniers. Kaplan reports, '[O]ne of the things that always flavors work there ... is the quantity of people who are there for personal reasons, who are looking for signs of relatives who died in the camps, and who work in an entirely different key than the so-called "disinterested" scholars' (113). Witnessing the flow of amateur seekers who come to the library as if to a detective's office stimulates private stories even in professionals who will issue 'dry archival report[s], fit for a public' (103). These stories allow 'work to take place, answers to be found.' They are 'fragile but necessary contingent ingredients of archival work, they are the private process that is erased as soon as it succeeds in producing a bit of truth. This is perhaps the common denominator of all archival passion – the sense that even the smallest result is "a bit of truth"' (115). Acquiring that bit of truth, according to the suppressed story of archival passion, requires entrance into the archival space, literal and imaginary.

Since the verisimilar representation of actual locations matters to the plot, characterization, and atmosphere of romances of the archive, it is all the more important to confront one of the most influential recent uses of the term 'archive,' as employed by intellectual historian and philosopher Michel Foucault. For Foucault and his followers, the archive is not limited to a place, real or imagined. His definition of archive as 'the domain of things said' claims the word for something other than collections of books and papers. Foucault's archaeology of knowledge focuses on those discourses of power (such as natural history, political economy, or clinical medicine [*Archaeology* 126]) that exist in time, beyond individual contributors, books, and ideas. Intrinsically placeless, but rather distributed through many locales and times, these discourses elude pinning-down in a particular spot or individual. A Foucauldian archive cannot be 'visited,' and ordinary scholarly methodology will not function properly in it. Foucault writes:

> Instead of seeing, on the great mythical book of history, lines of words that translate in visible characters thoughts that were formed in some other times and place, we have in the density of discursive practices, systems that establish statements as events (with their own conditions and domain of appearance) and things (with their own possibility and field of use). They are all these systems of statements (whether events or things) that I propose to call *archive*. (128)

Foucault's ideas not only dislocate the archive from location (a library, a nation, a culture), but also from traditional ideas of coherence, order, continuous identity, and fixed truth:

> I do not mean the sum of all the texts that a culture has kept upon its person as documents attesting to its own past, or as evidence of a continuing identity; nor do I mean the institutions, which, in a given society, make it possible to record and preserve those discourses that one wants to remember and keep in circulation. (128–9)

Instead, the archive in Foucault's usage means something much more encompassing: it defines the mode of statements, makes possible their enunciation, and governs their functioning (129).[16] The archive according to Foucault is not in a particular place because it must contain all of us and all of our statements and actions (past and present), whether we speak professionally, or as sisters, mothers, consumers, citizens. To attempt to confine this discourse (made up of all the practices and communications within a social institution) in a limited set of sites can only be to act on a fantasy of power and control. Thus, to take the Foucauldian view, archival research that seeks recorded evidence in a particular locale or set of places risks missing the forest for the trees, the Foucauldian archive for the collection of documents. Furthermore, a Foucauldian understanding of the archive requires the researcher to acknowledge the social, political, economic, and personal circumstances that condition any truth-claim or announcement of a discovery. Ideally, this conception of the archive reveals the way discourses serve power, and aids the resistance to discursive regulation. At the very least, it endorses self-consciousness about human limitations in truth-seeking.[17]

Lest this theoretical excursion seem rather far afield from the world of Byatt's novel, I juxtapose these excerpts from Foucault with their parodied version from *Possession*. Though he demonstrates from the first scene his practical understanding of the archive as a site, and the researcher as a truth-seeker, Roland also 'knows himself' in proper post-Freudian fashion. He is a product of his poststructuralist training:

> Roland had learned to see himself, theoretically, as a crossing-place for a number of systems, all loosely connected. He had been trained to see his idea of his 'self' as an illusion, to be replaced by a discontinuous machinery and electrical message-network of various desires, ideological beliefs and responses, language-forms and hormones and pheromones. Mostly he liked this. He had no desire for any strenuous Romantic self-assertion. (*Possession* 424)

Byatt depicts Roland struggling to reconcile the theoretically aware way of understanding his situation, for he has fallen in love with Maud, with a finely tuned sense of place, simultaneously meaning location, rank, and social station in 'the real world':

> [I]n the social world to which they must both return from these white nights and sunny days – there was little real connection between them. Maud was a beautiful woman such as he had no claim to possess. She had a secure job and an international reputation. Moreover, in some dark and outdated English social system of class, which he did not believe in, but felt obscurely working at gripping him, Maud was County, and he was urban lower-middle class, in some places more, in some places less acceptable than Maud, but in almost all incompatible. (424–5)

Against both this real-world sense of placement and the theoretical denial of continuous identity Byatt works a plot that drives her characters from location to location, from London to Lincoln, from home to abroad, from library to LaMotte's family seat, to the Yorkshire coast, to France, to the churchyard containing Ash's grave.

In a book that is ostensibly about two scholars who spend a lot of time reading, Byatt emphasizes the yoked travel plot and the love plot; in traditional romance fashion, even Roland and Maud's separations contribute to their shared quest, as Red Crosse and Una's do in Spenser's *The Faerie Queene*. The episodes in which Roland and Maud travel together to Yorkshire and Brittany add simultaneously to their knowledge of Ash and LaMotte and to the development of their love affair. The location of the documents they seek matters in multiple ways, permitting the journey away from their home contexts (being in France frees each of them to behave in unexpected ways), bringing them together to collaborate (despite their seemingly unbridgeable differences), allowing them to meet the helpers who hand over key documents previously unknown (a practical justification for a delightful sojourn in sunny Brittany), and, as in Yorkshire (where they unwittingly visit the same Boggle Hole discovered by LaMotte and Ash a century earlier), permitting them to enjoy the déclassé pleasure of retracing a writer's footsteps. The representational insistence on the actuality of place sets up and vouches for the discovery of selves as well as documents.

MATERIAL TRACES OF THE PAST REVEAL THE TRUTH

Despite all the sharpness of her criticism of academics, Byatt's novel rescues both modern-day characters from the sterility of their scholarly existences through a rejuvenating romance about learning. As I have suggested above, Roland and Maud discover their true and best selves by finding out the truth about Ash and LaMotte. A significant portion of the gratifying fantasy of *Possession* lies in Byatt's decision to make much of the hard evidence accessible: Roland and Maud may not find absolutely everything, but they have letters, diaries, photographs, and answers to many mysteries by the end of the novel. The representation of material traces of the past and the stories they reveal to an intellectual adventurer animates the historical element of romances of the archive. As Sabine Hotho-Jackson argues, Byatt demonstrates to her fictional researchers that 'the past is made of real myth-defying people,' provoking 'a humanising reassessment of the critics' myths' – those doxa of poststructualism and postmodernism that at first impede love and truth-seeking ('Literary' 118). Documents, photographs, imaginative re-enactments, sections in pastiche, or subplots set in earlier periods and apprehended by magic: in some way or another a romance of the archive leads the researcher to the evidence. If the contents of archives sometimes seem familiar to scholars, as do *Posses-*

sion's imitative literary texts, they also can surprise. The archives of Adam Mars-Jones's *The Waters of Thirst* comprises a collection of pornographic magazines. Robert Harris's *Fatherland* leads the researcher to a doctor's bag containing the only records of the Final Solution.

The researching character may arrive at the archival text on the first or last page of the novel. There may be one key text, or many scattered clues. Romances of the archive employ literary imitation (pastiche) and description of art objects (ekphrasis) when they present documents and images in their clue-revealing specificity. Extended ekphrasis brings visual objects such as photographs and paintings to the reader's inner vision; this strategy, too, has deep roots in the Spenserian romance that underlies novelistic versions of romance. Either as embedded texts or as secondary narration framed by a present-day fictional world, pastiche enables contemporary British novelists to claim the history of English letters within their fictions (though the use of pastiche alone does not make a novel into a romance of the archive). *Possession*'s elaborate pastiche becomes a romance of the archive when the story details the search for and reaction to the texts through which Roland and Maud reach the Victorian story. To set the other salient limit, historical reimagining of times past may not bring the material traces of that past into the hands of a researcher; hence, Byatt's twinned novellas, *Angels and Insects* (1992), though also set in the Victorian period, cannot be considered romances of the archive. When the archival material invokes an earlier period, it may be remote or recent, a single period or a sequence of different times, rendered realistically, through quotation of documents, or in fantastic re-creation.

Though the documents can be located, scholarly understanding is by necessity incomplete. This small reservation about the accessibility of truth through a romance of the archive is a far cry from the radical undercutting of the traditional values of history associated with postmodern theory and fiction. Even the redoubtable Hayden White admonishes his readers that they should refrain from applying his literary readings of historical discourse to the activity of research: '[W]e should ... discriminate between the activity of historical research (historians' study of an archive containing information about the past) and that of historical writing (historians' composition of a discourse and the translation of it into a written form). In the research phase of their work,' White continues in a vein that could raise no objection even from the most traditional scholar, 'historians are concerned to discover the truth about the past and to recover information either forgotten, suppressed, or obscured, and of course, to make of it whatever sense they can' (*Figural Realism* 7–8). That this effort must attempt to overcome gaps in the record falls into the category of what historians 'have always known,' in the words of Gertrude Himmelfarb: 'Historians, ancient and modern, have always known what postmodernism professes just to have discovered – that any work of history is vulnerable on three counts: the fallibility and deficiency of the historical record on which it is based; the fallibility and deficiency of the historical writing of history; and the fallibility and subjectivity of the historian' ('Telling It As You Like It' 159). If we adapt the terms historian and history to embrace literary scholars and literary historians, Himmelfarb's enumeration of the fallibility and deficiencies of scholarship serves as a more than adequate template for the situation of *Possession*, one that underscores Byatt's conservatism. Like Byatt, Himmelfarb strenuously insists upon the difference between these well-known limitations of history and the conclusions of postmodernism:

> [T]he frailty, fallibility and relativity of the historical enterprise ... are very different from the tidings brought by postmodernism. For the presumption of postmodernism is that *all* of history is fatally flawed, and that because there is no absolute, total truth, there can be no partial, contingent truths. More important still is the presumption that because it is impossible to attain such truths, it is not only futile but positively baneful to aspire to them. ('Telling' 159–60)

Byatt demonstrates that the quest for truth, though necessarily unfinished, does lead to an improved understanding of the past, one that is positively beneficial, not baneful. Both Ash and LaMotte scholars have laboured under serious misconceptions about the lives of the two poets, who are not even suspected to have known one another before Roland and Maud's discoveries. The intense conversation of the two scholars brings together bodies of knowledge that have been separated, since Ash has belonged to the literary establishment and LaMotte to the feminist critics. Sharing knowledge, swapping reading lists, and tapping into hitherto ignored or inaccessible networks leads the scholars to richer and better understanding of both poets. A pattern of allusions, shared lines, vocabulary, and other textual clues impel the questers to seek proof, in the form of extra-textual evidence. Particularly when the researchers know enough to achieve the rare and special insights that go under the name of intuition, their imaginative leaps permit significant discoveries to be made.

In making the evidence available and intelligible, *Possession* and most contemporary romances of the archive differ markedly from the teasing of postmodern historiographic metafictions. In the small number of post-modern romances of the archive, the proof and the facts, once grasped, then shimmer and disappear like mirages, or go up in flames. Insubstantial, inaccessible, or fugitive, the answers to scholars' questions and the evidence for their arguments dwindle so dramatically in works such as Carol Shields's *Swann* (1987) that believing in the existence of an actual subject and tangible documents requires a leap of faith. Though each item at one point exists in the story world, by the time of the climactic conference on the works of 'folk' poet Mary Swann, all her published works, her manuscripts, her photographs, and her acquaintances have been either stolen, destroyed, or discredited. Whether the reader takes this novel as the ultimate postmodern send-up of fact-finding, as an indirect psychological novel about the thief who conspires to erase Mary Swann, or as a theological fiction urging the necessity of belief in the absence of tangible evidence, Shields's reversal of the romance of the archive emphasizes the urgency of the search itself. In more than one postmodern novel, however, the frantic activity of research leads to less knowledge, or knowledge so trivial as to be a joke. In Julian Barnes's *Flaubert's Parrot*, to take a celebrated example, the amateur scholar *does* find out why two entirely different Flaubert museums can claim to display the actual parrot Flaubert had on his desk during the writing of 'Un cœur simple,' though both claims are guesses represented as fact. But who cares which museum has the 'true parrot'? (*Parrot* 188) – only the obsessed Flaubert buff and narrator, Geoffrey Braithwaite. In this case, an excess of evidence is as baffling as too little proof.

Braithwaite's quest begins when he finds two sites, each with the 'authentic' parrot on display. The search peters out when he finds more: of the fifty Amazonian stuffed parrots in the Museum of Natural History, from where Flaubert and then the rival curators of Flaubert collections all borrowed their parrots, three remain: 'They gazed at me like three quizzical, sharp-eyed, dandruff-ridden, dishonourable old men ... Perhaps it was one of them' (*Parrot* 190). A more tantalizing discovery occurs early in the novel, when the Gosse scholar Ed Winterton claims to have found correspondence revealing Flaubert's and Juliet Herbert's love affair. Having taken the trouble to acquire the correspondence, read it, and tell Braithwaite about it, however, Winterton reveals that he has burned the letters. The narrator rages: 'Did this criminal, this sham, this failure, this murderer, this bald pyromaniac know what he was doing to me? Very probably he did' (47). Scholarship devolves into an irritating squabble between unreliable narrators. Though the quest for knowledge appears degraded and trivial, an ironized version of the romance of the archive motivates the plot and character of *Flaubert's Parrot*. Barnes's stout resistance to any feel-good conclusions about learning and discovery announces his postmodern disdain for communicating and valuing significant truths about the past.[18] Mouldy and bug-infested, the evidence is a row of stuffed parrots incapable of squawking even their rote lines. As Linda Hutcheon observes, *Flaubert's Parrot* 'openly assert[s] that there are only *truths* in the plural, and never one Truth; and there is rarely falseness *per se*, just others' truths' (*Poetics* 109).[19]

Historiographic metafiction, Linda Hutcheon's valuable term for postmodern novels like *Flaubert's Parrot*, overlaps in a small set of instances with romances of the archive. Written with an awareness of postmodern historiography, or, in Hutcheon's words, 'a serious contemporary interrogating of the nature of representation in historiography' (*Politics* 50), historiographic metafiction renounces grand theories and heroic victors in favour of textuality and the points of view of losers or non-combatants (51). It is intensely self-conscious and self-referential: in thematizing the 'turning [of] events into facts through the filtering of archival documents,' historiographical metafiction focuses on 'the process of turning the traces of the past (our only access to these events today) into historical representation' (57). Fallibility, incompleteness, and the inevitable fictionalization of the past undermine the possibility of truly knowing it: 'What this means is that postmodern art acknowledges and accepts the challenge of tradition: the history of representation cannot be escaped but it can be both exploited and commented upon critically through irony and parody' (58). Hence, historiographic metafiction does not merely correct historical narratives, but undercuts the practice of creating discursive wholeness from scraps of evidence. Furthermore, the destabilizing achievement of these postmodern versions of the past can be applied by back-formation to accepted historical narratives: 'Historical meaning may thus be seen today as unstable, contextual, relational, and provisional, but postmodernism argues that in fact, it has always been so. And it uses novelistic representations to underline the narrative nature of much of that knowledge' (67). Narrativity thus becomes the signal weakness of history and the most powerful device of postmodern fiction.

The shared narrative form of fiction and much historical writing makes this sort of critique across disciplinary lines especially powerful – and, to the defenders of traditional history, especially exasperating.[20] Here is Gertrude Himmelfarb in high dudgeon: '[T]he postmodernist imagination is uninhibited and unapologetic. It is then, liberated from the delusion of "fact fetishism" and persuaded of the "fictive" nature of all history, that creative interpretation may take the form of fictional history ... Postmodernism entices us with the siren call of liberation and creativity, but it may be an invitation to intellectual and moral suicide' ('Telling' 164–5, 173). With the very idea of historical truth discredited and indeterminacy endorsed, even the historical novel, from this perspective, seems to have relinquished its old role of richly imagining contexts and creating avenues on which key historical moments and figures can be more nearly approached. (In fact, historical fiction is alive and kicking in the contemporary period, invigorated by its feisty dialogue with postmodernism, feminism, poststructuralism, and postcoloniality.) If old-fashioned scholarship looks a bit green around the gills in most postmodern fiction, the scholars still committed to creating it and the readers who hope to continue consuming it cannot be blamed for their protest, though perhaps we need not anticipate suicide and soul-death for them. As Himmelfarb concedes, postmodernism attracts relatively few historians across the profession. Yet she worries about the younger generation: '[H]ow can they resist it when it carries with it not only the promise of advancement but the allure of creativity, imagination, inventiveness?' ('Telling' 170).

Indeed, the words of G. Kitson Clark begin to sound oddly quaint, though he published them in 1958, in the early decade of the contemporary period: 'Your work,' he assures Cambridge graduate students in history, 'will not be a waste of your own and other people's time only if you feel that the subject on which you are working is one about which you are anxious to discover the truth, because it is important that the truth about that subject should be discovered' (*Guide for Research Students* 8). It is one thing to criticize the time-wasting squandering of energy on the gathering of trivia, as Byatt does in *Possession*. The constipated Blackadder and the defensive Beatrice Nest seem destined never to complete their scholarly editions. But Byatt's emphasis on the value of expertise, however stingily or unfairly used, ensures that the best aspects of scholarship survive in the younger generation, as represented by Maud (expert on liminality and guardian of the gates of a feminist resource centre far from the British Museum) and Roland (new critical close-reader, allusion-spotter, nascent poet). Much of *Possession*'s energy comes from the recovery and celebration of old-fashioned scholarly practices in a day of high-falutin' theory, practised by the likes of the chameleon and sexual adventurer Fergus Wolff, who sees the aim of scholarship as getting to the next international conference at a luxurious hotel (*Possession* 302). The fact that Maud Bailey is a feminist critic, conversant with but not professionally yoked to the theory industry, allows Byatt to stage relatively sceptical conversations about the spirit of the age. This helps her show the complication of her young scholars' perspectives on their subjects, as they imaginatively and resourcefully overturn the critical pieties constructed by the older generation. Their legitimate discoveries make this more than predictable rebellion; what Roland and Maud learn also forces them to buck the trends of their own generation. Literary history has been told incorrectly by their elders: those with incomplete information and political or personal agendas. But it can be corrected, filled in, and even brought to a television audience by the right kind of adventurers. In Byatt's vision, their striving for the truth may be a lark, but it is certainly not a waste of time.

If romances of the archive do not always correspond to postmodern historiographic metafictions, texts in Hutcheon's category do often share with romances of the archive an interest in representing research and the interpretation of documents. They differ radically in their attitudes towards the search for truth. By far the bulk of romances of the archive endorse the view that the truth is worth seeking. It can be recognized, interpreted, and presented to an audience. I have already commented upon the peculiar fact that, in contemporary British fiction, romances of the archive appear most often far from the borders of the campus or university setting, in novels of gay life, in historical adventures, in fantasies about alchemy and hermeticism, in Condition of England novels, and in counterfactual tales of the future. Romances of the archive are not hemmed in by a conventional set of academic settings;[21] in fact, they often entail liberating travels through space and time. Their bookishness is closely allied to plot, for where campus novels steer their characters away from archives and expose the limitations of book learning, contemporary romances of the archive aver that the intellectual quest can still be a worthy adventure. For this reason, I include fictions that represent postmodern challenges to more traditional ideas about representing the past, but I subordinate them to the more numerous examples in which truth can be located. This does not mean that I take an uncritical view of the 'truths' promulgated by numerous romances of the archive.

POSTIMPERIAL DISPOSSESSION

'Why must the English now always apologise?'
(*Possession* 401)

No sooner has the Ash–LaMotte correspondence been discovered than issues of proprietorship erupt. Will the letters suffer deportation to a swanky American library? Byatt alludes to a real situation facing British critics of British writers: many of the documents they need to consult are located in the United States. In this scenario, the possessor of a significant set of papers announces that the collection is up for sale to the highest bidder, patriotic hearts sink, and rich American universities scoop up another piece of British cultural heritage.[22] The process continues into the present day, when in the competitive bidding for contemporary authors' papers, for instance, well-endowed American libraries often prevail (or express interest while home institutions overlook opportunities). *Possession* reverses the normal course of events. Its conservative fantasy flouts American money. It corrects American feminist criticism, which has celebrated Christabel LaMotte as a lesbian writer. It rewards its English hero Roland not with a job at an American college (as many of his real-life compatriots sought after 1988), but with competing offers from universities in Hong Kong, Barcelona, and Amsterdam. The invigorating and financially rejuvenating resource of *Possession*, Victorian literature and eminent Victorians, turns Roland into a valuable commodity for export into the postimperial academic marketplace. Europe and the vestiges of the Empire come through for this latter-day Orlando.

The comical anti-Americanism of *Possession* depends upon residual discomfort with the shift in global power and cultural authority in the past half-century. Edward Shils summed up British intellectuals' feelings about this development in 1955:

Then, too, there was America. From a harmless, amiable, good-natured, powerful, ridiculous, loyal ally – a sort of loutish and helpful nephew – it suddenly seemed to develop into a huge challenging empire, wilful, disregarding Britain, criticising Britain, lording it over Britain, and claiming to lord it over everyone everywhere. Loyal British backs were arched at this peril ... Patriotism in this atmosphere was nurtured by anti-Americanism. ('Intellectuals' 9)

Byatt's novel reanimates this now rather mouldy rhetoric, the cultural version of which features a Hollywood-produced mass culture destroying British arts and heritage. Though the Americans of *Possession* have grown up enough to be real scholars, the characterization of Cropper as a movie cowboy reveals his genealogy as a pop-culture bogeyman. Part rich exporter of national treasures and part P.T. Barnum, Cropper is happy to leave a projected image behind, so long as he can have the real thing for his private collection across the Atlantic. The British needn't apologize in *Possession*, for now they are the ones who stand to lose. As Shils presciently observed in 1955, the victim-position can possess its own potency: '[A] feeling of being bereft of something, a feeling of loss, enhance[s] the sense of national identity' ('Intellectuals' 9).

This strand of the novel, in which Byatt emphasizes possession and access to recovered British literary treasures, reveals one aspect of the politics of archives and conceals another. She makes the case by appealing to sentiment, dramatizing the scene of persuasion by placing it on television. When the novel's flamboyant American feminist critic, Leonora Stern, announces to Shushila Patel, sari-clad television talk show host, that '"The days of cultural imperialism are over, I'm glad to say"' (*Possession* 404), she means that the newly discovered letters of Christabel LaMotte and Randolph Henry Ash ought to stay in Great Britain, instead of being whisked away by her countryman, the insidious rich American collector Mortimer Cropper. In *Possession*, the underfunded scholars of postimperial Britain heroically race, battle, and even cooperate with one another to keep English literature in the British Library. Doing so requires producing a sound-bite that will persuade the viewers of Ms Patel, who admits to reading only 'modern American and postcolonial English' (400). The defenders of English literature must persuade the British public that the contents of the literary archive matter enough to spend money on keeping it at home. Byatt shows that a stirring love story can overcome the apathy of the public, rejuvenate interest in home-grown literary products, and help to win the attention of the recently educated, multicultural population of postimperial Britain. She plays the heritage card in defence of literary history. When she invokes the competing literature of American and postcolonial writers, Byatt places Britain and British writing in the sympathetic role of underdog. The fact that British libraries and museums still contain treasure troves gathered from around the world lies concealed, for Byatt does not invite closer scrutiny of the imperial history of collecting and acquisition.

Invoking politics when discussing a novel so apparently light-hearted may revolt readers, but as I hope to demonstrate, political visions of contemporary Britain and its relation to its past run through even the fluffiest romances of the archive. As Jacques Derrida comments in a footnote in *Archive Fever*, 'there is no political power without control of the archive.' Most importantly for Derrida, the quality of a democracy can always be evaluated by 'the participation in and the access to the archive, its constitution, and its interpretation' (4n). On the one hand, a forbidden or repressed archive reveals state power exerting its authority unfairly over historians or, as in Orwell's *Nineteen Eighty-Four* (1949), over the evidence-bearing texts themselves. On the other hand, a state that fails to collect and protect the materials that belong in its archive risks cultural memory loss. *Possession* triumphantly defeats the forces of contemporary forgetfulness, while at the same time inducing selective amnesia about the past.

Byatt's romance of the archive represents just one use of a recovered past, by no means the only possibility explored by contemporary novelists. In *Traces of Another Time*, Margaret Scanlan emphasizes an alternative view. She sees in the works of Anthony Burgess, Elizabeth Bowen, J.G. Farrell, Iris Murdoch, Thomas Kilroy, Paul Scott, and Doris Lessing an expression of the ultimate uselessness of the past:

> History as presented in the contemporary British novel is neither glamorous nor consoling. It is too diffuse to offer lessons, too unfinished to constitute a space into which we can escape; and we ourselves, implicated in the failures of the past, cannot even enjoy its ironies comfortably. Whatever the authors' professed politics, their novels resonate with a profound pessimism about the consequences of public action. What actuates these fictions is not, then, a confidence that the past will teach us how to behave, but a quieter conviction that it is better to know than to remain ignorant, even though what we learn is the enormous difficulty of understanding our lives historically. (*Traces* 16)

Romances of the archive acknowledge and even dwell upon this difficulty of managing the nexus of the personal and the historical.[23] Novels like *Possession* set up the obstacles enumerated by Scanlan in order to stage their triumphant overcoming by research questers. Self-aware, theoretically informed, and motivated by a desire to know, the romancers of archives restore to history its glamorous, consoling, and admonitory powers.

While presentism and antiquarianism may be absent from postmodernism, as Holmes and Linda Hutcheon concur (Holmes *Historical* 55; Hutcheon *Politics* 71), these views and other alternatives from historiography predating postmodernism frequently appear in romances of the archive. The subsequent chapters demonstrate that reading a wide variety of romances of the archive opens up a broader range of historiographical questions, such as: What kinds of relationships of the past to the present day do romances of the archive propose? If the truth is out there, who is it for? Does the past gain value only as present-day characters apply its lessons? Does commerce, or an idiosyncratic idea of personal heritage, trump history? Does the Whig interpretation of history (dedicated to elucidating stages in human progress towards parliamentary democracy) live on in contemporary fiction, or have antiquarianism, canon-bashing, postmodernism, and nostalgia for lost worlds denuded it of its enduring narrative power? I will seek to explain why romances of the archive so often turn to questions about Britain's role and the history of the British Empire. As we will see, the fictional consideration of the uses of the past leads contemporary novelists to diverse conclusions about literature, history, memory, evidence, the value of alternative perspectives, heroism, and culpability.

3

Wellsprings

The romance of the archive arises out of a rich tradition of precursors – British, American, European, and Latin American. Though later chapters establish the specific uses to which contemporary British writers put its various inherited traits, this chapter undertakes the genealogical work of identifying sources for the key elements of recent British romances of the archive. The description I proffer in the preceding chapter suggests that a romance of the archive contains character-researchers, endowed with the corporeality and round psychology of the realistic novel; romance adventure stories, in which research features as a kernel plot action, resulting in strong closure, with climactic discoveries and rewards; discomforts and inconveniences suffered in the service of knowledge; sex and physical pleasure gained as a result of questing; settings and locations containing collections of papers; material traces of the past revealing the truth; and evocation of history, looking back from a postimperial context. Each of these elements, alone and in combination with its fellows, appears in so numerous a collection of literary works that every reader could propose a unique set of potential influences. The sources and analogues I examine in this chapter thus do not make up a definitive, closed list, but suggest instead some of the representative texts and literary sub-genres from which recent romances of the archive arise. Each example invokes the prehistory of at least one key trait of romances of the archive, though in some rich texts many more can be found. From sixteenth-century allegorical quest romances to twentieth-century pulp fiction, the romance of archive inherits a complex set of characteristics. These it reworks, responding to an end-of-the-millennium impulse to scrutinize, defend, expose, and celebrate, and otherwise come to terms with Great Britain's imperial past.

The following pages offer a series of exhibits from a variety of older texts, presented more or less chronologically, but not so arranged to suggest a development or progress from nascent to fully developed romances of the archive. These wellsprings can be located both in the traditional realistic novel and in romance genres. Indeed, the link between a library and national history pre-dates the novel as a form. In Edmund Spenser's *Faerie Queene* (1596), the link between romances involving big old books and Britain's national ambitions plainly shows. Gothic novels (particularly those of the nineteenth-century gothic revival) contribute, among other things, atmospheric settings, the overwrought psychology of the questing character, climactic scenes of revelation, and an emphasis on secret messages and conspiracies unveiled. Henry James's novella *The Aspern Papers* (1888, 1908) suggests the combination of scholarly research, discomfort, and misplaced desire, rendered in a modern psychological style. James's distaste for romance climax revises the sexual bargain into an obstacle to truth-seeking. Inaccessible or disappearing truths, we will see, pre-date postmodernist literary fiction.

British and American thrillers encompass the sub-genres of dime novels and pulp fiction: gothic horror, spy novels, and adventure fictions all contribute to the romance of the archive. H.P. Lovecraft's tales explore the traces of ancient evil revealed by ill-advised questing in archives best left alone. John Le Carré's cold war spy thrillers place the textual dimension of espionage and counter-espionage in a conspiratorial context, representing the competition and sometimes overt hostility between British and American operatives. Later romances of the archive revisit this theme. Quest romances live at the movies, where researchers such as 'Professor' Indiana Jones discover threats to democracy. Here the adventure spy thriller returns to its gothic roots when Steven Spielberg invokes the ancient powers of the Ark of the Covenant and the Holy Grail.

Though detective fiction usually eschews magical or supernatural agency, its epistemological thrust guarantees that the truth can be found. Blind alleys and dead ends in the investigation only delay the ultimate revelation of answers. From Wilkie Collins's *The Moonstone* (1868) on, the interpretation of character, circumstances, motives, and physical evidence eclipse textual analysis in most mysteries. Arthur Conan Doyle's 'The Adventure of the Musgrave Ritual' (1893) is a notable exception and a *locus classicus* for the interpretation of textual evidence in detective fiction. In the twentieth-century police procedural, archival research often appears in close proximity with the more exciting activities of detection, but it is normally represented in the most truncated and sketchy fashion. Josephine Tey's *The Daughter of Time* (1951) makes forced inactivity into an excuse for romancing the archive, as a bed-ridden police detective works to exonerate Richard III of his crimes, revealing him to be the victim of Tudor propagandists' conspiracies.

Finally, the international success of Umberto Eco's *The Name of the Rose* stimulates the recent efflorescence of British romances of the archive. Eco's popular novel presents a powerful literary model for fiction that asks questions about finding the truth in the face of official obfuscation, and it represents politically motivated manipulation of the past and the historical record. Though the author and setting are Italian, Eco makes a subtle, humane, and rational British scholar the hero of the book's intellectual quest. The combination of William of Baskerville's successful decoding of the labyrinth and its hidden truths with the catastrophic destruction of a valued past strikes a chord both nostalgic and pessimistic. This mood particularly suits fictional explorations of the uses of the past in the wake of the 1982 Falkland Islands conflict. With the exception of the antecedents to contemporary romances of the archive, the several dozen novels I discuss in detail in this study all date from after 1982,[1] and the end of this chapter proposes a set of literary, historical, and cultural contexts as circumstances influencing the surge in British romances of the archive from the 1980s to the present.[2]

THE BOOKS IN THE LIBRARY OF THE HOUSE OF ALMA

Writing nearly four hundred years before the Falklands crisis and the late-twentieth-century literary response to decolonization, Spenser associates corporeality, a library housing Good Memory, and books of nationalist, imperial history that establish the appropriate uses of the past for specially qualified readers and defenders of the soul's house. These readers are Sir Guyon, the Knight of Temperance (whose adventures in the company of his sidekick the Palmer make up the bulk of Book 2 of *The Faerie Queene*) and Prince Arthur, the magnificent young leader. Both figures engage in an episodic progress in order to develop characters modelled along Aristotelian lines; they are functionaries in an allegory, not realistic, psychologically convincing characters. When he defends and then tours the House of Alma in cantos 9 and 10, discovering the history books that lie in the library located in the head of that corporeal house of temperance, Guyon enacts the romance of the archive within a great sixteenth-century English allegorical romance, doing his part in the education of Prince Arthur as he acts out his own self-fashioning.

Spenser represents the House of Alma as the fleshy container for the soul and as the home of a real girl rescued from beseiging forces by Sir Guyon and Prince Arthur. Amazingly, after seven years of being besieged, Alma is still a 'virgin bright' (*FQ* 2.9.18 l.1). She invites her defenders to penetrate the fortress, which is built not of brick but of perishable flesh. The visitors note the entrance and exit, mouth and anus. Each part of the face, mouth, and throat is rendered architecturally, and allegorical figures represent bodily functions. Alma arranges safe passage between the rows of armed warders (the teeth) into the Hall (the gullet) and into the stomach and organs of digestion. Perhaps out of virgin modesty, Alma does not take her guests to the sex organs. However, after being entertained by damsels in the goodly Parlour (the heart), the knights are finally led by Alma up the spine into the stately Turret, the head (*FQ* 2.9.44 l.8). Three rooms in the tower contain sages:

> The first of them could things to come forsee:
>> The next could of things present best aduize;
>> The third things past could keepe in memoree,
>> So that no time, nor reason could arize,
>> But that the same could one of these comprize
>> (*FQ* 2.9.49 ll.1–5)

The third sage, employing memory to help men and faeries alike comprehend events and their causes and consequences, guards a remarkable chamber, 'th'hindmost roome of three' (*FQ* 2.9.54 l.9). This chamber we will examine closely, for it suggests many of the traits of the rooms and containers represented with such conventional particularity in romances of the archive.

The room of memory seems ruinous and old, but strong curving walls (the skull) make the container strong. Memory, the man of 'infinite remembrance' (*FQ* 2.9.56 l.1) looks a wreck – an 'oldman, halfe blind' (*FQ* 2.9.55 l.5), but he can recall with clarity all the events of the past. The records are laid up in a sturdy chest, incorruptible and immortal, yet the room itself is decorated with decayed records, emphasizing the miraculous quality of the old man's memory:

> His chamber all was hangd about with rolles,
>> And old records from auncient times deriu'd,
>> Some made in books, some in long parchyment scrolles,
>> That were all worme-eaten, and full of canker holes.
>> (*FQ* 2.9.57 ll.6–9)

The promise of perfect recall and complete knowledge, a fantasy embedded deep in the sources for romances of the archive, is mitigated by the works of time. Even in Spenser's allegorical temperate House of Alma, age, decay, and decrepitude threaten impeccable recall. Furnishing the old man (Eumnestes, or Good Memory) with a helper, Anamnestes (Reminder), remedies the failings of human brainpower and creates a character-type, the minion – or archivist's apprentice – in which access, continuity, and preservation may be vested:

> A litle boy did on him still attend,
> To reach, when euer he for ought did send;
> And oft when things were lost, or laid amis,
> That boy them sought, and unto him did lend.
> (*FQ* 2.9.58 ll.4–7)

When Prince Arthur and Sir Guyon enter the library, however, they do not need the help of Anamnestes or Eumnestes to find the perfectly appropriate volumes. Research is a matter of being the right character in the right room at the right moment. The ancient books practically jump into the hands of the designated readers, *Briton moniments* for Prince Arthur and *Antiquitie of Faerie lond* for Sir Guyon. Though the knights are otherwise represented as men of action, the histories ignite curiosity in Guyon and Arthur. 'Whereat they burning both with feruent fire,/ Their countries auncestry to vnderstond,' the two knights 'Crau'd leaue of Alma, and that aged sire,/ To read those books; who gladly graunted their desire' (*FQ* 2.9.60 ll.6–9). Spenser then employs the scene of avid reading in order to interpolate, in Canto 10, a chronicle of British kings from Brutus to Uther, and 'rolles of Elfin Emporours,/ till time of Gloriane' (*FQ* 2.10 epigraph). Thus, the human Prince Arthur learns his personal and national history, from Trojan Brutus (implicitly) to the Tudors, while Guyon bones up on the faerie empire, leading up to the reigning Gloriane (who also represents Queen Elizabeth of Spenser's present day).

Though these chronicles parallel one another, the faerie history is presented more briefly and with less emphasis on trials and tribulations. Both chronicles come together to teach Arthur, Guyon, and Spenser's Elizabethan readers a self-justifying legend about the ancestry and reign of Elizabeth and the expansion of the empire that begins under her supervision. Spenser recasts here a well-worn mode, of epic narration in the service of imperial history that comes out of Vergil and the Roman context. He works in a more contemporary frame of reference – competition for dominion in the new world, an area unknown to the classical writers. The proem to book 2 of *The Faerie Queene* invokes this context, with reminders of the growing known world: 'Many great Regions are discouered,/ Which to late age were neuer mentioned' (*FQ* 2. Proem 2 ll.4–5), including Virginia. In order to sanction the expansion, exploration, and dominion of Tudor colonial activities, Spenser has Arthur and Guyon study (on the one hand) a heroic chronicle of how Britain came to be united under its right ruler and, on the other, the annals of a legendary fairy empire. Spenser's imaginary *Antiquitie of Faerie lond* attests to the natural dominion of the faerie kind: 'Of these a mightie people shortly grew,/ And puissant kings, which all the world warrayd,/ And to them selues all Nations did subdew' (*FQ* 2.10.72 ll.1–3). Since Gloriana is the descendent of this imperial race, her actions fulfil the destiny more laboriously achieved by imaginary and historical figures named in the chronicle of Britain.

The book that Arthur reads relates the actions of the human antecedents of the sovereign Queen, telling how

> The land, which warlike Britons now possesse,
>   And therein haue their mightie empire raysd,
>   In antique times was saluage wildernesse,
>   Vnpeopled, vnmanurd, vnprou'd, vnpraysd,
>   (*FQ* 2.10.5 ll.1–4)

By occupying, populating, fertilizing, naming, and making it memorable through noble deeds, the ancestors of Elizabeth establish their dominion over a land only in use by Giants and naked half-beastly men, who are quickly driven off the territory they pollute. Drawing on Geoffrey of Monmouth's twelfth-century *Historia Regum Britanniae* as a main source, and on the standard sixteenth-century chroniclers (including Holinshed) as supplements, Spenser assembles in sixty-four verses a condensed narration of British history up until Uther Pendragon. Either the account ends with the coming of Arthur, or Prince Arthur is magically prevented from continuing to read into what would be, for him, the future. Arthur reacts to his historical reading with gratitude to his country:

> At last quite rauisht with delight, to heare
>   The royall Ofspring of his natiue land,
>   Cryde out, Deare countrey, O how dearely deare
>   Ought they remembraunce, and perpetuall band
>   Be to thy foster Childe, that from thy hand

Did commun breath and nouriture receaue?
How brutish is it not to vnderstand,
How much to her we owe, that all vs gaue,
That gaue vnto vs all, what euer good we haue.
(*FQ* 2.10.69 ll.1–9)

The purpose of encountering the past is to discover indebtedness to the
country itself, created through the efforts of his ancestors, but now represented as a nurturing foster mother responsible for all that is good in the
present. The rational soul of the House of Alma finally resides in these
Good Memories. Understanding, which separates men from brutes,
amounts to an enumeration of debts. The way to repay that debt, Spenser
suggests, is to act out the destiny of the faerie race, which sanctions the
imperial rule of Gloriana. Yet Arthur and Guyon are temporarily immobilized, so beguiled by novelty, and so inspired by the natural desire to
improve their country's condition (*FQ* 2.10.77 ll.1–2) that they can scarcely
tear themselves away from their studies for supper. The demands of plot
and of temperance intervene, and Alma brings them 'half vnwilling from
their bookes' (*FQ* 2.10.77 l.8). The lessons of the past would be of no use if
the action heroes who are to implement them get addicted to reading.

Spenser poses and solves one of the hazards of fictions that require
characters to sit down and study. Scholarship is necessary, but it impedes
action: the denizens of the archive must be drawn away from their books,
interrupted before they are satisfied. They must keep moving in order to
continue learning. A further risk lies in extensively quoted history or
vividly represented historical documents, for these secondary texts can
dilute the interest in the surrounding adventure plot. A romancer of the
archive does not succumb to the antiquarian's impulse, forever collecting,
compiling, and adding detail to the recovered past. Instead, brief encounters with uncompleted narrations pique interest and drive the questing
action forward. The fascination with fragmented, lost, concealed, or suppressed documents, discovered before the inevitable amnesia of Good
Memory destroys all access to the past, receives its amplest development in
gothic fiction, one of the most important sustainers of romance conventions during the first two centuries of the English novel.

GOTHIC CONVENTIONS: 'THE TRUTH IS OUT THERE'

Contemporary romances of the archive owe a great deal of their atmosphere and their conspiratorial plots to gothic fiction. As in many popular

kinds of contemporary film and fiction, gothic settings, character types, storylines, and devices such as embedded stories or peculiar dream-states abound in romances of the archive. John Fowles's *The Magus* (1966) exemplifies the evocation of the uncanny repetitions of gothic in a contemporary research narrative. Gothic fiction bequeaths to Fowles and his metafictional cohort the often-employed set of conventions whose prevalence Eve Kosofsky Sedgewick notes: 'A fully legible manuscript or an uninterrupted narrative is rare; rarer still is the novel whose story is comprised by a single narrator, without the extensive irruption into the middle of the book of a new history with a new historian; rarest of all is the book presented by the author, in his or her own person, without a pseudonym and an elaborate account of the provenance and antiquity of the supposed original manuscript' (*Coherence* 14). Contemporary romances of the archive make frequent casual use of these trappings and strategies of gothic, committing to its full generic array of characteristics only in certain cases. Some recent romances of the archive, such as Susan Hill's *The Mist in the Mirror* (1992), cleave so closely to the pattern of gothic tales that they can best be understood as imitations of the form as popularized in the Victorian revival or in the early-twentieth-century ghost stories of M.R. James. Many more quote gothic devices within tales governed by other generic conventions, the archival romance unleashing gothic forces into more rational story-worlds. Others fuse gothic with its descendent genres (sensation fiction, detective fiction, and thrillers) to create up-to-date versions of big Victorian novels. Whether one comes by one's gothic through reading Ann Radcliffe, or by watching *The X-Files* on television, its conventional entanglement with irrationality, ambiguity, madness, darkness, evil, and hidden crimes that come back to haunt you still possesses the power to discomfit and thrill.

Writers of romances of the archive draw on both the themes and structures of gothic fiction in order to impart the thrilling agitation of suspense to their readers. The intense feeling with which characters respond to revelations about the past carries over from eighteenth- and nineteenth-century gothic and sensation fiction into contemporary mystery thrillers and the Lovecraftian sub-genre called gothic horror. As in gothic tales, romances of the archive emphasize the location of secrets or hidden messages in boxes, chests, and cabinets (or other pieces of furniture with concealed compartments). Finding secrets hidden in this fashion (perhaps after anonymous prompting or mysterious warnings) may endanger the life or sanity of the quester. The unspeakable contents or occult power of the letters, diaries, scraps, recipes, maps, or suggestive lists contained in gothic hiding-places unleash hazardous knowledge about the past that is often better off contained, sealed, buried, or cast in a crevasse. Several of M.R. James's *Ghost Stories of an Antiquary* (1904) reverse the scholarly treasure hunt, beginning with research scenarios and ending with the destruction of documents or the re-interring of caskets. More than one of James's antiquarians ends a broken man, unhinged by knowledge of demonic forces.[3] Unlike the Spenserian history that inspires gratitude in its princely readers, gothic offers for ordinary consumers the dark side of the past: dispossession, murder, incest, rape, bigamy, forced religious conversion, drugs, slavery, and miscegenation. In gothic fiction, researching history means investigating crime.

It has not escaped the notice of critics of gothic that the genre rises and gains popularity (from the first phase of the 1760s to 1820s) during the period when late-eighteenth-century capitalism finds materials and markets in a growing empire. The coincidence of timing (which is of course also true of the British novel in all its modes) underscores what theorists of gothic have observed: that it contains a 'very intense, if displaced, engagement with political and social problems' (Punter *Literature of Terror* 62). To some commentators, gothic represents a challenge to the ideology driving that imperial expansion, while other critics, particularly those focusing on the later nineteenth-century gothic revival, see in it a convenient imaginative space in which to work out guilt about mistreating other races and appropriating their lands (while allowing the continuance of the profitable British adventure).[4] Cannon Schmitt has persuasively argued that the nineteenth-century debate about empire is elaborated in gothic fictions' encounters with others, aliens, and monsters (*Alien Nation* 16). In accordance with the Manichaean logic now strongly associated with Orientalism as described by Edward Said, an English self-understanding arises out of the characterization of exotic difference and depravity. Schmitt argues that 'gothics pose as semi-ethnographic texts in their representation of Catholic, Continental Europe or the far East as fundamentally un-English, the site of depravity' and 'present and enact productive (though not necessarily benign) workings of power ... represent[ing] and enact[ing] the formation of England conceived as a nation and of English national subjects' (*Alien Nation* 2, 10). It thus follows that those investigations of history in romances of the archive that are marked by gothic conventions sustain gothic's political interests. As a sort of story manifestly unreal and fictive, gothic continues to provide a vehicle for the symbolic or allegorical working-through of vexatious topics and hot-button issues in disguise. Racial strife, diseases such as AIDS or the Ebola virus, technologies that outpace ethics (cloning and genetic engineering), terrorists, religious extremists, survivalists, and millennial cultists all get ground through the mill of gothic, particularly in the fast-reacting medium of the television series. Gothic functions as a mirror that shows us, in its distortions, who we are in relation to what worries us.

That these contemporary preoccupations might best be revealed through the scrutiny of evidence from the past feeds the conspiratorial plot lines of gothic fiction since the eighteenth century. Though the conspirators, evil agents, and original criminals vary (they may be monks, Jesuits, Freemasons, white slavers, alchemists, deposed goddesses, and so forth), gothic posits a world of hyper-consequence, in which past actions continue to yield their often dire results generation after generation. This view of an infectious source urgently compels research, interpretation, and action, and it is from gothic that the romance of the archive draws the spectacular closing gesture of destruction. Too hazardous to be known by more than an elite few, the discovered truth is put to the torch, in a humanitarian gesture of forbidding that simultaneously enhances the vicarious thrill of the reader who has voyeuristically taken in the results of the quest for knowledge. The destruction of gathered evidence paradoxically enforces the possibility that 'the truth is out there,' to quote the slogan of *The X-Files*. Lack of proof hijacks rational explanation, deviating from normality to those alternative trajectories featuring supernatural, otherworldly, or otherwise inexplicable forces. Particularly when confronting discomforting aspects of contemporary political reality, the lure of gothic's conspiratorial explanations can be felt in many romances of the archive.

'PENETRATION FAILS': THE CASE OF *THE ASPERN PAPERS*

I delight in a palpable imaginable visitable past – in the nearer distances and the clearer mysteries, the marks and signs of a world we may reach over to as by making a long arm we grasp an object at the other end of the table. The table is the one, the common expanse, and where we lean, so stretching, we find it firm and continuous. That, to my imagination, is the past fragrant of all, or of almost all, the poetry of the thing outlived and lost and gone, and yet in which the precious element of closeness, telling so of connexions but tasting so of differences, remains appreciable. With more moves back the element of the appreciable shrinks – just as the charm of looking over a garden-wall into another garden breaks down when successions of walls appear. The other gardens, those still beyond, may be there, but even by use of our longest ladder we are baffled and bewildered – the view is mainly a view of barriers ... We are divided of course between liking to feel the past strange and liking to feel it familiar; the difficulty is, for intensity, to catch it at the moment when the scales of the balance hang with the right evenness. (Henry James, 'Preface' to *The Aspern Papers* x)

In James the past is an imaginary place that can be visited, or almost reached, despite the barriers that time puts in our way. Historians tend to care whether the past with which they engage seems strange or familiar, because perceptions of similarity and difference in turn govern the uses to which historical interpretations can be put. The novelist in this case represents the alternative possibilities in order to create a work imbued with 'intensity' ('Preface' x). In his novella *The Aspern Papers*, James shows how an enthusiast hopes to plunder the past for souvenirs and augmented knowledge of a famous poet, while the living woman who knew the poet works to prevent the researcher from achieving his aim. Her goal, however, is not the protection of reputation and guarding of privacy so often motivating the destruction of personal papers, but the entirely materialistic aim of securing the best price for what she possesses. Though crass, she acts to benefit another, her penniless niece. The researcher, in contrast, sets out to victimize the ladies in order to gratify an acquisitive wish. James's novella raises many of the ethical questions that bedevil researchers in romances of the archive.

In earlier passages of the preface quoted above, Henry James establishes the historical model for the fictional characters treated in *The Aspern Papers*. Though for his story he changes the names and locations, James explains that it struck him as extraordinarily romantic that while living in Florence he should have overlapped with 'Jane Clairmont, the half-sister of Mary Godwin, Shelley's second wife and for a while the intimate friend of Byron and the mother of his daughter Allegra' ('Preface' vii). Despite never seeing her, and in fact hearing of her 'long survival' after it is no longer possible to see her 'in the flesh,' James values Clairmont (actually Claire, not Jane, as James mistakenly asserts) as a symbolic link with the past: 'I felt myself more concerned with the mere strong fact of her having testified for the reality and the closeness of our relation to the past' (vii). Though James declares, 'I delight in a palpable imaginable visitable past' (x), his novella explores a scenario in which an unscrupulous scholar attempts to breach the barriers fancifully figured above as 'garden walls' to do more than contemplate visiting the past, in the form of old ladies formerly connected with dead poets. Instead he wishes to lay hands on it, so long as it is safely inanimate.

The scholarly narrator of the story, obsessed with securing the literary remains of romantic poet Jeffrey Aspern, introduces himself under false pretences and an alias into the Venice home of Miss Juliana (the elderly former lover of Aspern) and Miss Tina (Juliana's middle-aged 'niece') Bordereau. The Misses Bordereau's surname suggests both the border and the bureau that would have to be violated in order to acquire the letters and papers of Aspern. James explores the monomania and the sterility of the scholar, setting the latter's desire for the papers against his revulsion from the actual physical contact that would be required to secure them. He boasts at the outset that he will 'make love to the niece' (*Aspern Papers* 14), and he does flirt with Miss Tina whenever he gets a chance. He recoils, however, from the bargain she offers after her aunt dies, to swap marriage for access to the papers. The narrator already stands self-confessed as lacking 'the tradition of personal conquest' (22), but he has been willing to spend a great deal of money to get a chance at the papers, and he has certainly invited Miss Tina to imagine a romantic connection. When the scenario goes beyond flirtatious bantering, the narrator panics. It is possible, after all, that Miss Tina would be satisfied with little more than financial security, but the intimacy that titillates the narrator when it is immured in the past inspires horror in the present. When the narrator returns after ignominiously fleeing the scene of the proposal, Miss Tina reports that she has burnt the papers, one by one, in the kitchen fire; only a portrait of the poet survives. In the end, it hangs as a souvenir of failure above the solitary narrator's lonely writing desk. The concluding words of the story emphasize what has not been achieved: 'When I look at it I can scarcely bear my loss – I mean of the precious papers' (143).

Getting in touch with the past through research turns out badly for the erstwhile romancer of the archive in this psychological portrait of a scholar's failed humanity. It is vital to recall what the narrator does not notice: that we have no evidence of the existence of the papers that drive him to lie, sneak around in the dark, and trifle with the affections of a pathetic old maid. Though Miss Juliana herself is hidden in plain sight, like Poe's purloined letter, the letters of Jeffrey Aspern appear nowhere in the fiction. They are always offstage, or purported to be inside an impenetrable container. To the narrator the letters are more real and certainly more desirable than the woman who knew Jeffrey Aspern intimately. From his perspective, she offends by still existing, grasping money and bargaining for an outrageous rent, yet her imminent death menaces him with the possibility that she will destroy the compromising papers. Where are the papers? Miss Tina's ambiguous exclamation – '"Oh she has everything!"' – the narrator regards as 'precious evidence' for their existence (*Aspern Papers* 78), but thirty pages later he still wonders where they are hidden, in the bedroom, in a 'battered box,' in a 'tall old secretary ... a receptacle somewhat infirm but still capable of keeping rare secrets' (100). Miss Tina's blush, apprehended by the narrator when he stares at the secretary, may be the verification he seeks, but it may also be the moment in which Miss Tina conceives the details of a tall tale about the papers. One does not have to be a Freudian to imagine yet another reason for an old maid's blush when a man stares with such interest at a 'receptacle somewhat infirm but still capable' of containing mysteries (100).

The bizarre liveliness and attractiveness of objects in the tale is matched by the creepy treatment of women as vessels or relics of the dead. In one of many gothic traces in the story, Juliana herself – the inspiration for 'Aspern's most exquisite and renowned lyrics' – has become a terrible relic, a ghastly creature whose green eye-shade masks a face the narrator imagines as a 'death's-head' (*Aspern Papers* 23). Though distaste and horror predominate, the narrator's homosocial[5] desire is aroused by his first being near Juliana: '[H]er presence seemed somehow to contain and express his own' so that the narrator feels 'nearer to [Aspern] at that first moment of seeing her than [he] ever had been before or ever ha[s] been since' (23). James lays bare the tawdriness of the scholar's wanting to shake hands with her, feeling 'an irresistible desire to hold in [his] own the hand Jeffrey Aspern had pressed' (30), and seeking a receipt in the spirit of the tricky souvenir hunter after an autograph (42). The story relates a sequence of rebuffs to these desires, until the narrator retreats in shock at the possibility of consummation in the person of Miss Tina. (Her age and obscure parentage makes it possible that she is the illegitimate child of Aspern and 'Aunt' Juliana – not that the narrator suspects this.) Getting in contact with the past opens up a strange array of avenues, not all of which lead to the truth. Miss Juliana herself declares: '"The truth is God's, it is n't man's: we had better leave it alone"' (90). Leave it alone is just what the narrator cannot do.

The compulsive masochism of the research takes a sadistic turn as privacy is violated, for the impenetrable regions of the ladies' Venice mansion are associated as much with pain as with the inaccessible letters. The narrator comically notes that he looks in from his station in the hall 'with my heart beating as I had known it to do in dentists' parlours' (*Aspern Papers* 16). The gothic fear comes down a notch with the introduction of a bathetic tone reminiscent of Jane Austen, but James brings overwrought emotions back up again in the climactic scene of 'research.' The narrator sneaks into Miss Juliana's rooms, hoping to open the secretary and steal the papers (he fantasizes that Miss Tina has unlocked the desk for him). He gets caught in the act: 'Juliana stood there in her nightdress, by the doorway of her room, watching me; her hands were raised, she had lifted the everlasting curtain that covered half her face, and for the first, the last, the only time I beheld her extraordinary eyes. They glared at me; they were like the sudden drench, for a caught burglar, of a flood of gaslight; they made me horribly ashamed' (118). The consequence of this violation on Miss Juliana is more permanent than the temporary humiliation of the narrator. She falls back in a seizure and dies not long afterwards.

In this novella, the material traces of the past become terribly corporeal, the desiccated body of a woman replacing the paper traces of the dead poet's passions. James elliptically reminds the reader that human bodies are the most palpable connection other humans have with the past – physical resemblance, memory, inheritance, and family lore all requiring first the creation of a younger generation out of the bodies of women. What in Spenser's House of Alma begins as an image of nurture and promise for a bright future turns through the researcher's revulsion into a rejection of continuity and humanity. Selfish acquisitiveness guarantees that the papers will elude the researcher. In this seminal story of a hidden archive, nothing comes to fruition. Long before postmodernism arrives to destabilize the idea of facts and certainties, the truth remains beyond the fictional researcher's grasp. James accomplishes this in a characteristically modern fashion, through psychological portraiture. The personal obtuseness of the researcher contributes to the representation of monomania, or single-minded obsession, which (in combination with ethical breaches) makes a founding gesture for romances of the archive. Miss Juliana, in control of a scheme to match her antagonist, and Miss Tina, reacting to her humiliation with the only dignified action left to her, are also round characters, capable of surprising in a convincing way, to apply E.M. Forster's test-phrase.[6] James gives the characters of his quest plot the bodies and minds of modern fiction.

Nonetheless, many ingredients of an old-fashioned romance adventure plot remain, with great dashes of Gothic flavouring. Penetrating the Venetian house; trespassing and approaching the forbidden secretary; killing the old lady with shock; fleeing the scene in a gondola: all these plot events add action and adventure to the narrative, in which most of the story time must actually be devoted to the researcher cooling his heels. The enhancement and exaggeration of the normal events of research are to be repeated in virtually all romances of the archive after James. By way of contrast, realistic reports of actual researchers are inevitably abbreviated to contain their inherent dullness. James's contemporary Frederick Rolfe, whose thinly veiled autobiographical novels were published under a variety of pseudonyms (most famously 'Baron Corvo'), describes a researcher's routine in a far more recognizable fashion. Several months of steady scholarly work receive this compressed summary:

> All day long, he lived in the British Museum, studying, discovering unknown Medici MSS. and some unpublished holographs, following clues, and generally collecting the atmosphere and the background on which to place his figures 'vividly and picturesquely to suit the Library Public' (whatever that chimera might be). When the Museum closed, he went back to his cave, and grappled with his day's notes ... The abominable electric light of the Reading Room damaged his eyes. The enormous consumption of cerebral tissues (which his work involved) demanded augmentation of nourishment. His carnal appetite astonished him; and his pound a week went almost all in food. In the course of his work, it became necessary for him to go about the country after Medici documents; and his means did not suffice ... After all, a man cannot work eighteen hours a day during seven days a week, on insufficient food and with total absence of recreation, without feeling the strain. (*Nicholas Crabbe* 70)

Gone are the gondola excursions, the confrontations in walled gardens, and all the accoutrements of the vacation splurge. Though James's wealthy researcher avoids the hunger and fatigue that afflict a poor man like Corvo's Crabbe, he does emphasize the discomforts and inconveniences ensuing from his quest. He must keep up the tedious pretense of loving flowers and gardens, when in fact he is a sterile character not at all at home in the greenery. He must spend more money than he intends. His calculating flirtation with Miss Tina leads to a mortifying scene. As Miss Tina correctly asserts, there is no pleasure in the house she shares with her aunt (*Aspern Papers* 39). The story ends with the narrator's regret, but not with his repentance. To the encyclopedia of key traits present in *The Aspern Papers* strong closure can be added: the unyielded documents are fed (offstage) one by one to the flames. In the end, James indicts the very desire that he writes of so romantically in his preface. An accessible past reached through records shows itself to be an unwholesome fantasy, verging on necrophilia. Transformed from a picturesque vista of garden walls into a locked cabinet within a forbidden room, the barriers gain symbolic power as James's corrupt researcher fails to get beyond them. Inside the house, under the mattress, locked in the secretary, and into the stove, the papers (and any truths they might reveal) dodge and weave, to remain out of reach when the researcher's powers of penetration fail.

REVEALING CONSPIRACIES – FROM PULP FICTION TO THE MOVIES

A researcher in a horror story, a thriller, or an action-adventure tale is far less likely to be thwarted like James's protagonist than to be sucked into a terrifying conspiracy or to discover knowledge too horrible to be borne by mortals. The genres found in pulp-fiction magazines such as *Amazing Stories, Weird Tales, Black Mask*, and *Thrilling Adventures* have a continuous life in popular culture, passing from print form into the movies and television, and then back again into popular fiction.[7] In these formulaic stories, the researcher uncovers the evidence of dark forces at work in the world. These powers go by different names: Freemasons, Jesuits, Fifth Columnists, Mormons, Nazis, Elders of Zion, Soviet spies, IRA splinter-groups, the Mafia, Sauron, and Cthulhu. Within these Manichaean fictions stereotypes govern the sketchy characterization of the bad guys against whom good guys must struggle for the sake of future freedom and prosperity. Diverse representatives of the dark side share the common tactic of abusing the freedoms of open, democratic societies. They exploit secrecy and oath-taking, use blackmail and informants, and evoke fear of revenge, death, and the destruction of civilization. In the most extreme cases, researchers discover cults or secret societies in which vicious practices – human sacrifice, cannibalism, and black magic – awaken occult powers that weaken the fabric of civilization.

H.P. Lovecraft, one of the acknowledged masters of horror fiction, often employs an over-curious researcher. In different ways in the stories 'The Call of Cthulhu' (1928), 'The Dunwich Horror' (1929), and 'The Haunter of the Dark' (1936), Lovecraft shows the alteration of a researcher's state of mind, from rationality and scepticism to horrified belief. In the earliest story, Lovecraft's myth of an ancient species of aliens receives its fullest exposition, through the efforts of a young researcher drawn into investigating the cult of Cthulhu after he looks into his dead grand-uncle's papers. He discovers the presence of malevolent monsters that communicate from their tombs by entering the dreams of artists, musicians, and sensitive souls. The call of Cthulhu leads to destruction and madness, as the behavior of murderous voodoo practitioners and 'mongrel' worshippers in the cult of Cthulhu illustrates. Indeed, the newspaper clippings gathered from the world press suggest that the destructive suggestions of the telepathic monsters lead to all forms of human misfortune. The rationality of the narrator, aspiring anthropologist and grand-nephew of a professor of semitic languages, dissolves into superstitious dread as a direct result of his successful researches:

> The matter of the cult still remained to fascinate me, and at times I had visions of personal fame from researches into its origins and connections. I visited New Orleans, talked with Legrasse and others of that old-time raiding party, saw the frightful image, and even questioned such of the mongrel prisoners as still survived ... What I now heard so graphically at first hand, though it was really no more than a detailed confirmation of what my uncle had written, excited me afresh; for I felt sure that I was on the track of a very real, very secret, and very ancient religion whose discovery would make me an anthropologist of note. My attitude was still one of absolute materialism *as I wish it still were*. ('Cthulhu' 148)

The Great Old Ones whose cult the researcher uncovers are in fact dreadfully physical, as the images produced by dream-tormented sculptors or uncovered at ancient sites have hinted. Huge, squid-headed, octopus- and dragon-like, the monsters are not flesh and blood, though they thrive on the psychic food of human sacrifice. They can transform themselves into sea creatures, but they are extraterrestrial predators, as disgusting as they are dangerous, 'the green, sticky spawn of the stars' clutching at their victims with 'flabby claws' (157).

The only protection humankind can hope for is ignorance, for knowledge leads to enslavement and the madness of worshipping monsters or fruitlessly attempting to propitiate these ancient enemies of humanity. The narrator reflects on the results of his research:

> [T]here came the single glimpse of forbidden eons which chills me when I think of it and maddens me when I dream of it. That glimpse, like all dread glimpses of truth, flashed out from an accidental piecing together of separated things – in this case an old newspaper item and the notes of a dead professor. I hope that no one else will accomplish this piecing out; certainly, if I live, I shall never knowingly supply a link in so hideous a chain. I think that the professor, too, intended to keep silent regarding the part he knew, and that he would have destroyed his notes had not sudden death seized him. (130)

Thus, the discovery of the horrifying truth about an ancient evil force that threatens to consume and obliterate life on earth begins by chance and leads to a deliberate conspiracy of silence. The only way to combat the threat of Cthulhu, Lovecraft's researchers discover, is to stop the transmission of knowledge. Lovecraft's readers, of course, get automatic exemptions from the prohibition, so they can share in the fearful delights of horror.

In several of Lovecraft's tales, the quest for forbidden information destroys the researcher. In 'The Dunwich Horror,' an appetite for arcane knowledge betrays the quester's obscene hybridity. A creature only partly human, residing in the haunted western Massachusetts hills beyond Lovecraft's fictional 'Arkham,' Wilbur Whateley ensures his own transmogrification by chasing down occult lore in texts such as the invented 'hideous *Necronomicon* of the mad Arab Abdul Alhazred.' Possessing only an inherited copy of this magic book, an English translation by the Renaissance mage and scientist Dr Dee, the agoraphobic Whately is driven to extreme measures – leaving the house:

> Correspondence with the Widener Library at Harvard, the Biblioteque Nationale in Paris, the British Museum, the University of Buenos Ayres, and the Library of Miskatonic University at Arkham had failed to get him the loan of a book he desperately wanted; so at length he set out in person, shabby, dirty, bearded, and uncouth of dialect, to consult the copy at Miskatonic, which was the nearest to him geographically. Almost eight feet tall, and carrying a cheap new valise from Osborne's general store, this dark and goatish gargoyle appeared one day in Arkham in quest of the dreaded volume kept under lock and key at the college library. ('Dunwich' 173–4)

The librarian, Dr Armitage, declines to lend the book to so disreputable-looking a patron, correctly guessing that the scholar is scarcely human, and perhaps therefore ineligible for the usual library privileges. He alerts the guardians of special collections about Whateley's quest and hears later of the monstrous being's 'grotesque trip to Cambridge, and of his frantic efforts to borrow a copy of the *Necronomicon* at Widener Library. Those efforts had been in vain, since Armitage had issued warnings of the keenest intensity to all librarians having charge of the dreaded volume' ('Dunwich' 177). Back at Miskatonic, Whateley breaks into the genealogical reading room, garners the last bits of knowledge he requires, and releasing a fetid miasma, turns into a tentacled alien. The thorough contamination of the reading room only hints at the consequences of seeking knowledge of the cruel beings, whose goal is to 'wipe out the human race and drag the earth off to some nameless place for some nameless purpose' (202). Even as Dr

Armitage explains the threat to humankind, he emphasizes namelessness: the safest path lies in refusal of knowledge.

No tale of Lovecraft's better illustrates this principle than 'The Haunter of the Dark,' in which a dogged researcher and writer of occult horror stories becomes obsessed with an old disused church on Federal Hill in Providence, Rhode Island. A mysterious being has been shut up in the darkened church, where an unorthodox sect called Starry Wisdom once practised its rites. Warned repeatedly by the spooked neighbours and a garrulous cop, and knowing that a newspaper reporter on the same case disappeared thirty years earlier, Robert Blake insists on pursuing the line of questioning that results in his death. He breaks into the church to explore. Readers of Lovecraft and gothic fiction recognize the warning signs when Blake comes across shelves of forbidden books in a rear vestry room – no good can come of the lore recorded in these disintegrating volumes. Worse still, Blake carries off a leather-bound book inscribed with 'entries in some odd cryptographic medium' ('Haunter' 106), hoping to solve the riddle that ought to be left alone. The discovery of the missing reporter's skeleton and notebook only stimulates Blake to further efforts in decipherment. He works in secrecy, under a half-comprehended compulsion, terrified by the knowledge he amasses, and even feeling remorse for what he has enlived by letting daylight into the darkened church. A terrible smell, a flash of lightning, and Blake's last notes reveal his hideous end: 'Ia ... ngai ... ygg ... I see it – coming here – hell-wind – titan-blur – black wings – Yog-Sothoth save me – the three-lobed burning eye ...' (120). More suggestive than conclusive, the story lives up to Lovecraft's own definition of the weird tale as more than a gothic rehash:

> The true weird tale has something more than secret murder, bloody bones, or a sheeted form clanking chains according to rule. A certain atmosphere of breathless and unexplainable dread of outer, unknown forces must be present; and there must be a hint, expressed with a seriousness and portentousness becoming its subject, of that most terrible conception of the human brain – a malign and particular suspension or defeat of those fixed laws of Nature which are our only safeguard against the assaults of chaos and the daemons of unplumbed space. (*Supernatural Horror* 15)

H.P. Lovecraft died in 1937. Very shortly afterwards, the nuclear age brought with it fear of forces that could be released in a way that seemed to defy the fixed laws of nature. During the ensuing cold war, writers such as John Le Carré could evoke sensations as chilling as those elicited by

Lovecraft's 'literature of cosmic fear' (*Supernatural Horror* 15) without requiring aliens and monsters of obscure celestial origin.[8] The Soviets, close at hand, proved sufficiently sinister and powerful to underwrite another sort of popular thriller influencing romances of the archive, the cold war spy novel. Arising out of imperial romances such as Rudyard Kipling's *Kim* (1901), spy thrillers carry out in the twentieth century the glamorous activities earlier associated with the Great Game. This label describes the undercover activities of agents of the British secret service in India and the 'uncharted' East. Critic Jon Thompson describes the key traits of the espionage novel in a way that reveals its relationship to later romances of the archive:

> [T]he dramatic suspense and interest of these novels derives largely from the predicament of the protagonist, who typically is responsible for the destiny of a group or nation by searching for the knowledge that will allow him to protect the interests of the collective he represents ... [I]t is no longer just the fates of individuals that are at risk, but, in the case of England, and English literature, the fate of a proud imperial nation; indeed, in many cases, what is at stake is the course of history itself. (*Fiction, Crime, and Empire* 85)

The search for knowledge typically demands travel, disguises, brushes with mortal danger, and study, for the intellectual component (whether searching secret files, decoding intercepted messages, mastering difficult languages, or recovering hidden documentation of evil-doing) makes the spy novel especially bookish, for an adventure. It also tends to require a masculine protagonist, though exceptions exist. Martin Green defines adventure as featuring 'a series of events, partly but not wholly accidental, in settings remote from the domestic and probably from the civilized ..., which constitute a challenge to the central character, ... [who] performs a series of exploits which make him/her a hero, eminent in virtues such as courage, fortitude, cunning, strength, leadership and persistence' (*Dreams of Adventure* 23). In British espionage novels, these characteristics belong especially to British spies, secondarily to a select group of their Soviet adversaries. Doltish, over-reliant on technology, and blinded by their sense of superiority, American operatives as often as not get in the way of the successful completion of missions to save the free world. Despite Green's suggestion that the adventure hero could in fact be a woman, spy novels from Kipling and Buchan to the present tend to be masculine adventures. This is not to say that they feature no female characters; indeed, women often turn up just when the espionage novel turns to the library.

With an oddly revealing trace of the spy thriller's generic ancestry in gothic horror, John Le Carré's *The Spy Who Came in from the Cold* (1963) places its main character Alec Leamas in an archive, the Bayswater Library for Psychic Research (*Spy* 29). The thrill has nearly gone out of such a location, however: no copies of the *Necronomicon* appear there, only a sterile collection of shelves and indices guarded by an old maid and an ancient curator who suffers from shell shock. Leamas has been sent to this location to set up an exposé that will ultimately save a British spy, for in the library a young woman with communist sympathies works. Leamas is put in place to seduce her. Their love affair is an 'operational convenience' (211) in a conspiracy that results in their disillusionment and deaths; they are shot down as they attempt to cross the Berlin Wall. Though unusually intelligent, Le Carré's spies are not always smart enough to avoid being used; in this they prefigure the protagonists of Robert Goddard, who also fall victim to seductresses with predictable regularity.

Sometimes, however, knowledge is the best defence against those who would exploit any weakness. The unfaithfulness of his wife can only harm the spy who fails to understand that he has been betrayed. In Le Carré's *Tinker, Tailor, Soldier, Spy* (1974), George Smiley has been at least temporarily obstructed by Soviet spy-master Karla's scheme to protect his British mole by suggesting the mole's adulterous liaison with Smiley's wife. Despite the embarrassment, Smiley keeps his head. Impeccable research carried out by means of covert photography and theft of files can only carry Smiley so far in his quest to decode 'Witchcraft,' to reveal the mysterious 'Source Merlin,' and to root out the mole who has penetrated the Centre of British intelligence (gothic traces remain in these code names). The scenes of 'getting hold' of documents ('in Smiley's dictionary, read "steal"' [*Tinker* 165]) contribute nerve-wracking tension that scenes of mere 'reading, comparing, annotating, cross-referring' cannot supply (208). The larcenous element of the spy's research undergirds the trope of the just thief in the romance of the archive: he who will use and interpret documents properly has a superior moral claim on their possession. Furthermore, when everyone's credibility has already been undermined, the documentary evidence matters enough to seize by any means.

Because records are fallible, lost, or razored out, however, Smiley must rely on human memory to fill in the gaps, and this strategy also goes a long way to solving one of the central aesthetic problems of the research narrative in spy-thriller mode. Le Carré confronts one of the representational dilemmas facing the recorder of research squarely – watching someone else read is extremely boring: 'A very dull monument,' Smiley reflects as he surveys the files, 'to such a long and cruel war' (*Tinker* 129). The interviews with participants, witnesses, and skilful researchers who have been put out to pasture enliven the narrative significantly. These conversations also provide Le Carré with the means to interpolate interpretive keys to the behaviour of characters, in the form of views uttered by Smiley's interlocutors. If the contemporary romance of the archive picks up from spy fiction the often-employed theme of sexual betrayal by temptresses and adulteresses (the honeytrap), it also preserves an alternative female character type, the brainy woman, as we see in Le Carré's ruined but still brilliant Connie.[9] Though she is drunk and debilitated, Connie can recall research she carried out years earlier. She also puts her finger on the central weakness of Bill Haydon: recruited 'before "Empire" became a dirty word,' he belongs to the last generation of spies attracted to the Great Game, proud to be Englishmen, trained to 'rule the waves,' only to find the Empire all gone (111–13). Connie's hints are confirmed by Haydon's embittered confession in the last pages of the novel: '[T]he Suez adventure in '56 finally persuaded him of the inanity of the British situation, and of the British capacity to spike the advance of history while not being able to offer anything by way of contribution. The sight of the Americans sabotaging the British action in Egypt was, paradoxically, an additional incentive' to betray his country, and in the process his friends and co-workers (340). The memory of global status becomes the excuse for treason in a postimperial world. It is up to Smiley, who also belongs to Haydon's generation, but who lives more equably with diminishment, to break the cycle; as he reflects, 'somewhere the path of pain and betrayal must end' (326).

Fictional spies, like the researchers who work for intelligence agencies, spend a lot of time in the sedentary activity of reading, which always presents a challenge for filmmakers who adapt this kind of novel to the screen. Movies represent research economically, with shots of library stacks, papers spread out on messy tables, and characters studying photographs or computer screens. Though so much of the ratiocination of the spy thriller depends upon a research scenario, film versions must abbreviate the scenes devoted to actions so fundamentally dull to watch. (*Three Days of the Condor* [1975] is a good example of a research film; it tellingly compresses the action that James Grady's novel presented in *six* days.) Despite this limitation, film paradoxically glorifies research and historical knowledge, particularly in action-adventures. Movies such as *Indiana Jones and the Last Crusade* (1989) and *StarGate* (1994) keep the conventions of late-nineteenth-century imperial romance fresh and weave research stories into their quest-plots. Mysteries, romances, westerns, thrillers, fantasy, and science-fiction films and television shows educate viewers the easy way, with a knowledgeable interpreter on hand to spell out the steps in problem-solving or information-seeking. No translation, sustained study, or prior knowledge is needed. The romance of the archive gains from these precursors a convention of easiness; readers need not be professional scholars, for they can share in the discoveries of the archive by reading over the character's shoulder while the process of discovery transpires. Whether the researcher gazes at a sequence of pin-up photographs or reads a book containing the secret history of the world, the discovery and interpretation shared with the reader make up key components of an intellectual adventure that requires no sweat.

The easiness of action-antiquarianism comes through in print form, as well. Book critic Michael Dirda, in a sequence of reviews for the *Washington Post Book World*, describes a contemporary international sub-genre, the 'antiquarian romance.' In a review of Lawrence Norfolk's *Lemprière's Dictionary* (1991), Dirda defines antiquarian romances by the following traits. They 'juxtapose the present and the past, disclose awesome, frequently game-like conspiracies at work in history, draw heavily on some branch of arcane learning (chess, Renaissance hermeticism), provide a trail of scholarly "documents," pastiche earlier styles of speech, offer "intellectual" conversation, and emphasize a Gothicky atmosphere of mystery and foreboding. Not the least, they are frequently long, leisurely and deliberately old-fashioned, or seemingly so' ('Secret Masters' 1, 14). Dirda remarks that 'they are not simply tales of wonder, but tales specifically about the wonder of reading and the pleasures of scholarship. The main character must nearly always learn to interpret correctly a game, a document, a painting or a book, and thus discover the extraordinary behind the ordinary' (14). The interpreter/researchers update the pursued and pursuing quester of Lovecraft's weird tales or Le Carré's spy thrillers. They are classically trained scholars and autodidacts, at home in the Warburg Institute and in cyberspace, undaunted by the information overload, fragmentation, truncated sound bites, and constantly upgraded software of the contemporary moment. The conspiratorial atmosphere and the gaming, decoding, and hacking of their protagonists derive from the cold war genres of metafiction and spy thriller. The formal resemblance of these books to Victorian novels (they tend to be very long) accounts for the readability of fiction that, in a more challenging form, might repel readers who suspect or resent difficulty. Many of these 'up-to-date sensation novels' have been best-sellers in the United States ('Secret Masters' 14).

They celebrate the kind of reading, learning, and interpretive skill that the condition of postmodernity impossibly demands of citizens of the world, without actually asking it of readers. Romances of the archive draw liberally from these popular novels, especially from Umberto Eco's *The Name of the Rose*, itself a hybrid of historical fiction, romance adventure, philosophical novel, and mystery.

DETECTIVE FICTION

Detective fiction depends upon the accessibility of facts and the possibility of interpretation of actions, personal character, and material evidence by a figure gifted with superior intellectual powers. The detective begins with knowledge and skill, continues with questions, seeking, and interpreting, and ends by revealing the truth. Plots of questing and discovery contain recovered stories of crimes, for thinking and interpreting lead to answers about what happened in the past. Though postmodern variants of detective fiction sometimes emphasize the ultimate unknowability of past actions and motives, the mystery novel in its classic forms reassuringly arrives at answers after delays and divagations that recapture the difficulty of intellectual questing for the reader who follows along. Detective fiction has sometimes been labelled as a conservative genre because it implicitly promises to arrive at answers, solve crimes, and restore order by quelling the uncertainties that create the disturbances of plotting. Even in the hands of its finest practitioners, detective fiction is unabashedly formulaic, and an important ingredient in a satisfying mystery is the revelation of the truth. This is not to say that detective fiction raises no questions about the nature of a truth that can be recovered through investigation.

From the very first detective novel in English, Wilkie Collins's *The Moonstone* (1868), the genre has addressed problems of knowledge, as Brian McHale observes when he calls the detective novel the pre-eminent 'epistemological genre' (*Postmodernist* 9). An epistemological fiction poses questions about the location, transmission, status, alteration, and limitations of knowledge.[10] This does not necessarily imply that epistemological fiction endorses fixed truths. Indeed, the solution to the mystery in *The Moonstone*, in which the most dedicated quester after truth turns out to be the unknowing guilty party, creates a new set of irresolvable epistemological problems. Franklin Blake takes the diamond while in a drug-induced trance; he cannot recall his actions, but re-enacts them with the help of the hybrid character Ezra Jennings. Those in a position to reveal his guilt beforehand have refrained from doing so, for he is a gentleman, not a criminal type. Blake is not in on the secret of his own actions, which we are to understand as so far out of character as to complicate the assessment of blame. Yet in the end, the very gentleman who so assiduously organizes the taking of testimony about the crime stands revealed as the thief. Collins undermines the reader's confidence in coherent, consistent selves with reliable self-knowledge. Furthermore, by empowering Ezra Jennings to reveal the truth through an experiment that ignores expectations about characters who occupy certain social positions, Collins allows the denizens of an English country house to be subjected to the scrutiny of Jennings, a hybrid offshoot of imperial adventuring. That the truth comes out of this strategy, not from the investigations of the English detective, suggests that those possessing alternative perspectives may be more likely to arrive at true stories about the past. Romances of the archive adopt this assumption and imitate detective fiction when they use outsiders and marginalized figures to uncover the true history that has been obscured by official versions.

Many more traits of romances of the archive find their source at the wellspring of detective fiction. Such fiction often relies upon the material textuality of evidence, though most often speech and physical traces preoccupy the investigator. Assembling collections of documents that offer parallel testimony and allowing the reader to interpret the contradictions and nuances that arise from their comparison has proved an enduring narrative strategy in both detective and high-modernist fiction. The interpolation (embedding) of key bits of textual evidence within the narration exhibits the scattered sources from which a crime story can be reconstituted. From the very start, detective fiction proposes that a true story about the past can be discovered by an investigator of unusual intellectual powers, despite the plethora of perspectives and the limitations of the fallible minds giving their conflicting versions of the story. Since the reader of mysteries is often invited to anticipate the revelation of the reconstituted chain of events at the end of the story, detective fiction privileges difficulty over easiness, in order to allow the successful puzzler to feel a sense of accomplishment, superiority over less astute readers, and kinship with the brilliant detective. It is no wonder that professors of English are so dedicated to detective fiction.

Two subsets of detective fiction bring us closer to the romance of the archive: the historical mystery and the mystery in the library. In the former category, some detective fictions revisit famous mysteries of the past, or use a setting in an earlier period to bring the reader close to a historical event or famous character. Here the writer of detective fiction can indulge

in writing revisionist history without adhering to the professional historian's pesky requirement, citation of sources. The convention of the detective's personal brilliance and the expectation of truth-discovery are sufficient
to endorse the revelations of historical mysteries. In one of the founding
examples of this type, 'The Adventure of the Musgrave Ritual,' Sherlock
Holmes describes to his chronicler Watson 'a very singular business'
('Musgrave' 249), in which a tawdry story of seduction, betrayal, and
murder contains a deeper historical mystery.

The tale begins with a messy stack of documents, which Holmes will
neither destroy nor clear away. Watson complains, 'His papers were my
great crux. He had a horror of destroying documents, especially those
which were connected with his past cases, and yet it was only once in every
year or two that he would muster energy to docket and arrange them ...
Thus month after month his papers accumulated, until every corner of the
room was stacked with bundles of manuscript which were on no account
to be burned' ('Musgrave' 248). For the reader this disorder represents not
only the quirk of a genius who can be roused from indolence by an
intellectual challenge, but also the abundance necessary to sustain a serial
narrative. Each bundle contains a story that Watson might one day be
privileged to tell. One day Holmes responds to Watson's pestering by
pulling out a tin chest full of records of special cases, pre-dating his
association with Watson, his 'biographer' (248). Out of a 'small wooden
box, with a sliding lid, such as children's toys are kept in' Holmes produces
'a crumpled piece of paper, an old-fashioned brass key, a peg of wood with
a ball of string attached to it, and three rusty old discs of metal' (248–9).
These objects are the material traces of a mystery: the document that sets it
off; the tools employed in the decoding; the key to the treasure chest; and a
few of the coins that lay with the object that Holmes identifies as the
crown of the executed king, Charles the First of England. Though the
Musgraves of the time of the story do not realize it, they are the guardians
of the Royal Stuart crown. Hence, when Watson inquires, '"These relics
have a history, then?"' Holmes replies, '"So much so that they *are* history"' (249).

The history that Holmes recovers for his aristocratic school friend has
been forgotten until Brunton, Musgrave's butler, disappears. Musgrave has
dismissed his butler after discovering him rooting around in family papers;
Brunton behaves strangely for a few days and then vanishes. The solution
to this mystery leads Holmes to the royalist history of the Musgraves. As
Peter Brooks observes, '[T]he spatio-temporal realization of the story
witnessed as Holmes plots out his points on the lawn at the last opens up a

vast temporal, historical recess, another story, the history of regicide and restoration, which is brought to light only because of the attempted usurpation of the servant' (*Reading* 26). Both Brunton and Holmes in turn recognize that the 'strange catechism' passed down from father to son in the Musgrave family may be interpreted as a map ('Musgrave' 253). The butler Brunton, a highly intelligent former schoolmaster, seeks treasure; the disinterested Holmes finds history. The Musgraves, who have forgotten the meaning of the ritual they preserve, end up with the crown after a bit of 'legal bother' ('Musgrave' 258). Brunton does not live to be disappointed by his discovery, for he is murdered by his accomplice, a housemaid whom he has seduced and abandoned. Holmes suggests that she may have fled England in a voluntary act of transportation. The class and gender elements of the mystery underscore Conan Doyle's thinking about the possession of history. The Musgraves have preserved but forgotten it. The upstart butler recovers it to steal it. The wronged woman tosses it in a pond: she cares nothing for it once she is avenged. Only Holmes possesses the necessary combination of wit, mathematical ability, practical imagination, and historical sympathy to understand it. Too late to be of any use to the Stuarts, the crown of Charles becomes a conversation piece at the seat of the Musgraves. Thus, a middling man and a housemaid initiate a criminal plot that Holmes's empirical problem-solving turns into a classic tale of heritage restored. The discovery that the Musgraves once had royalist sympathies changes nothing significant about the understanding of the past. The crown in the house merely emphasizes the long tenancy of the family in their ancestral home. Revealed by Holmes's brainwork, the valuable entrusted to an aristocratic family underwrites the aristocratic values of the Musgraves.

In contrast, some historical mysteries seek to overturn received interpretations or popular understandings of historical events. One of the best known of this sort of mystery is Josephine Tey's 1951 novel, *The Daughter of Time*. In this unusual mystery novel, the detective Alan Grant has been immobilized by an embarrassing accident, falling through a trap door in pursuit of a criminal. An actress friend brings a set of portraits to the detective, who prides himself in his ability to read character in faces. Gazing at the face of Richard III, he sees not 'the monster of nursery stories,' 'the destroyer of innocence,' nor 'a synonym for villainy' (*Daughter* 23), but a sympathetic human character:

Someone used to great responsibility, and responsible in his authority, Someone too conscientious. A worrier; perhaps a perfectionist. A man at ease in a

large design, but anxious over details. A candidate for gastric ulcer. Someone,
too, who had suffered ill-health as a child. He had that incommunicable, that
indescribable look that childhood suffering leaves behind it. (22)

The murderer of the princes in the Tower cannot be reconciled with
Grant's estimation of the character of the man in the portrait. With the help
of a gung-ho American research assistant, Grant works his way from the
monstrous Richard of the Tudor propagandists to a fully rehabilitated
innocent king, slandered by those who deposed him, blamed for their
crimes, and cruelly immortalized as the villainous hunchback of Shakespeare's *Richard the Third*.

Although Grant discovers at the end of the novel that his defence of
Richard's character has been anticipated by vindications written in the
eighteenth and nineteenth centuries, making an original discovery matters
less than the novelized re-presentation of the case for a new generation of
readers who have already taken in the character assassination of Richard.
Tey sets these dupes of popular history up as a perennial problem for
'research workers,' who deal only in facts and the hard evidence. As
Carradine, the young American research assistant opines, 'Truth isn't in
accounts but in account books' (*Daughter* 101). Narratives of events,
motivated by personal and political agendas, cannot be trusted, whereas
the reasonable investigator can draw solid conclusions from records. Yet
the detective and purveyor of truth will always come up against those who
already believe a false version promulgated in stories. (An analogous case
for the American context – where it must be acknowledged, few students
have any opinion whatsoever about Richard III – would be the common
slander that Abraham Lincoln owned slaves.) Tey's metaphor for this
problem is 'Tonypandy.' Today's historical accounts of the troubles in
Tonypandy (arising from a 1910 strike in Welsh mining villages) suggest
that Winston Churchill nearly called out troops and the London Police
to quell the riots, but did not have to do so. Yet in Churchill's 1950
campaign for election, his Labour opponents accused him of setting
troops on trade unionists (Morgan *People's Peace* 112). Tey's 1951 novel
comes to Churchill's defence by attacking those who fail to contradict
the exaggerated tale of government troops shooting down Welsh miners
(*Daughter* 99–100).

The curious thing about Tey's 'Tonypandy' lies not in the discovery that
false versions of events exist, but in who takes the blame for this. Retailed
for political reasons by those who seek to smear the opponent, false

history becomes the responsibility *not* of those who told the lie, but of those who failed to contradict it. Tey's inspector Grant rails: 'The point is that *every single man* who was there knows that the story is nonsense, and yet it has never been contradicted. It will never be overtaken now. It is a completely untrue story grown to legend while the men who knew it to be untrue looked on and said nothing' (*Daughter* 100). Let down by historians and by eyewitnesses alike, the detective takes refuge in a return to the world of crime-solving, where relativism and political motivations have no place, where fairness and ordinary morality govern: 'The values of historians differed so radically from any values with which he was acquainted that he could never hope to meet them on any common ground. He would go back to the Yard, where murderers were murderers and what went for Cox went equally for Box' (203). As we will see, the common-sense views of a self-styled simple, no-nonsense investigator often appear in romances of the archive to debunk the misrepresentations of both authoritative histories and popular beliefs.

THE NAME OF THE ROSE: THE MYSTERY IN THE LIBRARY

Those mysteries taking place in libraries, archives, or museums often interweave their present-day crime plots with deeper mysteries about the past, in which historical, philosophical, scientific, or theological ideas figure prominently. Umberto Eco's manifestly intellectual novel *The Name of the Rose*, though at first rejected by fourteen publishers in the United States, appealed to readers accustomed to historical novels and detective fiction and surprised Harcourt Brace when it became a best-seller. It had already done well in Europe and Great Britain; eventually it was made into a film starring Sean Connery.[11] *The Name of the Rose* showed novelists and publishers that novels of ideas could succeed commercially as well as critically. Its success in Britain stimulated the publication of a host of successors, including A.S. Byatt's *Possession* and the translation of Eco's own less successful novel *Foucault's Pendulum* (trans. 1989). Eco brought the romance of the archive to its contemporary apotheosis by combining witty allusions to metafictional precursors such as Jorge Luis Borges, learned discourses on medieval church politics, theological discussions of the nature of laughter, and a detective story featuring William of Baskerville, a British Franciscan with Holmes-like skills and an admiration for the ideas and inventions of Roger Bacon. As A.S. Byatt observes, *The Name of the Rose* satisfies readers' appetite for plot. Reacting against the *de rigueur* openendedness of modern fiction, novels like *The Name of the Rose* exploit 'the formal structure of the detective plot even while doing something quite different with it,' to the delight of readers (Byatt in Wachtel *Writers and Company* 87–8).

Like G.K. Chesterton's Father Brown stories, *The Name of the Rose* approaches problems of knowledge along theological and empirical avenues. The novel places the establishment of truth in a high-stakes context: the backdrop of the story involves the rooting out of heretics by inquisitors and the political machinations of churchmen intent on retaining power in the world (William of Baskerville comes to the abbey with a diplomatic mission, to bring together the Emperor's envoys and the Pope's legation). Believing the politically incorrect truth (*Rose* 152, 234), or imagining that the 'truth will make you free' (272), can lead to the stake. As the vehicles of ideas, books (like bodies) are threatened with prohibition and destruction. In the face of this dangerous situation, William insists on the possibility of alternative kinds of wisdom, the truths of simple people, and empirical verification of hypotheses (304–5). He is a British humanist hero, who believes with Roger Bacon that the aim of learning is to 'prolong human life' (74) and that laughter is a sign of man's rationality (131).

Each of the key traits of the romance of the archive appears in Eco's novel. Eco lovingly invokes a medieval world with all its furnishings: some of the most effective passages of the novel show how powerfully carved and painted representations work on their beholders. Yet the historical element does not get in the way of a fast-paced plot; William and his Moriarty-like adversary Jorge of Burgos square off in roles set by detective fiction, observed by Adso, a less intellectually gifted side-kick whose narration makes the tale easier for ordinary readers to follow. A story about monks need not go far to bring in discomforts and inconveniences; nor is it a surprise when an interval of sexual adventuring temporarily distracts Adso (*Rose* 246–7). William intuits almost immediately that the murder mystery conceals a deeper conspiracy, and he discovers that the crimes stem from deeds that 'originate in the remote history of the abbey' (445), when a certain book was stolen and hidden in the library (466). With postmodern self-awareness William emphasizes to his young colleague that he solves the mystery by accident (491).

Many aspects of the mystery William does deduce, however, and the plot lingers on the research and interpretation required to unravel the labyrinthine library in which Aristotle's lost work on comedy lies, as the exciting climax reveals. The forbidden book hidden in the room labelled *finis Africae* jeopardizes all those who know of its existence, for its protector Jorge will do anything to prevent the spread of Aristotle's views dignifying human laughter (*Rose* 473). Jorge becomes an image of the Antichrist who deforms piety and passion into obsession and sinfulness, according to William's final meditation:

> Jorge did a diabolical thing because he loved his truth so lewdly that he dared anything in order to destroy falsehood. Jorge feared the second book of Aristotle because it perhaps really did teach how to distort the face of every truth, so that we would not become slaves of our ghosts. Perhaps the mission of those who love mankind is to make people laugh at the truth, *to make truth laugh*, because the only truth lies in learning to free ourselves from insane passion for the truth. (491)

The traditional strong closure of gothic fiction is recapitulated when the library goes up in flames, destroyed by the desperate antics of its mad librarian, who kills himself by devouring the poisoned pages of the book he has sought to preserve.[12]

One of Eco's most striking contributions lies in the rendering of the setting he creates to decode and then destroy – the labyrinthine library. Its contents are unmatched in medieval Europe, yet its architecture is not designed to distribute truth, but – in the most generous interpretation – for 'delaying its appearance' (*Rose* 286). The luminous Scriptorium, where the monks consult, illuminate, and copy the works that have been brought out from the stacks, embodies 'the spiritual principle that light incarnates, radiance, source of all beauty and learning' (72). As yet innocent of its perils, Adso remarks that the place seems 'a joyous workshop of learning' (72). Yet the library's chained catalogue is designed to baffle rather than to reveal; it lists volumes in the order of their acquisition, which makes knowledge of the contents of the library a body of arcane lore, passed from librarian to librarian, and zealously protected from wider dissemination (75–6). In the Aedificium's labyrinthine stacks, tricks with mirrors (172) and booby traps using hallucinogenic drugs (174–5) foster the rumours that magic protects the works of learning (89). Having penetrated the stacks only to become thoroughly lost, William and Adso discover the shapes of the rooms and their mystifying labels (drawn from the Apocalypse of John). Later William uses this knowledge to create a map of the library, working from the outside. In the end he discovers that the contents of the rooms, the labels, and the relation of the rooms to one another (in a tip of the hat to Jorge Luis Borges's 'The Library of Babel') correspond to locations on the map of the world (314). This system exists to hide books (a goal perversely described by Jorge as 'preservation' [399]), but as Adso gradually realizes under William's tutelage, knowledge cannot be locked away in hidden volumes:

> Now I realized that not infrequently books speak of books: it is as if they spoke among themselves. In the light of this reflection, the library seemed all the more disturbing to me. It was then the place of a long, centuries-old murmuring, an imperceptible dialogue between one parchment and another, a living thing, a receptacle of powers not to be ruled by a human mind, a treasure of secrets emanated by many minds, surviving the death of those who had produced them or had been their conveyers. (286)

This conversation is intrinsically multicultural and multi-vocal; Adso's recognition of dialogue's powers shows that he has come a way from the younger self who hopes for fixed truths and solid answers.

Shortly afterwards, we find William teaching Adso a relativist lesson. Adso spots a copy of the Koran on the library's shelves and comments, 'The Koran, the Bible of the infidels, a perverse book ...' William corrects him: 'A book containing a different wisdom than ours' (*Rose* 315). In contrast to Jorge's view that the library testifies to truth and error (129), William's vision of the knowledge contained in and represented by the labyrinth is inflected by its Borgesian sources, acknowledged by Eco in his 'Postscript' (515). Readers familiar with the teasing fictions of Jorge Luis Borges will recognize the allusion to 'The Library of Babel' in the hexagonal rooms, air shafts, and contents of the Aedificium, to 'The Garden of the Forking Paths,' where a book and a maze are one and the same, and to 'Tlön, Uqbar, Orbis Tertius,' where a research narrative turns into an exercise in world-making (*Ficciones* [1945], trans. as *Labyrinths* [1962]).[13] Eco transforms these hints from Borges into a library that is a labyrinth and a map of the world; by rendering it so persuasively as a physical place, Eco invites readers to believe in the characters and books that move around inside it. His hero William's realization that the labyrinthine space of conjecture 'can be structured' but 'never structured definitively' ('Postscript' 526) draws the line of connection from the medieval past to the contemporary period in which Eco writes. His conclusion gives an answer for our times. If we sympathize with Adso, crying out in frustration, '"Why won't you tell me where the truth is?"' we acknowledge with William that '"the most we can do is look more closely"' (*Rose* 205).

CONDITIONS FOR GROWTH OF A NEW GENRE

After the success of the English translation of *The Name of the Rose*, a remarkable number of romances of the archive appeared in Great Britain. In an interview, A.S. Byatt acknowledged that she composed her novel *Possession* in part as a response to *The Name of the Rose*.[14] Other novelists are not on record as directly responding to Eco, but the timing of the vogue for romances of the archive in the 1980s and 1990s correlates strikingly to the publication and enthusiastic reception of Eco's novel in translation. A number of conditions existed that made the time ripe for an explosion of romances of the archive and for their success with readers. In literary terms, the 1980s and 1990s provided particularly fertile ground for the growth of a newly popular kind of British fiction reconsidering the uses of the past. Detective fiction already had a solid audience; historical fiction was enjoying a resurgence. The market for serious literary fiction had been boosted by the publicity garnered by Booker Prize–winning novels. Betting agencies set the odds on the short-listed authors, and each year promised a new controversy arising from the judging or from the behaviour of writers at the award ceremony; whatever the cause, sales of serious literary fiction were up. The competition between a cohort of younger English novelists and their postcolonial counterparts intensified, while both parties' works got more attention and commanded higher advances, as a result of increased sales.[15] In 1992 W.H. Smith capitalized on the British public's appetite for prizewinners by inaugurating its 'Thumping Good Read' award, which has gone to popular novels and genre fiction, including the successful paperback fiction of Robert Goddard. Goddard's conspiracy thrillers, often taking the form of romances of the archive, are reported to be the favourite contemporary fiction of John Major;[16] in any case, the former Conservative British prime minister was not alone in his enthusiasm for tales that re-examined the past through research narratives.

The commercial context – the changes in the publishing market and reviewing establishment, and the discounting made possible by the end of the Net Book Agreement – does not by itself explain why British novelists so frequently succeeded with research narratives engaging with the past. For this we must recognize that they took on history in novels that were easy to devour (they were for the most part formally undemanding). These fictions were driven by the familiar conventions of adventure or detective fiction and populated by an enjoyable array of stock heroes and villains. Finally, they addressed a question whose pertinence had recently been refreshed by the Falklands adventure. An intensification of feeling about British heritage, encouraged by Margaret Thatcher's Conservative government, and further enhanced by the patriotic upswell following the Falklands war, created a climate in which recovering and visiting the past through library research enjoyed renewed potency. The pervasive rhetoric of decline that afflicted Great Britain during the years following the Suez crisis emphasized either the neglect of her history and her historical roles, or lamented the transformation of the British Isles into one big open-air museum or heritage theme park. One way to combat the sense of lost glory was to revisit the past to vindicate British imperial history; another common strategy sought excuses for present postimperial malaise in history. Imitation of period style, or pastiche, enjoyed a vogue during the 1980s and 1990s, as it called up imagined voices from earlier centuries. These voices uttered a wide range of views, not at all in unison. The romance of the archive proved a flexible vehicle for expressing a variety of perspectives on history. Lacking consensus about the appropriate uses of the past in contemporary life, culture, and politics, but acutely aware of a past demanding reinterpretation and inviting exploration, British novelists weighed in on the 'heritage' question with their romances of the archive.

4

History or Heritage?

In the 1930s, historian Carl Becker reminded his colleagues that an ordinary man paying his coal bill might embark upon a research project that resembled, in all its fundamental strategies and actions, the making of history.[1] The story of events and consequences assembled by the good citizen refers to the most mundane occurrences in the past, but it results in a satisfying conclusion in the present – money owed gets paid on time to the proper person. To Mr Everyman, the uses of the past and the purposes of history, for which he would employ no such grandiose language, serve him unobtrusively as he follows the trail of a mystery – who supplied his coal? Finding the answer, he remains in good standing with the coal purveyor, and ensures a warm home for his family in the future.

For this late-twentieth-century reader, Carl Becker's anecdote calls up a poignant set of associations, having little to do with history. I grew up in western Pennsylvania, where soft coal was being strip-mined when I was a child. I know what a hillside looks like when it has been peeled away. I know what the winter air smells like when neighbours burn coal in their furnaces. The house I grew up in, perched on land riddled far below with mine-shafts, has on its flank a cast-iron door that was once connected by a chute to a coal bin (though we used a big old 1930s gas furnace). These bits of trivia could be connected to histories of industry, technology, and unionism, to global economics, and to the politics of big business and the environment. But they are not. Carrying the burdens of emotion and nostalgia (not for coal mines, per se, but for a childhood spent in the final decade of western Pennsylvania's heavy industry), they belong to the antithetical realm of 'heritage.' Intensely regarded, highly personal, often quite specifically local or regional, the materials of heritage overlap with historical evidence. This in itself can enhance feelings of pride and significance, for most people with little interest in history at least know if their own families, ancestors, and places appear in the historical record, even in the most obscure ways. Becker's relativism might be seen as ultimately authorizing the highly personalized perspectives on the past expressed by heritage narratives; certainly the freewheeling subjectivities of postmodern historiography render the myths or mistakes in heritage narratives less vulnerable to puncturing or correction. Calls to embrace, elevate, defend, or preserve heritage evoke strong responses in most people, not excepting intellectuals. We define our traditions and identify valued aspects of our past differently, but most people have some strong feelings about their heritage.

I open in this personal fashion because the contest between history and heritage often employs terms denigrating the popular and successful 'heritage industry'[2] in its many forms, and critics sometimes express contempt for those wooed by it. While on the one hand sanitized, sensationalized, self-deceiving, marketable versions of the past deserve to be criticized for debasing history in the interest of tourist-trail heritage, on the other hand readers, movie-goers, and travellers should not be blamed for enjoying themselves. This chapter takes no position in the history-heritage debate. It avoids endorsing a hierarchy of values in which history (detached, scholarly, dispassionate, accurate) trumps heritage (nostalgic, dysfunctional, inexact); nor does it lobby for the reverse, in which heritage (popular, inspiring, authentic, belonging to all of us) outdoes history (academic, hyper-specialized, politically correct, irrelevant). Instead, the following pages provide a sketch of the attitudes towards the past inhering in various controversies, trends, and policy decisions about British history and heritage in the 1980s and 1990s. Arguments about the preservation and marketing of British heritage, the status of evidence, the value of chronology and primary documents, the merits of a celebratory nation-based school history curriculum, the perils of racism, or, alternatively, the identity politics of multiculturalism permeate the public sphere. A British novelist of this period need not be steeped in academic historiographical debates to engage in the popular discussion of history and heritage.

Contemporary romances of the archive make substantive contributions to this ongoing debate about the uses of the past. The context brought to light in the first section of this chapter illuminates those features of romances of the archive (especially their treatment of the past and expression of attitudes about history) that mark them as the products of their time. I then consider in the following sections romances of the archive written by two British novelists – Barry Unsworth and Peter Ackroyd – who represent strikingly different visions of the uses of the past. Both Unsworth and Ackroyd earn their contrasting views about history and archives through experience. They represent the small subset of novelists who have logged many hours in libraries and special collections, doing research for the creation of historical fictional worlds. They go beyond the typical historical novelist's use of history when they write the research experience into romances of the archive. As we will see, however, this real-life experience in the archive does not result in identical views about the uses of the past. Instead, it points up the extremes that define the outer limits of the debate. Postmodernists, revisionists, relativists, and proponents of the dethroned 'new history' will find much that is congenial in Barry Unsworth's implicit historiography and explicit criticisms of heritage. Paradoxically, for his novels are often described as postmodern, Peter Ackroyd's celebratory engagement with monuments, places, and writers of the English tradition give lovers of London, of Englishness, and of a continuous British heritage much to appreciate. Indeed, Ackroyd's combination of formal experimentation and historical pastiche demonstrates how closely related heritage and postmodernism can appear. In the words of Robert Hewison, the foremost authority on the heritage industry, 'the rediscovery and representation of the past as an entertainment mediated by the heritage industry is an aspect of the post-modern condition' (*Culture and Consensus* 221). Before turning to lengthier discussions of Unsworth's *Sugar and Rum* (1988) and *Losing Nelson* (1999) and Peter Ackroyd's *Chatterton* (1987) and *The House of Doctor Dee* (1993), I take a brief look at Penelope Lively's novel *The Road to Lichfield* (1977). It provides an avenue for a quick tour of some of the recurrent themes of the history-heritage debate. Lively's first novel for adults is a romance of the archive that articulates some of the key issues taken up by many subsequent British novels.

The Road to Lichfield tells the story of a crisis in the life of Anne Linton, a middle-aged woman whose father lies dying in a nursing home in Lichfield. In the course of visiting her father, clearing out his desk, and settling his affairs, she acts out the most common kind of archival quest experienced by ordinary people. Reading his private papers, she discovers that he had a long relationship with a woman not her mother. Not as a result of this knowledge, but not coincidentally, Anne Linton indulges in an adulterous fling with a friend of her father. Her repeated trips to Lichfield thus serve two purposes, continuing her affair with David Fielding, and carrying out her daughterly duties. They take her away both from her family, and from her half-hearted efforts to prevent the destruction of an early fifteenth-century cruck-frame farmhouse, one of a few surviving old buildings in her town (*Road* 36–7). The construction crew's schedule and her father's impending death force these trajectories to share an endpoint, desired or not. In one of the most effective passages of the novel, Lively has Anne Linton visit the site of the razed cottage and rehearse the emotions she may feel when her father finally stops hanging on. Confronting the bulky, infested mound of debris, she is 'surprised to find that she felt really quite unemotional about the whole thing. It was bound to happen ... Stopping it was never really possible at all though of course they were perfectly right to try ... One should have at least recorded it in some way before it went' (166). Exploring the analogy between the human life cycle and the fate of inanimate old things raises questions about what characters are supposed to feel and do in the face of passing time. Lively emphasizes the inadequacy of our responses and the futility of our efforts, and she undermines the felt certainties of family lore by employing a mixture of perspectives on events of the past to demonstrate that different participants carry away clashing versions of what happened. Access to these alternatives depends upon accidents, and the dying man's reveries can only be witnessed by the reader.[3] Anne Linton thinks that if something cannot be preserved, it ought to be recorded. But what version, whose version, should be kept? Lively shows her characters discovering how little they know their intimates: siblings, parents, children, lovers. These insights extend beyond the personal realm, for inhibited by loss of information and conflicting accounts, how well can anyone possibly comprehend the past? Even though the plot of this personal tale treads the familiar floor plan of the domestic novel, then, Lively less predictably includes a set of questions about the status of history and the nature of heritage.

Lively lampoons the uses to which her contemporaries put the material remnants of the visible past, even as she alludes to the threatened discipline of history, particularly in its old-fashioned narrative form. She seems at first to be mounting a defence of sensitive preservation of artefacts and of chronological narrative history, though the turns of the plot and the discontinuities of the novel's storytelling call these impressions into question. By beginning with characters invested in the past, Lively invites the readers to sympathize with the historically minded underdogs. Both Anne Linton and her lover David Fielding have a stake in the teaching of history, as they discover in an early conversation. Anne teaches O-level history part-time at her local comprehensive; David is a schoolmaster. While Anne has her doubts about 'the lessons of the past,' David feels endangered:

'Another historian,' said David Fielding, 'we're an unfashionable lot.'
'What do you mean?'
'The tide's against us, hadn't you noticed? People haven't got much time
for the past nowadays. They want vocational instruction.'
'Oh, come,' she said. 'I can't entirely agree with that. I should have
thought it had never been more popular, literally popular. Cheap Book Club
editions of history books all over the back of the *Radio Times*; millions of
people tramping round stately homes every weekend; the last hundred years
in some aspect or other being re-hashed on the telly every time you turn it
on.'
'The past as entertainment.'   (*Road* 28)

Lively's novel goes on to reveal that the past is its unvarnished self, capable
of shocking and embarrassing when its evidence is turned over by bankers,
husbands, or bulldozers. Whether it instructs or not depends upon what
sort of lesson is looked for. David's paranoia about the status of the
discipline is more than justified by a later turn in the plot, when Anne
learns that the comprehensive where she teaches plans to eliminate O-level
History and her position. Dead wood, an outdated concept, history is to
be replaced by the more relevant social-science option (*Road* 87, 88). As
another fictional history teacher, Graham Swift's Tom Crick, learns from
his headmaster, history – 'a rag-bag of pointless information' inspiring
only gloom and nightmares of nuclear annihilation – is to be cut from the
curriculum (*Waterland* 19). In the 1970s and early 1980s school history did
suffer from comparisons to social-science subjects and practical, vocational training, even as proponents of new methodologies attempted to
break away from traditional teaching methods emphasizing facts and
chronology. Both Lively and Swift record the painful moment when
history was often stigmatized as an irrelevant subject. (As we will see, the
later 1980s and 1990s witnessed the partial revival of school history as
a part of the National Curriculum, an educational reform underpinned by
a Conservative nationalist agenda.) Economically invoking the paradox
of a simultaneously threatened history and flourishing heritage, Lively's
novel echoes a commonly voiced complaint and its most typical rejoinder:
the past has never been so popular.
    Anne Linton's accepting view of a benignly popular heritage alters as a
result of her experiences with the ad hoc committee formed to prevent the
destruction of Splatt's Cottage. Not only do the committee members seem
silly, pathetic, and ineffectual, but their cause also comes to look less noble
when Anne discovers that the cottage is in an advanced state of decay from

dry rot (which would cost a fortune to arrest) and that the building site is slated for conversion to housing for the local elderly (*Road* 77). The developer of the land recalls that his grandparents had kept the cottage nice-looking, but cherishes no illusions about living in a damp, inconveniently situated house with no running water (123–4). The possibility of present usefulness exposes the sentimentality of newcomers who would preserve the relics of the past as idealized architectural exemplars. When at the end of the novel bulldozers reveal the shallow grave of abused children who died (half-starved, perhaps the victims of infanticide) in Splatt's Cottage, the past becomes an outright embarrassment, no longer 'dead posh' (57) and the object of energetic defence, but a reminder of pain, dirt, hunger, crime, and shame. Similarly, antique objects can be esteemed so long as their use is not too specifically recalled – obsolete agricultural implements hanging on the Pickerings' walls compel admiration as 'super shapes,' but Miss Standish's recognition of a dibble and recollection of its use in the fields is curtly terminated as an irrelevant digression from the preservationist business at hand (82). Converted to wariness of the 'disagreeable' past (190), Anne Linton considers the veneration of old things 'wrenched' from their contexts: 'It was as though by displaying what had gone before and making an ornament of it, you destroyed its potency' (178). The novel's doubled plots of discovered adultery make a tiny sample of a potent past uncomfortably available, and endorse leaving the truth behind, without 'harping on what's done with' (215). The novel supports the young's desire to leave behind the failures and horrors of the previous generation, and proffers a memorable image: the child who peers into the window of Splatt's Cottage expecting to see eels is unsurprised by the discovery of the skeletons, for she has always known the old house contains 'something nasty' (177).

The heritage version of the past cherished by preservationists, keepers of the National Trust, Tory MPs, and countless visitors of the burgeoning number of museums and historic sites in Great Britain eschews for the most part real or imagined nastiness. Though its outlines can be rather misty, the heritage represents a past in which British people can feel pride. Patrick Cormack, an influential politician who has a sideline as a 'heritage adviser' to a conservation and restoration company, and who has headed up both the All-Parliamentary Committee for the Heritage and the Heritage Coordination Group, takes a stab at a definition:

When I am asked to define our heritage I do not think in dictionary terms, but instead reflect on certain sights and sounds. I think of a morning mist on the Tweed at Dryburgh where the magic of Turner and the romance of Scott both come fleetingly to life; of a celebration of Eucharist in a quiet Norfolk church, with the medieval glass filtering the colours, and the early noise of the harvesting coming through the open door; or of standing at any time before the Wilton Diptych. Each scene recalls aspects of an indivisible heritage and is part of the fabric and expression of our civilization. (Cormack *Heritage in Danger* 11–12)

Landscapes, buildings, art objects, religious ceremonies, and even the weather can be part of the heritage. Certainly the works of British writers, artists, composers, artisans, and architects (particularly those from earlier centuries) contribute to a prized collection of achievements lending lustre to Great Britain as a nation and to British culture. As Robert Hewison chronicles, the unlikeliest sites and subjects are marketed as aspects of the visitable past; the detritus of abandoned industrial areas become museums commemorating an idealized workers' past, in a bid to attract tourism where industry has failed (*Heritage Industry* 15–27). One might agree with the boosters of a strategically marketed British heritage, who hope to harvest tourist dollars and inculcate national pride simultaneously, or one might fret with Hewison that a nation so 'hypnotised by images of the past' will fail to imagine its future with sufficient creativity and vigour (*Heritage Industry* 10). Either way, an observer of British culture in the latter part of the twentieth century would certainly see many signs of a cherished past – preserved, restored, and defended.

Regardless of the actual figures, the widespread perception that Great Britain has suffered a decline in economic well-being and global status arises out of the experiences in the 1970s of inflation, unemployment, the failures of the welfare state, loss of industry, and, in the Thatcher years, of recession, downsizing, and the underfunding of universities.[4] Against this backdrop, an emphasis on a more positive past can seem a natural reflex, an understandable impulse of nostalgia, a calculated program on the part of conservative politicians, or a pernicious evasion of responsibility for the present and future. Though Tories have led the way in defending the British heritage (particularly those tax-burdensome English country houses), conservatives have also criticized the substitution of heritage for religion. After a day of heritage-site visiting, a character in one of Alice Thomas Ellis's novels laments that the world has become 'a theme park and the people who thronged its artificial stage were not actors but puppets, strung along by the faceless conglomerates, the unimaginably powerful corporations that ruled the Western world' (*Fairy Tale* 84). Ellis's fictional version of contemporary Britain, like Fredric Jameson's postmodernism of late capitalism, proves debilitating to its deluded inhabitants, pursuing their recreations: '[T]he people believed they had taken over but it was Mammon whose interests were being so abundantly served here' (84). Without the right traditions to protect them, Ellis's characters barely escape with their lives and sanity from the Tylwyth Teg, the Welsh fairies who use human females for reproductive purposes and who eat the men that come their way. Only by accident does a scrap of scripture spring to the lips of a threatened male in time to avert his murder by a fairy (208). Ellis suggests that traditional values acted out in the spirit of New Age sentimentality only make human beings vulnerable to manipulation – both by multinational corporations and by the fairy gamekeeper who keeps an eye on the humans in the fairy preserve.

Not everyone in Great Britain would welcome a return to the traditional Christianity that Ellis recommends in her fiction. To the diverse citizens of a multiracial and multicultural nation, English heritage can seem a source of pride or an unfortunately exclusive, even racist, burden. In the 1980s and 1990s, the appropriate attitudes about surviving material traces of the past have been hotly contested, as social, developmental, industrial, and agricultural needs press against more symbolic claims for resources.[5] In the ongoing controversies about the fates of historic sites, buildings, art objects, and personal papers (especially those belonging to figures already icons of British heritage, such as Sir Laurence Olivier), compelling economic and patriotic arguments appear in the news, as competing constituencies articulate rival versions of the heritage most deserving protection, purchase, or preservation.

Though the tourists' desires command especial attention, even they have a variety of ideas about the British heritage they pay to encounter. It is this diversity of opinion on the 'Quintessences of Englishness' that Julian Barnes sends up in his satirical novel *England, England* (1998). 'Potential purchasers of Quality Leisure' rank the Royal Family (1), Big Ben (2), the Union Jack (11), Thatched Cottages (18), Stiff Upper Lip (21), Beefeaters (24), Double-Decker Buses (30), Winston Churchill (37), the Battle of Britain (39), Queen Victoria (43), and the Magna Carta (50). Equally present are traces of a populist 'history from below,' with the Manchester United Football Club (3), Pubs (5), God Save the Queen (13), TV Classic Serials (27), Gardening (32), Marks and Spencer (38), Breakfast (44), and Wembley Stadium (47). Unsuppressed in Barnes's list are those quintessences embodied in the Class System (4), Imperialism (10), Snobbery (12), Hypocrisy (31), Perfidy/Untrustworthiness (33), Whingeing (42), Emotional Frigidity (46), Flagellation / Public Schools (48), and, edging out the Magna Carta by one notch, Not Washing / Bad Underwear (49) (*England, England* 83–5). In Barnes's dystopia, an entrepreneur seeks to recreate this marketable England on the Isle of Wight. Correct product placement of a 'nation of great age, great history, great accumulated wisdom' will answer those 'classic historical depressives ... who think it's our job, our particular geopolitical function, to act as an emblem of decline, a moral and economic scarecrow. Like, we taught the world how to play cricket and now it's our duty, an expression of our lingering imperial guilt, to sit back and let everybody beat us at it' (39). Barnes's satirical pastiche of the argument about the relationship of British history and culture to its present and future role contains strong echoes of voices from the past several decades' policy debates.

HISTORY AND HERITAGE IN THE NATIONAL CURRICULUM

Between the late 1970s and the late 1990s, the teaching of history in British publicly funded schools underwent a series of transformations in which observers can read aspects of the historiographical argument about history and heritage. As in an allegorical drama, 'Old Fashioned History' found itself displaced by a 'New History' invigorated by social-science methodologies and changes in pedagogical techniques.[6] Separated from traditional narratives of national pride and differing from the facts and dates studied by elder generations, this new history in turn found itself vulnerable to charges of redundancy. Downsizing of history departments and replacement by more relevant or practical options ensued. Curricular reform driven at least in part by a conservative nationalist agenda then brought History back as a required subject, though not for students of all ages. The reinstated History owed as much to a memory of traditional history as to the inventive pedagogy of the teachers who implemented the new curriculum. At each stage, teachers, policy-makers, legislators, and even the prime minister have weighed in on curricular matters perceived to be at the heart of Britain's identity and direction as a nation.

The 1970s and 1980s saw the spread of the 'New History,' which integrated some of the techniques and topics of social history and social science into the school history curriculum. In part responding to new understandings of developmental psychology, innovators moved away from traditional chronological narration.[7] The teaching of facts and received knowledge about (primarily) British history yielded some ground to thematically organized units emphasizing the scrutiny of primary source materials, the acquisition of critical thinking skills, and the cultivation of empathy.[8] During the 1970s and 1980s, both world history and local history received greater attention in some classrooms, as autonomous teachers tested new ways of cultivating a sense of the past in their students.

At the same time that these liberal reforms encouraged the teaching of history as a mode of inquiry and raised questions about the value of traditional school history, however, teachers on the ground worried that the entire subject was in jeopardy, to be displaced either by more modish social-science options or by more practical vocational subjects. Critics of the new history reviled its evident multicultural, anti-racist thrust as inappropriate social engineering and sought to seize control of the teaching of school history to advance more upbeat, patriotic, future-minded aims.

In the 1980s the National Curriculum Working Group devised and implemented a set national curriculum emphasizing the basics of British history.[9] These basics re-centred the curriculum on British national history and heritage. Adopted in 1988 as part of the Education Reform Act (and consolidated with a few refinements in the 1996 Education Act), the National Curriculum History prescribed a program of historical study for students aged five to fourteen. Considering that its proponents pitched the National Curriculum History as a restoration of history to a central place in compulsory education, it is ironic that for 14 to 16 year olds at Key Stage 4, history became an option (English, math, science, physical education, technology, and foreign language remained as required subjects). Hence, the same history teachers who were required to adapt to a centrally controlled set curriculum with assessment by public examination of students at Key Stage 4 also faced the difficulty of keeping history available as a viable option for 14- to 16-year-old students. The adoption of the National Curriculum History did not end history teachers' fears of being made redundant or being relegated to second-class status. The discussions on the bulletin boards of British government–sponsored web sites such as the National Grid for Learning suggest that, in the late 1990s, history teachers still felt that their subject was threatened, even as they worked to achieve the new aims set out by the National Curriculum.[10]

When it was implemented in 1988, the National Curriculum History was praised for restoring the traditional narrative history recalled by parents and grandparents. The Romans, the Anglo-Saxons, and the Vikings were followed by highlights including medieval realms, Tudor times, and Victorian Britain. (The extent to which these traditional topics had really disappeared during the years of the new methodology is a matter of some debate.) The National Curriculum History firmly emphasizes monarchs, major events, personalities, and period labels, at least in the goals set out for teachers. Chronology gets top billing among the key elements of study, followed by range and depth of historical knowledge and understanding, interpretations of history, modes of enquiry, and organization and communication.[11]

According to its advocates, familiarity with the basic elements of the national past, to be gained through the National Curriculum History, would equip students to be citizens of a democratic nation. They would carry away more knowledge than the random fragments proffered by the skills-based curriculum of the 1970s and 1980s, and they would not be contaminated by the relativism of academic history (Little 'National Curriculum' 326). Critics charged that the story of the development of a great nation-state with its characteristic parliamentary democracy glossed over darker episodes in British history. Even in the revised version, one seeks in vain for the history of the Empire apart from the voyages of discovery of Sebastian and John Cabot, the acts of Union, and the growth of trade. When a non-European society is to be studied, the options curiously omit any of those places altered by their domination by the British. No account of postwar decolonization is prescribed. This is an upbeat history: the Irish famine and the Holocaust are nowhere to be seen in the mandatory years of study. The cataclysm of the First World War is embedded in a local history option, while the Second World War receives stronger emphasis in a unit on 'Britons at War' – the world wars are to be encountered through the home front.[12] Of course, in the hands of real teachers any of these topics could be rendered in a more nuanced fashion, but critics complained that the emphasis on developments in government, industry, transport, and technology imply a tale of progress indistinguishable from the Whig interpretation of history eschewed by most professional historians since 1945.[13]

At the heart of the contested changes in the teaching of school history are differences in the perceived aims of history. Should it make students feel good, or feel guilty, or – for the goal of cultivating empathy has come in for particular criticism – 'feel' anything? Should Members of Parliament and the prime minister be able to craft a history curriculum designed to make citizens proud of their nation, even if that means glossing over the slave trade, the exploitation of the Irish, and the ugly side of war? Should history teaching be used to illustrate the progress of the nation, with an emphasis on continuities, or should schoolchildren be introduced to the radical differences of remote periods in the past? Most commentators agree that in its best form history teaching moves past praising and blaming to stimulate curiosity about causes and effects, to develop interest in (and tolerance of) the different practices and cultures of the past, and to hone critical-thinking skills by contemplating change over time. Though academic historians are prone to criticize 'presentism' (the interpretation of the lessons of the past through the lens of current concerns), educational policy-makers tend to assume that school history ought to have some bearing on the 'now' in which students live, and on the future they will help to create. Looking at the past for the sake of the future may lead to nostalgic desire to recover lost ways of life, or it may inspire change and reform, but much depends upon what stories about the past can be freely shared.

The choices made by the National Curriculum are perceived to limit the freedom of history teachers (who must think of the exams their students will face), and make the omissions from the official list seem especially galling to those who have worked up effective units on topics not mentioned by the list.[14] (Some educators and advocates successfully lobbied to get the topics adjusted.)[15] A disheartened teacher writing in the left-leaning History Workshop Journal described her reaction to the 'dilemma at the heart of the National Curriculum' history:

> Post-colonial Britain staggers towards the end of the twentieth century under a mountain-load of imperial pride, imperial guilt, and accumulated imperial history. The national Curriculum is a nationalist curriculum designed to off-load this legacy, to re-equip the nation's children with an acceptably insular British (possibly European?) outlook for a different era. If the museums, the archives and even the families of the nation are bursting with inconvenient, uncomfortable reminders of past imperial glories which have lost their aura, then these historical reference points must be stowed safely away into tissued boxes on the shelves of some locked store-room. For the children of innermost England, and most especially for the ex-colonial strangers who are settling amongst them, national history must be recast in the mould of the desired future, rather than that of the tarnished, no-longer-profitable, imperial past. (Bush 'Moving On – and Looking Back' 192)

The evidence suggests that the fight over the school history curriculum is indeed part of 'a cultural struggle against the previously dominant liberal, social-democratic ideology and an assertion of shared values and unity against a multi-ethnic, pluralist and increasingly divided society' (Little 'National Curriculum' 327). Liberal critics see its promulgation of an airbrushed past as reflecting nostalgia for past glories embodied in a celebrated heritage.

From the conservative perspective of novelist and biographer A.N. Wilson, embracing heritage protects national interests: '[I]f we taught our children history with a little more honest and unaffected pride in our national achievement we should not need episodes like the Falklands War to lift national morale and make us believe in England again.'[16] The heritage version of school history, according to its Tory promoters, ought to persuade British schoolchildren that they live in a great country with proud traditions and a distinguished patrimony:

> This is an extraordinary country, one which has rough passages of which to repent perhaps, but whose creativity and achievement are a beacon to others and ought to be taught to each generation. We are not like Croats or Serbs, who pick the ruins they have created for better days. We are a great civilization, the mother of others throughout the English speaking world, and a wellspring of the highest achievements in the practice of government, law, trade, industry and the life of the mind, the sense and the spirit. We traduce Britain's glory if we teach a history which makes us seem just like anybody else.[17]

If these goals are to be taken seriously, as they are by the crafters of the National Curriculum History and by the curators of countless heritage sites, then the meditation on those 'rough passages' that may call for repentance becomes a vexatious duty, to be undertaken not just by professional historians and cultural critics, but also by ordinary citizens.

Romances of the archive, as we will see, show fictional characters endeavouring to come to terms with a British past unexpurgated of its rough patches. Gravitating to the gaps in school history, revisiting glorious episodes with a critical eye, and attempting to recuperate heritage sensations from periods rendered inert or shameful by academicians, romancers of the archive enact and criticize their culture's fascination with the uses of the past. Usually the writer of the romance of the archive happily rides the wave of popularity. Few authors satirize British ideas about their history and heritage with such anatomizing energy as Barry Unsworth.

'THE FEEL OF THE PERIOD': BARRY UNSWORTH'S *SUGAR AND RUM*

Barry Unsworth is best known outside Britain as the Booker Prize–winning author of *Sacred Hunger* (1992), a massive historical novel about the eighteenth-century slave trade.[18] As his regular readers know, nearly half of his thirteen novels contain a historical element, invoking for part or all of the fiction a distant place and time. Turn-of-the-century Constantinople, Renaissance Venice, medieval Yorkshire, eighteenth-century Liverpool (and other points in the triangular trade routes) have appeared in *The Rage of the Vulture* (1982), *The Stone Virgin* (1985), *Morality Play* (1995), and *Sacred Hunger*, respectively. In *Sugar and Rum* (1988) and *Losing Nelson* (1999), Unsworth meditates on historiographical problems through representations of archival research, conducted by the central characters, in both novels would-be writers. Unsworth has also made a specialty of representing the psychology of afflicted characters, including the 'blocked' writers of his archival fictions. Neurotic, obsessive, haunted, and even delusional, as in *The Hide* (1970) and *Mooncrankers Gift* (1973), these distressed figures populate Unsworth's fictional worlds with social misfits who nurse grievances and occasionally stage brilliant comic interventions in the ordinary world's solemn occasions. Unsworth has a gift for creating scenes comically riven by gaffes, awkward behaviour, and random weirdness. In both *Sugar and Rum* and *Losing Nelson*, Unsworth equips his oddball characters with knowledge of the past and hampers them with historiographical problems. His characters experience these difficulties about the uses of the past as personal and social problems.

In *Sugar and Rum*, Unsworth winds the historical, psychological, and black-comedic strands together to produce an unusually astringent consideration of the uses of the past. He shows how research in the historical sources (the documentary traces of Liverpool's eighteenth-century slave trade) yields a strikingly different 'feel of the period' than that produced by clichéd imaginative re-creation. He suggests that unregulated capitalism leads to barbarous mistreatment of fellow human beings, and not only back in slavery days. He asks why the unpleasant truths about the past are so unacceptable both to the descendents of victims and to those who inherit the riches of the perpetrators. He shows how absorption in a deeper, more remote past rewards the attention of those who wish to avoid the unsavoury aspects of the more recent, documented past. Unsworth poses these serious questions about history in a novel that also sends up the staging of English heritage by social-climbing conservatives.

The main character and central consciousness of *Sugar and Rum*, Clive Benson is a historical novelist suffering from a writer's block. In the story, Benson has come to Liverpool to consult the archives located in a city that was once a major port in the slave trade. In lieu of writing, Benson conducts research on his projected book on the eighteenth-century slave trade. Unsworth embeds in the novel scenes of Benson's research; some of the key documents appear as exhibits of a true eighteenth-century period style. Not precisely autobiographical, but informed by experience, *Sugar and Rum* contains a report on the nature of historical research when it is conducted in an atmosphere unfriendly to those stirring up the past. Contemporary residents of Liverpool are shown to be reluctant to admit a connection to those unpleasant old days. In a recent interview, Barry Unsworth recalls the 1980s, when he went to Liverpool to serve as the writer-in-residence at the university. Shocked at the 'dilapidated and deprived' city and the 'highly politicised nature of the university,' Unsworth suffered a fifteen-month-long writing block (he has published novels at three- or four-year intervals throughout his thirty-year career). Unsworth says that he worked through his writer's block by fictionalizing it in Clive Benson.[19] In real life, Unsworth published *Sacred Hunger*, a novel suggested by the imaginary project of Clive Benson, four years after *Sugar and Rum*.[20]

Speaking about this later novel, which shares with *Sugar and Rum* an eighteenth-century setting, Unsworth makes the connection between the 1980s and the eighteenth century explicit: 'For me, the Eighties was an appalling period in British political life. We saw not only the condoning, but the enthronement of greed. The slave trade seemed a perfect metaphor for what was going on – the profit motive, pure and simple.'[21] In the present day of *Sugar and Rum*, Liverpool suffers from urban blight, unemployment, poverty, homelessness, and a despairing, violence-prone citizenry. The theory of correspondences that allows Clive Benson to connect random occurrences with his private obsessions invites the reader to understand the current state of the city as a consequence of its guilty past, though other characters offer critiques that place the blame for urban decay on policy-makers of the day. *Sugar and Rum* does not answer the question of causes outright, leaping as it does over the intervening centuries, but the novel underscores the similarity of eighteenth-century and late-twentieth-century profiteers. In *Sugar and Rum*, Clive Benson becomes the avenging agent who violates social convention by reintroducing the repressed historical memory of Liverpool's investment in the slave trade to the inhabitants of the lovely eighteenth-century homes built on its profits.

The synopsis so far does not do justice to the baroque complications of Unsworth's plot in *Sugar and Rum*. Benson's current work, and his past, enrich the novel with characters, subplots, and variations on the themes of history and heritage. Benson, though a published author, is a marginal figure who ekes out a living by tutoring the Fictioneers, a hapless set of would-be writers. Jennifer Colomb, one of Benson's students, is at work on *Treacherous Dreams*, a historical romance set in an anachronistic eighteenth-century. "'Do you think I'm getting the feel of the period?'" Jennifer Colomb asks, only to discover that her teacher has not recognized the eighteenth century despite her attempt to capture 'the true accent of the time' (*Sugar* 92–3). In rejoinder, the ensuing three pages of quotation from historical documents convey Benson's unwelcome, corrective version of the 'accents of the period' (93). Unsworth interpolates a slave ship physician's observations, traders' logs, insurance records, and contemporary descriptions of implements used to force feed 'sulky' property (93–5). Though these documents speak with the unmediated voices of authentic records, Benson remains at a loss as to how to use them properly. This problem is solved when he is reunited with Hugo Slater, under whom he served in the Second World War.

The shared war experience that connects Benson to Slater, now a wealthy inhabitant of a country house, brings out their differences about the past and provokes Benson into making a violent intervention in Slater's pet project, a theatrical production that makes grandiose claims for the heritage of Slater's property. The path leading from Benson's Liverpool to Slater's country house is labyrinthine. First, Benson catches a glimpse of Killer Thompson, a comrade from the war, tracks him down in his squalid squat, and discovers that their former second lieutenant and impresario has done well in life. Hugo Slater lives nearby on a property putatively associated with the Battle of Brunanburh (A.D. 937). Back in the war, Slater used the production of ENSA-style entertainments as an avenue to avoid dangerous postings, and in the process used his men (*Sugar* 79).[22] Since then he has prospered in the entertainment business. He plans to stage a pageant celebrating the Battle of Brunanburh as the first united English victory over a foreign invader, in full-blown Festival of Britain style. The heritage spectacle is produced for the purposes of Slater's social advancement, a fact that outrages Benson both as a historian and as a former subordinate. Especially galling is the discovery that, during the war, Slater fails to protect Walters (Benson's partner in the cross-dressed comedy routine of the *Beachhead Buddies*). The performer is killed in action, while the director manoeuvres himself further away from the hazardous front.

As a result of this discovery, Benson and his Fictioneers disrupt the pageant to embarrass the social climber Hugo Slater. In the climactic scene of the novel Killer Thompson is discovered to have murdered Slater, avenging the death of their comrade more directly than Clive Benson has intended. In the contest over ownership of historical meaning staged by *Sugar and Rum*, it is not the conscientious intervention of the liberal researcher that trumps the conservative heritage fantasy of the capitalist. A raving disreputable homeless man who has saved his army-issue knife for all these years settles the score. Though Unsworth does not invite an allegorical reading of *Sugar and Rum*, the backdrop of rioting in inner-city Liverpool[23] suggests a pattern in which victims rise up to maim and murder their oppressors, whose crime is not just their prosperity, but their desire to forget what really happened back in the discomforting past.

In *Sugar and Rum*, Unsworth takes pains to defy a Whig interpretation of the nation's progress. In his influential 1931 polemic *The Whig Interpretation of History*, Butterfield argued that historians had made the error of siding with Protestants and Whigs, praising changes that led to the current state of affairs and interpreting the past in the light of the present (*Whig* v). The twinned impulse to quest for origins and to discover an unfolding logic in history marred historical thinking with a story of progress proving certain figures or ages right because they seemed to be the sources of present-day institutions and practices (42–3). In Butterfield's view, this habit blinded historians to the radical difference of the past (11), led to false assumptions about causation (12), and encouraged simplification of the past by creating a 'short cut through that maze of interactions by which the past was turned into our present' (26). Worst of all, the Whig interpretation tempted the historian to 'forget the sufferings of a generation' and easily 'assert that the original tragedy was no tragedy at all' so long as the following generation managed to 'make the best of it' (88–9). Benson's condemnation of Hugo Slater epitomizes the rejection of progress, but as we will see, Unsworth creates a complicated structure of more and more remote pasts to debunk the Whig interpretation of history thoroughly.

In *Sugar and Rum*, Unsworth explores the vulnerability of the past to misrepresentation by considering the contemporary uses of three historical periods: the Second World War years, the eighteenth century, and the tenth century. Nesting flashbacks of war experience within the present-day narration, Unsworth invokes the modernist fiction of memory (with its reliance on narrators of questionable reliability) within a romance of the archive. Benson's research narrative takes the reader to the eighteenth century, a period accessible through the historical record, but nonetheless likely to be romanticized in its re-creation. Most susceptible of all to the manipulation of heritage re-enactors is the hazy tenth-century Battle of Brunanburh, the subject of a poem in the *Anglo-Saxon Chronicle* (most readers know it in Tennyson's version). The sequence of ever-more remote pasts correlates with a pattern of history abused; the deeper we go, the more likely we are to find misrepresentation of the past for private purposes. Even the lived history of the Second World War cannot be completely grasped by observers who were participants.

Unsworth literalizes a favourite metaphor, the labyrinth, in depicting his narrator's war experience. Benson and his fellow soldiers are caught in an area of Italy where opposing sides are entrenched in 'the Moletto Stream, a tangled maze of watercourses' (*Sugar* 70). Called the 'Wadis' by soldiers with North African experiences, the maze of stream beds is a treacherous murder ground. Unsworth takes pains to show that the cost of climbing out of the stream bed into the daylight is death, and that the cost of believing in one's ability to navigate the maze is death of a comrade. Surviving the labyrinth burdens the living with guilt for killing enemies and more guilt for failing to protect comrades. It leaves the living victim unable to compose a straightforward narrative, relying instead on a mystical (or paranoid) sense of connections. Because Unsworth's characters (mad and sane) always have something at stake, it becomes impossible to disentangle an objective, innocent version of the events narrated. Though the reader comes away with a sense of who is to blame for unnecessary deaths, everyone with a tale to tell has a motivation, often an ignoble one, and this warps both experience and memory. Yet it is worthwhile, Unsworth suggests, to strive for understanding, particularly when the entertainment industry has apparently captured the past.

Wounded by his wartime experience of being used in the trenches and on stage, Clive Benson makes a career as a historical novelist, continuing to take on disguises while seeking the healing truth. The woman he meets and imagines his Muse is named Alma, which can be read both as the Italian 'soul' (as in Spenser's *Faerie Queene*) and as the Latin 'nourishing.' Because Alma's birthday happens to fall on May 22, the same day as the breakout from Anzio, Benson hopefully imagines his relationship with her as a cure for alienation and artistic crisis. Merely questing for facts will not heal him, for the archival element of the novel represents, among other things, Benson's growing understanding of how human beings come to use other humans. Delving into the unsavoury records of the slave trade deepens Benson's wounds. After a morning calculating the extent of Liverpool's responsibility for and profits from transporting half a million slaves in a ten-year period, Benson is paralysed by the understanding that '*We would do it again*' (*Sugar* 151).

To prevent the terrifying repetition of crimes against humanity, those with historical knowledge are obliged to pass it on to the public. Throughout the novel, Benson struggles to find a venue to express his knowledge. All his audiences except the mentally ill homeless reject his news of the eighteenth century. Early on Benson meets a history master who advocates presenting children with a 'balanced view' (*Sugar* 42). '"A balanced view of the slave trade?"' Benson is incredulous: his view of history invites moral evaluation of rights and wrongs, and he sees the desire for balance as a cover-up: '"We tend to think a balanced view is virtuous ... Especially when it is applied to our crimes. We are not so keen on it when there are profits to be made"' (42). In any case, the children have only got so far as the Wars of the Roses, and are unlikely to hear about either fascism or slavery. Unsworth shows that the historical view is blocked by fantasy as well as ignorance. No scruples about accuracy afflict Hugh Slater, whose pageant of the Battle of Brunanburh embodies the heritage view of the uses of the past. Slater has no interest in modern history. He rebukes Benson for his comments on the source of the wealth that built the country house Slater owns. Slater's materials for constructing his heritage fantasy are the contested and contradictory traces of a battle about which history records only a date and names of commanders (Aethelstan and Eadmund lead the English; Constantine and Anlaf lead the Picts and Vikings). According to Slater, however, the location and meaning of the Battle of Brunanburh are clear:

> [T]his wasn't just any battle. It was one of the great battles of our history. Athelstan was the first Saxon King to have effective rule over the whole of England. The army he was commanding was an English army – not Mercian, not West Saxon, not Northumbrian. *English*. North and South burying their differences, fighting as one nation to repel the foreign invader. (178–9)

The pageant commemorating this battle, staged on a site Slater is 'convinced' lies on his land (178), will celebrate 'the forging of the English state and nation by dramatising scenes from the life of King Athelstan, very loosely constructed, with interludes and entertainments' (179). As a children's choir rehearses Blake's 'Jerusalem' (the same hymn with which the Festival of Britain dedicatory service concluded),[24] Slater glosses his intentions in the language of an advertisement: '"Traditional songs expressing the unity of England and our great heritage. That is the theme of the whole show – unity"' (177). Athelstan is rewritten as the architect of a property-owning democracy and hero of the *nouveau riche* Slater. Benson's comment that the Liverpool slave trade perfectly exemplifies a property-owning democracy (188) could not be less welcome in the home of the heritage impresario who asserts '"We hear a lot about division these days from the gloom and doom merchants. The North-South divide, all this stuff about two nations. England is one nation ... can't help but be, considering our history. Chains forged like that are not broken by local discontents, or local malcontents either. They are forged in steel"' (180). Unconscious of the aptness of his metaphor, Slater resolutely ignores any aspect of the national past that could induce a bad mood.

Hugh Slater's pageant reasserts the Whig narrative of progress with cartoonish simplicity; according to the actor playing St Columba, the appearance of the saint in Athelstan's dream predicts not only victory in battle, but 'Agincourt ... the Armada, Shakespeare, the Spinning Jenny, the Steam Engine, the spread of Empire' (*Sugar* 186). Like his near namesake, the Fictioneer Jennifer Colomb, the dress-up version of Columba of Iona is unperturbed by anachronism, so long as the proper feelings are elicited. The clanking chains of a pain- and crime-filled history haunt no one but Benson, that is until Slater is murdered in a revenge killing, vulnerable in the end to the return of the repressed.

Like Butterfield, Unsworth holds out hope that specificity and detailed analysis will result in the recognition of the past for the sake of the past. Yet he also dramatizes the limitations of Butterfield's antidote to the Whig interpretation. The heritage view of national progress will always seem more upbeat and appealing than the detailed description of remote times. As in Benson's case, research that becomes an end in itself can paralyse those with historical knowledge, or result in an incommunicable hyper-specialization. Finally, Butterfield's view that historians ought to suspend judgment about history is rejected implicitly in *Sugar and Rum* and demonstrably in *Sacred Hunger*, where historical fiction takes a stand as it invokes the past. Unsworth endorses here and in subsequent novels a detailed, particularized, unflinching study of the past with all its warts and wrinkles. The exercise of critical evaluation and moral judgment about the past in the best cases then enhances the possibility of self-criticism in the present. An uncensored critical encounter with the past thus yields intellectual, moral, and political benefits in the present, but as Unsworth demonstrates in *Losing Nelson*, the failure to achieve these liberal aims of the sympathetic imagination runs the risk of soul death.

HERO-WORSHIP AND THE PATHOLOGY OF RE-ENACTMENT
IN *LOSING NELSON*

The necessity of making judgments about the actions of historical figures and denouncing nationalist, imperialist history receives its strongest treatment in the barbed comedy of Unsworth's most recent novel, *Losing*

Nelson. His main character and first-person narrator Charles Cleasby devotes his life to the daily re-enactment and commemoration of events in the life of Horatio Nelson, the hero and martyr of the Battle of Trafalgar. Like Clive Benson in *Sugar and Rum*, Charles Cleasby is at work on a book – in this case a hagiographical treatment of the life of Lord Nelson. As in *Sugar and Rum*, Unsworth focuses on a period of blocked creativity. Charles Cleasby cannot get beyond Naples 1799, a disgraceful episode in which Nelson apparently colludes with disreputable forces, tricking and then handing over Neapolitan freedom fighters and their families to be executed (*Losing* 35–42). Cleasby's identification with his subject is so complete that the contemplation of the Nelson of Naples provokes a nervous breakdown.

Cleasby starts out a wounded figure, whose mother abandons him in childhood (she decamps to India [*Losing* 17]) and whose father terrorizes him with his joy in killing (57). Rather than seeing the need, in these circumstances, to disavow the imperial inheritance, Cleasby idealizes an English hero of the British Empire, who in his view 'lives in the memory and gratitude of the whole nation' (27). We do not need to be told, though Unsworth manages it, that one can be 'British enough' without worshipping Nelson (27). Throughout the novel, Cleasby chronicles his own obsessive behaviour without openly acknowledging his coping mechanisms as symptoms of a graver malady. In this respect, with Nelson taking the place of the fallen idol Lord Darlington, *Losing Nelson* can be seen as a rather darker version of Kazuo Ishiguro's treatment of a narrator's painful state of denial in *The Remains of the Day* (1989).[25] While the butler Stevens evokes pity in the reader, however, Cleasby's narration is calculated to provoke first laughter, then distaste, and ultimately horror. Cleasby's imitation of his 'bright angel' Nelson's breaking the line makes him more than a 'dark twin' (*Losing* 8). He represents the worst kind of useful past, which erupts into the present with murderous violence. Hero-worship; the history buff's habit of dwelling on detail; the feel-good versions of English imperialists; and bloodless heritage battle re-enactments – in *Losing Nelson*, Barry Unsworth represents these as the products of a pathological inability to face the truth.

Unsworth's indictment of the heritage celebration of English heroes rests on his characterization of his narrator. Cleasby reveals tremendous agitation if he cannot re-enact each event of Nelson's life on time, that is, on the day and hour that they occurred (*Losing* 2). Like a faithful participant in a liturgical calendar, he does the events commemoratively, with little respect for chronological order. Sometimes a sustained naval battle requires that he stay on duty for several days running, moving his model ships around on his blue glass basement table, until a confrontation at sea has been fully staged. He describes his lonely life and awkward social interactions, for which he compensates by merging with Nelson in his moments of triumph. Readers can see that Cleasby indulges in masturbatory fantasies about Emma Hamilton, Nelson's mistress, and that he comes dangerously close to losing himself to the imaginary persona of the psychotic. At moments Cleasby's 'I' becomes a 'we,' or, even worse, the 'I' of Nelson. This intense identification makes critical detachment impossible for Cleasby, as his typist and interlocutor Miss Lily points out. Rather than accepting that his hero was an imperfect human being deserving of criticism, Cleasby fuses with the dark side of Nelson, committing a symbolic murder of an innocent child near the site of Nelson's betrayal of the Neapolitan revolutionaries.

Obviously, we do not look to characters such as Charles Cleasby for a realistic representation of archival research or the sceptical inquiry of the historian. While Penelope Lively's Anne Linton sorts through her dying father's papers, she meditates on 'the fitful evidence about people's lives' that survive as scraps: 'They told you facts, but facts stripped of the whole truth' (Road to Lichfield 23–4). In Sugar and Rum, Clive Benson immerses himself in the records of the slave trade to try to get at a more honest version of the past than that on show in heritage pageantry. These novels avow that historical knowledge is hard come by and difficult to integrate with the self-interested present-day version of how things were. The archive becomes the site of striving for understanding in the face of incomplete knowledge and indifference or hostility to the truth. Losing Nelson reverses this paradigm by showing the obsessional practices of Charles Cleasby in his library and the lethal results of his preoccupation with an imperial hero.

Already the master of all the dates and events in his subject's life, Cleasby does not need to do research in order to attain fresh knowledge of Lord Nelson: he has that already, returning to well-known books only to check references. Instead, he uses historical sources like mind-altering drugs: 'I needed more text,' Cleasby thinks as he attempts to call up Nelson's voice, 'only by some more continuous reading could I get any closer' (Losing 107). Reading becomes a device of self-hypnosis by which Cleasby conjures up Nelson. The books on Cleasby's shelves serve as talismans, which he superstitiously touches on the spine as he treads his study like Nelson pacing the deck:

Approach the bookshelf, choose a book ... Choose a word in the title. You can choose any word, but once you have chosen, you must keep to it ...

Forefinger of the right hand, touch the word, then straight across, six paces, touch the wall with both palms flat against it, thumbs horizontal but they musn't touch. Then six paces back to the shelves, touch the word again. Very soothing. (121)

This strategy of moving about in his library serves Cleasby's mollifying purpose as he struggles to find a way to exonerate Nelson of the crimes of Naples (234–43).

Cleasby populates the world of historical debate using the same reani-mating personification that brings Nelson and his contemporaries to life. The scholars who have tackled the problem of Nelson's behaviour are fleshed out, dressed, and given imaginary personalities according to their support for or disapproval of Nelson (*Losing* 262ff, 293). These shadowy representatives of the historical profession command more respect from Cleasby than do live interpreters, as several hilarious episodes demon-strate. Cleasby has no patience with the tour guide's presentation on board HMS *Victory* (218–25). A popularized and dramatized version of Nelson's last victory and death elicits only scorn. Yet if this episode shows Cleasby to be opposed to the callowest marketing of English heritage by those who know only a memorized script, he certainly has no truck with recent trends in academic history, either. To his disgust, levelling believers in history from below have infiltrated even the halls of the Nelson Club, where Cleasby is disturbed by the denizens' interest in dockyards and 'humble heroes' (70–1).

When Cleasby makes his presentation on 'Two Episodes in the Making of a Hero' to a sparse audience at the Nelson Club, he is goaded by a novelist clearly representing Barry Unsworth; the walk-on character is introduced as the author of a long historical novel on the slave trade (*Losing* 181). Cleasby sizes up his creator in a rare moment of metafictional frame-breaking: 'I didn't much take to this man; he didn't look the sort who would take pride in our country's great past' (181). In the ensuing encounter Unsworth makes fun of Cleasby's failure to respond to contem-porary interests in race and gender, even as he mocks his own fictional persona as equally confined by prurient hobbyhorses – the fictive novel-ist comments, "'It would be interesting to know ... whether Nelson ever had a black woman'" (184). Unsworth's conclusion appears to be that nineteenth-century-style epic history, reduced to the fragments of epi-sodes in the life of a hero, simply cannot answer late-twentieth-century questions. The very grounds of morality have shifted when Nelson can be characterized as a serial killer.[26] At the same time, however, Unsworth captures in his self-satire the preoccupation of contemporary history with knocking heroes off their pedestals; his fictionalized representative doesn't recognize Nelson in his portrait (181), but he avidly speculates about the hero's opportunity to enjoy the sexual favours of enslaved black women (184). Cleasby's complete lack of sympathy for another character's enthusiasm for David Bowie (190–1) points up failings in his character and in contemporary historical discourse. We are meant to feel that Cleasby would be a better person if he could see the similarity between his infatuation with Nelson and Hugo's ardour for Bowie, but Unsworth also implicitly criticizes contemporary culture for allowing pop stars and historical figures to appear as equally viable options in the cafeteria of choices for fans who lack fulfilling lives of their own. Even if Unsworth cannot regret the passing of a hero-worshipping epic history of the English navy triumphant, he does suggest that present-day people lose when history becomes a mere hobby of the mentally unfit.

Like *Sugar and Rum*'s Alma, the sceptical interlocutor of *Losing Nelson* serves as the temporary moral centre of an unravelling fictional world. To Miss Lily, Cleasby's amanuensis, Nelson is little more than a media phenomenon, a travelling road show of marketable heroism (*Losing* 89). Lily's scathing interpretations of Nelson's indifference to his wife's situation (28–9), his infidelity (194–7), his willingness to throw away men's lives on meaningless escapades (46–7), and his fighting for blood money (157–9, 199) shock and intrigue Charles Cleasby. Indeed, Unsworth temporarily misleads the reader into hoping that Miss Lily can bring about the redemptive life change that would be required to save Cleasby from his obsessions. In striking contrast to the feel-good conclusion of many romances of the archives (from Byatt's *Possession* to Charles Palliser's *The Unburied* [1999]), here immersion in the past does not result in the recovery of balance, pleasure, and deepened humanity. Though *Losing Nelson* possesses each of the traits of a romance of the archive (including strong characterization, a quest plot, and a sustained encounter with the British imperial past), Unsworth employs the journey towards strong closure to bring his character into collision with the truth. Cleasby's trip to Naples reveals no material trace of Nelson (322–3), who is reviled there as the assassin of freedom fighters, if he is remembered at all. Cleasby must seek access to the historical site by purchasing a ticket to a Donald Duck exhibition – even a delusional history can only be glimpsed beneath a cartoon palimpsest (318–20). When research fails to provide the desired answer to the anxious questions of the re-enactor, Unsworth suggests, hero-worship is revealed at its pernicious worst. Unable to refute the local expert who knows the Italian sources (326–7), Charles Cleasby declares his ultimate interpretation of Nelson by murdering an innocent to emulate his hero. When he finally breaks through to join the past with the present, Cleasby's historical sense causes only damage.

PASTICHE AND PLAGIARISM: PETER ACKROYD'S REAL AND FICTIVE RESEARCH

Peter Ackroyd stands out among the small company of contemporary novelists who haved logged many hours in libraries and archives (beyond Barry Unsworth, these include Michael Ondaatje, A.S. Byatt, Anita Brookner, Patrick O'Brien, Rose Tremain, Timothy Mo, and J.G. Farrell). The author of ten novels and five biographies, Ackroyd spends hours every work day in the British Library. Typically, he researches the next book, either fiction or non-fiction (Ackroyd considers this generic difference insignificant), while he writes the current project. For many years Ackroyd wrote film and book reviews for regular deadlines, and he has conducted his career as a full-time writer with business-like consistency, handing over contracted volumes to his publishers right on schedule. This experience pertains to his romances of the archive in two possible ways. On the one hand, his familiarity with research makes Ackroyd a very experienced informant, whose representations of archival quests can be expected to be accurate about the mechanisms and practices of scholarship. On the other hand, the lists of activities in Ackroyd's daily planners demonstrate the monotonous truth of what he often tells interviewers about his boring life: almost every day he adheres to the same routine of writing, reading in the library, and going to the gym.[27] This routine might make a novelist less likely to glamorize research. The following pages compare Ackroyd's actual research practices for biographies and novels to his representations of research in his romances of the archive, *Chatterton* (1987) and *The House of Doctor Dee* (1993). As we will see, Ackroyd's treatment of archival research intersects in productive ways with his belief in the cyclical repetitions of time and his imaginative boundary crossing from the present world to its layered pasts. Though the 1992 novel *English Music* makes the case more explicitly than either *Chatterton* or *The House of Doctor Dee*, both of the romances of the archive under consideration here also reveal Ackroyd's fascination with English heritage.

How, then, does Ackroyd conduct research? First, he stays at home in London most of the time. Unlike the jet-setting international questers of many romances of the archive, Ackroyd travels mainly to perform book tours, to do brief stints as a visiting writer, and to vacation. He finds much of what he needs without leaving the British Library. Much of the rest of his material he gathers by writing letters to far-away collections and requesting photocopies. Early in his career, Ackroyd scored a critical success using this approach. Even without the cooperation of T.S. Eliot's widow, Valerie Eliot, Ackroyd managed to gather a large collection of unpublished Eliot letters from the universities and libraries that hold them. Very few curators demanded that he come in person. (By contrast, private holders of Eliot correspondence in the main closed ranks and honoured Mrs Eliot's request that materials be withheld from scholars and biographers.) Undaunted, Ackroyd produced an excellent biography without once quoting the interdicted texts.[28] Only his biography *Blake* (1995) required extensive visiting of foreign collections to see the images first-hand. (When preparing *Chatterton*, he crossed town to see the Henry Wallis painting of the poet in the Tate Gallery, as his characters do in the novel.) For his biographies, Ackroyd makes the most of the materials he can find close at hand, rereading the published works of the authors he depicts, combing the secondary sources, and doing relatively little work in foreign archives. For his fiction, Ackroyd's recourse to letters stands him in good stead when it comes to writing about unfamiliar activities or places. For instance, when he was at work on *Hawksmoor* (1985), he consulted with Julian Symons, a prolific author of crime fiction, about how to get information on the police.[29] Friends helped out with symptoms for ailing characters, such as Charles Wychwood, who dies of a brain tumour in *Chatterton*.[30] Professional genealogical researchers provided tips on how a character seeking information about a sixteenth-century house in Clerkenwell would go about finding it.[31] Using annotated period maps, Ackroyd placed his imaginary house of Doctor Dee at an address reviewers recognized as the offices of the *New Statesman* in the 1980s (the period when Ackroyd worked at the *Spectator*, also located in Clerkenwell).[32] This combination of desiring accuracy and simultaneously making revisions to correlate with personal associations (or to make trivial jokes) characterizes much of Ackroyd's historically based fiction. He gets the period detail pretty much right, with pastiche that sounds '70 per cent convincing to knowing readers,' as Claude Rawson estimates it, 'a high rate of success for extended exercises.'[33]

By the time Peter Ackroyd set about writing *Chatterton*, he had already published a sequence of three novels in which he honed his skills of imitation. The slightest of these books, *The Great Fire of London* (1982) bore a relationship to Charles Dickens's *Little Dorrit* (1857). For the admirable ventriloquism of *The Last Testament of Oscar Wilde* (1983), narrated in Wilde's voice, Ackroyd steeped himself in Wildeana. He drew up a collection of Wilde's witticisms, and composed more in Wilde's style. These he distributed systematically through his manuscript.[34] Discovering with this novel that he had a gift for reproducing the style of another writer or period, he went on to rebuild London after the Great Fire of 1666 in *Hawksmoor* (1985). Commenting on his method, Ackroyd describes how he immerses himself in texts of the period, in order that his own language and imagination might attach themselves to a subject, such as Thomas Chatterton, who as a teenager invented the medieval poet Rowley and published forged 'discoveries' of Rowley's verse.[35] Thus, *Chatterton* becomes not only a literary revivification of the marvellous boy, whose career ended in apparent suicide at age seventeen, but an exploration of the art of fiction according to Peter Ackroyd. That art nervously celebrates what Ackroyd presents as a continuum, beginning with research, leading to imitation and a liberated imagination, and ending with forgery, plagiarism, and death. If the romance of the archive in Peter Ackroyd offers a way of becoming one with the dead through their writing (*Chatterton* 84–5), it also exacts a punitive toll. Of three distinct research narratives in *Chatterton*, two end in early death. The dire consequences of inviting too close a relationship with dead letters complicate Ackroyd's message about the uses of the past.

For the central figure of the novel, Ackroyd begins with literary history. Chatterton himself digs in the muniments room of St Mary Redcliffe, discovering fragments of church records and ancient manuscripts. When these materials help the young poet find a voice (albeit the voice of a fictive medieval poet), the past prompts genius into language and suggests a way to make saleable goods out of old junk. Chatterton's method of joining passages from many different sources in order to create something that appears to be new jibes with Ackroyd's views: 'There is no such thing as originality. The history of English Literature is really the history of plagiarism. You can't escape the voices of the past, but why should you want to?' (Morris 'Word Up' 75). The novel itself suggests not only that an escape from the extreme form of anxiety of influence may be desirable, but also that one can achieve it (as Ackroyd has) by abandoning poetry for fiction. Not coincidentally, Ackroyd told Steve Morris around the time he was working up *Chatterton*, 'Poetry is just a sideshow these days. Prose is the dominant mode of expression' ('Word Up' 75). Ackroyd published his last volume of poetry (and the first in more than chapbook format), *The Diversions of Purley* (1987), in the same year as *Chatterton*, a novel he described in an interview as a 'threnody for poetry' (Leivick 'Following'

27). Ackroyd does not imagine an escape route for Chatterton into the emergent area of authorship, the novel, but he does defend the poet against the traditional charges of despair. Ackroyd imagines that the young poet does not die a suicide, but poisons himself accidentally with an overdose of arsenic and opium (a cure for gonorrhea). Though the disappointments of a writing life do not directly kill him, the trajectory that brings Chatterton from Bristol to London ends in his death.

In one of the several present-day plot lines, the reader meets another doomed romancer of the archive. Charles Wychwood is an unsuccessful poet who becomes convinced that an old portrait depicts Chatterton as a middle-aged man. Charles embarks on a scholarly quest that takes him from a bookshop to Chatterton's old stomping grounds in Bristol. There he receives in odd circumstances a set of old manuscripts that appear to show that Chatterton lived on, secretly to author many of the great works of eighteenth-century poetry, including verses by Thomas Gray, Christopher Smart, and William Blake. Unfortunately, this theory is based on forged documents, and Charles is in no shape to write it up. Both Charles's wife and son (in different ways) blame Chatterton for Charles's avoidance of responsibility, his failure as a poet, and his death from a brain tumour. His habit of eating books and papers emblematizes the condition of contemporary poets, consuming words but unable to bring original language into print.

In a mild and self-satirizing *apologia*, Ackroyd presents prose as a healthier choice – if it is indeed 'rude to imitate people' (*Chatterton* 44) and if the past is 'out of fashion' (89), novels and biographies provide forms for containing both impulses and reaping a profit, as well. All the novelists finish the story on their feet. Charles's acquaintance Flint, a novelist, biographer, and amateur palaeographer, goes from success to success despite his lack of sincerity. The ribald aging novelist Harriet Scrope, with whom Ackroyd identifies himself (Morris 'Word Up' 75), feels so defensive about telling the truth that she cannot write her own memoirs. She fears – and survives – the discovery of the plots she borrowed from a forgotten Victorian novelist for several of her early novels. Also alive at the end of the novel is Charles's friend Philip Slack, whose work in a library leads him to a most disparaging view of the fate of published poetry (*Chatterton* 150). Slack also discovers Harriet Scrope's debt to Harrison Bentley in the only performance of true scholarship in the novel (70–1). In position to inherit Charles's wife, son, and research, he demonstrates his sensible intentions regarding the Chatterton story: he will turn it into a novel (232). Plagiarism, theft, and forgery (the novel also details a scheme to continue producing and authenticating new paintings by a dead painter) may be technically criminal, but they are also at the heart of creativity, going by the names of allusion, echo, and inspiration (87). Despite this apparent willingness to dismiss the policing 'guardians of the town' so feared by the plagiarizing Harriet Scrope (97), the novel censures the wrong way of using the past. Caught by his son licking the dust he has just wiped off the old portrait, Charles asserts, "'I'm eating the past" ... "I'm engaged in an act of research'" (15). Craving and devouring without producing something new seals the fate of a character who writes with an empty pen (127) and ends the story in a crematorium.

Chatterton also endorses a right sort of relationship with the past, through the intuitions of the child Edward Wychwood and the heritage sensations of the young Thomas Chatterton. A strong sense of place, combined with a boy's love of history, English literature, and antiquities can compensate for a missing father. Ackroyd's own father Graham Ackroyd abandoned his family when his son was a baby; though he often protests that he never writes from experience, Ackroyd's novels do often feature fatherless boys (*Chatterton, Hawksmoor*), or boys with feckless dads (*Chatterton, The House of Doctor Dee, English Music*). Ackroyd's fictive child Chatterton relates how he defies death as he haunts St Mary Redcliffe church, in a scene conspicuously marked with the tokens of romantic self-inventing poetic authority:

[B]eing a fantastic, forlorn and fickle little Fellow it seemed to me that I was entering my father's house (that in no Pious sense), and to my Fancy all the funerary monuments there became Images of him straitened in the death from which I wish'd to pluck him. So you see how I came to be so great a lover of Antiquity.

In those far-off Dayes I would put on my brown cloth coat, and my round hat, and wander into the Fields in the hope of finding hidden Tumuli or inscriptions upon Stones. I would lie down upon the cropped grass, or lean against a tree, and look with wonder upon the Church which so dominated the fields and alleys beside it. 'There,' I would say to myself, 'there is the spot where the lightning hit the steeple – and there is the place where they formerly acted Playes. On the west side, there, the old monks blessed the well on the feast-day of St Mary – and there it may be that my father used to sit on an evening, when he was tired of singing.' And all these things came together, so that I fell into a kind of Ecstacy. (*Chatterton* 82)

This intensely romantic vision, deliberately brought on by meditating on the visible remains of the past, and mixed with a cherished sense of loss, could come straight out of Wordsworth's *Prelude* (1850). The personalized, emotional, and potentially curative fiction of the past, which recognizes its genesis in the wishful fantasy of a boy, and jumbles historical periods willy-nilly, the better to reach an ecstatic state, pre-dates the postmodernism it resembles by a century and a half. Through the fabric of imitative styles Ackroyd drapes on his fictions (perhaps to distract his readers from a central romantic influence), Wordsworthian spots of time and gloomier Coleridgean reveries reveal his fundamental romanticism about the past. Research is prized for its capacity to invoke sensations of connection, not for revealing facts and truths. In Ackroyd's fiction, unanswered questions and unfinished quests serve the needs of a felt heritage better than achieved and static history. While the boy Edward shouts that he has found a rabbit hole to Wonderland, Philip Slack muses on the romance of the archive as a perpetual fragment: 'Why should historical research not also remain incomplete, existing as a possibility and not fading into knowledge?' (*Chatterton* 213).

The anti-historical sentiments expressed by Peter Ackroyd's characters, and repeatedly glossed by the author in publicity interviews, underscore the pragmatic aspects of his craft. When Ackroyd cobbles together voices from the past, collected from diverse period documents, he hopes to make fictional characters sound sturdy enough to carry their burdens of mysticism, literariness, and self-consciousness without collapsing into the two-dimensionality of mere copies. Ackroyd's historical pastiche at its best evokes the life and consciousness of past periods by speaking its lines again. Though he claims that he hopes to recapture a sense of English history for benighted present-day readers who have, in the past thirty years, lost a sense of the past, Ackroyd plays fast and loose with known details about his historical characters. He has commented with frankness that historical distance makes melodramatic plot elements seem less incredible, and that his juxtaposition of the present day with earlier periods is aimed at revealing the unknowability of the *present*.[36] His nervous repetitions of scenes of revealed plagiarism, or, as in *The House of Doctor Dee*, scenes in which an author has unconsciously rewritten a book that already exists (*House* 223), can be understood as disclaimers in which Ackroyd disavows originality: as he frequently states, all books come from other books. Thus the deep past, the English tradition, and the library stacks authorize not only whatever Peter Ackroyd creates in the present, but the identity of their present creator.[37]

In combination with occasional bursts of modernist homage in his writing, these opportunistic uses of the past have encouraged critics to describe Ackroyd's novels as historiographic metafictions, indebted to American metafiction of the 1980s and 1970s, to Latin American magical realism, and to the work of his postmodernist contemporaries.[38] Ackroyd stoutly denies this, linking his 'magical realism' to the romances of Philip Sidney and Edmund Spenser, and dismissing the imputation that he might be part of a late-twentieth-century movement: 'It all goes back a very long way, and these modern phases are simply attached to very ancient forms of narrative' (Onega 'Interview' 219). As Ackroyd would have it, his writing pays homage to the English tradition represented by his favourite characters: Cockney visionaries, William Blake, political radicals, and music-hall artists. Of his seemingly postmodernist craft, Ackroyd tells Onega, 'No, it's English ... This combination of high and low, farce and tragedy, is something which is innate in the English tradition. Dickens, of course, is the great example. Shakespeare, too ... [A]s far as I am concerned, it's just part of the inheritance that goes back as far as a thousand years. It's nothing really to do with postmodernism' (218). The terms of Ackroyd's dismissal explicitly invoke the heritage version of the uses of the past. Ackroyd's imaginative celebration of London, Englishness, and mystical connections across time illuminate the presentist strategies of heritage thinking.

THE MYSTICAL CITY UNIVERSAL: TIME COLLAPSE AND
ENGLISH HERITAGE

Presentism usually means one of two things to historians, neither particularly complimentary.[39] It can describe the failure to recognize the radical strangeness and difference of the past; thus, a version of history emphasizing continuity, recognition, and 'roots' may be labelled presentist. It can also mean the selection and use of historical knowledge to serve present or future ends; hence, a school curriculum designed to foster good citizenship by emphasizing only positive features of a nation's past may be seen as presentist. The label of presentism in either case strongly suggests the neglect or deliberate suppression of knowledge that would interfere with feel-good recognition and celebration. Critics of heritage (such as Barry Unsworth) often cite these failings when they deride the theme parks, the pageantry, and the mythic commemorations that are the heritage industry's stock-in-trade. Frequently representing time as circular, collapsible, or permeable, and often asserting that history is merely a product of the present for the present, Peter Ackroyd would seem to be vulnerable to these criticisms. Another kind of presentism, however, inheres in Ackroyd's romantic evocation of past time made palpable or visible to those who tread in the right paths, read the right old books, and fall into reveries while hearing the right old music. The little boy whose grandmother took him on tours of Dickens's London and whose mother brought him home from the museum in time for a sung afternoon mass has never outgrown his love of London, English writers, and English music.[40] Ackroyd revisits these subjects with inexhaustible fascination in his poetry, his biographies, and his novels. That he does so without cleaning up the past (in fact he often lingers on old vices), and without rendering the historical encounter as especially redemptive for his present-day characters, reveals the structures of gothic horror undergirding his fictional world-making. As in gothic, for Ackroyd the present is the meeting place of all our pasts. Some of the success of Ackroyd's formula lies in the combination of love and dread, of sensations that blend déjà vu and the frisson of horror. The terrors and discomforts of the past enhance key heritage themes, such as marvelling that our ancestors could have lived through those dark, unpoliced, danger-ous, and nasty times, at least long enough to reproduce or to create the objects and traditions they have left to us.

Early in his career, Ackroyd employed gothic conventions to their usual macabre ends. In *Hawksmoor* he imagined a fictive architect, Nicholas Dyer (based on the real architect Hawksmoor, 1661–1736), who enacts Satanic rites by spilling the blood of murder victims into the foundations of his churches – spooky edifices placed to etch out a pentagram on the fabric of a rebuilding London. The historical traumas of plague and Great Fire then erupt into the late twentieth century, where a detective coyly named Hawksmoor must solve the murders that have somehow occurred in spots of time collapse. In *The House of Doctor Dee*, however, Ackroyd takes up similar gothic ingredients (the old building in a London neigh-bourhood, the fractured family, the practice of sexual magic, the alterna-tion of past and present storylines) to show the inheritance from the past in a more positive light. He does so by writing a double romance of the archive, which works in two times four hundred years apart. The connec-tion between Matthew Palmer, the narrator of the twentieth-century plot, and Doctor John Dee, Renaissance mage and narrator of the sixteenth-century story, Ackroyd renders literally. Matthew Palmer (his name sug-gests a light version of Bunyan's or Spenser's questing heroes) wants to understand the very old house in Clerkenwell he has inherited from his father. His researches reveal that it once belonged to Doctor Dee (only in the story – the historical figure lived in Mortlake). Dee, too, has a research project: to discover a method of creating life (ironically, his laboratory assistant in spiritual researches takes the opportunity to poison Dee's wife). The novel suggests that Matthew Palmer is the surviving creation of Dee, his 'little man,' or homunculus. According to the recipe for maintaining artificially created life, the homunculus must return to its maker or place of conception for a recharge once every thirty years. Thus, each character, half-comprehending, has an interest in the other, and connecting visions or hauntings allow the past and its future, or the present and its past, to interpenetrate one another. Ackroyd understands that the awfulness, filth, pain, bad smell, diseases, and crimes of the past are part of what makes the past so thrilling, but as the allegorical visions towards the end of the novel make plain, love (not horror or remorse) is the goal of existence, and light is its medium. Thus, Ackroyd handily reverses the suggestions of *Hawksmoor*, deploying the gothic elements to celebrate felt connections across time, the formation of true families of soulmates, and the healing of fractured relationships. The past plays the role of a restorative nature, capable of bringing on 'that blessed mood,/ In which the burthen of the mystery,/ In which the heavy and the weary weight/ Of all this unintelligible world,/ is lightened' ('Tintern Abbey' ll.37–41).

It is perhaps not accidental that the London young Wordsworth found so rebarbative Ackroyd draws upon as the restorative and ceaselessly fascinating source (his subjects Blake and Dickens were more enthusiastic Londoners). London's deeply layered past incarnations, so different from the present cityscape, live for Ackroyd in cherished continuities of function.[41] Political and religious radicals, mystics, and prostitutes reuse the same locales through the centuries. Furthermore, the present contains the traces of the past in human and verbal forms, though houses and streets may be unrecognizably different. Ackroyd writes:

[I]t is possible to walk down a street and glimpse a face, or gesture, which seems to have sprung from some past time. These same gestures and movements, even the very words themselves, have been repeated and revived over many generations in that precise place. I have seen medieval faces, Elizabethan faces, eighteenth-century faces, and in that recognition I realized that in London it is possible to understand everything within the eye of eternity. ('Same Old Haunts' 7)[42]

One need not be an aristocrat to inherit a share in Ackroyd's London; he uses his working-class background and his appreciation of London in its variety to lay claim to Englishness broadly. Though he declined to participate, Ackroyd's contribution to the heritage boosting of the eighties was recognized when in 1988 MP Patrick Cormack invited him to join a conservative advisory committee for the arts and heritage.[43] Profoundly uninterested in multiculturalism and postcolonial writings, mistrustful of union with Europe, and actively hostile to the influence of American literature, Ackroyd seeks to make the English tradition about which he feels so ardent accessible in popular writings.

Striving like Doctor Dee to distill his reading and synthesize knowledge through the combinatory alchemy of authorship (*House* 67, 275), Ackroyd labours among his books to enliven connections to the past that shares space with the present. If professional researchers like his character Matthew Palmer feel 'at odds with the rest of the world,' they are also 'travelling backwards' on behalf of the rest of us, who are stuck moving forward (*House* 13). The romance of the archive, no matter the subject of the research, brings the related pleasures of déjà vu and enhanced identity: '[I]t is as if I were entering a place I had once known and then forgotten, and in the sudden light of recognition had remembered something of myself' (13). This self-discovery requires of the historical researcher the brazenness of the grave robber as he digs into the past. Finding the sixteenth-century parish records in bound volumes (eschewing the available microfilm), Palmer 'savoured the stink of dust and age. It was as I were lifting down corpses wrapped in their shrouds. And of course this was precisely what they contained – names, signatures, the long-dead set down in lists, lying one upon another just as they might have been buried under the ground' (89). In an authorial meditation that appears at the end of the novel, Ackroyd vacillates between the ineffable but well-lit place of visionary recognition and the tangible bodies decaying in his prying hands. Asking 'What is the past, after all?' he hopefully votes for the combination of discovery and invention that comes out of the act of writing, 'discovering it within myself, so that it bears both the authenticity of surviving evidence and the immediacy of present intuition' (275). With a Shelleyan sense of poetic authority and the market savvy to switch genres to fiction and biography, Ackroyd crafts an approachable past, mapped onto recognizable places, and rich in the sources of English traditions, habits, gestures, and turns of phrase.

The present in which we live becomes in Ackroyd's handling a palimpsest of imagined pasts, recovered not for the sake of historical accuracy or revisionist narrative (though he sometimes achieves these goals along the way), but to heighten the sense of connection, continuity, tradition, and repetition. Though he sometimes lampoons heritage, as when in his abandoned filmscript *Albion* he shows demonstrators picketing against urban renewal that would jeopardize the Borough Prison, carrying signs reading Leave Our Heritage Alone, Ackroyd prefers an unsavoury past or a fictive, imagined past to no past at all.[44] This becomes for Ackroyd an article of faith in a liturgical approach to history.

Speaking on the subject of creative writing, Ackroyd explicitly confutes the common wisdom that aspiring novelists ought to write what they know. He urges writers not to report, but to invent. If they are fortunate, the words they use may take over and give them the past that they seek. Rather than indulging in nostalgic re-creation or traditional historical fiction, Ackroyd argues, the writer ought to try to visualize the past by looking at the present. This results in clearer vision of the present, as well as guaranteeing the receipt of an inheritance from the past. Ackroyd admits that the recipe he suggests verges on a visionary manifesto.[45] In this romantic version of the uses of the past, a strong sense of difference and remoteness is not lost. Nor can everything be recovered: Ackroyd's characters deplore the destruction of the British monastic libraries (*House* 40). The past can show through into the present and the future can be glimpsed from the past in visionary scenes that do not automatically favour earlier times. In the *House of Doctor Dee*, the late-twentieth-century office buildings deplored by Prince Charles become the gleaming towers of Doctor Dee's vision, arrived at after traversing the labyrinthine lesson in an allegorical Garden of Love. Knot gardens and glass-clad skyscrapers both belong in Ackroyd's mystical city universal, a place that present characters reach by scholarly questing. Matthew Palmer speaks for Ackroyd:

> Once upon a time I was afraid of libraries. Those shelves of books formed a world which had, almost literally, turned its back upon me; the smell of dust and wood, and faded pages, induced in me a sense of melancholy loss. Yet I began to repair my life when I became a researcher and entered the past: then one book led to another book, one document to another document, one theme to another theme, and I was led down a sweet labyrinth of learning in which I could lose myself. It has been said that books talk to one another when no one is present to hear them speak, but I know better than that: they are forever engaged in an act of silent communion which, if we are fortunate, we can overhear. (*House* 129)

With a tip of the hat to Umberto Eco, Ackroyd rescues the library from destruction and deconstruction to create a church of the past, in which worshippers can eavesdrop on the sacramental time-slip enacted by books among themselves. This testimonial distillation of the romance of the archive represents the treasured inheritance Ackroyd bequeaths to his characters and readers.

5

Time Magic and the Counterfactual Imagination

Perhaps it may die out in a positive age – this power of learning to shudder. To us it descends from very long ago, from the far-off forefathers who dreaded the dark, and who, half starved and all untaught, saw spirits everywhere, and scarce discerned waking experience from dreams ... As the visible world is measured, mapped, tested, weighed, we seem to hope more and more that a world of invisible romance may not be far from us.

Andrew Lang, 'The Supernatural in Fiction' (279)

TIME-SLIP FANTASY

The elaborate conspiracies and supernatural explanations of romances of the archive receive their fullest exploration in time-slip fantasy fiction for adults. Time-slip or time-shift stories are a popular variety of fantasy fiction in which characters travel back and forth between times, or otherwise evade the conventional limitation of characters to their life spans and fixed periods of existence. Like Peter Ackroyd's *The House of Doctor Dee*, the more fantastic romances of the archive flirt with the collapse of time and distance by making research a hazardous, magical activity that threatens to obliterate the self, as the object of research takes over or menaces the researching subject. Lindsay Clarke's *The Chymical Wedding* (1989) and Nigel Williams's *Witchcraft* (1987) exemplify two common variants of magic in the archive, unleashing into the contemporary (rational) world the ancient power of hermeticism, on the one hand, and the perverse obsession of the early modern witch-hunter, on the other. Though a vivid sense of the past and the fascination of its discredited powers imbues these novels with the gothicky feel of historical fiction, the successful containment of the dangerous archive's contents emphasizes the necessary distance between then and now. In the mode of H.P. Lovecraft, these novels embody antiquated powers, but use secrecy to buffer and protect the present from full knowledge of past crimes and ancient evil. Neither the resurrectionist impulse of romantic historiography (in which passionate archival research rescues the past from oblivion and gives voice to the silenced dead)[1] nor the antiquarian's obsessive desire to collect every detail about a vanished period accounts for the power of the past in time-slip romances of the archive.

Supernatural agents – spirits good and evil, powers ancient and otherwordly – erupt into rational worlds through the rifts opened up by curious researchers. As Andrew Lang noted a century ago, the enduring fascination of ghosts, spirits, and visionary experiences paradoxically depends upon the dominant rational view of explainable phenomena. Time-slip romances of the archive, a national specialty according to Colin Manlove (*Fantasy* 198), begin in that recognizable, post-Enlightenment world of scientific hypothesis and experimentation. The humanist-quester digs around in papers that tell of different times; as a result of this meddling, forces that controvert science and utilitarian, earth-bound thinking enact their disruptive interventions. These errant powers can only be understood (and defeated) by the completion of the romance quest in the archive. The threat of failure is almost invariably presented in the form of a menace acceptable to late-twentieth-century codes of plausibility, the descent into madness.

The familiarity of this sort of story in fiction and film derives largely from the huge number of time-slip fantasies for children. Though children's fantasies rarely feature archival research, the time-slip element often enables solution of a mystery and always entails adventures in the past. Perhaps the best-known research narrative for children is E.L. Koningsburg's Newbery Medal–winning *From the Mixed-up Files of Mrs. Basil E. Frankweiler* (1968), which takes place in the Metropolitan Museum of Art. More commonly than textual archives, machines, vehicles, talismanic objects, and magic-saturated places effect the transition from the present day. Abbreviated encounters with texts, such as the message in the bottle of Lucy M. Boston's *The River at Greene Knowe* (1959), the apprentice's indenture of Penelope Lively's *The Ghost of Thomas Kempe* (1973), or the handbook of wizardry in Diane Duane's *So You Want to Be a Wizard* series (1983–90), can play a role in stories of time-shifts. Lacking a knowledge of Latin and experience in palaeography, child protagonists are less often called upon to interpret difficult texts or delve into full-scale research projects. In obeying some of the conventions of plausibility, these fantasies more often call upon a child's skill in music (as in Susan Cooper's *The Dark Is Rising* sequence [1973–7]), where a well-trained voice or a capably handled instrument provides the special artistry and aptitude to open a passageway between fictional worlds, between present and past. Once in the historical otherwhere, the children conveyed by time-slip act out a variety of dramas drawn from adult thinking about historiography, developmental psychology, and theology.[2]

A large number of time-slip fantasies are frankly evangelical, providing access to remote times in which the realm of the spirit can be addressed without provoking squeamishness about proselytizing. Yet the purposes of time-slip episodes go beyond an allegorical rehash of Christian theology. They include witnessing the past to initiate a character into history and historical thinking, and in the process cultivating empathy in the face of radical differences. The correction of an error in the past (sometimes one committed by an ancestor of the child protagonist) or the intervention in history about to go the wrong way makes the child into the very person of historical agency without whom a key event would have turned out differently. Setting to rest a wandering ghost often leads to a mystery plot requiring voyages into the past; in a gentler mode, solace for loneliness can be found in the companionship of long-dead children (as in Philippa Pearce's *Tom's Midnight Garden* [1958] and Lucy M. Boston's *The Children of Greene Knowe* [1954]). Indeed, the slipperiness of time periods in tales of haunting means that the characters from the past appear in the present before the modern child can safely join them in their remote hometime. The Manichaean heresy of equally balanced good and evil powers has an undiminished appeal for both children and adults, but only the rare children's fantasy makes the threat of annihilation vivid. Philip Pullman's trilogy *His Dark Materials*, which at first appears in *Northern Lights* (1995) to be an alternative-world fantasy, but reveals itself in *The Subtle Knife* (1997) and *The Amber Spyglass* (2000) as a most Blakean or Miltonic depiction of time collapse, is exceptionally horrifying: the victims in these novels face not just their mortality, but something like soul-death when they are separated from their daemons.

Time collapse appears in a darker and more threatening guise in most time-slip fantasies for adults. The character who can cross the normal boundaries of death and dissolution is more often presented as demonic; the researcher who seeks to make a real connection with past lives is more often understood as flirting with metaphysical horrors. Adult time-slip fictions emphasize three elements less commonly present in the children's books: archival quests as a mode of connection with the past; erotic experiences confirming the violation of the normal time scheme; and the threat of fatal consequences and insanity for the main participants. An uneasy interrogation of historical escapism often accompanies the representation of time-slipping, as in Daphne DuMaurier's 1969 novel *The House on the Strand*, in which each 'trip' into the Cornish past requires a stronger dose of a hallucinogen that ultimately causes paralysis in the obsessed researcher. Altogether grimmer books than the sometimes danger-filled but happily resolved children's fiction, adult time-slip fantasies also engage with theology, but gravitate towards satanic powers, addiction, demonic possession, and rites such as exorcism. Madness lurks just around the corner. The erotic use of the archive to call up stimulating visions or salacious partners links sexuality with violent or mortal consequences, so that discovering history passes from a titillating to a devastating activity.

In Kingsley Amis's *The Green Man* (1969), Maurice Allington, the dissipated and debauched proprietor of a haunted inn called The Green Man, becomes obsessed with the ghost of a late-seventeenth-century cleric, Underhill, who is supposed to have murdered by dismembering his wife and a neighbour. In a nineteenth-century compendium of *Superstitions and Ghostly Tales* Maurice finds a reference to Dr Underhill and learns that a fragment of his journal survives in the library of All Saints at Cambridge. The nineteenth-century compiler stimulates Maurice's curiosity by remarking that 'this relic ... is not worth the pain of the perusal' (*Green Man* 104), and sure enough, when he finds it in its hiding-place in the college library, Maurice reads of Underhill's sexual adventures, which appear to depend upon channelling an ancient power from the pre-Christian past. Maurice digs up Underhill's grave to get his talisman, collaborates with the ghost of the long-dead doctor, and discovers that the cost of the erotic visions Underhill conjures up is the human sacrifice of his daughter to the Green Man, the ancient god of the woods. The deceiving doctor is revealed to be a seventeenth-century serial rapist and murderer, whose voracious spirit would continue his killing spree in the present. The terrifying, animated tree-like Green Man is nothing less than an old demon from ancient British times, the sort of pagan deity John Milton optimistically described as bowing out on the morning of Christ's nativity. Milton had the advantage of religious faith; the drunk and doubting Maurice, representative late-1960s Englishman, is predictably vulnerable. With the help of an exorcism performed by a disbelieving priest, Maurice rescues his daughter at the last moment, thwarts the dark powers of the past, and confronts his own mortality. *The Green Man* exemplifies the gothic-psychological variant of the time-slip romance of the archive, in which a contemporary character comes to terms with his frailties through a confrontation with the dire consequences of fulfilled desire.

In Amis's happily ending tale, the dangerous magic of the past is quelled by the present-day character who is ultimately improved rather than fatally wounded by the effects of his researches. Yet the uses to which time-slip romances of the archive generally put the historical encounter defy the expectation that wisdom and maturity will be gained by questing in the archive. Attaining knowledge of the past becomes too dangerous when supernatural agents and dormant conspiracies are stirred to malevolent life. If the survivors of the time-slipping archival quest learn any lesson, it is to stay out of harm's way by avoiding the past, and to focus on the ordinary, everyday task of living in the present. Having proffered the menacing thrills of historical understanding, the fantastic romance of the archive finally endorses a humble, private, insular, domestic, and quietist version of contemporary Englishness. The troubling materials of British imperial history invoked by these novels must be shut away and locked up like a dangerous trace of Cthulhu.[3]

MAGIC IN THE ARCHIVE

In this chapter I refer to three recent British novels in which research becomes a hazardous activity transpiring in magic-saturated archives: Lindsay Clarke's *The Chymical Wedding*, Nigel Williams's *Witchcraft*, and Lawrence Norfolk's *Lemprière's Dictionary* (1991). Lindsay Clarke's Whitbread Prize–winning novel employs a time-slip plot connecting contemporary researchers with a pair of Victorian hermeticists. The break in the transmission of occult secrets is believed by the late-twentieth-century characters to be responsible for all the ills of modern society, particularly the imminent threat of nuclear holocaust. The reconstruction of the Victorian hermeticists' lost work leads to bodily takeover, in which the characters lose control even as they enact scenes of sexual magic. Ruined relationships follow, mimicking the destroyed lives of the earlier period. (In the Victorian plot, a clergyman who goes out to India is driven mad by erotic temple carvings; back in rural England, his guilty conscience drives him to self-mutilation.) The past is revealed as the receptacle of horrifying and embarrassing secrets, and those who fixate on it appear out of touch with present exigencies. The American warplanes thunder in and out of the nearby airbase, emblems of Britain's lost status and mortgaged future.

Nigel Williams's *Witchcraft* also seeks an explanation for the decline of Great Britain, as a television screenwriter pursues a dangerous quest into the activities of a seventeenth-century witch finder, Ezekial Oliphant. Though Williams never makes it entirely clear where the researcher's delusions end, his character does narrate from a mental institution. Jamie Matheson has been driven mad by the past. He weaves an exculpatory tale in which the misogynist Oliphant takes over his body to rape, attempt to murder, and continue hunting down witches during Matheson's blackouts or periods of lost control. Though the 'real' Oliphant is also presented in autobiographical narration as a misunderstood victim of child abuse, neglect, sexual exploitation, and unfortunate historical circumstances, the reader has no way of knowing whether the politically correct period pastiche is supposed to be more true than the revelation that Oliver Cromwell, scourge of Ireland, was a witch. Though a Victorian hoaxer may be responsible for planting the document describing the perverse activities of Cromwell and his coven of political cronies, that antiquarian died insane, leaving open the possibility that Ezekial Oliphant was in control there, as well. In *Witchcraft* three questers after truth find only madness, and the novel closes with a fourth researcher in imminent peril.

For the creepy revelations of time-slip romances of the archive to achieve their startling effects first requires plausible intellectual quests beginning with rational kinds of curiosity. In these fantasies, the representation of archival research and the depiction of places containing collections both cleave quite closely to recognizable realities – at least long enough to establish a credible research scenario. *Witchcraft* opens with a hilarious and entirely probable scene in which the dubiously credentialed screenwriter Jamie Matheson attempts to gain access to the British Museum reading room. No sooner does he pass the portal guarded by the suspicious young man than he begins incompetently searching for Truth in a catalogue he does not understand. Yet in a scene reminiscent of Spenserian researches, the one appropriate text leaps immediately to hand. Matheson is not in the library half a day before he locates a published work by his seventeenth-century subject and makes eye-contact with the luscious palaeographer with whom he will soon be fooling around. Impatient with the narrow precision of academic history (the subject of his undergraduate study), Matheson prefers to imagine characters, thus bringing them to life. His rash wish expresses a commonly felt disappointment with the stories told by professional history: '"Wouldn't it be wonderful ... if they found a witch who wasn't an example of the oppression of women or the durability of outmoded belief systems in rural areas but actually *was* a witch?"' (*Witchcraft* 29).

No sooner does Matheson have sex with Anna, the redheaded expert on paper, ink, and handwriting, than Ezekial Oliphant, witch-hunter and condemned witch himself, begins to speak in his head. In short order Anna leads him to a chest full of handwritten papers pertaining to his quest. Thus, the adulterous sex not only gets Matheson closer to the sources he seeks, but it activates the magical takeover of his body. Soon the researcher is speaking in his subject's voice. We might pause to juxtapose this chain of events, moving as it does from ordinary activities in the library to extraordinary access to the past, with the words of Richard Altick, chronicler of scholars' adventures: 'Literary research is frequently dull and laborious beyond description, and even the most devoted scholar will admit as much. Much of it ends in despair, because history, however briskly prodded, simply refuses to talk. A great deal of it, furthermore, gives the world nothing but a heap of uninteresting and unusable facts dredged up from the silt where they might just as well have remained to the end of time' (*Scholar Adventurers* 3).

In *The Chymical Wedding*, as in *Witchcraft* and *Lemprière's Dictionary*, the buried facts are the most fascinating, useful, and hazardous elements of lost or deliberately suppressed systems of knowledge. Lindsay Clarke's novel, like A.S. Byatt's *Possession*, juxtaposes an archival quest transpiring in the 1980s with a Victorian past. Unlike Byatt's nineteenth century, the historical period delved into by Clarke's researchers is difficult to reconstruct. The aging poet Edward Nesbit, amateur student of hermetic mysteries, is thwarted by a language barrier. He has gained access to the family papers of an old school friend, whose Victorian ancestors include a father and daughter who sought to write up the secrets of hermeticism. As we learn from the sections set in the nineteenth century, Henry Agnew, the elderly father, suffers from ill health and a Casaubon-like writer's block as he attempts to encode the mysteries in verse. His unmarried daughter Louisa, who has dedicated herself to aiding her father, offends him by producing a gloss of these mysteries, in a prose treatise, *An Invitation to the Chymical Wedding*. She and her father burn all the printed copies of the book, after he judges it all too revealing of matters that should be kept safely in the dark. Jealousy also plays a part. To Edward and his American lover Laura, the loss of this knowledge and the break in the chain of oral transmission of the hermetic secrets account for the disastrous state of contemporary life.

Turning base metals into gold, the usual job of the alchemist, is the least of hermeticism's duties in this novel. No less an evil than nuclear warfare has become possible because the hermetic mysteries are no longer practised by mystic brothers and sisters, magical guardians of the universe. While the ancient fertility goddess 'Gypsy May' still stands guard over the land, embedded in the wall of the parish church, American warplanes scoot in and out of the local air base, where we are to understand the nuclear warheads reside. Edward's urgent research is driven by more than idle curiosity, for he hopes to reconstitute the protecting mysteries put to the torch by the Victorian adepts. He has gained access to the sort of archive scholars dream about – the private library of an old family in their country house: '[T]he air was still as a church in there, the rainy light playing through the leaded windows with their view across the parkland and the lake. It was a dream-chamber, redolent of leather and polish and the scented dust of books. And, yes, smelling of centuries of privilege, too, of aloof refined seclusion' (*Chymical* 216). The library contains a superb collection of rare works on hermeticism and, more importantly, the hand-written file cards of Louisa Agnew. Unfortunately, neither Edward nor his psychic girlfriend Laura can read these documents. In a rare touch of realism about obstacles in the way of archival questers, Edward lacks Latin. Luckily, Alex Darken – young poet, cuckolded husband, and pro-tagonist of the contemporary plot – appears. Initiated by a reading of the family tarot cards, tested and credentialed by his symbolic dreams, Alex Darken can aid materially in the research because he has Latin (*Chymical* 185). Possession of this key to the closed documents of the past unleashes nothing less than magic from the archive. Before long Alex and Laura are copulating on the very spot on the lawn where the whole print run of *An Invitation to the Chymical Wedding* was incinerated. Taken over by forces they do not understand, they learn that the practice of sexual mysteries can wreak destruction as well as heal. The intuitions and special insights of female characters are idealized by Clarke, but his Jungian imaginings are never far from their misogynistic underpinnings, in which Eros and Thana-tos together threaten the initiate with madness and physical wounding. The price of forging a compact with a mystic sister is paid when the mystic brother, the Anglican priest Edwin Frere, castrates himself. This horrific act Clarke renders political by tying Frere's self-destructive madness to his missionary work in India, to his adverse reaction to the fertility goddess 'Gypsy May,' and hence to the consequent cold war plight of Great Britain. Both *The Chymical Wedding* and *Witchcraft* propose that dark and demonic forces are at work in history, or perhaps even more alarm-ingly, that an ancient feminine goddess still wields destructive power.

The fear of calling up such forces interpenetrates all the novels under consideration. Lawrence Norfolk's *Lemprière's Dictionary* invokes Ovid's *Metamorphoses* as a fourteen-year-old boy witnesses a terrifying transformation:

> Opened, a monstrous, formless mouth, like the victim of an hideous burial, the face decayed and interlaced with roots which writhed and tore through its surface, falling away in clods. The face was crumbling away and beneath it a dull glint shone feebly. He tried to work his tongue, his throat was knotted and dry. The black slash of its mouth writhed, its lips splitting in tatters, peeling away until the bronze figure beneath began to emerge. It melted then recomposed. It softened, then redefined. It formed only to collapse. Its aspects shifted second by second, each complete metamorphosis being the herald for the next. But through it all the bronze eyes remained fixed and focused on the young man who breathed in quick, shallow gasps, chest tight, limbs rigid on the bed. (*Dictionary* 29)

By far the worst thing about seeing this monstrous shape-shifting is John Lemprière's conviction that he has called it up. As the novel reveals, no one mortal can be held responsible for the century and a half of misdeeds that keeps a 'god who tears his face out of the ground' stalking the earth for revenge (30). Instead, a group of perverse conspirators are to blame.

The influence of Thomas Pynchon can be felt in *Lemprière's Dictionary*'s tracing of the intersection of religion, magic, and conspiracy theories, but its London setting and its postimperial historical preoccupations make it a characteristically British novel.[4] This history-twisting romance of the archive reimagines the origins of the Honourable East India Company, which after its first voyage, falls under the control of secret owners. Norfolk's rollicking historical thriller begins with the revelation that the controlling interest in the British East India Company, chartered by Elizabeth Tudor in 1600, actually belongs to a group of nine French Huguenot entrepreneurs. The nine have absorbed the debts and most of the subsequent profits of the original investors, who lose their shirts when the ships come back full of pepper just as a market glut reduces its value. The treasonable secret agreements, in this fictive alternative timeline, last undiscovered until the eve of the French Revolution. At the time of the present day of the novel, the late 1780s, approximately 4 per cent of the world economy is owned and controlled by the tiny cabal. In a fiction dedicated to elucidating the use of commerce for vengeance, the shift in ownership of and responsibility for an exploiting empire rewards careful examination. Though *Lemprière's Dictionary* is an extraordinarily silly novel (in it giant whirlpools suck ships from the Thames into the cavities of a petrified giant's body lying beneath London, malevolent robots disguised in garden statuary await delivery to the conspirators who would bring down France, and political radicals released from jail by Henry Fielding take ship as pot-smoking 'Pantisocratic' pirates), it reveals in vivid detail the excesses of fantastic romances of the archive, which are among the most widely read versions of the fictive research quest. *Lemprière's Dictionary*, Lawrence Norfolk's first novel, was published when the author was only twenty-seven years old. It won the 1992 Somerset Maugham Award, and after becoming a hardcover best-seller in Germany, went on to sell over half a million copies worldwide.[5] I emphasize for a reason the popularity of novels like *Lemprière's Dictionary*, *Witchcraft* (which was later adapted for British television), and *A Chymical Wedding* (for which John Boorman wrote a screenplay).[6] The ideas about the past contained in these novels reach and appeal to broad audiences.

Though vulnerable to attack as irresponsibly warping facts and chronology, or for playing fast and loose with real history, time-slip fantasy fiction ordinarily escapes the censure of cultural watchdogs by appearing in so manifestly unserious a guise. Even the critics of postmodernism who recognize time-slip fantasy as a characteristic mode of abusing the past rarely deign to comment on actual examples. In correcting that omission, I also suggest that the uses to which time-slip fantasy puts historical materials point up the vagaries of the counterfactual imagination. Fantasy takes up the past to reshape lost worlds in which the stuff of English heritage – landscapes, mists, religious faith, forests, old buildings, ancient paths, prehistoric monuments, and time-honoured village practices – connect directly to urgent plots and motivated adventurers.

The vividly imagined green world of Middle Earth and all its offspring are juxtaposed in fantasy with a mechanized and death-dealing modernity. Colin Manlove describes the nostalgic impulse of the genre:

[M]odern English fantasy ... is written from within a sense of fragility. What was had was being lost: the wild country, the relation between man and the land, the certainty of a God and of a moral order, the sense of identity in the tyranny of commerce and regulated life, and gradually, piece by piece, England's own power in the world. In all this sense of continual slippage and loss, the impulse to preserve, to draw a protective circle, to look to an imagined glorious past for consolation was strong. (*Fantasy* 198)

In the formulaic fantasy versions of the romance of the archive, the en-

counter with the past propels the researcher (and reader) towards supernatural and conspiratorial explanations. The combination works in a self-
validating and self-undermining fashion at the same time; since the rational
world disapproves of both models of causation, the 'discovery' of magical
agency and hidden networks of power can be attractive. Despite the anti-
materialism of these fantasies, the truth revealed by supernatural intervention takes material form. As Richard Hofstadter observes, paranoid writing
insists on the compilation of evidence before making its leap to extreme
explanations (*Paranoid* 36). Even if the proof is destroyed by fire or flood,
the reader is urged to understand that it really exists. The archive holds its
occult traces all along, awaiting the initiate who can interpret them to a
crudely rational world. This flirtation with believing in discredited historical causes also contributes significantly to the threat of insanity invoked by
writers who reveal through archival quests the existence of avenging angels, witches, and cyborg conspirators.

THE COUNTERFACTUAL IMAGINATION

All fantasy fiction is counterfactual, as its theorists from Philip Sidney
forward have avowed. In his *Apology for Poetry* (c. 1579), Sidney praises
poets for their capacity to create fictive worlds, alternatives to the 'brazen'
natural world (*Apology* 15). The fictional worlds of poets' invention are
defined by their counterfactuality, 'another nature' full of things 'either
better than nature bringeth forth, or quite anew, forms such as never were
in nature' (14). Unlike the historian, 'loaden with old mouse-eaten records,
authorizing himself for the most part upon other histories, whose greatest
authorities are built upon the notable foundation of hearsay' (24), the poet
can imaginatively bring forth truer lovers, more constant friends, more
valiant heroes, juster princes, and more excellent characters in order to
teach and delight more effectively than even the moral philosophers (15–
23). Though imitation of reality has its place in Sidney's influential theory
of fiction, the poet's power rests in his ability to depart from the brazen
world of fact, records, antiquities, and examples from history. Fantasy is
by no means the only sort of literature to take its counterfactual licence
from these ideas, but since the nineteenth century it has been a perennial
and popular mode of alternative world-making, especially for British
writers.[7] Their creation of counterfactual universes, according to more
recent theoretical reformulations, makes fantasy and science fiction representative ontological art forms, 'the non-canonical or "low art" double[s]'
of literary postmodernism (McHale *Postmodernist* 59).

The questions posed by ontological fictions, according to Brian McHale, run from 'Which world is this?' and 'What kinds of worlds are there?' to 'What is to be done in this world?' and 'Which of my selves is to do it?' (*Postmodernist* 10). These questions suggest the counterfactual underpinning of world-creation, and raise the possibility that all fiction begins with the invention of impossible alternative worlds.[8] Time-slip fantasy foregrounds the fictive nature of world-creation and rests on the most counterfactual of assumptions, the possibility of moving backwards into the past or forwards into the future. Characters who enter worlds that ought not to contain them may do so by stepping back and forth through time, or by surviving impossibly long, as Septimus does in *Lemprière's Dictionary*. Just as a fantasy's secondary world corresponds through a series of contrasts to the 'real' primary world from which it departs, counterfactual fictions keep the alternative 'true' version close enough to the imagined alternative as to depend on history. Knowing that French Huguenots did not own the East India Company, and that the citizens of La Rochelle did perish in a seige on that Protestant stronghold, sets a limit on how far from the accepted historical narrative the counterfactual novel's imaginings can move. Fiction that employs counterfactuality reminds its readers of the points of connection to the actual sequence of events in time, for to untether it entirely is to lose the advantage of the contrast with the imagined alternative.

Though counterfactuals find their commonest expression in alternative time-line fiction, they have roles to play in the philosophy of possible worlds, in logic, and in history. In the hands of historians like Hugh Trevor-Roper and Niall Ferguson, counterfactuals provide an entertaining but not unserious way of thinking about the outcomes and causes of events. As Ferguson explains in the opening essay of his collection *Virtual History*, cliometric calculations in the field of new economic history have provided some of the most prominent (though not unassailable) examples of the uses of counterfactuality in historical analysis aspiring to empiricism (*Virtual* 17–18). Other uses in history are more clearly imaginative, taking off as they do from large or small events that turned out differently by accident or intervention. Ferguson defends counterfactual thinking in history as a logical necessity for the examination of causes. The historian must test a putative cause by wondering what might have happened in the absence of that cause. He also embraces the Rankean principle of attempting to know the past as it really happened, and argues that historians ought to include those possible outcomes that commanded the attention and shaped the behaviour of people in the past, even though they did not come to pass in the end. Rigorous counterfactual thinking in history is thus limited to those alternatives actually contemplated by contemporaries (*Virtual* 87–8). If, as most historians believe, the search for universal determining laws of causation is an impossible and undesirable quest, Ferguson offers a methodology by which historians can 'make tentative statements about causation with reference to plausible counterfactuals, constructed on the basis of judgements about probability ... inferred only from such statements by contemporaries about the future as have survived' (89).

Counterfactual fiction is not bound by these limitations, but it shares some of the imaginative historian's aims: investigation of conditions and causes, revisionist rewriting, and the pleasure of indulging in games of 'what if?' It explores alterations to the lives of known historical figures; it adds ingredients, imagining the impact of unrecorded persons and movements; it violates the laws of chronology; it changes the outcomes of events both celebrated and obscure to spin out new plot trajectories. The scale of the event altered in relation to its counterfactual double varies dramatically. In Joan Aiken's Dido Twite books, the Hanoverians conspire to steal the throne from the descendents of the Stuart kings – there has been no Glorious Revolution. Keith Roberts's *Pavane* (1966) imagines a Catholic England, preserved from Protestantism by a Spanish victory against Elizabeth's navy. Chaos theory has lent the counterfactual a vivid image of colossal differences stemming from infinitesimal causes, such as the proverbial beating of a butterfly's wing that stirs up a hurricane half a world away. The plot extremes to which counterfactual fiction gravitates are suggested by the sub-genres most given to alternative-world scenarios – fantasy, science fiction, mystery, and thriller. The uses of the past in these sub-genres point to those aspects of history most susceptible to reinterpretation and rewriting from a postimperial perspective. Thus, while romances of the archive in counterfactual time-slip fantasy may not tell the reader much about real history, they do reveal quite a lot about the attractions of alternative outcomes, exonerating determinist causes, and supernatural agents.

Lawrence Norfolk's *Lemprière's Dictionary* employs counterfactuality in the creation of small details and major structural elements of the novel, beginning with its handling of temporality. Historians of all but the very recent past must assume that the actors in and witnesses to the events they seek to understand have died, leaving behind only records of one kind or another. In the ideal cases the inadvertently created traces of actions and the more deliberate forms of testimony (diaries, memoirs, speeches) can be examined by a historian. Combined with knowledge of the period, this incomplete and fallible information allows a historian to create a narrative of events and an interpretation of contexts, conditions, causes, and motivations. The most basic limit on a historian ever proving the accuracy of those narratives and interpretations is time: the actors, agents, witnesses, and sufferers of consequences are no longer alive to contradict what history has to say about them. *Lemprière's Dictionary* contains a past (the early 1600s) nested within a more recent time (the 1780s). More than one influential character in the novel has lived through more than a century and a half of intervening time. Not only does their survival into the present complicate the recovery, through the research narrative, of the truth about the past, but it represents two different kinds of transmogrified historical agency. Living too long, unscrupulous businessmen become moral and physical monsters, whose efforts to arrest aging take a perversely material-ist turn. When they attempt to recruit John Lemprière to join them, it is never clear that they need more than his whole, young body parts. Alter-natively, the dead of La Rochelle, who would ordinarily succumb to oblivion and obscurity, combine to create a spirit-being in Septimus. Thus, a five-month-old child finds his death and release delayed until he fulfils the traditional function of a vengeance-seeking ghost. Not only do these time-slipping survivors of ordinary human limitations participate in Lemprière's quest for historical understanding, making their conflicting pitches for his sympathy, but they also interfere in present events. Most unruly subjects of investigation, these agents from the past not only attempt to cover up their actions, but they threaten the life and sanity of the researcher.

The reader comes to understand Lawrence Norfolk's manipulation of ordinary temporality through the confusions and clarifications experi-enced by the title character, John Lemprière. Here, too, Norfolk works in a counterfactual fashion. Historical fiction often works with the known details of a historical figure's life to provide a base for the author's psy-chologizing, interpreting, and revising. As Georg Lukács famously ob-served of the historical novel in the tradition of Walter Scott, recognizable historical figures sometimes appear on the fringes of the narrative, placed to give a more fully developed character a 'brush with history' (*Historical Novel* 39, 45). Though in both cases much of the detail provided must be created by the author, verisimilitude and accuracy are desired effects of the invention. As a counterfactual fantasy fiction, *Lemprière's Dictionary* han-dles historical figures differently. The title character John Lemprière, as well as several minor figures such as the magistrate John Fielding, are lifted from history. Their imagined biographies, however, are produced out of whole cloth.

The real John Lemprière, author of the 1788 *Bibliotheca Classica; or, a*

Classical Dictionary containing a full account of all the Proper Names mentioned in Antient Authors, bears little resemblance to the protagonist of Lawrence Norfolk's novel *Lemprière's Dictionary*. There are a few tenuous connections between biography and fiction. According to the brief memoir by F.A. Wright that appears in modern editions of the dictionary, the Lemprières were indeed an eminent Jersey family. John Lemprière, unlike the precocious autodidact of the novel, went to school at Winchester and proceeded at age nineteen to Pembroke College in Oxford University. Before reaching his majority he began work on his dictionary, not at the suggestion of a mysterious cabal, but possibly in imitation of Samuel Johnson, who might have been remembered by the older Fellows of Pembroke College (Wright *Memoir* vii–viii). After a short stint of schoolmastering at Reading, Lemprière finished his work at Oxford and took holy orders. By 1792 his career was well launched: he assumed the headmastership of Abingdon School and married not the daughter of a prostitute (as Norfolk characterizes his love interest), but a young lady of Abingdon. He became the father of a large family and neglected his duties as a clergyman and schoolmaster; as his biographer puts it, he 'relaxed into the life of contemplative leisure which was all too common among divines in the eighteenth century' (*Memoir* ix). After a few job changes representing a less than distinguished career as a teacher and schoolmaster, Lemprière retired to one of his clerical livings. He died of an apoplectic fit in 1824. Nonetheless, he wrote a practical book that is still in use more than two centuries after it was first published.

Lawrence Norfolk simply jettisons most of the unpromising material of John Lemprière's life. Instead, he presents a figure prone to visionary experiences, some supernatural and some faked to look like scenes from the classical literature he knows by heart. For instance, he wanders into the Jersey woods one day and finds a neighbour girl, Juliette Casterleigh, bathing naked by a waterfall. While he hides, watching, his father is murdered before his eyes, torn apart by hounds like Actaeon. Driven to London by his father's death, Lemprière discovers the quest that has apparently been interrupted by the murder. His father, like a sequence of ill-fated Lemprières before him, has tracked through painstaking detection the covert activities of the Cabbala, those entrepreneurial secret masters of the East India Company. Despite his father's efforts to stop the quest from being taken up by his son, John Lemprière embarks upon an archival search that leads to the discovery and destruction of the nine – or eight, for Lemprière is led to believe that his ancestor Francois was one of the original nine secret investors. Apparently threatened by the existence of yet another questing Lemprière, the eight conspirators plant the idea of writing a classical dictionary in Lemprière's head, collect the signed pages of manuscript, periodically stage gruesome murders in tableaux from classical mythology, and (in the end) set Lemprière up to look like a perverted (if unusually erudite) serial killer. Reaching D, Lemprière naturally writes up a piece on Danae, famous for receiving the attentions of the god Zeus in the form of a shower of gold. Then his Jersey neighbour Casterleigh, the mastermind of Lemprière's psychic torture, arranges the murder of a woman of the town – Lemprière witnesses her death from a shower of molten gold poured into her mouth. Thus, the dictionary that makes Lemprière's name is transformed into a signed, dated series of bizarre premeditations. The magistrate John Fielding is expected to put two and two together, though as it turns out, he suspects Lemprière only temporarily. If this were not enough to unhinge an already unstable character, Casterleigh also arranges to throw his adopted daughter Juliette in Lemprière's path at various occasions, only to reveal that she is the young man's half-sister. As with many of the revelations of this plot, it is set up by Lawrence Norfolk only to be reversed, and the reader later learns that Juliette and Lemprière (who have already consummated their love affair) have *not* committed incest. Before Lemprière and Juliette sail off together at the conclusion of this convoluted plot, Lemprière has passed through the mouldering archives of the East India Company to discover the truth about the Cabbala, resisted the temptation of joining them to replace his sinister ancestor (Francois, it turns out, has stayed alive and in control of the group for the better part of two centuries), and he has participated in the destruction of their subterranean stronghold by both fire and water. The career of the real John Lemprière pales in comparison.

The radical departures from the biography of the actual author of the *Classical Dictionary* make Lemprière a more appropriate protagonist for a romance of the archive. By depriving Lemprière of his formal academic training, and emphasizing his autodidacticism, Norfolk turns Lemprière into a gifted amateur author and researcher. The scene in which he humiliates his former tutor (*Dictionary* 43–5) emphasizes his total mastery of classical literature, a mastery he has achieved through dreamy preoccupation with the world of books, the only things this nearsighted character can see. Lemprière's intellectual attainment contrasts with his general personal incompetence, which is not much improved when he gets spectacles. The fictional Lemprière bumbles along in a hazardous city – mobs gather, assassins stalk, and buildings implode all around him, but like Mr Magoo, he comes to no lasting harm. This invulnerability arises partly from the generic blessing bestowed on amateur researchers by romances of the archive; they find their way into potentially contaminating realms, but their innocence protects them like the virgins in gothic novels. Lemprière has an additional advantage, for he has a well-placed ally. Throughout the story, Lemprière receives timely assistance from Septimus, a friend with an ambiguous relationship to the Cabbala. The actual John Lemprière benefited from connections with influential men, but their sphere of activity was the clerical world of university and school. The counterfactual link to adventurers and conspiratorial masterminds significantly glamorizes Lemprière's Jersey connections and connects his quest to a supernaturally motivated revenge plot.

That plot turns on three counterfactual 'what ifs,' combining the imagined failure of the first voyage of the East India Company, its bail-out by a group of Huguenot investors operating out of La Rochelle, and the consequences for their covert business when Richelieu (Louis XIII's chief minister) ends the Huguenot rebellion with the 1627–8 seige of La Rochelle. Though the Edict of Nantes allowed Huguenots freedom of worship and political rights, religious warfare erupted in Huguenot towns in southern France during the 1620s. This rebellion was finally quashed when the English fleet failed to relieve the beseiged Rochelais. In Lawrence Norfolk's fiction, the English navy tries none too hard to aid their Protestant brethren, but neither do the investors, who have a secret passageway in and out of La Rochelle (they use it to move their riches, the unlaundered yield of the East India trade). Disgracefully, they do not help their compatriots and co-religionists escape; this means that they sacrifice their own families. In the last crisis of the Rochelais, witnesses claim that they see an angel or winged spirit escaping the burning city; readers of the British version of the novel later come to understand that Septimus, Lemprière's friend, is actually this magical Sprite, still alive after one hundred and fifty years. (The American version omits supernatural explanations.) Tossed from the ramparts as a five-month-old baby, this infant son of Francois Lemprière is transfigured by absorbing all the souls of the dying Rochelais. Septimus lives on as an avenging angel, inspiring Lemprière after Lemprière to hunt down the conspirators. He completes his task and ascends to heaven only after the destruction of the members of the Cabbala.

They, in turn, have no qualms about siphoning off the wealth of the growing British Empire, for they can imagine that the failure of the English Navy is to blame for the destruction of their home. Their true enemies, however, are the Catholic monarch and church hierarchy in France. Here Lawrence Norfolk steers a little closer to the history of France, when he characterizes the entrepreneurial La Rochelle men as a covert power bloc, the businessmen who will underwrite the debts and supply the secret weapons to bring down Catholic monarchy and priests in the French Revolution. This counterfactual plot line resembles an old conspiracy theory, initiated by a French cleric, Abbé Barreul, who held that the Order of Freemasons orchestrated the French Revolution in order to set up a rationalist government.[9] In Norfolk's version, the rationalism turns into a technological nightmare, for the Cabbala plan to supply (and control) the revolutionaries with an army of automatons. Their other weapon is their wealth, for they can bring down nations simply by calling in debts.

The source of this extraordinary wealth is India, plundered by the East Indiamen in counterfactual fashion just as in history. If it were not enough to have the Cabbala pursuing Lemprière and scheming to destroy the French king, Lemprière questing to uncover the murderous Cabbala, and Septimus (the disguised Sprite of Rochelle) urging on the exposure of the conspirators, Norfolk adds a representative of the Empire's subcontinental victims. Nazim, a trained assassin of the Nawab (representative middle-man in the East India trade), comes to London to track down and kill those who have surgically altered the Nawab's last spy into a scarcely human clockwork robot (*Dictionary* 298). Vaucanson, one of the Cabbala, has made a specialty of creating automatons that look like humans on the outside; one of them, a stone-eating marvel, is on exhibit as a curiosity in London. Norfolk adds a technological counterfactual to the mix by imagining the vogue for mechanical clockwork toys as an immediate precursor to full-fledged robotics, allowing prosthetic combinations of man and machine. By the end of the novel we learn that several of the Cabbalists are themselves surgically altered robots, nearly impossible to kill unless you know how to choke their mechanical insides.

Thus, in Lawrence Norfolk's alternative reality, the most lucrative operation of the growing British Empire is run not by British merchants, but by Frenchmen. In addition to their betrayal of the Rochelais, their exploiting trade, their habitual deceptions, their murdering, their interfering in matters of national security, and their nasty habit of torturing women, these treasonous entrepreneurs invite our disdain by spending their money developing perverse technologies. To top it off, the most powerful among them are not even recognizably human anymore. This novel is far too fanciful to compel reading in a political allegorical mode, but it should not escape notice that its condemnation of Empire handily removes responsibility for exploitation and crimes against humanity far from the ordinary population of British investors fingered by the more historically minded Barry Unsworth. Where Unsworth's *Sugar and Rum* makes the point that every eighteenth-century lady or retired cleric with a little bit of money invested in the funds underwrote and profited from the slave trade, Norfolk plays down slavery, emphasizes Indian riches, and empathizes most with the exploited English (whores, sailors, sea captain's wives). All this is made much more palatable by the counterfactual ownership of the East India Company by traditional enemies of the British Empire.

The Protestantism of these infiltrating Frenchmen does not render them less sinister. At the Seige of La Rochelle they leave their Huguenot community behind; their unnatural use of technology allies them with no denomination, but with the irreligious commercial, technological developments of modernity. They are hierarchical, secretive, and contemptuous of the masses they manipulate into mob violence. With neither constituency to serve nor public outlets for extravagant charitable gestures, the members of the Cabbala spend their money on private theatricals, obscene toys, and elaborate schemes to corrupt and control. Just as in a Mafia story, hereditary privilege keeps the family business in the family, and weaker members are ruthlessly used, abandoned, or eliminated. The victims of the East India trade, or of the local operations of the Cabbala, matter most in the novel when they are cruelly treated family members, though the novel sketchily acknowledges more remote sufferers. The mission of the angelic Sprite of Rochelle is to seek vengeance for the abandonment of the doomed Huguenots. Locally, London lawyers and retired shipbuilders work to expose the Company's faked loss of ships, and the River Thames itself seems to cooperate with their plan to rout the Cabbala from their subterranean hideout. Though the assassin Nazim has been sent out by his boss the Nawab, who knows that he is losing his cut of the profits, apparently Muslim and Hindu victims of the Company's extortionate practices have no supernatural defenders. Indeed, they get no defence, for the novel ends with the destruction of the Cabbala, not the East India Company itself, and for all we know at the conclusion the Company retains control of the subcontinent until 1857, when the British government takes over in the wake of the Indian Mutiny.

A great deal of counterfactuality goes into the construction of the characters and plot of *Lemprière's Dictionary*, with economic, historical, technological, and political details deliberately altered. Temporality itself is manipulated to allow characters in robot and shape-shifting spirit form to survive long past their natural life spans and operate both in the early seventeenth and late eighteenth centuries. It requires an effort of will to find any serious historical thinking going on in this fantasy fiction of abnormally long-lived secret owners of the most lucrative component of the British Empire. Yet the elaborate evocation of both periods (the early 1600s and the 1780s) makes more than casual use of the past. The novel is filled with references to real people (in addition to the magistrate Fielding, a melancholy Boswell makes a brief appearance), and it attempts to capture the smells, sounds, foods, fashions, suffering, and pleasures of the past. It cannot fairly be charged with the callous indifference or failed empathy for which critics put postmodernism in the dock. Indeed, its elaborate representation of women's hunger, loneliness, sexual exploitation, torture, and murder makes the female body the symbolic ground of past suffering. The most enduring emblem of the Cabbala's crimes is the corpse of a woman whose stomach has exploded from being filled up with gold. If money hurts in *Lemprière's Dictionary*, it mainly hurts women, and both crowds and readers are expected to respond with horror to the unchecked activities of the conspirators. Yet the novel's recurrent scenes of voyeurism and manipulation of the incest threat complicate both its equation of femininity with suffering and its correlation of historical understanding with masculine agency. The research narrative within this romance of the archive strongly endorses the possibility of finding the truth in records and collections of papers, righting historic wrongs, destroying evildoers, and rescuing the endangered girl who is about to become the plotters' next sacrificial victim. It also relies on a narrative desire for ever-escalating scenes of violence, in which yet another woman is forced to display her naked body to strangers, or suffer violation by the winner of a drinking game, or swallow molten gold, or be burned alive with her children, or have her throat slit like Iphigenia. This sequence of horrors justifies Norfolk's final annihilation of the Cabbala, but it also titillates his readers. Norfolk boasts that his novel succeeded without a single sex scene, and this is technically true.[10] However, *Lemprière's Dictionary* shows how sadistic scenes of violence against women can make an effective substitute for sex, as pornographers since the Marquis de Sade have known.

Several points about Norfolk's fictional handling of past suffering stand out. First, the crimes of the Cabbala are significantly more spectacular than mundane investment in imperial profiteering, and the pain of their victims is dramatically visualized. This has the odd effect of suggesting that what was really bad about the Empire was the way it tortured white women. The remote and mainly voiceless victims of imperial expansion fade from view. Second, the exhibitionism and exaggerated cruelty of their crimes show the kinship of the Cabbala with other easily stigmatized groups – the well poisoners, child murderers, abductors, enslavers, and bogeymen of the conspiratorial imagination. Jesuits, Jews, Mormons, and Masons have all been painted in similarly garish colours. Since the Cabbala are an entirely imaginary group, and as far as we know unforgivably heinous, they need no defence from fair-minded Clio. Yet it is worthwhile to observe that the characterization of wholly evil conspirators in fiction almost inevitably justifies their punitive annihilation.[11] This would be irrelevant to considerations of the uses of the past, were it not for the currency and perennial attractiveness of conspiracy theories as historical explanations.

The conspiracy theory is one of the most popular forms of the counter-factual imagination. The furor stirred up in academic circles by Oliver Stone's films, which he presents and markets as 'historical,' illustrates the threatening potency of conspiratorial explanations.[12] Other forms of causal explanation pale before the demonically motivated conspiracy. Though influential historians such as Richard Hofstadter have helped explain the recurrence of the paranoid style, few professionals would give credence to most of what conspiracy theorists believe – 'the existence of a vast, insidi-ous, preternaturally effective international conspiratorial network designed to perpetrate acts of the most fiendish character' (Hofstadter *Paranoid* 14). Yet to regular people, the existence of secret societies, fraternal orders, hierarchical religious denominations, crime families, government agencies, incomprehensible bureaucracies, the super rich, political parties, interna-tional Communism, ethnic minorities, and multinational corporations can encourage the imaginative surrender of political agency to the secret pow-ers who pull the puppet strings. Historians seeking documents from closed archives may concur; as Marc Bloch observes, '[T]he spirit of the secret society is inherent in all corporations' (*Historian's Craft* 75).

Though there is a long history of European conspiracy theories featur-ing groups like the Freemasons, the conspiratorial explanation may in the cold war years be an especially American habit of mind.[13] The publishing history of *Lemprière's Dictionary* reflects this American taste for con-spiracy. As Lawrence Norfolk tells the story, he sought publishers in Britain and in the United States simultaneously. The American publisher thought that readers would balk at the supernatural elements of the fiction, so Norfolk agreeably removed them.[14] This editing has the effect of em-phasizing the conspirators' agency and radically reducing the competing power of the victims of La Rochelle (embodied in the British edition by the avenging spirit Septimus). A fictional world that operates along the lines of a Manichaean contest between good victims and evil conspirators shifts towards one in which an individual protagonist gets caught up in the webs of intrigue. As I show in my discussion of Robert Goddard's thrillers (in chapter 7), this kind of plot line *can* be given a distinctively British spin. The more important point is that the intellectual quest of the romance of the archive often reveals the past to have been shaped by the actions of an enemy conspiracy, led by an evil mastermind. Richard Hofstadter describes the type as a 'perfect model of malice, a kind of amoral superman: sinister, ubiquitous, powerful, cruel, sensual, luxury-loving. Unlike the rest of us, the enemy is not caught in the toils of the vast mechanism of history, himself a victim of his past, his desires, his limitations. He is a free, active, demonic agent. He wills, indeed he manufactures, the mechanism of history himself, or deflects the normal course of history in an evil way' (*Paranoid* 31–2). In time-slip fantasies the masterminds made up according to the paranoid template are chillingly capable of reaching out of the past to menace the denizens of the present day. When magic empowers the historical subjects conjured up by the ardent questing of romancers of the archive, the past is no longer a neutral set of events whose traces can be rendered useful by historians or purveyors of heritage. Nor is it simply available as a grab bag of styles for postmodernist allusiveness. It becomes instead the unsafe container of undead agency.

The fantastic romances of the archive treated here exhibit an excess of displaced agency, in which supernatural forces and conspiratorial powers exempt ordinary mortals from the responsibility for causes and consequences. Counterfactual sequences of events are created in these fantasies in order to imagine history driven by determining forces – demons, old gods and goddesses, and avenging spirits. The researcher who uncovers the secrets of history by meddling in archives is often to blame for awakening a malign spirit and must struggle to seal it up again in its catacomb or destroy it utterly. Though a terrifying truth about the past is located, exposing the evidence to present inquiry endangers those characters who feel compelled to seek historical understanding. Containing, concealing, or covering up the path back into the past seems the wisest choice when a researcher-character faces bodily takeover by old-time sociopaths, surgical alteration by death-defying cyborg makers, or even simple insanity and death threats. Only then will the imperfect but relatively stable, ordinary, and recognizable everyday world be safe to inhabit. Resisting the temptations of the still potent forces of the past (who offer sex, power, infinite riches, even world peace) restores time – especially the present and the future – to its proper position.

6

Custody of the Truth

Detective fiction inhabits a dramatically different mental universe than the one created by time-slip fantasy fiction, with consequences for the historical thinking in those romances of the archive that take on its conventions. In its classic forms (the whodunit or puzzler, the hard-boiled detective story, and the police procedural), it puts its trust in the availability of facts and the likelihood of their correct interpretation. In its postmodern form, the metaphysical detective story calls attention to this trust by emphasizing the 'ambiguity, ubiquity, eerie meaningfulness, or sheer meaninglessness of clues and evidence' and the 'absence, falseness, circularity, or self-defeating nature of any kind of closure to the investigation' (Merivale and Sweeney 'Game's Afoot' 8). As I show in this chapter, romances of the archive appear in all the common forms of detective fiction, not only in the metaphysical variant. The conclusions of these research narratives about the accessibility of the truth very often cleave to the more traditional view that the meaning of clues can be extracted by an intelligent investigator, reconstructed into a narrative of what really happened, and presented to the reader in a satisfying conclusion. Furthermore, the materiality of the evidence turned up in the archival quest tempers the postmodernism of those romances of the archive adopting elements of metaphysical detective fiction: the truth can still be discovered, despite the slipperiness of evidence and the limitations of the detective. Responsibility for recovered knowledge remains the more vexing problem, for the archive can hide the truth until it is decoded by the present quester, and it can activate the automatic device of displacement that means 'not *us*, now, but *them*, back then,' but it cannot resolve how the detecting researcher and the present generation manage their freshly acquired and sometimes unwelcome understanding of the past.

Detective fiction has been described as a representative 'epistemological' kind of fiction, in contradistinction to 'ontological' fantasy and science fiction. In asking questions about knowledge, such as 'What is there to be known?; Who knows it?; How do they know it? and with what degree of certainty? ... What are the limits of the knowable?' detective fiction typically destroys illusions for the sake of revealing a truer version of things (McHale *Postmodernist* 9, 16). This strategy creates an illusion of lifelikeness that is backed up by other traits of the genre. Time and space typically behave realistically; causes and consequences can normally be described in terms of human motivations (including the deviant impulses of the criminally insane). Though a crime, usually murder, disrupts the social order, its perpetrator can almost always be identified and punished. The implicit promise that thorough investigation, rational evaluation, and the application of the detective's impressive skills will result in the solution of the crime and the restoration of order has given detective fiction the reputation of being a conservative genre. Certainly it is consoling to imagine that rips in the social fabric can be systematically mended, though it is less soothing to focus on the imagined crime wave chronicled by detective fiction generally.

The quest for truth about what happened in the past may, as in fantasy, endanger the researcher, but the detective and any amateurs involved in investigating the crime are threatened by fallible human criminals, not by the devices of supernatural masters. Often taking place in accurately described locations, and adopting procedures used by real investigators, detective fiction creates mainly verisimilar fictional worlds. However, its plots are not governed solely by conventions of realism; indeed, structured to elicit what Peter Brooks calls the anticipation of retrospection, they have often been interpreted as the very essence of fictive storytelling.[1] Less theoretical evidence of their fictiveness can also be marshalled: for instance, murder mysteries in series featuring amateur detectives require abnormal numbers of unnatural deaths to occur in their proximity, yet these characters rarely fall under the suspicious scrutiny of the authorities. Many more implausibilities could be listed, but they are all subsumed by detective fiction's indulgence of romance's habitual pattern – questing for a talismanic representation of the truth. Mysteries reassure their readers that answers can and will be found, if only the right methods are applied by a sufficiently gifted detective. Read in great numbers and watched by even more in their film and video versions, detective fictions offer a compelling alternative to postmodernism's doubts about stable truths and retrievable evidence. By the end of the typical mystery story, the facts about the past have been located.

This pattern of closure by resolving mystery and finding truth becomes one of the standard templates for romances of the archive. As I suggest in chapter 3, 'Wellsprings,' romances of the archive owe to detective fiction their plots of research and revelation, many of their typical characters (including the amateur sleuth), and their conviction of the likeliness of discovering the truth. Though contemporary ideas about the past are assumed to be shot through with postmodern scepticism about arriving at 'a truth' or 'the facts,' detective fiction and romances of the archive validate both the process of research and its end results.

The historian Robin Winks, who is also an authority on detective fiction, hazards a guess about professors' well-known enthusiasm for the genre:

> The methods of analysis applied by the scholar are in many cases the methods used by the fictional detective to arrive at the right answer. Deductive logic, inductive reasoning, close textual analysis, the interrogation of evidence, the search for incongruities, patterns, and causal relationships: these will be found in literary criticism, philosophy, philology, history, indeed in a dozen disciplines in the social sciences and humanities. ('Foreword' ix)

Winks indirectly suggests that professional scholars and academics (from among whose ranks several well-known authors of detective fiction arise) indulge in reading this kind of popular fiction because it makes their own work practices seem more glamorous and exciting.[2] His overt point, however, is plainly stated: both scholars and fictional detectives use those methods to 'arrive at the right answer' ('Foreword' ix).[3] Very few detective novels or romances of the archive miss the opportunity to close with the revelation of the truth. As Michael Wood observes, however, recent detective novels 'place us in a world where a mystery's solution is called for but is finally the least of our problems.' Having found the answers that are sought only poses new problems: 'the frightening question is what to do with the truth when it surfaces; what it means, who can be trusted with it' ('Contemporary Novel' 967). Though the past is not the residence of supernatural agents who threaten to disrupt the present, it becomes in contemporary detective fiction the location from which troubling truths are unearthed. Once it is discovered, truth must be dealt with somehow. All four of the archival mysteries treated in this chapter value the discovery of truth, and suggest that knowledge be used to censure the guilty. Like the detective fiction that makes judgments, romances of the archive raise questions about purposes, causes and effects, and morality. Robin Winks observes that, like history, 'such fiction appears to, and occasionally does tell one what to do' and 'set[s] the record straight' (*Modus* 119). If not all of the guilty parties end up in the dock, exposed in public, or dead themselves, they do receive clear judgments on their moral and ethical failings, as well as their criminal acts. Historical knowledge becomes an instrument of discovering and blaming the guilty; thus, the custody of the truth becomes one of the most charged problems taken on by these romances of the archive.

This chapter treats four mystery novels that entail archival quests: P.D. James's *Original Sin* (1994), a police procedural; Robert Harris's *Fatherland* (1992), a hard-boiled detective novel; Peter Dickinson's *Some Deaths before Dying* (1999), a classic whodunit featuring a very bright old lady as sleuth; and Margaret Drabble's *The Gates of Ivory* (1991), which comes the closest to representing the metaphysical detective story in an archival romance. P.D. James and Peter Dickinson are both the authors of many mysteries and popular novels in other genres. Robert Harris has made a specialty of historical thrillers after writing a series of non-fiction books about the media, including an exposé of the co-conspirators in the Hitler diaries scandal in *Selling Hitler* (1986). Since he began as a journalist, it is perhaps not surprising that his novels depend upon careful research; he makes a hard-boiled detective-researcher his main character in his debut novel, *Fatherland*. Margaret Drabble writes serious literary fiction that in the case of *The Gates of Ivory* borrows plot devices from mystery novels and employs an archival quest to locate a missing person. In fact, all four novels follow missing-person mysteries to their revelatory outcomes through research in archives. Their internal storylines gravitate towards some of the most traumatic periods of the twentieth century, its war years. They provide relatively accessible treatments of the topics often taken up by historians in studies of memory. The first three novels all reach back to the Second World War, while Drabble's refers to a more recent conflict in Pol Pot's Cambodia. All four novels have something to say about Britain's role in twentieth-century wars; they employ and question theological, political, and personal frames of reference for making moral and ethical judgments about human behaviour in exceptionally stressful circumstances.[4]

The Gates of Ivory takes the missing-person mystery to Cambodia, where the parts played by postimperial Britons (journalists, human-rights observers) emphasize the altered status of the British in the international sphere, no longer in charge, and by no means pre-eminent representatives of civilization and decency. Despite this, the English sojourner who traces her lost friend does in fact arrive at something like evidence of his demise, in the form of a filmed testimony from the very person who sent his collected literary remains back to England. The villainous Khmer Rouge end up looking – individually – like ordinary human beings, capable of fellow feeling and acts of kindness. Drabble's novel is not alone in demanding the revision of stereotypes about heroes and criminals, and making the job of blaming the guilty that much more complicated. That the victims of history may themselves guard guilty secrets readers of both P.D. James's *Original Sin* and Peter Dickinson's *Some Deaths before Dying* are reminded. In *Original Sin*, a murderer operates in the ironically named Innocent House, taking vengeance decades later for the wartime betrayal of his family in hiding. He attempts to replicate the absence of his own missing family by killing the children of their betrayer. *Some Deaths before Dying* explores the morally ambiguous actions of a group of men bound together by their shared experience as war prisoners of the Japanese. Among the many things they will not talk about is their execution of one of their number for playing false with the leader they idolize. The missing of Robert Harris's *Fatherland* overwhelm the ordinary variants of the lost runaways, the kidnapped, or the murdered: Harris constructs a counter-factual history, in which the victorious Nazis have unified Europe in a German empire and carried out the Final Solution, eliminating all of European Jewry. Writing history as it did not happen strengthens Harris's condemnation of the Nazis (though the fiction requires readers to sympathize with the travails of an SS *Sturmbahnführer*) and underscores his implicit celebration of the British role in stopping Hitler from achieving his aims – in real life. In each of these novels the survival of an archive guarantees that answers about the missing can be ascertained. The archives' materiality does not compensate for the absence of the dead or betrayed, but it ensures that a historical narrative can be composed. The truth-finding genre of detective fiction thus intersects with the imperatives of the archival romance to enhance the verdicts of national guilt and innocence that accompany more individual statements of praise and blame.

The novels discussed in the following pages use mystery and thriller formulas to explore the past and single out agents of malfeasance. The past revealed by the archival quests in the mystery version of romances of the archive has paradoxical uses. On the one hand, it exposes the cruelty, greed, and murderousness of people who have enjoyed the esteem of society. The archive holds the facts that knock war heroes from their pedestals, tarnish the image of institutions and governments, and besmirch the reputations of admired figures. Seen this way, the archive's contents threaten the boosterish agenda of heritage thinking. No shibboleth is safe when the quester enters the archive: the assiduously concealed truth will out, and it will not be flattering. On the other hand, the success of an ordinary researcher in winkling out the truth from its hiding places celebrates the capacity of revisionism to right historic wrongs, to identify false memories. At least in open societies, these romances of the archive suggest, the official version can be corrected, myths can be exploded, and conventional pieties can be challenged. The archive and the state represent different interests in these fictions; the quest for the truth operates outside the law, with the hardest work demanded of truth-seekers in totalitarian regimes. Even there, fiction optimistically asserts, romancers of the archive can achieve their goals.

APPRENTICES, PROFESSIONALS, AND AMATEURS

P.D. James's *Original Sin* is one of her Adam Dalgliesh mysteries. Poet, detective, and, by the time of this story, an intimidating Commander in the Scotland Yard hierarchy, Dalgliesh presides over the investigation of a series of murders at Innocent House, the Thames-side headquarters of the Peverell Press. Though earlier Dalgliesh mysteries such as *Devices and Desires* (1989) employ his perspective for much of the narration, this late entry into the series emphasizes his younger colleagues' points of view. Dalgliesh, or 'AD,' as they privately refer to him, represents consummate professional investigative skill, the daunting achievements of a senior colleague, and the inscrutable boss who must be pleased if advancement is to be won. Though there is no reason why both Kate Miskin and Daniel Aaron might not rise in the ranks, for both are dedicated and intelligent, the novel sets them up for contrasting fates. Both are marked out by conspicuous differences that complicate their career paths. In its most superficial version, James's question might be paraphrased this way: will being a woman or a Jew prove more challenging to success in Scotland Yard? (James makes the difficulties of women in detection her central subject in earlier novels such as *An Unsuitable Job for a Woman* [1972].) P.D. James approaches several more serious problems through the contrast between the two apprentices, Inspectors Miskin and Aaron, and by further comparisons with the professional Dalgliesh and the amateur researcher Gabriel Dauntsey. Contrasting judicial and moral codes, James asks whether the end of justice is best served by professionals representing the law, or by impassioned amateurs who deal out reprisals in the mode of an eye for an eye and a tooth for a tooth. She unsurprisingly concludes that a successful policeman cannot ally himself with a murderer, no matter how just the avenging killer's motives may seem. Yet she also suggests that the amateur's intense desire for proof (and the sympathetic investigator's fellow feeling for the amateur's quest) leads more surely to the truth and the solution of the mystery than any amount of diligent interrogation of suspects, interpretation of material evidence, or scrutiny of circumstances. *Original Sin* tells the story of a balked investigation in which too few discoveries will stick in court. It concludes without a trial, the murderer self-confessed and a suicide, and one of the principal investigators disgraced for attempting to aid and abet the avenger. The plenitude of answers required for a satisfactory close to a mystery novel the archival research provides.

Working through the rich archives of the Peverell Press (a fictional independent publishing house, established in 1792),[5] Daniel Aaron discovers the material traces of crimes committed in the remote and more recent past, and in the process solves the mystery of the current murder spree. The theological language of James's title, *Original Sin*, demands that the earlier crimes be considered sins, the roots of evil in the present generation. The title also invokes a world of religious faith that James represents as dwindling to an empty place inhabited by a few lonely women – an Anglican nun (sister of one of the victims) and Frances Peverell, one of the story's main characters. The remainder of the characters, major and minor, are sometimes aware of their lack of religious feeling, but few regret the post-Christian nature of their existences. Though James makes plain the decency of the agnostic characters (who comfort the lonely and care for the sick just as well as believing Christians), she also allows Frances a miraculous escape from the murderer, and in doing so implies the presence of an unseen *deus ex machina* to whom efficacious prayers can be made. This one exception to the overall pattern only enhances the general effect of godlessness and faithlessness in the novel. James draws her readers' attention to the ideals that survive the jettisoning of grace, faith, and trust in God, and she suggests that loyalty to family, friends, and employer does not stand up well to the trauma of murder. Furthermore, James emphasizes the strong feelings that many of the characters have about their homes (not only the denizens of the grand imitation-Venetian palace Innocent House, but also the residents of humbler cottages and flats) and shows how easily hospitality and generosity can be abused, privacy violated, and gardens despoiled. In short, the novel's irreligious emphasis stops short of disbelief in sin. The crimes transpiring in the immediate plot and uncovered through archival research testify to the continuing influence of greed, wrath, overweening pride, and vengefulness in human behaviour. James is particularly hard on the hypocritical compromises that ambitious people make in order to carry out their intentions.

Devoted mystery readers should be forewarned: the plot synopsis that follows is rife with spoilers, for to discuss the archival quest is to reveal answers to mysteries as well as the objects of blame. James gives her readers plenty to deplore: the hypocrisy of a celebrated hero of the French resistance (who is not above exposing a few hidden Jews to ensure the continued goodwill of the Nazis), the vengefulness of a Jewish survivor (who acts as investigator, judge, jury, and executioner), and the murderous greed of the original builder of Innocent House (who pushes his wealthy young wife off a balcony to free up funds to finish construction). All three of these stories come to light through evidence in writing, stored in the archive of Peverell Press.

From the very beginning of *Original Sin*, the top-floor archive is an overdetermined site. On the one hand, it possesses the typical traits of the stacks, consisting of 'a large cluttered room filled from floor to ceiling with metal shelves tightly packed with files and bundles of papers. The racks ran from the windows to the door with just enough room to walk between them. The air smelt of old paper, musty and stale' (*Original* 13). Attached to this area is a small workspace, the little archives room. Two dead bodies are discovered here, one a suicide and the other a victim of murder. The reader later learns that for many years the former director of the Peverell Press conducted a clandestine love affair in the archives room. The perfect place for unobserved meetings because no one would think of going there, the archives room is the portal to a collection of records going back two centuries. Once the archive is transformed into a crime site, the papers that have gone unscrutinized for nearly that long undergo a transformation. No longer mere setting (arrayed in claustrophobic aisles of shelving), backdrop (dull archives set against sex and violence), props (the visual emblem of the tediousness of thorough police work), or detritus (to be weeded out to make space), the papers assume their central role as records and bearers of the tragic truth, sources of evidence and proof.

P.D. James arranges the novel in five parts, alluding to the five-act Renaissance revenge tragedy that plays so important a part in her earlier mystery *The Skull beneath the Skin* (1982). Entitled 'Foreword to Murder,' 'Death of a Publisher,' 'Work in Progress,' 'Evidence in Writing,' and 'Final Proof,' the five acts blend the terminology of the publishing world with the process of detection, in more and less successful puns. By the time the 'Final Proof' of the last act is revealed, the bodies litter the stage and the revenger is unmasked. He is Gabriel Dauntsey, once a promising poet, and author of distinctive verses about the Second World War. At Peverell Press he has served as poetry editor, working for Henry Peverell – the owner of the family business – and Peverell's partner Jean-Phillipe Etienne, hero of the Resistance in Vichy France. Dauntsey has not written much poetry since his early successes, devoting himself for forty years to his secret obsession – tracking down those responsible for the betrayal of his family. The official story he gives out to conceal his true quest is that his wife and two children 'had been killed in a British bomber raid on occupied France' (*Original* 163). Responding to an instruction of Dalgliesh (who intuits that the archives hold important secrets), Inspector Daniel Aaron finds the fruits of Dauntsey's research, which Dauntsey has cunningly wrought in the form of a proposal for a book (entitled 'Original Sin') about the quest to find those who exposed Jews in hiding. The professional investigator regards the work of the amateur with awe, admiration, and empathy. Dauntsey has gathered written evidence that his own employer, the 'genuine hero' Jean-Phillipe Etienne, is responsible for giving away Dauntsey's wife and children to be deported and murdered in Auschwitz. To avenge himself, Dauntsey imparts this contaminating family shame to Gerard Etienne, informing him by tape recording why he must die. Dauntsey murders (among others) both Gerard and Claudia Etienne, under the mistaken impression that they are the offspring of old Jean-Philippe. The hero of the resistance is in fact sterile and appears to feel little for his killed adoptive children. This ironic thwarting of Dauntsey's neatly designed revenge-plot does not make his murders any more or less criminal, but it undermines the satisfactions of retaliatory justice.

A further tragedy ensues from Aaron's discovery of Dauntsey's intentions. Aaron comes from Polish Jewish stock. He is an unbeliever who has ambivalent feelings about his inherited religion, his family obligations, and the burden of involuntarily representing to himself and others 'the evil of mankind' (*Original* 129). Though he wants nothing more than to prove himself to Adam Dalgliesh, he is hampered by feelings of resentment about his Jewishness: '[H]e couldn't reject his faith without feeling the need to apologize to the God he no longer believed in. It was always there at the back of his mind, silent witness of his apostasy, that moving army of naked humanity, the young, the middle-aged, the children, flowing like a dark tide into the gas chambers' (128). The empathy he feels for Dauntsey (once he discovers the file that reveals the murderer's motivation) he puts to use in a way that permanently wrecks his career. Aaron races to warn Dauntsey, and then allows the seventy-six-year-old revenger to commit suicide. His colleague Kate remonstrates with him, but Aaron is unrepentant: "'It must be comforting, never having to face a moral dilemma'" (425). The apprentice turns away from the professional world of 'criminal law and police regulations,' identifying himself instead with retribution for acts committed and suffered by another generation.

The forty-year gap between crime and retribution raises a historical question in a form familiar from the 1980s, when European public figures had to answer accusations about their activities during the war years. It also activates a rich literary tradition scrutinizing 'the sins of the fathers' and chronicling their consequences for the succeeding generations. The historical traumas of exterminating the Indians, enslaving blacks, and fighting a Civil War makes this a perennial theme for American writers such as Nathaniel Hawthorne, Mark Twain, William Faulkner, Robert Penn Warren, and Toni Morrison. In British literary fiction Puritan and Freudian ideas about inherited guilt have little purchase on representation before the contemporary postimperial period. Gothic fiction, one of the generic wellsprings of the romance of the archive, does provide influential paradigms for discovering the sins of the past and suffering their consequences, and some modern British writers (Elizabeth Bowen, Virginia Woolf, Ford Madox Ford) draw on gothic to imbue their fictions of memory with some of the horror of the sins of the fathers. From Wilkie Collins's *The Moonstone* on, British detective fiction has articulated the direst results of actions that have already become a part of history. P.D. James thus labels and makes prominent one of the tasks of detective fiction, acting as a proxy for more traditional Christian modes of confession and examination of conscience.[6]

It may appear in this account that James conveniently displaces guilt onto others – the Nazis, the Vichy regime, the imperfect members of the Resistance, and the vengeful Jewish survivors. Yet James takes pains to indict the British past as well. Daniel Aaron discovers in the archive an Anglican prayer book containing the written confession of the builder of Innocent House. Too cowardly to make a public confession, or to seek absolution from a minister, Francis Peverell describes in writing how he murdered his wife to continue his grandiose building project. He makes her death look like suicide and collects the money that she has tied up in protected funds. Then he directs his descendants to pass on his story, but keep his secret in the family (*Original* 288–9). In venerable gothic fashion, the subsidiary plot line (a snare) about the building of the inappropriately named Innocent House brings the problem of historical guilt home to roost in English history, an English family, an English business, and an English house.

Little more than the rumour of a bloodstain on the sidewalk where the murdered woman fell, this crime is remote – it embarrasses, but it does not inspire passionate retaliation like the recent past. James's novel, like Robert Harris's *Fatherland* and Peter Dickinson's *Some Deaths before Dying*, emphasizes the threshold between remembered experience and history. P.D. James shows history's hold on present-day people weakening as time passes, and she does not deplore this. Dauntsey may begin with a righteous quest, but he lets it become an obsession, which turns him into a serial murderer. Though it may seem absurd to judge the avenger as harshly as James and Dalgliesh do (empathizing with Aaron's sacrifice of his career is another option), the novel operates in a levelling fashion on ranked crimes and comparative suffering. Each death by murder is equally tragic, James reiterates; she makes a point of this through Dalgliesh's respectful treatment of the corpses of the friendless and unlikable. In *Original Sin*, the wrongs and injustices of the deeper past may be as bad or worse than those recalled by the living, but blame that takes the form of personal vengeance on the guilty threatens society more seriously than historical indictment. Continuing a cycle of vengeance beyond the immediate historical context, James suggests, is simply a crime.

RESCUING THE 'WRONG' HISTORY

Robert Harris's *Fatherland* imagines an alternative timeline in which Germany vanquishes the Allies in the Second World War. Peace with Britain (1944) is achieved after all the U-boats are fitted with new cipher codes, enabling an effective blockade around the British Isles.[7] Peace with the United States (1946) follows Hitler's detonation of a nuclear device in the air over Manhattan; a reconfigured cold war ensues (*Fatherland* 83). A toothless European Union enjoys the dominating sponsorship of the German Empire (196); King Edward and Queen Wallis of Great Britain are about to arrive on a state visit "'further to strengthen the deep bonds of respect and affection between the peoples of Great Britain and the German Reich'" (39). Stalin is disgraced as a genocidal villain (205), and Russia continues to fight on the much-extended eastern fringes of the Greater German Reich (a map shows the better part of the Soviet Union swallowed up in the *Reichskommisariat Muscovy*). President Kennedy of the United States is about to visit Berlin in an effort to warm relations between the rival superpowers. In one of the many clever jokes of the novel, the president is not the youthful hero of Camelot in the early 1960s of this counterfactual history. He is Joseph Kennedy, Sr, and, we are to understand, a right-winger who has made Charles Lindbergh his ambassador to Germany.

In Harris's counterfactual fictional world, the monumental buildings of Reich Minister Albert Speer have been constructed; rustic tourists back from the east for Hitler's birthday celebration gape at the gauche, dauntingly oversized architecture. The victorious Reich, now well into its second generation, enjoys its dominant position in global politics at the expense of serious social and political problems at home. The settlers for whom *lebensraum* was made want to come back home; the hardscrabble existence in the East does not live up to the propaganda that drew them there. Student dissidents are stirring up trouble. The continued war on the Siberian front drains resources and shows no sign of coming to an end, for the guerillas are funded by their American allies; the war dead get shipped home on night trains to conceal the number of casualties. Sex 'crimes,' including rape, mixed marriage, homosexuality, and adulterous sex with Polish labourers, are on the rise (*Fatherland* 12–16). Constant surveillance keeps ordinary citizens in line: Harris's main character Xavier March describes 'the German look,' a swift check left and right before speaking, and his characters seek out public parks and phone booths to converse about forbidden subjects (46). No topic is so shrouded in secrecy and deliberate mystification as the fate of European Jewry. As far as anyone in Germany knows, they were simply moved East. The archival quest in *Fatherland* solves the mystery of the disappeared Jews, and ends with the precious records of the implementation of the Final Solution speeding out of Germany in the possession of an American journalist. The free world will at last know the truth, though the primary investigator pays with his life for the accomplishment, or so the reader infers as the novel ends when March comes to the end of the line at the site of a dismantled concentration camp.

Xavier March, homicide investigator with the Berlin *Kriminalpolizei*, in his Waffen-SS *Sturmbahnführer* uniform represents the terrifying state power from which ordinary citizens shrink – on the face of it an unlikely character to reveal German crimes to the world. Yet he is also cut to the pattern of the American hard-boiled detective – middle-aged, divorced, estranged from his child, disaffected, and a drinker, he is himself under investigation by the authorities for insufficiently patriotic behaviour. Though he serves on a submarine during the war, he later becomes an outsider in a society that persecutes 'asocials'; his own son betrays him to the authorities for re-education late in the novel. His scepticism marks him out from his countrymen. In a sardonic mood, March reads the paper backwards, from sports to headlines, to get true news first and the propaganda last: 'even the Party had yet to devise a means of rewriting the sports results' (*Fatherland* 38). They nearly succeed in rewriting everything else, however, with Orwellian exactitude. On the outside of the Reichsarchiv building, a quotation from Hitler declares, 'FOR ANY NATION, THE RIGHT HISTORY IS WORTH 100 DIVISIONS' (234). On the inside, six floors of tightly controlled documents are transformed into official history or immolated in a furnace, '"the place where the wrong history goes"' (238). Before making the discoveries that will rewrite postwar history, March is just a homicide detective who investigates suspicious deaths. His curiosity about the previous inhabitants of his apartment labels him as a problem case; his work leads to the archival quest that will rescue the wrong history.

March is set up by individuals in the government to expose the Gestapo's serial murder of several old men, ostensibly faithful servants of the Reich. The Gestapo are ordinarily responsible not for regular crime, but for crimes against the state; their appearance at the crime scenes and in the murder investigation point to a deeper mystery (not the predictable collection of looted art which is too quickly revealed). Harris thus constructs a familiar thriller plot, in which the true enemy turns out to be the rival investigator, working for the other agency to cover up the truth while the protagonist attempts to uncover it. If Globus of the Gestapo has the backing of state power, March has the advantage of allies like Rudolf Halder, an academic who works in the Reichsarchiv on the official history of the war. Halder helps March identify the murder victims as senior civil servants, all of whom attended a secret interagency meeting on 20 January 1942 (*Fatherland* 240). Further research in race-and-chase mode leads to the chilling discovery of the consequence of that meeting, a replica of the historic Wannsee Conference at which plans were laid for carrying out the Final Solution. (According to his 'Author's Note,' Harris preserves the details of the conference, only altering the fates of the individuals attending for his counterfactual historical fiction.)[8] Having been given the unsavoury job of implementing Hitler's wish – the total elimination of the Jews – the fourteen participants in this meeting secretly save records of their activities and stow them in a locked box in a Swiss bank. At the time of the story, the surviving old men are being bumped off not by vengeful Nazi-hunters but by the Gestapo, who plan to eliminate all witnesses and records. The state's attempt to perpetuate the obfuscating 'right history' reveals not only its ruthlessness towards the architects of its success, but also the difficulty of its task when the records survive. As Holocaust historian Raul Hilberg observes in *The Politics of Memory* (1996), a document is more than an artefact or relic; it is a material part of history: 'It is the original paper that once upon a time was handled by a bureaucrat and signed or initialed by him. More than that, the words on that paper constituted an action: the performance of a function. If the paper was an order, it signified the entire action of its originator' (*Memory* 74). These traits make records especially threatening to a regime attempting to induce false memory in the rest of the globe as well as in its own citizens. Revealing the truth about the Holocaust at this time would jeopardize détente with the United States; discovering it results in arrest, detainment, torture, and death for the archival quester. Yet *Fatherland* tells not a despairing but a romantic tale: in Xavier March, Harris celebrates the potential of the single dissenting individual to correct the authoritarian state's mendacious history.

It is from an American journalist, twenty-five-year-old Charlotte Maguire, that March hears the rumour version of the fate of the Jews. He has a personal interest in the matter, having discovered a group portrait tucked behind the wallpaper in his apartment – the only trace of a vanished Jewish family (*Fatherland* 36). Safe for a day in Zürich, March hears the horrific, unlikely, and incomplete story from a young woman who has grown up despising German bogeymen: '"They say you scoured Europe for every living Jew – men, women, children, babies. They say you shipped them to ghettos in the East where thousands died of malnutrition and disease. Then you forced the survivors further East, and nobody knows what happened after that".' A handful of escapees '"talk about execution pits, medical experiments, camps that people went into but never came out of. They talk about millions of dead"' (204). Contradicted by the German ambassador, these rumours cannot be substantiated until March discovers the traces of the planning conference in the Reichsarchiv and subsequently the real trove of records, contained in a brown leather doctor's bag (293). Harris emphasizes the materiality of the bag and its contents, documents that he appropriates from the actual historical record and the real world where we do know, Holocaust deniers notwithstanding, what happened to the Jews. If Maguire can get these telling documents out of Germany and into the United States, she will take them straight to the *New York Times*. Having the facts changes everything: 'Without them, you had nothing, a void. But produce facts – provide names, dates, orders, numbers, times, locations, map references, schedules, photographs, diagrams, descriptions – and suddenly that void had geometry, was susceptible to measurement, had become a solid thing' (322). Though the truth can still be 'denied, or challenged, or simply ignored,' the facts provoke responses and reactions to something real (322–3). The German Reich will not be able to sustain itself in the face of the truth, Maguire predicts: 'You can't build on a mass grave' (323).

This prognostication resonates differently in the real world of 1992, in which a defeated but reunited and economically rejuvenated Germany had assumed a leadership position in the European Economic Community, to Great Britain's sometime discomfort. A Labour supporter and political columnist for the (London) Sunday *Times* (he quit this job after *Fatherland* appeared on the *New York Times* best-seller list), Robert Harris protests that he did not mean to equate the Europe of today with his counterfactual future world. Yet he pointed out in a 1992 interview that 'in 1942, the Germans did think of founding a European Economic Community, with a European central bank which Hitler wanted to base in Berlin. Now Chancellor Kohl wants to base it in Frankfurt. We're now seeing Berlin emerging as the capital again, and it will be the hub city of Europe. We've seen Eastern Europe collapse, and the Slavic people reduced to a state of penury, which Hitler intended. There's a power vacuum in Europe' and Germany, not victorious Britain, finds itself in the position to fill it. While Conservative politicians, led by Margaret Thatcher, sought at the time to exacerbate British fears of a German-dominated Europe, Harris claimed to feel no anti-German sentiments, merely noting that Germany, '50 years after the war, is emerging with many of Hitler's war aims coming true' (Whitney 'Inventing a World' C17). A journalist like his character Charlotte Maguire, Harris shares her view that a greater German Reich could not long survive the revelation of the facts about the Holocaust.

An international best-seller, translated into twenty-five languages, winner of bookseller' W.H. Smith's 'Thumping Good Read' award, Robert Harris's *Fatherland* reminds its readers in backwards fashion of what everyone in the postwar generations already knows about the Germany of the Third Reich. *Fatherland* ingeniously reanimates the numbingly familiar history by turning it into a crime story with two layers, the crime of commitment and the subsequent crime of cover-up. The guilt for both is pinned on the Reich itself, on Hitler who desires the Final Solution (but avoids committing his wish to paper), on those obedient and ingenious bureaucrats who devised the means for dispatching six million Jews with mechanized efficiency. *Fatherland* freshens the shock of that collaborative work by exhibiting the documents, the evidence of committee work, the signs of painstaking planning. In the language of the Russian Formalist critics, it defamiliarizes the object of its representation and helps the reader see it anew. Within the counterfactual world of the novel, the purpose of uncovering the German Empire's guilty secret is self-evident to March and Maguire. Publicizing the truth to the younger generation within Germany and to the world that appears ready to court the powerful regime demands that all risks be taken. Thus, *Fatherland* does more than remind readers of German guilt and shame for Nazi crimes against humanity; it also implicitly celebrates those doughty representatives of the free world who stopped Hitler, too late for the six million Jews and three million other victims of his genocidal plans, but soon enough to discover what happened before all the evidence could be destroyed. The counterfactual outcome of a degradingly subservient Great Britain (supplier of English maids and quality luxury goods), with a Nazi-sympathizing monarch courting Hitler's favour, underscores the British contribution, in real life, to Hitler's defeat, and to a 'right history' of his crimes.

CUSTODY BATTLES

The public, even global, significance of the recovered history in *Fatherland* represents the far end of a spectrum in which the past may be useful to multitudes, to nations, and to posterity. The release of the facts to a wider public becomes a matter of urgency. On the near end of the spectrum are those more private, personal, often familial stories of archival quests, in which a very few people care about the discoveries, and in which the objects of praise and blame are not regimes and states, but intimates – lovers, family, friends, and colleagues. Though on a world-historical scale these fictions are considerably lighter, they pursue truth no less passionately, scrutinize evidence no less assiduously, and endow their verdicts with no lack of gravity.

   Peter Dickinson's unusual mystery *Some Deaths before Dying* exemplifies this kind of romance of the archive. Here the research quest is carried out on behalf of a totally immobilized old woman, Rachel Matson, who suffers from motor neurone disease (ALS, the condition formerly known as Lou Gehrig's disease). Rachel works to come to terms with long-suppressed memories before she dies. In the end, the last living witnesses to the events she reconstructs agree to tell enough of their tales for her to understand the events that link two tragic betrayals, a murder and a disappearance. Dickinson characterizes the small circle of close friends within whose view these events take place as an almost impenetrable barrier to research. Closing ranks and protecting their own, the elder generation asserts its right to custody over its own stories. Dickinson thus shares the stuff of tabloids and sensation fiction with readers implicitly enjoined to respect the seal of the confessional. When at last the aged holder of the details shares the end of the tale of sexual betrayal, attempted blackmail, murder, botched duel, and punitive execution, he seems not like a murderer, but 'like any old man thinking about times long past and things long done with' (*Some Deaths* 251). Though there is plenty of guilt to share around, the second murder victim in the story – the long disappeared Fish Stadding – is shown to be the instigating villain, who only gets what he deserves for letting down the lads (132). Seducer, procurer, embezzler, ruiner of Rachel's marriage, disloyal friend, and dirty dueller, Fish none-theless benefits in death from the protective silence of a group of closely bonded men. If it were not for Rachel Matson's research at the end of the day, Fish would escape censure for practically all his crimes. As it is, only a few living characters possess the hard-won knowledge.

Even more radically constrained than Josephine Tey's hospital-bed-bound Alan Grant, Rachel Matson clings to her ability to think as her nerves progressively die off. While she can still speak, she receives a visit from Dick, her disappointingly greedy son, who is anxious to locate his dead father's antique pistols. One of the pair of 'Laduries' has shown up in a stranger's hands on an episode of *Antiques Roadshow*. Though Rachel has no interest in restoring the pistols to Dick, who has no right to them, the initial question of the missing gun leads her to ponder an unsolved mystery from many years before, when her husband was still alive. With the help of Dilys, her nurse, and Jenny Pilcher (the young woman who innocently seeks the *Antiques Roadshow* valuation), Rachel contacts the last survivors of the Cambi Road Association. These are the men who were imprisoned by the Japanese with her late husband, Colonel Jocelyn Matson, and they are the only ones who are likely to know what happened after Rachel shoots dead a blackmailing youth who has invaded her home to brag about his sexual knowledge of her husband. Rachel's research ulti-mately reveals that Major Fish Stadding, who embezzles the funds of the Cambi Road Association and promptly disappears, actually dies at the hands of his fellows for betraying Colonel Matson. Rachel also comes to understand that Fish is her husband's seducer, who during their imprison-ment turns her once passionate spouse into a homosexual, permanently altering his sexual orientation. Though Dickinson represents the homo-sexuality of his characters with some sympathy, he shows Rachel to have been wounded by the death of passion in her marriage, and outraged to the point of murder by the insolent young man who violates her privacy. So much trouble could have been avoided, the novel suggests, if keeping silence had not been such a perogative of her close-lipped generation.

Two different kinds of mute object emblematize the problems of custody of the past in the novel. Both are collectibles, the products of careful craft, and both possess value as aesthetically pleasing things. Neither the pistols (the separated pair of Laduries that instigate the mystery) nor Rachel Matson's photographs possess the power to speak, but both yield up testimony. The missing pistol shows signs of having been improperly cleaned after its last firing; the corrosive gunpowder has pitted some of the pistol's interior surfaces, as if to suggest that traumatic actions inevitably leave residue, physical evidence, on the surfaces of objects. The more revealing condition of the pistol lies in its location; figuring out why it has been held for years by a loyal member of the Cambi Road Association leads to more central questions about what happened. Unlike a police procedural, however, *Some Deaths before Dying* pays relatively little attention to the mechanics of analysing physical evidence. Instead, it attends to the re-evaluation of what can be seen and understood by studying a photographic archive.

Rachel Matson, though aged and incapacitated, has unusual resources as an archival quester. She is a serious photographer, who has a career's and lifetime's worth of images bound in volumes just outside her sickroom door. She has already organized and preserved her memories in narrative sequences of photographs; all she must do to gain access to a record of the past is to direct Dilys to the proper volume. Once she confronts the frozen images of her own making, however, she finds them unreliable, even treacherous. 'By insisting on the pure truth of the isolated instant,' still photography denies 'the shift and dither of reality' (*Some Deaths* 13). This distrust of photographic evidence, of the 'pure truth' of the aesthetically pleasing black-and-white images, Dickinson turns around in the course of his tightly constructed story. By the time Rachel concludes her investigation, satisfied that she understands what happened to her husband, to the young man she murdered, and to Fish Stadding, she sees that her own photographs contain the traces of the story she has recorded without recognizing at the time. The still photograph is thus vindicated as a special form of evidence to be scrutinized and interpreted by the archival researcher. In *Fatherland* and *Original Sin*, family snapshots of vanished Jews make these long-dead people seem more vivid, more present, to the researcher who discovers them. The climactic moments in some research quests, as in A.S. Byatt's *Possession*, are heightened by the description of photographic portraits that make final proof and unerring identification miraculously possible. If individual images in romances of the archive contain an excess of truth, collections of photographs that can be arranged and interpreted as stages in a reconstructed narrative have almost uncanny power to reveal the past, by capturing personalities and relationships as well as recording events.

The next chapter, 'Envisioning the Past,' gives detailed treatment to photographic archives in relationship to literary realism. The texts treated there complicate any simple equation between photographic representations and captured truths and are thus more in tune with contemporary views about the cultural construction of subjectivities and realities. Detective fiction's promise to interpret and come to conclusions makes mysteries especially prone to suggesting that photographs contain and reveal incriminating evidence. (Sir Arthur Conan Doyle's story 'A Scandal in Bohemia,' the first Sherlock Holmes tale, features just such a photograph, and the 1966 Michelangelo Antonioni film *Blow-Up* is a *locus classicus* for the ever-closer scrutiny of captured evidence.) In *Some Deaths before Dying*, Peter Dickinson shows his character reconsidering what can be observed in these carefully made and selected images of scenes from the past. Though they lie by freezing and thus privileging a single instant, photographs can capture the very essence of change as or even before it occurs. Rachel Matson thinks, 'The picture expressed a premonition of that change, a pivotal moment at which one kind of past began to become a different kind of future' (*Some Deaths* 229). At the time she makes the pictures, she seeks to retrieve images of her recovering husband after his ordeal in the Japanese P.O.W. camp. Her photographs document his return to health and normality, his restoration. Yet viewing the photographs in narrative sequence, she sees that she has arrested a different story in the albums, whose cumulative effect is to narrate her husband's turning away from her. Looking at the pictures of Fish Stadding and Jocelyn Matson, she sees that she has documented more than a friendship: 'Perhaps she had sensed something of it when she had originally compiled the albums, but at last she could see it clearly. Now the series of images seemed to her to portray something very like the history of a marriage' – though not her own (230). The truth recorded in the past survives her misapprehending, earlier viewings of her own images, to emerge with clarity as she looks back over her whole life.

The photograph thus has custody of information that is not always nor consistently revealed to the viewer, but it possesses something that is out of the control of both subject and maker: 'The camera can deceive in that way. Sometimes it may picture a self which the subject would prefer not to display, but just as often the apparent self is an illusion' (*Some Deaths* 229). If she expresses some doubt about whether a photographic portrait can capture the 'real' person, Rachel Matson finally endorses 'the kind of inward truth that was there in the photographs in her albums. Those two-dimensional black and white and grey shapes on paper were none of them the thing they showed, but its essence was in them' (238). Though the novel does not attempt to guarantee that any other viewer will ever see what Rachel Matson perceives in her photographs, it does chronicle the healing of her young accomplice, Jenny Pilcher, who is marked out by her receptiveness to Matson's photographs. Gazing into the eyes of the corpse-like old woman, Jenny sees the intelligent self bound inside the immobilized body, decides to help her, and proves instrumental in solving the mystery. Dickinson leaves his readers with the hope that the custody of the past will be awarded to a perceptive young person, rather than to a crude and greedy inheritor.

GOOD TIME AND BAD TIME

If conventional mysteries rather insistently arrive at the truth, contemporary novels adopting plots of detection focus the reader's attention on the difficulties of knowing what to do with the truth once it has been located. This is especially noticeable in romances of the archive that create the expectation of resolution through the use of mystery conventions, as we have seen in the preceding sections. As Michael Wood has observed, making the truth legible, manageable, or useful to others appears a vexatious project for the contemporary novel ('Contemporary Novel' 967). Some commentators would claim that postmodernism accounts for this thwarting of readerly expectations, and they would be right in many cases.[9] The metaphysical detective novel, according to Merivale and Sweeney, 'parodies or subverts traditional detective-story conventions – such as narrative closure and the detective's role as surrogate reader – with the intention, or at least the effect, of asking questions about the mysteries of being and knowing which transcend the mere machinations of the mystery plot' ('Game's Afoot' 2). This sub-genre of detective fiction emphasizes textuality as it represents a mystery as 'a maze without an exit,' investigated by a 'defeated detective' who is overwhelmed or baffled by ambiguous evidence that might help locate a missing person, a lost identity, or a doppelgänger. In the end, the story and the investigation both defy the mystery reader's desire for strong closure ('Game's Afoot' 8–9). Margaret Drabble's 1991 novel *The Gates of Ivory* handily represents the interpenetration of the romance of the archive and the metaphysical detective fiction. Liz Headleand is at the very least an unlikely detective, a professional interpreter, an amateur quester, and neither the wife, sister, nor lover of the man she seeks. Though Liz navigates the maze successfully – finding no body, but at least enough evidence to announce a death – Drabble flirts with anti-closure as her novel breaks up at the end. These traits all suggest a kinship with postmodern detective fiction.

In romances of the archive, however, a superficial resemblance to postmodernist fiction often clothes more traditional kinds of fiction, in which some kind of truth can be recovered from the surface confusions and obfuscation. The revival by contemporary writers of the Victorian multiplot novel contributes other means of undermining certainty and fixed meanings to the more trendy vocabulary of postmodern doubt. The limitations of individual perspectives, on the one hand, and the representational challenge of tracing the ripple effects of events through complex communities, on the other, both raise questions about the end results of quests for the truth. Drabble's *The Gates of Ivory* presents the reader with an updated version of the Trollopian or Eliotian 'great web' of society in the global village. Dispersing the narration between an old-fashioned knowledgeable, interfering narrator who focuses on a variety of characters' perceptions and an intermittent first-person narrator, out for herself, *The Gates of Ivory* uncovers the past with narrative plenitude, devoting significant stretches of story to history of different kinds. The mystery plot, though only one of multiple narrative strands, gives the story its forward momentum as it provides answers about the fates of missing persons.

Drabble's trilogy begins with Liz and Charles Headleand's New Year's party celebrating the end of the seventies in *The Radiant Way* (1987). In this novel of Thatcher's Britain, Drabble follows the fortunes of the Cambridge friends Liz Headleand, Alix Bowen, and Esther Breuer, who make up the three-legged stool of perspectives upon which she balances her investigative narrative. The second volume, *A Natural Curiosity* (1989), extends Drabble's relentless anatomy of Britain through the experiences and views of her three major characters: '"No," says Alix,' at the end of the novel, '"England's not a bad country. It's just a mean, cold, ugly, divided, tired, clapped-out post-imperial post-industrial slag-heap covered in polystyrene hamburger cartons. It's not a bad country at all. I love it"' (*Natural* 308).

In *The Gates of Ivory*, an international best-seller and critical success, Margaret Drabble brings to a satisfying close her three-volume diagnosis of the condition of England. Romances of the archive in their moral mode reiterate and revise the call to conscience familiar from Victorian condition-of-England novels. As Roger Bowen has observed, *The Gates of Ivory* places the condition of England in a global context, decentring Drabble's familiar fictional world by tracing Stephen Cox, Liz's absent friend, to Cambodia ('Investing' 279). In the process, Esther and Alix are relegated to minor subplots; the old triumvirate is reconfigured into Liz's story, Stephen's story, and Hattie Osborne's first-person narrative (Hattie is Stephen's literary agent). Holding together these disparate, criss-crossing, and disconnected trajectories is an old-fashioned overt narrator with a voice, and opinions of her own.

In their nineteenth-century form, these condition-of-England novels direct attention to the wrongs of the present and rely on a colonial geography of otherwhere to dispense with characters or to stimulate economic recovery at home. When postimperial condition-of-England novels like *The Gates of Ivory* use the archive to point at records of global problems touching Britain, they locate the sources of present losses in the now uncorrectable actions and intentions of the past, so that the Good Time of the West is implicated in the Bad Time suffered elsewhere in the world. This does not solve the problem of how contemporary characters are to go on, selfishly living in Good Time with full and awkward knowledge of the contiguous Bad Time.

This narrator announces the subject: 'This is a novel – if novel it be – about Good Time and Bad Time' (*Gates* 3). Bowen points out that these terms are redactions of George Steiner's language for discussing the Holocaust, adopted from William Shawcross on the Cambodian genocide ('Investing' 280–1). Cambodia stands for Bad Time in *The Gates of Ivory* and into Bad Time first Stephen and then Liz go, equipped with both deprecation of and desire for the heart of darkness. Drabble's Bangkok and Cambodia are departures for a novelist of the British middle-class experience. Her other travellers stick to airplanes, hotels, and restaurants, and in *The Gates of Ivory* she is still most at home in descriptions of tourists' venues. Yet she devises in the savvy Miss Porntip (a Thai beauty queen) a credible guide for Stephen as he gathers materials for a play about Pol Pot. Driven, as Roger Bowen points out, by a desire to plunder the 'gorgeous East' for his screenplay about Pol Pot (*Gates* 47), Stephen finds 'a relentlessly contemporary' place, where 'colonial adventure [has been] replaced by postcolonial proxy wars, by a regional holocaust' (Bowen 'Investing' 282). Miss Porntip knows better than to enter the Bad Time of the Khmer Rouge and Stephen's further explorations feel rather researched, as if

Drabble herself could not follow Stephen's misleading dreams into the misapprehended Conradian territory. In fact, she was denied access to Cambodia and made do by travelling to Vietnam and to refugee camps on the Thai-Cambodian border.[10] The impression of a bookish encounter with otherness is strengthened by the bibliography at the novel's end and by Drabble's indecision about her chosen form ('if novel it be' [*Gates* 3]), but it is also appropriate to its central thread, an archival quest that leads Liz Headland from the cryptic papers of Stephen Cox to Cambodia and to the end of Stephen's cold trail. Having fallen ill of fever while in the hands of the Khmer Rouge, Stephen Cox recovers enough to be taken to a clinic, where he dies (393). Not in the end a murder victim, Stephen Cox finds friends and comforters among the Khmer Rouge, who cannot be blamed for his illness. His doctor in the clinic is responsible for mailing the package that arrives on Liz Headland's desk. Thus Drabble indicates how human connections and global communications can actually cross the line between Bad Time and Good Time.

The story begins engagingly when a package containing a manuscript in Stephen's handwriting, papers, postcards, newspaper cuttings, and two joints of a human finger bone arrives in Liz's office and transforms Stephen's prolonged absence into a mystery. Liz Headland, a 'healer of hurt minds' (*Gates* 5) finds herself volunteering for a research quest to locate her missing friend, following his trail as in a 'police reconstruction' (319). Liz is a representative middle-class Briton, well meaning but generally inattentive to displaced people, refugee camps, and other consequences of the postimperial rearrangement of the world (23). The arrival of Stephen's 'orts and fragments' (23) impels her into the nightmarish Bad Time of recent Cambodian history. In Drabble's hands, investigating criminal regimes and following the fates of individuals who hope to understand them (those typically British envoys, human-rights observers; the 'relief worker, the photojournalist and the television reporter' [124]) becomes a specialized form of looking for trouble. These characters court both personal endangerment and the moral trouble of catering to the media-stimulated appetite for horror stories. The knowledge of atrocities garnered by those who follow their research quests into the danger zone, or by those who greet the few survivors, leaves recipients in a bind: 'We in Good Time receive messengers who stumble across the bridge or through the river, maimed and bleeding, shocked and starving. They try to tell us what it is like over there, and we try to listen ... We are seized with panic and pity and fear. Can we believe these stories from beyond the tomb? Can it be that these things happen in our world, our time?' (3–4). The burden of receiving testimony leaves the custodians of the truth confused and afraid; some kinds of knowledge of late-twentieth-century history impose impossible demands from which ordinary characters not surprisingly shrink. The quest itself can be hazardous in mundane ways: if finding the evidence of Stephen's death is not sufficient to warn off other questers into the Bad Time, Liz nearly dies of Toxic Shock Syndrome while in Bangkok.

The Gates of Ivory spills untidily in many directions, as if to demonstrate the narrator's hunch that 'for this subject matter, one should seek the most disjunctive, the most disruptive, the most uneasy and incompetent of forms, a form that offers not a grain of comfort or repose' (*Gates* 138). It proceeds by juxtaposing sequences and scenes, introducing a very wide range of characters and locations, formalizing the simultaneity that Drabble makes a major theme, and in the process enacting a crisis of confidence in novelistic representation: 'The mismatch between narrative and subject is too great. Why impose the story line of individual fate upon a story which is at least in part to do with numbers? A queasiness, a moral scruple overcomes the writer at the prospect of selecting individuals from the mass of history, from the human soup' (138). Thus, we find Drabble radically extending her favourite technique of itemized concurrence, as in the beginning of *The Radiant Way*, where she presents in sequence Alix at her dressing table, Esther walking, and Liz daydreaming as she prepares for the evening's party. They are separate, but they come together. The resistance in *The Gates of Ivory* to a sense of completion or of a neatly checked-off list of participants leads to a more provisional and untidy fictional world, one showing signs of what Roger Bowen calls 'aspirant post-modernism' ('Investing' 280). Only at the end of *The Gates of Ivory*, when the characters come together for the party – a memorial service for Stephen Cox – does Drabble allow herself the narrative satisfaction and inclusion of the extended checklist.

If the service, a successful 'Good Time post-Memorial party' (*Gates* 445), pleases the guests and at least temporarily unites the dispersed and disparate lives it is Drabble's special talent to enumerate and describe, it cannot sustain the promise of the hymn that declares '"Earth shall be fair, and all her folk be one!"' (440). Drabble undermines the social rituals she excels at describing; generic stresses fracture the occasion, which can only partly heal the rifts of late-twentieth-century existence. In a fictional world governed by the simultaneity and proximity of Good Time and Bad Time, the amazing Miss Porntip's flowers can arrive by airmail for the memorial service of her deceased lover, but the demands of thinking globally stagger the mind. Alix Bowen, hearing the hymn, reflects on

> the faltering unpractised note of heart-breaking optimism, extend[ing] equally to the toiling billions of China, to the Indian subcontinent, to the Americas, to the fragmenting empire of the Soviet Union, to the Iranians and the Inuit and the head-hunters of Irian Jaya and the whole stinking selfish murderous brutish greedy gazetteer of *National Geographic* folk colourful and colourless, rich and poor, oppressing and oppressed: in short to the whole four or five billion individuals that make up the population of the globe, of whom this ragged, tattered, fragmented, faithless gathering makes but a miserably inadequate representation. (440)

Lest we imagine that the novel is not up to the challenging task of representation so defined, Drabble ends with a unifying image from the fractal-driven patterns of life in the megalopolis. A traffic jam becomes a shared social situation, the inevitable ripple effect of an accident on the M4. The dispersed characters get caught in traffic, arrested as they unwittingly await the news of the End of History (445). For Drabble, the End of History is the anticipated failure of narrative, ironically to be announced by the story-spinning media to the voracious consumers of Good Time. Those in Bad Time should be so lucky as to be done with History, to be released from the excruciating contexts that make them the subjects of the Western imagination's (media) attention. Yet Drabble tellingly closes her novel before the announcement is made. Though they are isolated in their separate vehicles, Drabble places her characters in a rewoven great web in which consequences of actions half a world away are still felt, certainly but unpredictably, by the rest of the human community. To be sure, assembling evidence, finding satisfactory answers, hearing witnesses, and tracing movements in Drabble's great web requires good luck. As in George Eliot's fictional worlds, the tasks of praising and blaming are assisted by coincidences and fortuitous connections; as in Trollope's world, characters are inevitably known to others. The witness to Stephen Cox's death has been caught on film; Liz Headleand runs into the one person in the world who possesses that evidence, a friend of a person she already knows. Despite the population of the globe and the impossibility of comprehending our various experiences, in Margaret Drabble's novels chance occurrences and meetings underwrite assertions of coherence and interconnectedness. The characters from her previous novels provide the ties to children, acquaintances, former lovers, and professional contacts who turn out to populate even the most remote locations of the globe. The research quest thus becomes a matter of a sequence of recognitions, arrayed in a chain until the mystery has been solved. Thus, the romancer of the archive succeeds not because she is such a skilful interpreter, but because of her social position in a network of educated cosmopolitans. Stephen Cox, a Booker prizewinner, a person of a certain class, can be located. This might be consoling, but Drabble makes it equally unnerving.

The Gates of Ivory gives far less certainty and resolution to the characters within its fictional world than it offers to readers. It instead shows how the discovery of the truth can lead characters to feelings of thwarted obligation. Something ought to be done, but what? characters in *The Gates of Ivory* wonder. It come closest to postmodernism in those moments when the attempt to narrate the past itself appears a form of misrepresentation, an effect of the human desire to have answers that can be put in story form. In the world of the Bad Time, Drabble suggests, answers to missing-person mysteries are not so easily found. Mme Akrun perpetually asks, from an award-winning photograph, and in life, 'Where is my son?' (*Gates* 289, 336). This missing person may be anywhere:

> Mitra Arkun is a para-social worker in a resettlement centre in Montreal.
> Mitra deals in crack in Washington.
> Mitra is writing his life story in little red notebooks.
> Mitra is a born-again Christian.
> Mitra has murdered a fellow-refugee in a hostel in New Zealand.
> Mitra sits in front of a prison psychologist in New Zealand and confesses to multiple trauma.
> Mitra is working as a garden maintenance man in Kent. (341–2)

For the residents of Good Time who desire the conclusions to narrative enigmas, Drabble creates such a complex web of connections in the social world she depicts that the doubts, denial, and uncertainty expressed about knowing the truth become elements in realistic psychological and social portraiture. This self-aware and theoretically sophisticated novelist, who deftly combines elements of detective fiction with her investigations of the obligations of history, flirts with postmodernism but commit herself in the end to a more traditional representation of self and society, at least for residents of the communication age, the wired global village. She does this for an old-fashioned social-problem-novelist's reason – to awaken her middle-class readers to the reality they would rather not see. Yet if Drabble's fiction reveals a debt to Elizabeth Gaskell's inspired sermonizing, it also depicts with social and psychological verisimilitude the difficulty of responding to history, faced with the incomprehensible testimony of those who live in Bad Time. The final words of the novel contain Drabble's warning that the Good Time's wishes and opinions will be irrelevant when they are overtaken by the swelling numbers who burgeon in Bad Time. This parting trace of Orientalism is embodied in the figure of the missing Mitra Akrun:

> He will not step back through the gates of horn. He will march on, armed, blooded, bloodied, a rusty Chinese rifle at his back. Many have died and many more will die in their attempt to maim and capture him. He grows and grows, he multiplies. Terribly, he smiles. He is legion. He has not been told that he is living at the end of history. He does not care whether his mother lives or dies. He marches on. He is multitudes. (462)

As Drabble ensures, no one in Good Time wants custody of this threatening truth. Postmodern undecidability is by far a more comforting option, but she blocks the path. Brandishing her bibliography, she admonishes her readers with unwelcome references to real history. Like Fredric Jameson, Margaret Drabble makes a taste for postmodernism look like an evasion of responsibility.

7

Envisioning the Past

Many contemporary British romances of the archive are neither fantasies, nor detective stories, nor postmodern historiographic metafictions. This chapter considers a set of more conventionally realistic novels, linked by their shared interest in gender, sexuality, and identity. They consider these topics from a variety of angles. Alan Hollinghurst's first novel *The Swimming-Pool Library* (1988) features a gay researcher who discovers Edwardian adventures and betrayals through archival research. Adam Mars-Jones's *The Waters of Thirst* (1993) confronts the AIDS crisis through the parallel suffering of a terminal kidney patient, who happens to be gay. Robert Goddard's paperback historical-research thriller *Past Caring* (1986) links heterosexual men accused of sex crimes through a research quest into the times of Lloyd George and the Suffragettes. Stevie Davies's feminist archival quest *Impassioned Clay* (1999) brings to life the brutally silenced seventeenth-century female religious radicals when a lesbian historian delves into a personal and historical past. These novels all rely on traditional modes of characterization and plotting to tell realistic stories entailing episodes of archival research. The characters in these fictions exist in recognizable versions of contemporary Britain; their research quests draw them towards earlier periods of the British past where the people and problems they hope to understand dwell. The researchers themselves are fallible and limited, prone to errors of procedure and interpretation. Yet they successfully study historical documents, collections of photographs, and scientific reconstructions, discovering occluded truths and clarifying views of clouded pasts. Though supernatural agency, time travel, and the replete solutions of detective fiction are eschewed by these archival romances, evidence scrutinized in the proper frame of mind leads to the recovery of authentic voices. The romance in these realistic novels resides in the felt connections created and sustained by archival research, which brings into uncanny proximity the questers and the historical subjects they pursue.

Late in the history of the realistic novel, so late indeed that their stubborn employment of old-fashioned plot and character may itself appear a nostalgic symptom of a postmodern crisis in representation, realistic romances of the archive work to establish connections with people in the past for the sake of individuals in the present. The elucidation of human motivations, both in the past and in present-day plots, governs novels that cultivate the sympathetic imagination by showing characters at work to understand their beliefs, their sexuality, their mortality, and their positions in social worlds. If detective fiction employs the archival romance to make judgments, to praise and blame, the novels under scrutiny in this chapter more often labour to correct misjudgments by re-evaluating the past according to the revised standards of the present, especially with respect to gender roles and sexual orientation. Goddard's novel differs slightly, in that it offers a counterblast to present-day 'political correctness' by idealizing one of history's losers. Each of these novels could be criticized from a historian's perspective as indulging in presentism, since they do not hesitate to review the motivations and actions of historical subjects by standards of the present day, but they certainly cannot be held to account for failing to render verdicts. Michael Wood has observed of contemporary fiction a tendency to make understanding equivalent with forgiveness, to tolerate even as it judges: 'To understand everything *is* to forgive everything – or it would be if we understood everything, or anywhere near it. As it is, our impulse to forgiveness is just a name for our bafflement. We have lost our villains in the same way as we have lost our feeling for abnormality. There is a principle of tolerance here, of course, but there is also, more urgently, a sense of helplessness, as if we had mislaid the concept of justice somewhere and could not go back for it' (Wood 'Contemporary' 970). Romances of the archive in the social-problem mode attempt to defeat bafflement, identify villains, and restore responsibility for judging to fiction.

By accounting for the effects of historical events on ordinary people's lives, and making the past real again by emphasizing the feelings of historical subjects, romances of the archive put the sympathetic imagination to work. Thus, this subset of contemporary fiction can be observed carrying out one of the basic tasks of the traditional novel as conceived by George Eliot and Elizabeth Gaskell. That this moral training of the sympathetic imagination should be accomplished through exercises in historical research suggests both the personally renovating potential of intellectual encounters with the past and the continuing usefulness of realistic fiction in cultivating outrage for the purpose of making social and political changes. The tendency of these realistic romances of the archive to employ historical evidence as if it were accessible, yielding, and readily understood makes the connection of past to present easier to make and render transparently. The emphasis on achieving empathy with human subjects denies sharp differences of the past from the present, suggesting instead that present-day researchers with the right identities and emotional qualifications can better comprehend those who were misunderstood in the past than anyone who coexisted with them.

This is especially the case when the researcher shares with the historical subject some aspect of identity: in the novels of Hollinghurst and Mars-Jones, both questers and subjects are gay men; in Davies's *Impassioned Clay* a lesbian feminist recovers the voices of radical religious women bound to one another as 'yokefellows'; and (from a more central location in the political spectrum) Robert Goddard's *Past Caring* links in researcher and subject two misunderstood victims of accusations of sexual misconduct. In the face of contemporary doxa about the cultural construction of subjectivity, gender, sexuality, and even the body, romances of the archive profess faith in evidence that allows the quester to hear credible voices, touch tangible physical traces, and see photographic records of persons. The connections they make, though never actually breaching conventional time and space, verge on the weird. In an uncanny unhinging of agency, the researcher seems to be singled out by the quest, to be fated to be the one individual from the present who can reach into the dormant past to reanimate the interests of the silenced historical subject. Informed by liberal, feminist, and queer perspectives, these archival romances contain aged, unburied, and disease-threatened bodies. The overt eroticism of the questers imbues with desire their acts of envisioning and interpreting the extraordinarily yielding past, a feature that combines uneasily with these novels' testimony about corruptible bodies. Wanting to know – wanting for the right reasons, that is – virtually guarantees that the research quester will come away with the primary sources that put the flesh back on the silenced dead.

'HOW SEXY THE PAST MUST HAVE BEEN'

Few sorts of collections are traditionally preserved in such secrecy as private holdings of erotic or pornographic images, so it is perhaps inevitable that narratives of archival research would turn to the specialized, sometimes auto-erotic, scrutiny of photographs. While one ordinary reaction to images of people from the past is to feel impossibly distant from those 'fools in old-style hats and coats,' in Philip Larkin's words,[1] the photograph can also bridge the distance by making the object of its representation nearly present to the viewer. Romances of the archive incline to the latter attitude. As Roland Barthes attests, photography's artifice can make it seem truer to reality than reality itself; the photograph's inclusion of detail provoking attraction or distress (Barthes's 'punctum') permits the image to pierce, to prick, to touch the viewer in his or her real world.[2] Reaching into the image for evidence of a vanished person or way of life inspires close scrutiny of photographs in many research narratives, which are relatively rarely troubled with photography theory's nuanced disavowal of the photograph's evident realism.[3] The photograph in the archive vouches for the existence of the research subject in the past. Stephen Watt ruefully notes that 'in the wake of numerous interrogations of the cultural construction of such "realities" as subjectivity and gender, photography continues to be employed to corroborate and, at times, constitute versions of historical reality' ('Photographs' 58). Even when the image itself is clearly the product of staging or fictive crafting, or when the moment captured cannot sustain the weight of the truly representational that freights its interpretation, the photographic record of human bodies created by captured light possesses an unusual status in archival romances.

Perhaps it is, as Barthes intuits, that the very lifelikeness of the photographic image invokes the oppositional fact of death (*Camera* 32). In formal contrast, narrative fiction, as theorists of diverse perspectives have observed, bears a relationship to temporality; as Hayden White (glossing Riceour) puts it, '[T]he experiences of both "within-time-ness" and "historicality" can be dissolved in the apprehension of the relation of "eternity" to "death"' (*Content* 180). Thus, it is appropriate to find novels whose time-bound narrative structures intimate the inevitable conclusion of death while the backward-looking research narratives they contain dwell lovingly on photographic residues from the past. As Barthes would have it, these images simultaneously defy time's passing and remind the viewer that the body captured on film has irrevocably changed since the moment of the photograph's making. Bound into novelistic form through detailed descriptions, the discovered photographs activate the narrative devices of delay, commented on with elegance by Peter Brooks in *Reading for the Plot*, where delay is explained as the erotic resistance to narrative's mortal end point. Celebrating the sexiness of the past becomes part of the brave and futile work of Alan Hollinghurst's *The Swimming-Pool Library* and Adam Mars Jones's *The Waters of Thirst*. Representing research in textual, photographic, and film archives, Hollinghurst and Mars-Jones in different ways invoke a lost world – disappeared not so long ago – in these elegiac novels that insist on connections with a past before AIDS. In both novels, the archival research undertaken by the main character begins in the mode of voyeurism; the effect of their research is, at first, titillation. More unwelcome connections of past and present loom, as mortality converts the living and perceiving into the marked men of the death toll.

In *The Swimming-Pool Library*, Hollinghurst's Will Beckwith is proto-typically qualified to undertake a research project, having read history at Corpus Christi in Oxford (*Swimming* 37), but he couldn't be less interested in doing so. A chance encounter with an old man, Lord Nantwich (whose life he saves) and the discovery that they both frequent the same gay swimming club, the Corinthian, provide the personal connections that authorize a quest into a private past. The records of that past take the form of manuscript diaries, 'masses of papers' and images (81). Dedicated to time-consuming sexual adventuring, Beckwith resists the notion that he should write the memoirs of Lord Nantwich: 'It seemed at first a monstrous request, although I could see it was quite reasonable in a way. If he had had an interesting life, which it appeared he had, he could not possibly hope to write it up himself now. If I didn't do it, nothing might come of it. It was partly because I idly disliked any intrusion into my constant leisure – my leisure itself having taken on an urgent, all-consuming quality – that I instinctively repelled the idea' (81). When he relents, he at first finds the past in Nantwich's diaries full of trivia, unexciting, and parochial: 'It was the awful sense of another life having gone on and on, and the self-importance it courted by being written down and enduring years later, that made me think frigidly that I wasn't the man for it' (96–7). The research quest ultimately teaches Beckwith to be more interested in others' lives, not so contemptuous of the 'virtually useless annotation of ... life in a book for five years' (99).

Photographs, too, Beckwith learns to value for reasons beyond the aesthetic. At Nantwich's club he meets Staines, a photographer and collecter who advises Will never to destroy a photograph: '[I]t's a bit of life sealed in forever' (*Swimming* 43). At Staines's place, where Beckwith has gone to pose for a faux '*Edwardian* pic' (160), he encounters the alternative archive before the old photos are all sold off. The copious and inscrutable evidence of the scenes of Nantwich's earlier years strike Beckwith with the strange difference of the past:

Together we tugged out the wide shallow drawers in which hundreds and hundreds of photographs were laid up. Crazed, silky sheets of tissuepaper

interleaved the older prints and, pulled back, revealed anonymous society
faces of the Forties – I supposed – sulking, or smiling complacently ... It was
depressing to think of the scene of Charles' life crowded with such glossy
Mayfair figures, the women with their jutting busts and laquered lips, the
men with their conceited crinkly hair. (160)

Just as he is first put off by textual evidence of the past, and then intrigued,
Beckwith shortly revises his first judgment: 'I felt each picture encourage a
question, or hint at some urgent, tawdry secret' (160). More recent photographs may be part of conspiracies as well; Beckwith sees an envelope of
images of Colin, a character with whom he enjoys an erotic interlude, but
who claims to be a police officer when picked up by Beckwith's friend
James (222). Deceptive, dangerous, 'wildly naughty,' and apparently actually a policeman (235), Colin represents the shifty inaccessibility of the
man beyond the aesthetically pleasing fixed image.

   The researcher gets both a voyeuristic charge and a cross-generational
bond out of reading manuscript journals. The discovery that Nantwich's
life story contains fore-echoes of his own touches Beckwith, and he begins
to unthaw a bit with the old man (*Swimming* 129). This has a great deal to
do, at first, with the realization that the now decrepit old character Nantwich
was once an erotic adventurer and exotic voyeur in his own right, and that
he enjoyed access to those imperial playgrounds now closed to postimperial
Britons. The journals, as Christopher Lane observes, suggest that the
genealogy of racism includes a history of 'colonial desire,' enjoyed in the
golden days of Empire. Nantwich's experiences, according to Lane, show
that 'fantasies of national expansion and colonial splendour are inseparable
from homosexuality' (*Ruling Passion* 231). Hollinghurst presents this idea
critically, by demonstrating the pains of the inheritance of this fantasy by a
postimperial generation, and also by showing how cruelly the fantasy
contrasts with history. Although Nantwich appears to have received all the
benefits of his generation, Beckwith discovers that his own grandfather
(upon whom he depends for his luxurious apartment and indolent lifestyle) is an opportunistic gay-basher who persecuted and jailed Nantwich
in order to gain the peerage (*Swimming* 260, 264).

   The truth unleashed into the present by Beckwith's historical researches
not only destroys his self-satisfaction, but it mirrors in the present day the
police harassment of Beckwith's friend James, also a homosexual. The
news of an Edwardian sex scandal is not safely isolated in the past, for it
activates an unwelcome analogy with problems of the present day, and
clearly still concerns the living (the Edwardian period representing that

liminal area of the past which is still, just barely, within the reach of memory at the time of the novel). Postimperial London compares unfavourably with the Edwardian Empire that created it; Beckwith's black lover Arthur Hope belongs to a London of tower blocks – another world – where, when he ventures there, aristocratic Beckwith gets savagely beaten. Clearly the levels of risk vary according to class, race, and education, as well as the obviousness of one's sexual identity. In the face of these disparities, a sense of shared suffering links privileged gay men of separate generations. The reader is always uneasily aware that persecution ought to be the least of their worries, and that sympathetic connections are shortly to become lines of transmission.

Set in 1983, in the last days before knowledge of AIDS alters gay lifestyles in Britain, Hollinghurst's novel is permeated with ominous signs of the permanent changes to come. Revelling in the frank description of Beckwith's sexual adventures, the novel is an exercise in period nostalgia; it becomes perversely consoling to recall a (recent) time when the threats of hostile homophobes were among the worst life offered a gay man. As Michael Wood observes, the 'novel is a memorial to the randy, reckless world AIDS has depopulated' ('Contemporary' 984). Without mentioning the disease, it keeps the consequence of all those couplings ever before the reader. Beckwith catches whiffs of a trendy talcum powder called 'Trouble for Men,' which marks a random assortment of friends and strangers with a detectable emblem of the then undetectable virus. If the archival plot of *The Swimming-Pool Library* is in part about revealing the blindness of the researcher – he only discovers in Nantwich's diaries what all his friends and family already know about his grandfather – the account of the present is also marked with the signs of the scourge to come, seen, but not comprehended. The romance of the archive thus asserts that if we could go back in time, we might apprehend the evidence and notice the signs. Since we cannot, no exorcism, magic rite, or revelation can prevent the causes recognized in the past from erupting into the present and future with mortal consequences.

If the early years of the century are revealed by Beckwith's researches to have been no idyll for Lord Nantwich, Edwardian literature still represents a *locus amoenus*, a pleasant place of retreat, to Beckwith and his friend James. The patron saint of the novel's romance with the Edwardian is Ronald Firbank, modernist experimental author, aesthete, homosexual, and regular at the Café Royal, London's Bohemian headquarters. The link between the extreme ends of the twentieth century, Nantwich meets Firbank at the Savoy in his youth ('even then he belonged to another age' [*Swim-*

ming 167]). Nantwich possesses a fine first edition of Firbank's *The Flower beneath the Foot* (1923). In the last scene of the novel, Staines, the aptly named keeper of a film archive, shows Beckwith and his friend James a film that captures Firbank in his last days, in which he appears as 'a bona fide queen. He had on elegant unEnglish light suiting, with a bow tie and a broad-brimmed straw hat which gave him a sweetly arcadian character, at the same time as shadowing his face' (*Swimming* 285). This miraculous and unexpected photographic relic of Firbank is set against the vanished set of 'enigmatic beautiful nudes' of Colin, glimpsed earlier in the novel (162). While Firbank is found, the image of Colin disappears. Beckwith hopelessly rummages in the print drawer for the lost or removed images. The unexplained extraction of Colin's image from the collection serves as a grim hint of treachery and of the imperfect protection afforded by disguises. It also figures the brutal culling AIDS is about to visit upon the living. Firbank remains in the protective custody of the archive, but in the 'now' of the novel, living in a Firbankian style represents an aestheticized risk.

The times before and after AIDS establish the irreconcilable difference between characters' and readers' worlds in *The Swimming-Pool Library*, which guarantees an ironic reading experience. Adam Mars-Jones's *The Waters of Thirst* is firmly located in the time after the disease is known and more or less understood, but it too invokes a lost world – the past of sexual freedom. Terry and William become a couple just in time to find safety with one another, but William, the novel's narrator, suffers from congenital polycystic kidney disease. He undergoes dialysis and impatiently awaits a kidney transplant – the source of a great deal of the novel's unexpected humour, as William dwells on the reckless behaviour of motorcyclists, prime candidates to become kidney donors. *The Waters of Thirst* makes the point that gay men who don't die of AIDS die of something else, but William's disease, which leaves him with the same kind of pneumonia that HIV-infected people sometimes suffer, gives Mars-Jones a way of writing about AIDS without writing about it directly (in his earlier stories Mars-Jones made a mark as one of the first artists of the AIDS epidemic). The past of the novel's archive – a collection of pornographic magazines featuring an American film star named Peter Hunter – reaches back only so far as the dangerous early days of the epidemic, so that AIDS becomes the beginning and end of the narrative timeline in both story-time and in the reconstructed time of William's researches. If the auto-erotic 'one-handed research' conducted with magazines represents the safest sex in dangerous times, the images over which William pores are not immune to the disease.

Even the alternative fantasy world of the pornographic scenario is touched by the consequences of AIDS, as William's close scrutiny discovers.

The collection that forms the 'Peter Hunter archive' (*Waters* 48) must be assembled with ingenuity, for customs officials search the mail for offending materials. A friend in Scotland, 'the soft permissive North' (16), has better luck gathering pornography through the mail, and offers to send on any magazines featuring Peter Hunter. Thus, William follows Peter Hunter's career from his debut as a teen ingenue. Later the star owns his own concern, The Pure Net (an anagram of Pete Hunter), which means that he achieves the artistic control over images, rare for porn actors (108). William learns from an interview that Peter Hunter has taken to delivering a 'hot safe sex rap' in his live shows, which 'sows a seed of fear' about the star's health (108). The disappearance of Peter Hunter's buttocks inspires William to attempt a 'rudimentary sort of statistical analysis' to verify the trend 'away from full nakedness' (110–11). He sets to work, 'dating and cross-referencing' on index cards (111), plotting the appearance of body parts on sketches of a human form (115). At last William has hard evidence: Peter Hunter's body is going into retirement 'piecemeal as he came to fall short of his own standards of excellence' (115–16). Over time, less and less of Peter Hunter's beautiful body shows in these images; part by part, he succumbs to the disease that cruelly renders him unphotogenic. The simultaneous appearance of a sequence of posed pin-ups featuring the artist seem to be devised to falsify through magazines, as if a publication or consumers' beliefs could 'give Peter Hunter a clean bill of health' (117).

William discovers that these pin-up photographs appear to have been taken on a single day to simulate years' worth of shoots: 'I could assemble the marathon photo-session in strict sequence, though the photographs were scattered at meticulous random through a run of magazine issues' (*Waters* 118–19). The distressing conclusion is unwelcome: Peter Hunter is being 'held hostage ... by a terrorist that his bloodstream could only carry round and round his system' (120). The discovery drives William away from his fantastic refuge as the curator of Hunteriana (121), for his object of desire is as tainted with mortality as his own imperfect body. After a last-ditch kidney transplant, William's weakened immune system lands him in an AIDS ward with a case of non-HIV-related pneumonia. Locked into the decline towards death, William with his kidney disease and the AIDS sufferers no longer differ. Bound with coverings like grave-cloths, the inexhaustible Peter Hunter becomes an emblem of death, as the phantasmal conclusion to the novel suggests. William finds himself in bed with his dying idol: 'My head was buzzing with heat and thinking. Just as if I was looking at a Peter Hunter magazine and trying to deduce its hidden meanings, I started to wonder if this was another sly game' (174). The effort to find understanding of illness and mortality through close scrutiny of images is a dodgy business until hallucination does its verifying work to bring William and Peter together in death (181–2). The novel rapidly traverses the distance between voyeuristic sexual fantasy and mortality by means of research into a past that isn't really the past, but a parallel track of the present. The photographic image allows separate lives to merge in the visionary imagination of the beholder, erasing the distinctions between self and other and past and present. The conventional though often-contested equation of realism and photography thus becomes more complicated when the images appear within a romance of the archive, where descriptions of images can be layered genealogically and interrogated with a more than scholarly intensity.

'THE DEAD DO NOT DISSEMBLE'

As the recent television film *Shooting the Past* (1999) suggests, the photographic archive can capture the traces of life stories, or contain those traces until a gifted seeker and interpreter unlocks them by looking carefully. In that film an American businessman intends to close down a comprehensive library of photography that occupies the country house he has just purchased for conversion into a business school for the twenty-first century. Unsentimental and resolutely future-oriented, he threatens with obliteration an incomparable set of records about the past. The preternaturally knowledgeable archivist of the jeopardized collection startles him into sparing it by unearthing the photographic traces of the sensational life story of the American's grandmother. Luckily, she liked being photographed. The archive even contains a picture of the American as an infant perched on his grandmother's knee. Ocular proof of a connection to recorded and collected history on film persuades the American to preserve an extraordinary resource, a key to his own (and by implication) everyone else's past.

Shooting the Past represents in its plenitude one extreme limit case of the romance of the photographic archive; at the other extreme one finds those research narratives that reveal one single surviving image that verifies a narrative otherwise consisting of textual elements. Byatt's *Possession* and Robert Goddard's *Caught in the Light* (1998) both employ the rare, miraculously surviving image as final proof, invoking still unbroken connections with remote times by means of mute photographic testimony.

Raphael Samuel comments with sympathy in *Theatres of Memory* on the 'hallucinatory sense of oneness with the past which old photographs seem so often to induce (*Theatres* 374).[4] Romances of the archive in the realistic mode depend on that illusion when they describe the discovery of photographs.

To begin a quest with a photograph embodying mysteries of identity and occluded histories often correlates with assertions that felt connections with the past are more real than relationships in the present day. Robert Goddard exploits this idea in his first novel, *Past Caring*. The favourite living author of former prime minister John Major, Goddard has since 1986 turned out historical thrillers (the early ones issued in paperback) that typically feature imperfect but likable, mild-mannered protagonists who foil better-funded and less-scrupulous conspirators by being too stubborn to drop the mystery and too decent to be corrupted, or at least for long enough. As Nigel Jones points out, 'Goddard's men are the blinking, bespectacled Little Englander heroes for a post-imperial, post-macho, post-just-about-everything age, just as Major is the post-Thatcher prime minister ('Oh Yes' T10). These qualities make for protagonists with whom it is easy to sympathize, even when their own misdeeds are revealed.

Goddard suggests that the very traits making a character vulnerable to the machinations of manipulators with concealed motives also make him likely to succeed in his historical quest. With the right combination of alienation, curiosity, impolitic bloody-mindedness, and hidden wells of compassion, the Goddard protagonist (usually a middle-aged man with a chequered past) sticks to his task and uncovers evidence unknown even to the puppet-masters. *Past Caring* initiates this formula and in the process makes a liberal defence of decent Englishness in the face of postcolonial critics and those rapacious British profiteers who discredit the whole nation in their pursuit of money and power. The manipulation and betrayal of the gullible drive Goddard's convoluted plots, which seem to show that the ordinary guy, like unemployed, divorced, disgraced history grad Martin Radford of *Past Caring*, will always end up being victimized, especially when buried secrets are brought to the surface by their investigations. And so it transpires. His curiosity piqued by a photograph and a manuscript diary, Radford embarks as a paid researcher on a quest for facts that introduces him to three remarkable characters: an eighty-seven–year-old ex-suffragette, Elizabeth Latimer; the deceased memoirist Edwin Strafford, who loved and lost the suffragette, in the process ruining his political career; and Ambrose, Strafford's cider-soaked and aged nephew.

Radford's love for these individuals differentiates him from those villainous characters who would manipulate the past for gain, especially the acknowledged and unacknowledged descendents of the central villain Gerald Couchman, a bigamist. Radford's sympathetic quest leads to fuller knowledge of their concealed history than has ever been revealed, as three key documents come to light from their dispersed archival hiding-places. It also results in Radford serving a jail term for manslaughter when he kills the employer – Leo Sellick – who sets him on the quest. The researcher does not appear to profit, but in the end, the virtuous cultivation of empathy for the dead and the willingness to jettison any present-day advantage for knowing the truth about the past results in fabulous rewards. Radford inherits Strafford's Madeira estate. Elizabeth Couchman's fortune also comes to Radford, so he can live out his days comfortably contemplating the suffering of Strafford, the best friend he has never met. In a novel full of references to the poetry of Thomas Hardy, guilt, regret, and a consciousness of life's little ironies haunt the researcher. Radford writes to Strafford, long dead, '[I]f you had told me, my elusive quarry, what to expect from a quest after your past, I would never have embarked upon it. Your shade, which I tracked and moved in, envelops me now in this place of your displaced being' (*Past Caring* 5). Because of the historical quester's efforts, errors and misrepresentations of the past have at least been brought to the public by the press, though it takes a murder trial to get the wider world to share an interest in this particular history.

In *Past Caring* Goddard stages a debate about the uses and misuses of the past, the sentimental qualifications of the researcher, and the appropriate rewards for truth-finding. To do so the novel relates an imaginary revisionist history of an episode in early-twentieth-century British politics. Martin Radford's research reopens an Edwardian scandal, in which Lloyd George cuts a secret deal with Christabel Pankhurst, removing an obstacle to his political plans by ruining the proposed marriage of his Home Secretary (Edwin Strafford) to the young suffragette Elizabeth Latimer. In the fiction, George agrees to make votes for women a priority if Pankhurst helps him remove Strafford, who has already indicated his unwillingness to join Lloyd's planned coalition. In the short term Pankhurst keeps an able lieutenant for her movement by breaking up Latimer's planned marriage to Strafford; in the longer term Pankhurst thinks she wins extension of the franchise (*Past Caring* 218). This counterfactual scenario is typical of Goddard's cavalier use of history, which he studied at Cambridge. According to the author, he was not encouraged there by his tutors, who did not appreciate Goddard's 'habit for indulging in more liberal degrees of speculation than were regarded as academically acceptable,' as he explained in an interview with Tim Rostron ('Clever Plot' 21). Yet if his imaginary history does not always stand up to logical analysis,[5] he has clearly absorbed an academic's respect for documentary evidence and for the advantages of the historian's more objective assessment of the past. While living people always have ulterior motives, 'the dead do not dissemble' (*Past Caring* 71). (The traces the dead leave may of course be unreliable, but at least they are not around to interfere personally with the historian.)[6]

Goddard conveys with enthusiasm the voyeuristic pleasures of reading personal papers, the thrill of the scholarly chase, and the righteous satisfactions of revisionist history. These verifying experiences are set against a formidable array of antagonists, motivated by baser impulses: the heritage industry's desire for a tidied-up and marketable past; a distinguished family's efforts to control public opinion of their members and their business enterprises; the conspirators' urgent need to cover their tracks; and the academics' intellectual opportunism. The narrator and intellectual quester Martin Radford must earn his distance from these craven manipulators of the past. As we learn, he is covering up an unseemly affair with a student, the real reason for his abrupt departure from teaching. He comments, 'Historian though I was, I didn't mind laundering the past when it suited my purpose' (*Past Caring* 14). His feeling of being led 'towards something new or mysterious' initiates the renovation of his character through the research quest (24). Identifying with the suffering of the chronically mystified Edwin Strafford sets Radford on the road to self-improvement. Radford becomes less whiny, emulating Strafford's out-of-fashion stiff upper lip. He becomes more direct and confrontational with his ex-wife and her bossy relatives, empowered by his knowledge of their family. He makes friends of Strafford's remaining connections, Ambrose and Elizabeth. All of these changes contribute to his success in research. For if Goddard's fictional world is one in which truth has a tough time surviving contemporary and historical spin control, it nonetheless suggests that some evidence survives to controvert the assertions of the influential manipulators.

When wealthy avengers have academic historians in their pockets, truth's vicissitudes worsen. Goddard embodies this idea in Eve Randall, an academic who willingly participates in laundering the past to justify her salary and to transform her academic study of suffragism into a schlocky bestseller. Eve represents a stock character in Goddard's *oeuvre*, the seductive, devouring, all-too-intelligent, and fundamentally amoral female. An ambitious professional historian, Eve Randall on the one hand appears to possess genuine expertise, as her colleagues grudgingly acknowledge. She is a successful lecturer at Cambridge and a true archive hound who knows her way around the personal papers of the Pankhurst circle, as Radford acknowledges. On the other hand, Martin Radford attributes her popularity as a performer to her good looks, not to the quality of her lectures (which he finds rather fluffy). Most damningly, Eve Randall's possession of the Couchman chair depends on her willingness to accept the sexual advances of the predatory Timothy Couchman, whose family pays her salary.

Intellectually, Randall blows with the slightest breeze, revising her central thesis about the political savvy and efficacy of the suffragettes to suit the latest revelations about Elizabeth Latimer, Edwin Strafford, Gerald Couchman, Lloyd George, and Christabel Pankhurst. If they can be used to pad her monograph and make it over into a trade book, historical discoveries have their uses. Ordinarily, academic historians are caricatured as hopelessly overspecialized and oblivious to market considerations, but in Goddard's version, the feminist historian will sell out any aspect of her subject for the sake of making sales. One of the least realistic assertions of *Past Caring* is that authorship of a popular historical best-seller will enhance a historian's academic career; in this fantasy plot line, Eve Randall rides her sensational story all the way to Harvard. (The reformed and chastened character of the novel's end has finally earned her degree and completed a more sober treatment of suffragism.) Goddard also suggests that Eve seduces and then humiliates Radford to exact a feminist revenge for Radford's indifference to the fate of the teenager with whom he has an affair. What is Radford to do, periodically check in on his victim? Even in 1986 they called that stalking, as a more persuasive feminist character would be sure to know. Eve Randall's function is not to represent a three-dimensional feminist character, for the aged former suffragette, Elizabeth Latimer, occupies that role. Goddard employs Eve to jerk Radford around and elicit readerly sympathy for the hapless guy.

This sympathy carries the reader through the climactic episode, in which Radford becomes a killer. When Martin Radford thwarts Sellick's intentions by shooting him dead, he protects Strafford's Elizabeth and beats the revenger Sellick by exacting revenge for the earlier murder of Strafford. His bond with this man he has never met arises from his close reading of Strafford's memoir, including the Postscript that Radford discovers with the help of Strafford's nephew Ambrose. Both documents are presented in full, so that readers can share Radford's interest in solving the mysteries of Strafford's broken engagement, ruined career, and hounding by Sellick. Discovered by Radford inside a toy castle stored in the cluttered loft of the family home, which now belongs to the National Trust, the Postscript contains the proof of Gerald Couchman's deceits and crimes. In his final archival triumph in a novel full of documentary discoveries, Radford locates and reads the final instalment of the journal in the very attic where Strafford penned its last words.

This incendiary document inspires a great deal more action than most historical discoveries; members of the Couchman family do not hesitate at breaking and entering, ransacking, and issuing threats to gain control of the journal. In it, Strafford has transcribed his damning conversations with Gerald Couchman, who confesses the whole conspiracy. Couchman's defence of his crimes and his opportunism blends postimperial rage, class hostility, and an insouciant confidence that history can and ought to be controlled:

> 'The British have become hostages to history, triumphant in a war, but still queuing for meat rations while every black face round the world condemns us as imperialist ogres ... I have to kow-tow to a load of cloth-capped union leaders who call themselves a government ... You don't like the past? Then fiddle the books. Re-write your image until it fits the bill. You'd be surprised at how easy it is, as long as it's just paper and fallible memory.' (Past Caring 342, italics in original)

The character holding this assortment of views is discredited not for his implicit nostalgia for an imperialist, paternalistic, aristocratic past, but for his hypocrisy. What Couchman really yearns for is a permanent freedom from responsibility for his actions. He wants profit, pleasure, and public honours with no strings attached. His unacknowledged son Sellick makes Couchman's crimes representative of the English officer class, assuming that 'they could go and do exactly as they pleased, without let, hindrance or any obligation to those whose lives they disrupted' (430). This attitude on the part of a character might suggest Goddard's postimperial apologetics, except that he employs Couchman to isolate and contain British responsibility for imperial misdeeds. When Sellick condemns the 'peculiarly Anglo-Saxon vanity that the Empire was your playground,' Goddard has already emphasized Strafford's contrasting decency and responsibility. He suggests that colonial subjects are likely to remember the careless Couchman – 'they paid for his dalliance with their lives' (431) – not the moderate, conscientious Strafford.

Sellick's immoderate rage does nothing to win sympathy for the victims of British imperialism. Like the crabby women of the novel, postcolonial subjects fail to realize how good they have it. Sympathy with an aging suffragette does not translate into understanding of present-day feminists; indeed, Radford's experience of being vilified for inappropriate sexual relations with a minor only makes him empathize with the falsely accused Strafford, whose career is ruined by a sex crime he does not commit. Radford's sacrifice not only earns him the fabulous reward of the Madeira estate and an independent living, but it defeats the version of the past promulgated by those with axes to grind, the self-interested manipulators of the record. Goddard practically congratulates Martin Radford for killing Sellick. Postcolonial subjects' complaints about the behaviour of imperialist Englishmen are silenced in *Past Caring* by the perfect gentleman, who slays the cad for insulting a lady.

SILENCED WOMEN

By the end of the century and the millennium, the formula of the archival romance has brought success to popular writers such as Robert Goddard, Alan Wall, Robert Harris, Lawrence Norfolk, and Charles Palliser. It has proved in the hands of writers with more literary ambitions (A.S. Byatt, Peter Ackroyd, and Julian Barnes) to be a vehicle for creating some of their biggest sellers and crossover books that reach the larger popular market. Readers attuned to the larger field of contemporary British fiction will have noticed, however, the relative paucity of romances of the archive authored by women writers. Though A.S. Byatt's *Possession* (1989) is the best-known romance of the archive, and P.D. James's *Original Sin* (1994) would certainly rank among the best-selling, few British women writers contribute to the burgeoning production of archival romances. As I have earlier observed, Anita Brookner's novels sometimes feature female academics bearing the title of 'researcher,' but her fictions do not depict the activity of research in the way that Penelope Lively's do (in *According to Mark* [1984] and *The Road to Lichfield* [1977]). Margaret Drabble, in *The Gates of Ivory* (1991) and *The Witch of Exmoor* (1996), joins her sister Antonia Byatt as one of the few established women writers to employ the romance of the archive. Beyond these names there are very few.

Since contemporary British women writers have earned distinction for their detective fiction, their historical novels, and their time-shift fantasies for children, a lack of interest in the main ingredients of the romance of the archive cannot explain the gender imbalance. Broadening the scope beyond British novelists allows the critic to notice Canadian novelist Carol Shields's *Swann* (1987), American Martha Cooley's *The Archivist* (1998) and Katherine Neville's *The Eight* (1988), and several novels by postcolonial women writers, including Bharati Mukherjee's *The Holder of the World* (1993) and Keri Hulme's *the bone people* (1983). (The latter two novels receive my attention in the epilogue to this study, 'Postcolonial Rejoinders.') The fact remains, however, that male writers are responsible for by far the majority of recent British adventurous fictions of archival quests. Perhaps the burden of differentiating one's fictive scenario from A.S. Byatt's discourages women writers, for a strong and successful example in a genre can dampen imitation in the short run.

To extend the observation to the researcher-characters within romances of the archive reveals a similar discrepancy. Byatt's main character is a man, Roland Michell, though he cannot accomplish his quest without teaming up with the feminist critic Maud Bailey. Because writers of archival romances often include female researchers as sidekicks or antagonists, the numbers increase. Nonetheless, Byatt's Maud Bailey, Drabble's Liz Headland, Penelope Lively's Anne Linton, Tom Stoppard's Hannah Jarvis (a character in *Arcadia* [1993]), Nigel Williams's palaeographer Anna, Robert Harris's American journalist Charlotte Maguire, Peter Dickinson's exceptional protagonist Rachel Matson, and Robert Goddard's Eve Randall are still in the minority if all the archival questers of contemporary British fiction are enumerated.

During the course of writing this study, I often wondered why so few British women writers have adopted the increasingly popular formula of the archival romance. I was less perplexed by the dominance of male characters among the fictional researchers; writers seeking a broad audience and a sale of film rights take a risk when they employ female protagonists, as literary agents for mass-market fiction will confirm. Miss Smilla notwithstanding, female characters are perceived by agents and publishers as limiting the potential market for a popular novel. While female readers will happily cross the gender/genre lines to purchase and read thrillers, spy and detective novels, horror stories, and other traditionally 'male' subgenres of romance, very few male readers reciprocate outside the small market for serious literary fiction. Surely, I thought, many more women have the first-hand experience in the archives that sometimes inspires the composition of an archival romance or the characterization of a female researcher. As two male academics in Stevie Davies's novel *Four Dreamers and Emily* (1996) agree, times have changed:

'Ten years ago – or fifteen,' sighed Neil, 'women like Laurie Morgan had not been invented.'

'Forty years ago,' observed Stan, 'there were hardly any women about. Just one or two earnest bibliographers. And then of course if they married another member of staff that was it – career over – they got the boot.'

'A hundred years ago,' said Neil, 'they couldn't even be students. Of course,' he added, 'that was a damned unfair state of affairs.'

'I sometimes feel,' said Stan, tamping down the tobacco in his pipe with his forefinger, 'that the pendulum has swung a smidgeon too far the other way.' (*Four Dreamers* 171)

Romances of the archive by men and women record the presence of women in academia, though feminist scholars are not always presented in a flattering light. Robert Goddard's Eve Randall can serve as Exhibit A: a competent researcher who knows her way around the archives, but whose interpretations and conclusions are swayed by political and material considerations. She is also a classic variant of the *femme fatale*, only a few generations from Rider Haggard's Ayesha in *She* (1887). Though she is written as a chilly mortal in order to depict her thawing out, Byatt's Maud Bailey is not far removed from this formulaic creature – intellectual, beautiful, and terrifying. As Fergus Wolff allusively observes of Maud, 'She thicks men's blood with cold' (*Possession* 34). Though the eclipsing of the stereotyped mousy librarians in bad shoes by these glamorous and threatening feminists suggests at least in negative terms the increasing influence of women in research, I still wondered where Maud Bailey's female colleagues could be. Representational romances of the archive seemed to have skipped them.

Stevie Davies's *Impassioned Clay* (1999) goes a long way towards filling the gap. Davies is a feminist literary critic, historian, and novelist who left an academic post at Manchester University to pursue a full-time writing career. (She is an elected Fellow of the Royal Society of Literature and honorary Senior Research Fellow at Roehampton Institute in London.) The author of seven novels and thirteen books of criticism and history, Davies has direct experience with researching the past, training that infuses her most recent novel. In *Impassioned Clay*, which Davies describes as 'deeply autobiographical' (Nicolette Jones 'No Bridles' 11), she creates a feminist historian (Olivia) who from adolescence is haunted by unanswered questions about a skeleton unearthed in the back garden of the family home: '*Our spades rang off stones and broke the fibrous mat of roots that webbed the Cheshire clay. We shovelled earth from above her face, then feathered soil from a still hand which lay open to us ... With the nest of bones – some shattered, others entire – we salvaged the gravegoods of her Calvary: an iron crown'* (*Impassioned* 3, italics in original). The woman's remains reveal that she has been hanged and then buried wearing a 'brank,' also known as a scold's bridle.

The brank is a heavy metal helmet in the shape of a cage, designed to be locked shut on the head of a woman, forcing a long metal bit into the mouth. This device would not only prevent speech by smashing the tongue, but could shatter the teeth and break the jaw of the woman confined to it. It was a cruel and lasting punishment designed to mark the body permanently. The first-person narrator Olivia reflects that 'the space where her mouth had been did not ... grin as skulls were fabled to do. Only the poor smashed teeth and skewed jaw reminded me of the human agonies these bones had outlasted.' Haunted by an impression of the 'slack jaw's soundless cry,' Olivia must recover the identity and voice of the character so cruelly tortured (*Impassioned* 11).

The research narrative within *Impassioned Clay* tells the story of Olivia's intellectual quest. She discovers Hannah Emanuel, the seventeenth-century character who endures the brank for her unruly speeches and her persistent religious testimony. The texts reveal that she can no longer eat solid food after her release from jail, but only execution silences her effectively. The romance of the archive celebrates the survival of Hannah's words and the testimony of her contemporaries, including her 'yoke-fellow' and mate Isabel Clarke. In the long run, the voices released from old documents by Olivia thwart the punitive repression of the seventeenth-century authorities. Davies's scholarly work and the quest of her fictive Olivia work against history's 'mass silence,' reminding readers of 'a nearly forgotten generation of exceptions who dared to speak out in conditions of female repression, telling God-given and anomalous truths' (*Unbridled* 2). Scanty evidence, mistrusted sources, motivated excision of the record, and a more general neglect by authorities conspire to ensure that we in the present inherit a falsified version of the past, according to Davies's protagonist: 'History, gagged and branked, struggles in the silences that are left when dissident voices have been discredited. How do you know which silences are the pregnant ones? All that tearing up, shredding and burning of paper ... the ensuing silences brim with sadness for me; so too these muffled voices that survived the purge' (*Impassioned* 141). The scholar uneasily faces the challenge of reading the absences and filling the gaps.

The recovery work of Davies and a generation of feminist scholars has already had a practical effect, resuscitating the writings of women from periods that were once imagined to possess no female voices.[7] Having researched the period for her scholarly study *Unbridled Spirits: Women of the English Revolution, 1640–1660* (1998), a book that announces an intention to 'haunt' readers, Davies turns to fiction to exorcise the conjured characters, gestures, actions, voices, and strange stories of seventeenth-century religious radicalism. Davies writes, 'The record is fragmentary, cryptic, unsatisfying. Sources may be mendacious or bias-riven. But a well-woven fragment may [be] ... so vivid that a living eye glistens through the rubble of time and stares straight into ours; a face turns sharply out of shadow' (*Unbridled* 9). *Impassioned Clay* re-enacts the scholarly process in order to share it with ordinary readers, to give voice to characters otherwise confined to an academic book, and to finish the quest by means other than publication. Davies told Nicolette Jones that 'what I did in the novel is study my problem in laying the ghosts, confining them to the past' ('No Bridles' 11). Thus, Olivia ultimately restores the bones of Hannah to her grave, after discovering her full story, which Olivia's dead mother, a pious Quaker, posthumously initiates and completes.

Throughout the novel Davies emphasizes the continuities of the maternal line; despite their generational clashes, mothers, daughters, aunts, nieces, grandmothers, and great-great-granddaughters play vital roles in the preservation and recovery of female voices. The unidentified bones are discovered while digging a grave for Olivia's mother on the family property, and they are laid to rest again after Olivia's research gives a name, a face, and a voice to Hannah. When still alive, Olivia's mother admonishes her daughter, 'Be silent. Listen to the truth that is in you' (*Impassioned* 5). The novel concludes with a moment of silence held by Olivia and her beloved colleague Faith over the reinterred bones. Arriving at this peaceful reconciliation of past and present requires not only extensive research, but self-discovery. The research quest itself works towards Olivia's maturation, when she can live comfortably with her lesbianism and her loss of Faith, enjoying the rootedness proven by her genetic tie to Hannah Emanuel, who is buried with Olivia's mother in the back garden.

Like Maud Bailey's direct line of descent from the Victorian poets Randolph Henry Ash and Christabel LaMotte in *Possession*, Olivia's connection with the woman in the brank is familial, though it begins as an intellectual and emotional bond: '*Heart spasming, I reached down into the bed of clay to cover what was left of her hand with my right, my writing, hand; and she gripped me*' (*Impassioned* 3, italics in original). In the seventeenth century, while very much alive though imprisoned, Hannah

Emanuel makes a writer of her labouring-class yokefellow Isabel by teaching her to read and write; long dead, she makes a historian of her descendent Olivia. Matrilineal property rights underwrite the genetic connection and the vocational ties: Olivia's mother's people 'have agelessly inhabited this straggling homestead' Pinfold, where Hannah is discovered and where Olivia grows up (*Impassioned* 4). Olivia gets her father to turn the homestead over to her, as her rightful maternal inheritance (37); thus, she lays claim not only to her property, but to her history, for Hannah Emanuel's Isabel works on Pinfold Farm, meets Hannah there, lies with her under the attic beams, and buries her in a dell nearby so she can always visit the grave of her helpmeet. Finally, Hannah's child Grace marries into the family that lives at Pinfold and her offspring continue on that same plot. 'The truth that is in you' turns out to be an audible message about rooted identity and connection to a long line of women, not all of them conventional wives and mothers.

Olivia suffers in adolescence from a lack of mother love and in adulthood from loneliness. A combination of grief and bookishness drives her towards the compensatory research quest that results in the discovery of her descent from radical religious leaders (*Impassioned* 13). The heritage elements of her (abandoned) Quaker faith and her family's long residence in one spot are augmented by the garnering of academic credentials – Olivia prepares herself by reading history at New College, Oxford. Like Martin Radford in Robert Goddard's *Past Caring*, the quester's research develops from a passion that goes beyond the usual inspirations for academic projects: 'I started secret burrowings for the writings of women in the seventeenth century, which allured me with the kind of thrill most people of twenty keep for sexual discovery ... This was neither curiosity nor conscientious dedication to study: it was the ferocity of passion, secret and intimate' (*Impassioned* 34). Passion seems to guarantee results that may elude less-motivated questers – Olivia runs across Hannah Emanuel almost immediately, though she fails to recognize her (34). Later Olivia gets a second chance, finding 'Hannah Jones, *blasphemously calling herself Emanuel*,' a 'known heretic and scold,' accused of witchcraft and blasphemy, disowned by the Quakers, and sentenced to be 'branked and hanged' (67, emphasis in original). Vital information survives in surprising places; much of what Olivia discovers appears in the pages of a diary written by one of Hannah's enemies, the cleric Lyngard. Hannah's chestnut hair and green eyes, her heretical speech, her relationship with Isabel Clarke, and her bastard child are all recorded by Lyngard, who evinces an obsessive interest in the woman he torments. Passion guarantees the creation of the record, and passion authorizes its recipient, centuries later, to take custody of the documents. Olivia finds Isabel Clarke's testament glued into a makeshift envelope in the last pages of Lyngard's diary: 'In that moment of discovery, it seems impossible that the sealed envelope was not meant for me. Between those glued leaves, someone has deposited a letter, to be opened by the person most interested in those connected with the story. Who could be more passionately interested than myself?' (93). Like A.S. Byatt's researcher Roland Michell, who removes an autograph manuscript from the London Library, Olivia justifies her violation of scholarly codes of conduct: 'I did not think of my act as theft. The message simply belonged to me. I accepted receipt' (94). Olivia's later outrage at her mother's censorship and destruction of Hannah Emanuel's *Wilderness of Women* is not tempered by the reflection that she, too, has obstructed some later searcher's quest, especially so as she has resolved never to publish her absconded findings (159).

Though Olivia is an academic historian, her research quest represents a divagation from the professional path towards success and recognition. More personal impulses drive Olivia into the past, away from present dilemmas. She has not at the outset of the narrative accepted her lesbianism (*Impassioned* 58). The novel relates her friendship with and unrequited romantic love for Faith, a colleague, who later marries another colleague. Fear of rejection in the present is diverted into energy for Olivia's passionate quest: 'How safe such time-travelling passion seemed, beside the insecure bondings of the present tense. Should I find vestiges of this woman, she could not refuse my reading of her. Deep in the shadow world, she was subject to my light or none at all. Silent until I voiced her, she would be impotent to reject me' (67). Faith offers friendship, and flirts with more, but chooses a conventional heterosexual marriage, which breaks Olivia's heart. This plot line is echoed by parallels in the unfolding seventeenth-century story, for in order for Olivia to be her descendent, Hannah must bear a child. Her idealized bond with her sister-radical and yoke-fellow Isabel is temporarily disrupted when she becomes pregnant with a child evidently fathered by the charismatic James Nayler, a historical figure like many of Davies's characters. Having made their peace as a couple, the two women raise Grace as their shared offspring as long as they can. When she reaches adulthood, Grace proves more conventional than her mothers; she rejoins the local Quakers and marries into the family living at Pinfold Farm. Thus, Olivia's female line gravitates to a centre marked by a breast-shaped burial mound (*Impassioned* 5).

If the romanticized thematics of possession authorized by heritage, family ties, and passion guide Olivia through the thicket of documents with remarkable ease, she does encounter some realistic obstacles along the way. The Assize records for the year of Hannah's trial have been destroyed by an eighteenth-century fire, and the clerk of the Hesketh Friends Meeting does not reveal what he knows of Hannah Emanuel, though he refers to her as an unstable, delusional, perhaps schizophrenic woman who ran amok (*Impassioned* 70–1). Davies implies that sectarian interests can survive the centuries; contemporary Friends might not prefer to dwell on the history of the early days, embarrassed or shamed by compromises and the shift into quietism.

In Olivia's feminist interpretation, the ardent spirits of the women of the first generation of Friends are deliberately subdued by channelling Quaker women into good works and by discouraging public preaching. A fictional creation of Davies, Hannah Emanuel embodies many of the disruptive traits of the early generation of radical religious women. She cross-dresses in boy's clothing, thinks nothing of stripping to the waist while testifying in public, refers to the Spirit as 'She,' insists on her priority to the founders of the Religious Society of Friends (including the visionary George Fox), chooses a same-sex union, and bears a child out of wedlock. Convicted, transported, and returned from Turkey (where she gets a first-hand glimpse of the infidel, finding them less savage than the authorities at home), and finally hanged for repeated offences, Hannah is an embarrassment to the Quakers who disown her and (simultaneously) a danger to the vulnerable and awkward Olivia. Olivia's mother knows all about Hannah Emanuel (having discovered her in a genealogical quest), but she suppresses the evidence to protect her daughter, lest Olivia succumb to 'the glamour of distance' that might inspire twentieth-century imitation of seventeenth-century unruliness (*Impassioned* 156). The Quaker clerk John Hale keeps a pact made with Olivia's mother to withhold information from her impressionable daughter; he repents after seeing the wax model of Hannah in her brank displayed in the museum. He breaks silence and symbolically removes the brank from Hannah's historical voice, so that communication may be resumed. The goal of hearing these voices is met when Hannah and Isabel find an empathetic 'listener,' who can imagine their pain and their privation. Harshly judging those who repressed, tortured, and executed Hannah Emanuel becomes part of a rewritten past, in which female religious radicals not only existed, but also sacrificed everything for their convictions.

Thus, empathy leads the way towards pride in ancestors strikingly different from the conventional representations of seventeenth-century people. *Impassioned Clay* does more than demand sympathy for the suffering of long-dead religious radicals, renegade Quakers, and their detractors within and without the Society of Friends. It describes a feminist historian's quest to unearth the facts about obscure figures, to understand their motivations and relationships, and to hear their voices speaking through the centuries – for the benefit of those living today. Here Davies works in her most autobiographical vein, as comparison with her historical work *Unbridled Spirits* shows; the historian Davies insists that 'if there is a sense that we are all informed by the whole of the past (even those parts which seemed to flake away into oblivion), then these women ... being our past, are also part of us' (*Unbridled* 6). Attending to militant foremothers not only makes amends to them for their suffering and for historical amnesia, but also points up the areas where modern women fall short, failing to achieve or to avail themselves of 'an equal interest with the men of this nation,' in the words of Leveller women (8). The feminist recovery of activist female ancestors serves present-day aims, which are in turn dignified by the clear link to the historical record of resistance to oppression.

Though *Impassioned Clay* presents its feminist politics overtly, it also demonstrates the force of the maxim that the personal is political. Olivia is motivated not by abstract principles, but by the grip of the past upon her. She queries her tutor: 'Don't you hear them? ... The dead. Speaking. From the pages of books' (*Impassioned* 35); hovering between delusion and heightened imagination, she attests that the voices often have northern accents. Olivia deliberately cultivates historical interests with a local provenance, so that she can look at the present world and see through its lineaments to the past of the English Revolution. When she becomes a teacher herself, she takes her students outside into the streets of Manchester to imagine the past, to search for 'vestiges ... remains ... litter. Leavings. Traces' (42). It takes an especially inspired person to conjure up a lost world from these scraps, but at least they are located right outside, not on a far-away continent or locked in texts written in a foreign language. Though every page of *Impassioned Clay* celebrates difference, its past is strikingly English. Davies describes the peculiar insight of the researcher and professional historian, intent on treating the past 'as a foreign continent, with its own complex mental terrains,' but the Englishness of the residents of this past invites the 'recurrent sense of uncanny closeness, as if, with their audacious, God-driven energy, they were only a breath away' (*Unbridled* 2).

The research quest requires extensive work in collections of broadsides, ephemeral publications of the seventeenth century that have miraculously survived three hundred years. Like her creator, Olivia has a gift for hearing in these documents long-silenced voices from the past. If their words make it into the protective custody of antiquarian collections, if they survive fire, damp, and readers' carelessness, Davies writes in *Unbridled Spirits*, these books arrest the reader 'with a pang as if the dead got up and spoke forcibly, freshly, from the page, and the library stillness is filled with characterful voices arguing. The leaf, like a freckled face, bears all the signs of time, yet the voices retain their dissident energy ... Reading them, we listen to the voices from which our own tongue derives' (*Unbridled* 6). Reading in the John Rylands Library, where the bomb blasts of IRA terrorists luckily do not reach the collections, Olivia reflects that 'the old books, precious in the dimness of these sanctuaries, maintained their pacific time-travel, rocked by no explosion, though when you opened their pages, the seared, schismatic voices raged with passion always fresh and raw' (*Impassioned* 49).

As the title of the novel hints, the passionate voices represent only the textual part of the recovery work. Human flesh itself is resurrected in clay, for Olivia's work in court records, diaries, journals, and pamphlets is augmented by the scientific reconstruction of the face of the long-dead woman whose identity she discovers. Alexander Sagarra, a medical artist with expertise in the reconstruction of ancient figures, rebuilds the face, 'a real face, not a portrait, from the remains of a skull' (*Impassioned* 21). Like his real-life counterparts at Manchester, Alex employs the protocol for moulding and casting a skull, fitting pegs to mark established skin-thickness, then building muscle bundles made out of wide strips of clay onto a plaster cast of the skull. This enables Alex to craft the face methodically (60–1), using in the words of the experts 'the most logical and foolproof way of ensuring that the face grows from the surface of the skull outwards of its own accord and according to the rules of anatomy' (Prag and Neave *Making Faces* 30). The cartilage of the nose and the shape of the lips are guesswork, but the rest is created according to tested scientific principles that have helped forensic detectives identify victims (*Impassioned* 62).[8] Alex makes a copy of the 'Hesketh Maiden' in wax, which is exhibited wearing the scold's bridle under the caption 'Silenced Woman' (64). The same display that later inspires John Hale to surrender the testament of Hannah Emanuel spurs Olivia to pursue her research with unusual confidence: 'Despite knowing very well that records for the period of the Revolution and its aftermath are scanty, full of holes, I felt sure of finding her. Whereas Alex had modelled a face from the skull, it fell to me to breathe life into the static clay' (67). The clay head intrudes upon Olivia's consciousness with a strange surprise. Use of the Manchester protocol in rebuilding a face from a skull 'reduces to a minimum the possibility of subjective interference' (Prag and Neave *Making Faces* 30); proceeding scientifically, Alex crafts not only a reconstruction, but a life mask of Olivia, which reveals her to be the uncanny double of Hannah, the silenced woman (*Impassioned* 75).

The reappearance of Hannah's real face, so obviously related to her descendent Olivia, puts the burden on the contemporary scholar to build up her voice and her life story from the fragmentary record. Davies's work expresses no naiveté about the survival of evidence from multifarious lives in the past – little of it gets into the record. Further, her narrator reflects that the status of evidence is under attack even among historians: '[T]here were Facts Men, and there were Foucault's Men (there were no people, only discourses), and there were Doubt-your-Sources Men' (*Impassioned* 120). A practical researcher of any theoretical persuasion would be forced to acknowledge that even among the living, far more goes unknown and unrecorded than ever can become the materials for future scholarship. The great bulk of activity that made up life in the past escapes notice. A library clerk's mistake reminds Olivia that 'yesterday did not exist except in paper. No memo, no event. And without corroborating memory, everything depended upon a written record' (139). The historian acknowledges the frustration of gaps in the record, but the novelist is not bound by the requirements of academic scholarship. Thus, to a scholar the censoring excisions from Hannah's *Wilderness of Women* would be a permanent barrier to full understanding, but Olivia can unloose her imagination to fill the gaps with re-creations of unrecorded scenes. Fiction liberates the imagination, which in turn 'takes empathy, and more than a gift for the vivid collage of reconstruction' (120).

This special combination of knowledge and empathy can only be culti-vated, Davies suggests, by a living, feeling, physical person who sits still to read. In an unusual set-piece that confronts the central dilemma for action plots of scholarly research, Davies defamiliarizes the sedentary activity of the scholar:

Round this table we cajoled the dead to reveal their innermost secrets from the stretched integument of cows rendered into vellum and sheep limed into parchment. We consulted the beaten, bleached rags of our ancestors, sized with glue culled from hooves, for intelligence of the dead. Tanned and tawed skins of beasts stripped by illiterates from animal carcasses cradled the quires of pages on which we fed ... Thus I pondered, oozing sweat amongst my cerebrating fellow scholars, breathing in particles of powder, products of extinct slaughter-houses whose floors had once been slick with creatures' blood, questing among these mortal vestiges for a quickening of mental life. (*Impassioned* 124)

All too much is going on in this scene of research. In near silence, living creatures handle the decaying remains of animals to catch the words, the 'intelligence,' the 'innermost secrets' of the dead. The straining verbs – cajoled, consulted, pondered – suggest the serious labour involved in sitting down, turning pages, and dreaming. As Richard Altick acknowledges in *The Scholar Adventurers*, even 'the most devoted scholar will admit' that 'research is frequently dull and laborious. Much of it ends in despair, because history, however briskly prodded, simply refuses to talk' (3).

The mimetic romance of the archive strives to record the difficulties in order to enhance the scholar's triumph in finally envisioning the faces and hearing the voices from the past. The dreary hours of unfruitful work cannot be skimped. Yet it is not enough to be properly credentialed, dogged in pursuit of the facts, and passionate about the subject. For the mental life of the past to 'quicken' in the metaphorical womb/brain of the living researcher, other requirements must be met. Success depends on an exclusive sameness, a suitable match across the centuries. Recognition of an earlier self marooned in the past verifies the imaginative insights of the archival romancer. The right pairing of subject and quester – matched down to the facial bones and the mitochondrial DNA (reproduced without recombination down the maternal line) – makes a fetish of heritage.[9] Paradoxically in fictions that emphasize their subjects' marginal positions and exceptional experiences, continuities of nationality, location, religion, genealogy, gender, and sexual preference constitute privileged authorities that not only know, but also embody, the past.

EPILOGUE

Postcolonial Rejoinders

'The crucial difference between the major English literature of the first half of the 20th century and the major English literature of the second half is not that one was modern and the other postmodern,' Michael Berube recently announced in an opinion piece in the *Chronicle of Higher Education*. The late-breaking news: 'The crucial difference is that one was produced largely in the United States, Britain, and Ireland, whereas the other was ... a global English-language literature' ('Teaching Postmodern' B5). As teachers, critics, and wide readers of contemporary fiction know, this change has brought to the university syllabus, the Booker Prize short lists, and the shelves of better bookstores excellent works by a wide variety of authors who write in English but who would be wrongly described as English novelists. Added to the list of many celebrated American and Irish writers are eminent Canadians, Australians, New Zealanders, Nigerians, Kenyans, South Africans, Guyanese, Indians, Pakistanis, and writers from the Caribbean nations. To these the wide reader adds the many writers who have migrated from their original homes, so that some of the brightest lights of Canadian literature, for instance, hail from India and Ceylon (now Sri Lanka). Berube's discovery comes as no surprise to the scholars of later-twentieth-century British, Commonwealth, and postcolonial literature, who have participated in the transformation of their field of study. As this epilogue's brief survey suggests, anglophone postcolonial writers redirect the legacy of literature in English, shifting the emphasis of its array of interests, themes, and forms. The deployment of romances of the archive by postcolonial writers reveals a diversity of critical revisions of the research quest's encounter with the past.

In the recent decades upon which this study focuses, the 'English' novel has been invigorated by the fiction of anglophone writers from the Commonwealth and former British colonies, a phenomenon that has, in the main, benefited literary fiction generally. This point has been noted so often that it sometimes provokes peevish responses, like A.S. Byatt's in her recent volume *On Histories and Stories* (2000): 'Wherever I go in Europe, as well as in Britain, there are seminars on post-colonial writing where Salman Rushdie's wit about the Empire Writing Back is quoted, and his assertion that British writing before the Empire Wrote Back was moribund and that contemporary British writing is desperately in need of enlivening, is accepted without question (*Histories and Stories* 3). I agree with Byatt that 'a body of writing' including 'Burgess, Golding, Murdoch, and Lessing ... carries weight,' and that contemporary British fiction was neither 'moribund nor insular' before Salman Rushdie came along (*Histories and Stories* 3, 12). Though Byatt takes pains to defend him from neglect, Anthony Burgess himself contributed to a broader view of excellent fiction in English. In 1984, when after decades of writing book reviews he compiled his ninety-nine favourite novels since 1939, Burgess included American novelists, genre fiction, and works by R.K. Narayan, V.S. Naipaul, Wilson Harris, and Chinua Achebe. Despite occasional bouts of grousing in the press, novelists born and bred in Great Britain have generally been glad to share the English novel with their peers from Australia, Canada, West Africa, the Caribbean, India, and Pakistan.

The Booker Prize has played an important role in this reorientation, particularly in its recognition (in 1981) of Salman Rushdie's *Midnight's Children* (1980).[1] Though it can only tell a tiny part of the story of contemporary fiction's changing lineaments, the Booker Prize short lists and winners reveal some of the trend that has by the end of the century so profoundly altered the face of English fiction.[2] In the earliest years of the Booker Prize, first awarded in 1969, Anglo-Irish (Iris Murdoch and William Trevor), Canadian (Mordecai Richler), Australian (Thomas Keneally), and white South African writers (Nadine Gordimer, Doris Lessing – from Rhodesia – and Andre Brink) represented Ireland and former settler colonies belonging to the Commonwealth of Nations. In the 1970s Brian Moore and V.S. Naipaul represented Ireland (by way of Canada) and the West Indies (by way of England), respectively.

In the 1980s writers of the formerly colonized peoples of the Empire followed V.S. Naipaul onto the short lists when the novels of Indian writers Anita Desai and Salman Rushdie were recognized. After Rushdie won the Booker Prize in 1981 for *Midnight's Children*, the short lists became more inclusive. While white writers from Commonwealth nations or former colonies continued to appear (Doris Lessing and Thomas

Keneally, joined by younger writers such as the Australian Peter Carey; Canadians Alice Munro, Margaret Atwood, and Robertson Davies; South African writer J.M. Coetzee; and Irish novelists John Banville and Roddy Doyle), minority English writers (Kazuo Ishiguro and Timothy Mo) and writers of colour such as Keri Hulme (New Zealand) and Chinua Achebe (Nigeria) were also recognized. Between 1981 and 1985 only one English writer (Anita Brookner) won the prize; in the later 1980s English writers (Kingsley Amis, Penelope Lively, Kazuo Ishiguro, and A.S. Byatt) won, but the short lists were significantly more diverse than the lists of a decade earlier. In the 1990s shortlisted English writers have been overtaken by a majority of non-English winners: South African J.M. Coetzee, Indian Arundhati Roy, African Ben Okri, Irishman Roddy Doyle, Scot James Kelman, Sri Lankan Michael Ondaatje (who now lives in Canada), and Canadian Margaret Atwood. When the 1993 short list (Roddy Doyle, Tibor Fischer, Michael Ignatieff, David Malouf, Caryl Phillips, and Carol Shields) came out, the by-then-annual Booker Prize controversy absurdly centred on the absence of 'English' writers. Evidently Tibor Fischer, born in England and Cambridge educated, possessed a name insufficiently English-sounding to justify his Englishness (his parents are Hungarian emigrants). Sometimes the journalistic defenders of the English novel overzealously police the short lists. However, it is clear enough that recent lists (including J.M. Coetzee, Anita Desai, Ahdaf Souief, Abdulrazak Gurnah, Romesh Gunesekera, Caryl Phillips, David Malouf, Rohinton Mistry, Michael Ondaatje, and Ben Okri) have had less space for English writers, traditionally defined. (A further trend can be noted: as the short lists since the 1980s have grown more multicultural, they have also afforded fewer spaces for novels by women.)[3] It would, of course, be a mistake to imagine that the vitality of the contemporary British novel can be gauged solely by the increasingly multicultural Booker short lists. While the success of literary fiction since Rushdie's *Midnight's Children* can be linked to the national and ethnic diversity of the 'best of the young British novelists,'[4] many of the novelists who have risen to prominence in the past two decades are actually British writers, born and educated in the United Kingdom. This stands to reason. With a book-buying public to support them, publishers can encourage home-grown talent, as well as scout the best of the postcolonial field.

As I have suggested from the start of this study, the newly international dimensions of contemporary British fiction frame my reading of the ardently English romances of the archive. I have argued that romances of the archive become increasingly popular after the Falklands War, and that their emphasis on English heritage and national history coincides with the last decades of the Empire's slow demise. The emergence of the library and the archive as privileged cultural sites, and the elevation of research questers to popular protagonists, coincides with the broadening and enrichment of the English novel by its former colonial subjects, and with the theoretical articulation of a variety of well-publicized postcolonial views about the past. If one of the essential tools of empire-building was the collection of information, one of the characteristic postcolonial strategies is to reclaim, re-examine, and resituate that information, making the former margin the centre and source of representation, and recasting England's collections and administrative manoeuvres as depredation and manipulation.

REALMS OF HERITAGE

A.S. Byatt observes, 'One very powerful impulse towards the writing of historical novels has been the political desire to write the histories of the marginalized, the forgotten, the unrecorded. In Britain this has included the histories of blacks and women, and the whole flourishing and brilliant culture of the post-colonial novel.' Byatt suggests that the imaginative historical activities of the under-represented groups inspire other writers as well: '[T]he existence of these often polemical revisionist tales has given other British writers the impulse to range further historically and geographically than the immediately post-war social realists' (*Histories and Stories* 12). Both historical writing and revisionist historical fiction from alternative perspectives have roles to play in the redefinition of the literary heritage represented by and in the English novel.

Conducting original archival work and reinterpreting its results through critical, politicized theories contribute to what Ato Quayson character-izes as the 'subjunctive historiographies' of postcolonial subjects. These revisions of history, while 'steadfastly engaging with the past,' also 'pro-vide models of agency for the present' (*Postcolonialism* 48). Abdul R. JanMohamed and David Lloyd explain the need, from a minority or postcolonial perspective, for assiduous archival work and a 'sustained theoretical critique' – resisting prejudice, exclusion, marginalization, and racism in the present depends upon understanding the historical roots of powerful institutions, and on reversing their habit of selectively forgetting the past:

One aspect of the struggle between hegemonic culture and minorities is the recovery and mediation of cultural practices which have been and continue to be subjected to institutional forgetting. Thus archival work is essential to the critical articulation of minority discourse. At the same time, if this archival work is not to be relegated by the force of dominant culture to the mere marginal repetition of exotic ethnicity, theoretical reflection cannot be dispensed with. Such a theory would be obliged to provide a sustained critique of the historical conditions and formal qualities of those institutions which have continued to legitimize exclusion and marginalization in the name of universality. ('Minority Discourse' 8)

Just a decade later, the threat of 'institutional forgetting' has been replaced with milder exhortations not to forget the many heritages that make up a postimperial British national identity.

In *A Future for Our Past?*, a book on 'Heritage Studies' aimed at a sixth formers, the authors caution that 'this "national" heritage is just one heritage among many' and that 'each will be valued differently by different people' (*A Future* 4). Thus, conservation and museum work must 'resist political and commercial pressure to distort or deny aspects of the heritage, and respect the needs and views of minority groups and interests' (14). In this late-twentieth-century view, 'there are certain parts of the past which are either seldom preserved or seldom the subject of presentation ... until very recently, there were few museum displays about aspects of the herit-age of non-western Europeans despite the fact that Britain is a multicultural society today' (42). Yet the embrace of 'subjunctive historiographies' can devolve into views of the past inclusive to the point of absurdity. *A Future for Our Past?* points out with perfect neutrality: 'There are in the U.K. for example, a Welsh and a Scottish Gaelic heritage, a West Indian heritage, an aristocratic heritage, a railway heritage, a seafaring heritage, a noncon-formist heritage, a culinary heritage, a heritage of the labour movement, a heritage of the women's movement' (4). All are to be celebrated equally. The possibility that inheritors of these disparate traditions might have reasons to feel at odds with one another is acknowledged: 'Heritages may even define themselves in opposition to each other, by exclusion rather than inclusion. "Heritage" can mean racism and intolerance' (4). However, typical representations of a diverse heritage play down historical conflicts and tend to aim for the 'balanced view' so scathingly lampooned by Barry Unsworth in *Sugar and Rum*.

A trickle-down postmodernism provides an alternative to representing unresolved conflicts, hatred, crimes, and contested histories in the 'bal-anced' manner that makes a minefield out of heritage. It would start from the premise that most of the time we don't actually know what happened in the past, thus to describe unprovable statements as facts is misleading. It abandons the concept of 'truth' about the past and admits to a biased viewpoint from the outset. This form of presentation can be refreshingly alive and even exciting, discarding compromise to one side and putting in its place enthusiasm and boldness. (*A Future* 39)

As the co-editors of the influential anthology *The Post-Colonial Studies Reader*, Bill Ashcroft, Gareth Griffiths, and Helen Tiffin point out, postmodernism need not conflict at every juncture with postcolonialism, for 'the major project of postmodernism – the deconstruction of the centralised, logocentric master narratives of European culture, is very similar to the post-colonial project of dismantling the Centre/Margin binarism of imperial discourse' (*Post-Colonial* 117). Sharing interests in the operations of power, decentred discourse, the construction of experience through writing, and the slipperiness of representations; rejecting the Cartesian individual in favour of a subject located in language or discourse; and often adopting subversive representational strategies, postmodernism and postcolonialism have significant areas of overlap (*Post-Colonial* 117). However, the blithe abandonment of facts and truth in favour of a bold and enthusiastic presentation of a biased view does not satisfy all the demands of a postcolonial re-evaluation of history and heritage. Postcolonialists affirm the political agency of colonized peoples and attempt to hear the voices of silenced subjects. They are not served by the abandonment of truth and the jettisoning of facts, as they struggle to recover cultural practices and experiences of the past in danger of erasure or forgetting.

Some theorists would argue that the dissevering of present-day people from their pasts, and particularly from their collective knowledge of the past, has already occurred. In these circumstances, what French historiographer Pierre Nora calls 'realms of memory' (*lieux de mémoire*) substitute for 'settings in which memory is a real part of everyday experience' ('General Introduction' 1). According to Nora, globalization, democratization, mass culture, media, independence movements, and decolonization have swept away societies based on memory. Vestigial symbols are all that remain. These memory sites can be places, monuments, books, festivals, or anniversaries, but they embody only traces of an otherwise obliterated connection to the past (1–6).

Nora's analysis, though based in French history and responding to French historiography, suggests why postcolonial re-evaluations of the archive provoke such powerful responses. He establishes that modern memory is itself archival, relying 'entirely on the specificity of the trace, the materiality of the vestige, the concreteness of the recording, the visibility of the image.' The archive thus acquires a special status in a 'religion of preservation and archivalization.' The resulting collections are not in themselves history, and indeed they may even induce failures of memory: 'What we call memory,' writes Nora, 'is in fact a gigantic and breathtaking effort to store the material vestiges of what we cannot possibly remember, thereby amassing an unfathomable collection of things that we might someday need to recall' ('General Introduction' 8). In the face of this crisis, individuals have not given up on history. Instead, according to Nora, they have 'followed the lead of ethnic minorities in seeking their own roots and identities.' Though this practice atomizes memory, multiplying private memories and individual recollections, it 'requires every social group to redefine its identity by dredging up its past' (10–11). A discovered identity, complete with a recovered past, traditional animosities and grievances, and celebrated traits and achievements, yields a precious sense of belonging. In Nora's view, those who were 'left out of the official histories' led the way into the archives, but they were followed by 'practically every organized social group, and not just the intellectual or educated' (10). From this perspective, romances of the archive can be seen as documenting a popular pastime that arises out of the modern experience of discontinuity and severed connections. The archive itself, with its promise of records and traces that can create a sense of connection and belonging, becomes a realm of memory in its own right.

Contemporary British romances of the archive reveal a complicated set of postimperial responses to the postcolonial re-examination of the historical record and its literary counterparts. Byatt is not alone in observing 'the extraordinary variety of distant pasts British writers are inventing, and the extraordinary variety of forms in which those pasts have been constructed' (*Histories and Stories* 36). The imaginary archives of contemporary British fiction suggest not only a renewed interest in the uses of the past, however, but also a discomforting awareness of postimperial and postmodern conditions. Not obviously retreating to an embattled universality in response to the postcolonialists' overtly political criticism of the dominant culture, romances of the archive engage with complications and particularities of a recovered past, as if to re-stake their claim on critical re-evaluation while depicting a heterogeneous experience back in history. The vogue for romances of the archive documents a scramble for turf and implies that the scrutiny of historical conditions, powerful institutions, and the contours of the national past will not be totally surrendered to postcolonial theorists and global English writers. The undertones of nostalgia, defensiveness, and anxiety can often be discerned in the fictional excursions into history; regret about Britain's decline in global status and annoyance at the complaints of postcolonial subjects are common features of the 'present day' depicted in romances of the archive. Though sometimes romances of the archive contain excoriating self-criticism, they often contribute to nostalgic fantasies about the uses of the past. Particularly when heritage themes occlude historical thinking, the endogamous Englishness of the past discovered within romances of the archive can add to a celebratory narrative of homogeneity, continuity, native virtues, and cultural survival.

Recent literary-critical and historical efforts to emphasize the diversity and popularize the multiple identities of 'the Isles' notwithstanding, Englishness more often than not makes up the better part of Britishness, leaving Irishness, Scottishness, and Welshness to fend for themselves in the realm of symbolic representations.[5] This is to say nothing on behalf of the hybrid identities of the communities made up of the descendents of postwar immigrants from Africa, the Far East, the Indian subcontinent, and the Caribbean, about some of whom Zadie Smith has written with great humour and optimism in *White Teeth* (2000). Having noted the ways diversity and distinctiveness are embraced in public histories in the United States, Canada, New Zealand, and Australia, Nick Merriman observes:

> England has a history of cultural diversity even older than these countries, but it is a feature of the national past that is rarely studied, at least in mainstream academia. England's heritage is not an explicitly multicultural one: in the nation's vision of itself, settlers are absorbed into a 'Deep English' identity from earliest times. Indeed in this vision of England people are frequently absent, or at least tend to take second place to landscape, wildlife and material culture in the promotion of a notion of unchanging Englishness. The continued advancement of the idea of a homogeneous English historical identity when other nations are shifting their position is an issue worth examining further in relation to the postcolonial era and the rise of new nationalisms within the UK and the rest of Europe. ('Understanding Heritage' 383)

Postcolonial writers and British authors writing from the margins have already done much to alter this situation, but only the rare British romance of the archive treats the recovered past as material for a reconsidered national identity.

The more historically minded writers, particularly Barry Unsworth,

Peter Dickinson, and Stevie Davies, do the most to offer criticism of the past and of comfortable fictions about the conventional meanings of historical periods. More often, romances of the archive call upon the past to redress injury, to correct omission, to restore pride, and to shore up the desirable meanings of Englishness. The genre tends towards nostalgia, in which the 'evocation of some past state of affairs ... in the context of present fears, discontents, anxieties, or uncertainties' solves crises of identity by defying feelings of insignificance and discontinuity (Davis *Yearning for Yesterday* 34–5). While a few oppositional authors offer less glowing and more overtly critical treatment of the past, in which nostalgia withers in the blast of historical discoveries, more often a desire to escape present confusions drives the research quest. The archive rarely reveals a simple past, however, and the adventure plot's required obstacles and antagonists ensure further complications. The romance of the archive generally shows the past not as a tidy theme park, but as a world as full as the present of hazards, confusions, moral dilemmas, and consequential accidents. Courage, skill, judgment, and knowledge are required of archival questers facing the difficult truths they have turned up. The brainy protagonists of the research narrative may compare unfavourably to their prototypes in adventurous imperial romances, thrilling gothics, and cool detective fictions, but they preserve in British fiction a conspicuous place for the bookish hero, dedicated to the quest for truth.

HISTORY: NO PLACE FOR TOURISTS

Postcolonial writers – poets, novelists, and theorists – have not failed to notice the contemporary British predilection for romances of the archive. They have responded in a variety of ways, each of which provides a glimpse of how this characteristically British mode looks from the outside. The tantalizing thought of 1950, that 'in obscure towns of Australia and Canada, even in the remote hills of India, today may rest documents of untold value for English literary history,' has been reversed; English literary history no longer sets the standard of value (Altick *Scholar Adventurers* 96). Caribbean poet and Nobel Laureate Derek Walcott ruthlessly satirizes the sentimentalized desire for connection with a heroic past through his English archival quester Plunkett, a character in the epic poem *Omeros* (1990). Walcott contrasts Plunkett's fantasized connections to history with the visionary dream-questing of his protagonist Achille. Keri Hulme (a New Zealand writer of Maori and Scottish descent) relocates the genealogical search in *the bone people* (1984), turning the tables to reveal the site of original crime and child abuse in a broken family of the Anglo-Irish aristocracy. In his novels *The Shadow Lines* (1988) and *The Calcutta Chromosome* (1995) and in his remarkable non-fiction narrative *In an Antique Land* (1992), Amitav Ghosh re-envisions the romance of the archive for an interconnected global future, and characterizes the research quester as a subtle interpreter of hybrid identities. Bharati Mukherjee, who with Ghosh represents the burgeoning field of the Indian diaspora, reinvents the tropes of imperial romance, co-opting and resituating the archival quest in *The Holder of the World* (1993). In each of the postcolonial texts mentioned here, a different quality of the romance of the archive is tested and recast. Because many contemporary British romances of the archive contain ingredients of imperialist master-narratives still in their potent half-lives, the postcolonial reaction is often delivered with some satirical, even lampooning, force.

In the attenuated versions of nineteenth-century imperial romance and travel narrative, cultural encounters are still structured around Orientalist definitions of European exploring self and exotic other, object of a Western gaze. Sometimes erotic adventure provides the motivation. Alan Hollinghurst's *The Swimming-Pool Library* depicts Lord Nantwich's relationship with colonial subjects sympathetically, idealizing black and Arab men, and romanticizing the last days of going out to the far reaches of the Empire. These appear as an irrevocable golden age, when black lovers and eastern erotica could still be collected. Yet for all Hollinghurst's sympathy for the politically incorrect sexual politics of the Edwardian Empire, nostalgia finally does not override criticism of this outdated behaviour. Hollinghurst also shows that though present-day characters may have eschewed paternalism, they have kept the sexual gourmandizing, and he indicts his characters for this. In postimperial London, a relationship with an exotic other can be conducted nearer to home. Venturing to the tower blocks of notorious housing estates recaptures some of the dangers of the imperial romance, without the glamorously remote location. Christopher Lane interprets Hollinghurst's criticism of the residual imperial romance in this way: 'By representing his characters' fantasies as part of a vast confluence of racial and national difficulty, Hollinghurst demonstrates that Britain has become mired in a renewed vision of colonial splendour and global influence' (*Ruling Passion* 231). The refusal to give up on Empire in face of the facts results in pathetic re-enactments of the adventures of an earlier generation of colonial masters.

Though the imperial romance in the hands of H. Rider Haggard and John Buchan often takes African sites as its symbolic ground, and Arabia has its advocate in T.E. Lawrence, India is the pre-eminent locale for fantastic recreations of the heydey of British imperialism. In 1984, in response to a spate of films indulging in Raj revivalism, Salman Rushdie wrote scathingly that

> there can be little doubt that in Britain today the refurbishment of the Empire's tarnished image is under way. The continuing decline, the growing poverty and the meanness of spirit of much of Thatcherite Britain encourages many Britons to turn their eyes nostalgically to the lost hour of their precedence. The recrudesence of imperialist ideology and the popularity of Raj fictions put one in mind of the phantom twitchings of an amputated limb. Britain is in danger of entering a condition of cultural psychosis, in which it begins to strut and posture like a great power while, in fact, its power diminishes each year. The jewel in the crown is made, these days, of paste. ('Outside the Whale' 91–2)

With critics as articulate as Rushdie watching every move of the sentimentalists, it is no wonder that since the 1980s most British writers with a taste for history stay far from the subcontinental territory. Kipling, E.M. Forster, Paul Scott, and Rumer Godden were the last to do it in any depth before the impressive generation of writers led by Anita Desai, R.K. Narayan, and Rushdie himself laid claim to India's multiplicity of stories and complicated history for novels in English. First-hand knowledge and the variety of inside views take precedence over the insights of Western sojourners. As Hayden White, concurring with Fredric Jameson, writes, 'If one is going to "go to history," one had better have an address in mind rather than go wandering around the streets of the past like a *flaneur*. Historical *flaneurisme* is undeniably enjoyable, but the history we are living today is no place for tourists' (*Content* 164).

Historian Peter Hopkirk flagrantly ignores this warning and sets out to flout the opinions of 'sanctimonious critics' who have visited postcolonial views on *Kim* and Kipling (*Quest* 12). Having spent a career chronicling the Great Game of the Secret Service, he turns to a travelogue memorializing the source of his interest in spies, adventure, and India. The resulting book, *Quest for Kim: In Search of Kipling's Great Game* (1996), tells a non-fiction romance of the archive in which Hopkirk retraces the steps of Kim and Kipling's other characters through the altered landscape of independent India and Pakistan. The decline of British influence in this sphere Hopkirk presents as generally regrettable. Every time he enters a railway station, Hopkirk is haunted by images of the violent break with the British past; every train reminds him of those that pulled into their stations filled with corpses during the Partition riots. Yet Hopkirk keeps the reader aware of the continuities with the late-nineteenth-century world created by Kipling's novel, noting in each crowd of underfed children 'a young Kim' who carries on the immemorial craft of the street urchin. The task is to see through the excrescences of the present into the past of Kim.

The research quest Hopkirk undertakes is based on the assumption that Rudyard Kipling used a live model or an actual place for each detail of his richly episodic fiction. Thus, a quest that exercises the historical imagination relies on a stunted conception of the literary imagination, in which nothing can be made up from whole cloth. Naturally, Hopkirk can locate the major cities, the Wonder House, and the Grand Trunk Road. His desire to identify the model for each person and site in Kim, however, leads to futile searches through the archives. The stubborn fact of fictionality impedes him in research through 'the eight shelf-miles of records at the India Office Library' and their huge photographic archive for the original of Lurgan Sahib's shop on the Simla Mall (Quest 184). The collection of memoirs by former Raj officials, held by the library of the School of Oriental and African Studies at London University, yields no reference to the source (185–6). Hopkirk consults the living experts to no avail: '[T]he fact that two serious historians living on the spot were unable to locate it in what is really a very small town now made me wonder whether it ever stood among the shops on the mall, save in hearsay or as a piece of tourist folklore' (198). The possibility that Kipling invented the site for Kim's initial training in spy-craft Hopkirk does not consider, though he admits that Kipling may have transferred a shop and proprietor from another location. Hopkirk concludes only partly in jest that 'perhaps the answer would be for someone to open a small antique shop on the Mall, cram it with Tibetan and other exotic treasures, and call it "Lurgan Sahib's Original Oriental Curio Shop". If life in Britain becomes too unbearable, I might even consider it myself' (199). Thus, we find the locations of Kim transformed into realms of memory celebrating a lost imperial heritage.

In Derek Walcott's epic poem Omeros, the tourist's Caribbean still exists and drives the economy in which several of Walcott's central characters labour. That the past will not belong to tourists, as well, is one of the accomplishments of Walcott's new world epic. A hazardous vision-quest into the voyages of ancestors makes up a significant portion of the fisherman Achille's story. In contrast to the canoe-voyages of the seafaring Polynesians, the ancestors of Achille are transported against their will into slavery. Walcott takes Achille through a moment of sunstroke into a descent to an ocean underworld, retracing the path of the middle passage backwards to the Africa of his ancestors. The romance of the archive embedded in one of *Omeros*'s many subplots demonstrates, by contrast, British sentimentality about the past. It also inoculates the poet/narrator against historically based criticism by thematizing the failings of one who wants to make a gift of history to its black victims.

Major Dennis Plunkett, sufferer from a wartime head-wound, is a retired soldier of Cockney origins who has chosen St Lucia as his adoptive home. There he sets up as a pig-farmer and acts the part of an ex-colonial master. He seeks to make a connection with the place through archival research; reading history, he combs through texts for evidence of coincidences that would fulfil his wish to verify re-enactments of Homeric patterns. The satirical treatment of this impulse guards the allusive and heterogeneous poem against censure for getting the references to history and the classics wrong, by showing the vacuousness of a personalized antiquarianism.

As a boy, the narrator of the poem tells us, Plunkett wins 'the prize for an essay/ on the Roman Empire. In those days, history was easy' (*Omeros* 113). The postcolonial condition makes history significantly more difficult, and Plunkett is ill equipped to face the challenges:

> He had no idea how time could be reworded,
> which is the historian's task. The factual fiction
> of textbooks, pamphlets, brochures, which he had loaded
>
> in a ziggurat from the library, had the affliction
> of impartiality; skirting emotion
> as a ship avoids a reef, they followed one chart
>
> dryly with pen and compass, flattening an ocean
> to paper diagrams, but his book-burdened heart
> found no joy in them except their love of events,
>
> and none noticed the Homeric repetition
> of details, their prophecy.
>
> (*Omeros* 95–6)

Plunkett wishes for a history that can guide, advise, protect and console. Leaving his wife Maud to her Catholicism, he seeks an alternative cure for his symbolic head-wound. If the wounds of the narrative's black islanders symbolize the legacy of slavery and colonialism, as Jahan Ramazani has persuasively argued ('Wound of History' 406), Plunkett's affliction has to do with his wrong thinking. The way to live through the end of empire is not to dwell on its former glories; delusional fantasies about the uses of that past must be ended decisively to cure trauma.

Plunkett and his wife Maud are childless (*Omeros* 29) and recently bereft of their black maid Helen, who has made off with Maud's lemon-yellow dress. The women dispute whether it was a gift or a theft: 'that dress// had an empire's tag on it, mistress to slave' (64). Plunkett's response to the upset in his home, and his half-acknowledged attraction to the beautiful Helen, is to retreat into books: 'Plunkett decided that what the place needed/ was its true place in history, that he'd spend hours / for Helen's sake on research' (64). As the narrator of the poem comments damningly, 'Plunkett, in his innocence,/ had tried to change History to a metaphor,/ in the name of a housemaid' (270). In fact he uses his research to avoid doing anything active for Helen's sake, who is already inspiring jealous conflict between Achille and Hector. The fantasies he concocts for Helen soon yield to more private consolations, for anxiety about his failed paternity inflects Plunkett's quest. He invents a son by discovering an 'ancestor' in ship records of Admiral Rodney's crew: 'This was his search's end. He had come far enough// to find a namesake and a son' (94).

Midshipman Plunkett sails aboard *The Marlborough*, Rodney's flag-ship, when she engages in the 1782 Battle of the Saintes offshore St Lucia (*Omeros* 79, 84); before drowning, he witnesses the sinking of the French ship *Ville de Paris* (86). A more satisfactory solution than the creation of an embellished family tree, for which Major Plunkett pays cold cash, the invented relationship addresses Plunkett's yearning for a legitimate place in British society and a connection to St Lucia. He comes from ordinary people, but feels embarrassed and defensive about it. Mourning midship-man Plunkett gives the aging man a hobby that allows for amiable day-dreams about a long-dead precursor in St Lucia. Like Laurence Sterne's Uncle Toby (who also suffers from a debilitating war wound), Major Plunkett dedicates himself to memorizing and imaginatively recreating 'the greatest battle/ in naval history' (92), acting out the part of an 'arm-chair admiral in old age' (90). This project substitutes for the real trip Plunkett had once hoped to take: '[A]fter the war, he'd made plans to embark on/ a masochistic odyssey through the Empire,/ to watch it go in the dusk,' visiting the battles he romanticized in boyhood, from Concord, Massachusetts, to the hill stations of India.

Walcott's narrator regards this 'khaki Ulysses' with a critical eye (*Omeros*

263), showing his fascination with an absent war and a lost empire as an evasion of emotional life in the now.[6] Plunkett's desire to give Helen dignity by celebrating her historical significance fails because this Helen cares nothing for history. As Walcott himself comments, '[W]ho is Plunkett to pronounce this benediction of elevation to a height that would make her the equal of a white Helen? A mistake' ('Reflections 133). In contrast with the would-be historian Walcott places Plunkett's wife Maud, who prefers gardens to empires, and whose death jolts Plunkett out of his escapist research. Walcott suggests that the work of mourning an individual dignifies a character who otherwise appears lost in silly nostalgia for an imperial past in which he has no part. Grief, not the falsified heritage of antiquarian history, is the cure for Plunkett's affliction. Because Walcott's project is not entirely distinct from Plunkett's, it matters that both historian and poet turn away from their aggrandizing efforts to create the sublime out of humble materials (234). The poet/narrator's embrace of unelevated ordinary daily life, by the end of the narrative, answers the internal criticism that the poem aims at its own grand conception, and distinguishes Walcott's productive imaginative project from the ineffectual dithering of Plunkett's researches.

If the trauma of slavery underlies everything that Walcott's characters can or cannot accomplish and comprehend, Keri Hulme's 1985 Booker Prize–winning novel *the bone people* invests in discovering the various causes of psychic and physical wounds. An orphaned white child's body becomes the ground upon which abusive history writes its terrible story. The decoding falls to Kerewin Holmes, the part-Maori heroine of this novel by a part-Maori novelist, when she becomes involved with an abused child of unknown origins. Dumped by drug-running sailors on the shores of New Zealand, Simon is mute but intelligent. A sneak thief and petty vandal at his indeterminate age of six, seven, or eight, he smokes, drinks, and bears scars of beatings administered by his adoptive father, Joe Gillayley, a Maori. Though the reader witnesses Joe's violence, the novel reveals that Gillayley is not the only one to have tormented the child: '"He had some bloody funny marks on him when he arrived"' (*bone people* 328). The nature of these injuries suggests sexual abuse by members of Simon's unidentified captors, but the child's inability to speak makes investigating his identity and his traumatic history nearly impossible (86).

There are a few clues; these lead to an abbreviated research plot. Simon calls himself Clare, and possesses a rosary that runs through a signet ring, whose heraldic symbols Kerewin researches: '*Armed with the ring and the rosary, I went to the library. In Debretts, after hunting through a thousand dusty pages, found a saltaire with phoenix on flame-nest superimposed.*

Arms of a doddering Irish earl in his eighties. He had two sons. One died in World War II, and the other popped off in 1956. Remarried, with no issue, was the Irish earl. Fat lot of help' (*bone people* 66, 97, italics in original). Kerewin writes to the Irish earl, and learns that the jewellery belongs to a disinherited grandson, who is known to have visited New Zealand. This discovery links the ravaged boy to decayed Anglo-Irish nobility (99); later the novel confirms the relationship with an Irish heroin addict, long dead.

Given that Simon's adoptive father Joe serves jail time for nearly killing the boy, Hulme does not shield the Maori characters from her alter ego Kerwin's harshest judgments. By juxtaposing Joe's violence with the sadistic behaviour of Euro-trash drug-runners, however, she makes the point that European culture breeds criminals at least as vile as the child-abusing Maori man. Since a major part of the novel's epic narrative concerns Kerwin Holmes's effort to come to terms with her hybrid ancestry, it matters that the discoveries of child-violation indict Europeans and Maoris equally. The novel itself bespeaks its Western roots through allusions to Joyce, Tolkein, Charlotte Brontë, and Yeats. For a positive, sustaining heritage, however, Hulme relies upon the rich hoard of Maori symbols and cultural elements: greenstones, spirals, boundary markers, sacred gathering places, extended families, and venerated elders. The visionary dream-quest into the legacy of the Maori ancestors suggests a means for healing the wounded trio (Kerewin, Joe, and Simon/Clare). The novel ends with a reconstituted family all taking shelter under Kerewin's name, Holmes, homonym of 'homes.' Kerewin Holmes's research yields genealogical satisfactions that contrast sharply with the fantasized connections of Walcott's Plunkett, though it doesn't get Simon very far to be linked to the Anglo-Irish aristocracy. Neither writer imagines what Pierre Nora sees as racial and ethnic minorities' pioneering use of the archive in a search for real or symbolic roots.

Postcolonial writers do sometimes reflect on the purposes and pleasures of research as it bears on identity, no one more subtly than anthropologist and novelist Amitav Ghosh. In *The Shadow Lines*, Ghosh writes a research episode in which his central character pores over evocative old newspapers in order to comprehend his own childhood experience of communal violence. He searches in order to see the portents of the riots in print and to attempt to read the signs that might have been more accurately interpreted to avoid danger:

There is nothing quite as evocative as an old newspaper. There is something in its urgent contemporaneity – the weather reports, the list of that day's engagements in the city, the advertisements for half-remembered films, still

crying out in bold print as though it were all happening *now*, today – and the
feeling besides, that one may once have handled, if not that very paper, then
its exact likeness, its twin, which transports one in time as nothing else can.
So, looking at the paper that my father had read that morning, I knew he
could not be blamed for ignoring the stirrings of the silence around him: in
that paper there was not the slightest hint or augury of the coming carnage.
(*Shadow Lines* 227)

Lacking the printed words that would verify his experience, the narrator
cannot explain the death that has marked his consciousness (228), but the
unyielding newspaper still functions as a powerful memory site. It forges a
sympathetic connection between son and father and absolves the father of
blame for misinterpreting the silence and endangering the family. The gaps
in the record are thus dignified as the instruments of a later forgiveness.
Once the riots occur, the newspapers duly record them, as Ghosh's protagonist reports. Yet making the news does not mean becoming a part of
history: 'By the end of January 1964 the riots had faded away from the
pages of the newspapers, disappeared from the collective imagination of
"responsible opinion", vanished, without leaving a trace in the histories
and bookshelves.' In an evocative sentence, Ghosh sums up the fate of
experiences that do not make it into history: '[T]hey had dropped out of
memory into the crater of a volcano of silence' (230).

Amitav Ghosh's non-fiction narrative *In an Antique Land* relates the
author's experiences as an Indian anthropologist studying life in an Egyptian village in the 1980s. In a series of scholarly interpolations, Ghosh also
describes his research into the life of the Slave of MS H.6, an Indian man
belonging to a twelfth-century Middle Eastern Jewish merchant. Traces of
the Slave appear in his master Ben Yiju's papers, part of a treasure-trove of
medieval documents collected in a chamber of a Cairo synagogue. The
connection between a medieval Indian slave and a late-twentieth-century
Indian anthropologist are tenuous, but as in many romances of the archive,
a wisp of shared identity creates a sense of purpose. Ghosh writes, 'I knew
nothing then about the Slave of MS H.6 except that he had given me a right
to be there [in Egypt], a sense of entitlement' (*Antique Land* 19). The
textual traces of the Slave, though preserved in the Synagogue of Ben Ezra
for centuries, now lie scattered in university libraries and special collections in Great Britain and the United States. Ghosh retells the story of the
archival prospecting conducted by late nineteenth-century European scholars, who remove the contents of the Geniza (the chamber in the synagogue
dedicated to holding deposited papers) and bring them to Cambridge.

What looks to late twentieth-century eyes like licensed pillaging the victims do not protest: 'By the First World War, the Geniza had finally been emptied of all its documents. In its home country however, nobody took the slightest notice of its dispersal. In some profound sense, the Islamic high culture of Masr had never really noticed, never really found a place for the parallel history the Geniza represented, and its removal only confirmed a particular vision of the past' (95).

The recovery of a single thread of that neglected parallel history preoccupies Ghosh as he reconstructs the Slave's life story. He must work in documents composed in a colloquial dialect of medieval Arabic that is written in Hebrew script; to his delight, the regional dialect Ghosh has earlier learned during his fieldwork aids him in his research, allowing first comprehension and then the startling time-collapse that often surprises a romancer of the archive: '[O]ver the next couple of years, as I followed the Slave's trail from library to library, there were times when the magnifying glass would drop out of my hand when I came upon certain words and turns of phrase for I would suddenly hear the voice of Shaikh Musa [one of Ghosh's informants] speaking in the documents in front of me as clearly as though I had been walking past the canal, on my way between Lataifa and Nashawy' (*Antique Land* 105). Not only language but also cultural practices survive the intervention of centuries and the disruption of European colonization; Ghosh reflects, 'It seemed uncanny that I had never known all those years that in defiance of the enforcers of History, a small remnant of [the Slave's] world had survived, not far from where I had been living' (342). If the voices and practices of the past are still, however improbably, preserved in the present day, the lives of the medieval Middle Eastern merchants, their families, employees, and trading partners are recovered through stubborn old-fashioned scholarship. Ghosh goes over seemingly unimportant documents for the fragments that reconstitute a lost social world. His vivid reconstruction of a cosmopolitan, culture-crossing, trading, travelling, thoroughly networked individual suggests that the key concepts of postcoloniality – hybridity, migrancy, double-consciousness, race, language, identity, and cultural difference – are embedded in experiences eight centuries old. Postcolonial theorists may have articulated these ideas in their influential forms, but the miraculously surviving archive allows the romancer of the past to discover them in their original matrix: a life out of that all-but-lost parallel history.

Ghosh's non-fictional contribution to the romance of the archive suggests that its conventions for structuring and revealing encounters with history are not exhausted by the copious contemporary British examples.

He opens up an older and more foreign past than that upon which most British novelists dwell, but the central quest for heritage that shores up identity, even exceptional identity, remains. By reporting the experience of uncanny familiarity, by narrating his assiduous effort to follow the trail of fragments through the archives, and by insisting on the ultimate accessibility of enough of the truth to permit confident historical reconstruction, Ghosh affirms the function of the romance of the archive and dignifies research as more than just a nostalgic exercise on the grounds of a realm of memory.

However, Ghosh's later fiction reconsiders the romance of the archive from a more critical perspective. In *The Calcutta Chromosome*, research becomes a burdensome form of piecework for an intellectual worker bound to his computer, where the discovery of links between hybrid identities of the past and of the wired global future fails to liberate the quester. Watched by the laser-guided surveillance camera of his computer, Antar stares at inventories of the contents of offices in remote parts of the world. He has not been entrusted with the big questions that drive the research, though he knows his employer, the Water Council, seeks an explanation for the declining global water supplies. An expatriate Egyptian living in New York, Antar has been assigned inconsequential work to be conducted at home in solitude, with only the artificial personality of his computer to keep him company.

In one level of his narrative, Ghosh tells the story of Antar's research into the identity of a man whose degraded ID card appears on his screen. The nested layers of historical narrative explore a conspiracy involving malaria research conducted in late colonial days in Calcutta. To detail the plots and interconnections of this Pynchonesque novel would overwhelm this epilogue, for in one sense the entire fiction revolves around different forms of research, including medical experimentation, spying, and journalistic investigation. The archival element is presented in the dreariest possible terms, man and computer lashed to one another in unceasing day labour. A seemingly infinite knowledge base extends by the hour as the computer processes trivia; the human element seems necessary only to make the occasional prompting and to sort out the odd detail over which artificial intelligence stumbles. The researcher possesses little independent agency, working under surveillance as a witness to the mechanical turning over of the archive. Ghosh here presents the remnants of the past as an intolerable burden; history itself is an unstable zone of deliberate cover-ups and still-active conspiracies. Yet this situation, as in other romances of the archive, also provides a door into the past. Either magically or as a result of conspiracy, the technologies of holography and virtual-reality 'simultaneous visualization' connect individuals continents apart. The novel ends with the researcher poised on the threshold of an entirely simulated world, his subjectivity apparently co-opted by the objects of his research, who have sought him out in the first place. Even Antar's quest is not really his own. *The Calcutta Chromosome* remakes the romance of the archive into an Orwellian nightmare, in which Third World technicians suffer for the global appetite for information.

Bharati Mukherjee's novel *The Holder of the World* depicts a wired research quest that takes the plunge into virtual reality. Mukherjee celebrates a harmless virtual tourism, even as she embellishes the past with alternative characters and evidence. Commenting on the past by inventing materials to correct history's omissions need not embarrass a novelist; revisions by back-formation of the sources of canonical works have been a stock-in-trade of postcolonial feminist fiction since Jean Rhy's *The Wide Sargasso Sea* (1966), which tells the tale of Charlotte Brontë's Creole madwoman from Bertha's point of view. Mukherjee's *The Holder of the World* makes an unusual twist on the formula, rewriting the origin of Hawthorne's Hester as a white Indian-loving woman who wears a scarlet 'I' sewn to her sleeve. To this Mukherjee adds two fictive sources for Hawthorne's Pearl. The granddaughter of the woman guilty of miscegenation bears double marks of hybrid difference, for she is the offspring of Hannah Easton and an Indian prince (from the subcontinent). Black-haired and black-eyed, she is 'Black Pearl' (*Holder* 284). Her mother, Hannah Easton, known in Indian circles as the 'Salem Bibi,' or mistress of the prince, garners a legend in India that influences the iconography of the destructive Hindu goddess Kali (*Holder* 15). When she returns to her Salem home, the town gossips rename her 'White Pearl.' Hawthorne's great-grandfather, son of the witchcraft judge, frequents the household of the two Pearls. Family lore presumably does the rest in passing on these suggestive materials to the creator of Hester Prynne and Pearl. In contrast to Mukherjee's version, the adulteress and illegitimate child of Nathaniel Hawthorne's *The Scarlet Letter* (1850) appear less hybrid, less adventurous, less rebellious by far than their historical 'originals.'

The character who puts these startling discoveries together is an American woman, Beigh Masters, whose partner, Venn Iyer, is an Indian computer scientist. He and his colleague Jay Basu are at work on the virtual-reality simulation of 29 October 1989 in its entirety, to be achieved through the input and reassembly of all available data. She is a researcher employed by a rich collector to track down an elusive diamond once owned by a Mughal emperor. Privately she dedicates herself to discovering everything there is to know about Hannah Easton, a woman from Salem who ends up in the Mughal court in close proximity to the diamond (*Holder* 19). More than a few material traces of Hannah's existence survive. She is depicted in the jewel-toned paintings of Mughal miniaturists; her own inventive needle-work survives in museum collections. A remote relative of Beigh's through old New England family connections, Hannah represents the broadening effects of cultural encounters; her life prefigures the experiences and views of late-twentieth-century cosmopolitans like Beigh. Hannah refers to her voyage to India as her 'translation'; as Beigh observes, she takes pleasure in the world's variety, enjoys the transformation of her life, and refrains from negative comparisons: 'She did not hold India up to inspection by the lamp of England, or of Christianity' (*Holder* 104). Traced through books, paint-ings, engravings, trade records, journals, archival records, and verifying travel, Hannah's life story is in the end fed into Venn's computer to reconstruct the day of the disappearance of the Emperor's Tear, the fabled diamond. Wearing the helmet, goggles, and wired gloves of a virtual reality hook-up, Beigh Masters temporarily inhabits the body of Hannah's com-panion Bhagmati, and discovers the location of the diamond.

In this near-fantasy sequence, a version of the *Star Trek* Holo-deck provides the matrix for the ultimate merging of researcher and historical subject. Hooked to the system, Beigh shouts in a language she does not know, and relives the death of a participant in a historic seige, an accom-plishment more significant than discovering that the diamond lies in Bhagmati's grave. It appears at the end of the novel that Beigh will not pass on her knowledge to her employer, who is too future-oriented to respect the pain and sacrifice of historical subjects like Bhagmati. He might actu-ally violate her grave to get his loot. The technology of Iyer and Basu's devising, by way of contrast, supports an innocent form of time-tourism in which a virtual body-snatch can be staged harmlessly. Unlike Hopkirk's quest for the original of Lurgan Sahib's shop, Beigh Masters's search reaches the completion of perfect mind-meld. Retrieving a day in India in 1695 complete with reconstructed persons depends on the genius of the programmers and the capacity of the computer, but truth itself is accessi-ble: 'Everything that has ever happened is still out there, somewhere, like light from distant stars' (*Holder* 280). If Bharati Mukherjee's version of the research quest outdoes the most fantastic romance of the archive in its representation of an accessible truth, it also pointedly revises the object of the search. Historical insight achieved by knowing a hitherto obscure woman's life story counts more than finding the diamond; Hawthorne's 'source' materials are given priority over the canonical text. The play with hybrid identities, world travel, and cultural confrontations writes post-colonial thematics deep into the early colonial days of both Massachusetts and India. There was no time, Muhkerjee implies, when subjects were not already hybrid, already encountering others, or already reinventing themselves through forced or voluntary relocations.

'ANYWHERE BUT THE HERE AND NOW'

Fictions of archival research provide sturdy vehicles for the narrative exploration of vital questions for postcolonial and postimperial subjects alike. Which of our many pasts do we choose to know and retell? How will we adjudicate the rival claims of history and heritage in a multicultural twenty-first century? Romances of the archive cannot answer these questions directly, nor do they agree in their versions of history, but they do insist that sufficient traces of the past remain for the imaginative rediscovery of the truth. Their heroic questers strive in spite of postmodern uncertainties to deliver the goods, which the historically minded reader can only resolve to evaluate with some scepticism. Even when romances of the archive err in details, flout received wisdom, espouse retrograde political views, or revel in counterfactual scenarios, they cannot be denied their passionate interest in the uses of the past. As Steven Connor has observed, novels do not play a neutral role in the creation of History out of events in the past (*English Novel* 130). Clad in the guise of thrillers, detective fictions, fantasies, and popular novels of quests for identity, romances of the archive make an adventure out of the contest over historical interpretation.

The historian Alice Kaplan writes not about fiction, but in a personal mode about her professional work. Her insights about confidential tales of real historical research illuminate the fictional versions treated in this book:

> They are versions of epic. Odysseus's travels, Diogenes' search for the honest man – or the reliable fact. They are redemptive detective fictions with their single problem, their crime, waiting to be solved at the center of the labyrinth. Archival work is an epic, but is also a dime novel, an adolescent adventure story. It is a mixed up genre whose tropes and figures cross over, multiply, intertwine. ('Working' 107)

Throughout this study I have argued that romances of the archive are a pervasive form of contemporary British fiction, widely dispersed among a whole range of sub-genres of the novel. The epic quester, the adventurer, and the dime novel's hard-boiled detective show the way for the amateur scholar to be reborn as an action hero. Furthermore, the ongoing arguments about the uses of the past that appear in romances of the archive are enhanced in different ways by their various generic surroundings. Concentrating on the diversity of these narratives reveals the range of views they contain about history. Romances of the archive quarrel about who deserves to have custody of the past. They often offer revisionist or frankly counterfactual versions of history. They disagree about whether secrets must be kept for our own protection, or revealed to bring the culpable to justice. They make characters with dubious credentials into crack researchers, and they sometimes assert that identity itself is the key that opens the lock-boxes of the past. For every romance of the archive that makes the reader doubt whether the truth can be found any more or anywhere (a recent version of this sort comes, surprisingly, from A.S. Byatt in *The Biographer's Tale* [2000]), half a dozen others attest to the accessibility of buried secrets, if only to a properly equipped quester.

In an extension of my primary observation about the diversity of views about history offered in romances of the archive, I observe that 'postmodernism' inadequately describes the whole form and content of the contemporary British fictional scene. While postmodern texts contest traditional ideas about fixed truths or accessible facts, or lead from text to text in playful infinite regression, many other novels employ strategies derived from psychological realism, detective fiction, fantasy, and even children's fiction to recover connections with the past and reveal truths that have been buried in mouldering heaps of paper. I have suggested that the decades so often characterized as postmodern times also see a critical re-evaluation of the past from postcolonial and feminist perspectives. I see the reassertion of British glory in the post-Falklands decades as answering anxieties provoked by the Suez crisis and Britain's postwar decline in global status. During and after the Thatcher years, a hotly contested debate about the history and heritage that ought to be taught to schoolchildren also makes its mark on fiction that considers the uses of the past.

Though I have kept a tight focus on archival romances, much of what I argue in this book could be applied to contemporary historical fiction more generally. A writer of both historical fictions (*Angels and Insects*) and archival romances, A.S. Byatt is especially well qualified to speculate on the reasons for the contemporary turn to historical fiction. She suggests that nothing attracts writers so effectively as interdiction: because contemporary writers 'have in some sense been forbidden to think about history,' many of them have 'taken to it' in defiance of poststructuralist theory (*Histories and Stories* 11). Her erstwhile biographer in *The Biographer's Tale* consciously decides to give up trying to become a postmodern literary theorist, adopting instead a quest for facts that would have the status of things (*Biographer's* 3). In some sense Byatt offers in this novel an anti-romance of the archive, with a tiny, unheroic protagonist whose autobiographical impulses ultimately subvert the biography of a biographer that he sets out to write. When the things and texts and even photographs of his subject turn up, their meanings are mysterious or oblique. In Byatt's words, '[A]ll he finds are fragments of other random lives ... overlapping human stories which make up the only available tale of the biographer' (*Histories and Stories* 10). The novel testifies to the way in which one's reading, or research, can end up being the most enduring part of one's identity; Byatt has written before about the invidious notion she reiterates here, that readers can only 'relate' to the present (93). In Byatt's view the compelling story is 'a tale of the lives of the dead which make up the imagined worlds of the living' (10). To disdain history or to warn writers off the past would, in this view, effectively dam up one of the wellsprings of the imagination.

Byatt acknowledges that writers seek paradigms in history to approach contemporary problems, and she recognizes the force of 'political desires' to investigate and recover unremembered pasts (*Histories and Stories* 11–12). She suspects that both activities are paradoxically stimulated by the 'vanishing of the past from the curriculum of much modern education' (93). This thought resembles Patrick Wright's idea that nostalgia is born out of the devaluation of historical consciousness (*Old Country* 20), except that for Byatt, what arises out of ignorance and neglect may begin as nostalgia, but continues as a positive and creative activity. Ultimately, Byatt argues, the attraction of the historical for the contemporary literary artist lies in the aesthetic opportunities it affords: the 'need to write coloured and metaphorical language, to keep past literatures alive and singing, connecting the pleasure of writing to the pleasure of reading' (*Histories and Stories* 11). In the face of contemporary spin control, truth commissions, false memories, and patently ideological use of language, something like 'fun' or 'pleasure' might still be proffered by the past. This is an appealing explanation and one that honours the reader's role in enjoying fictional encounters with history.

Yet for every influential defence of the historical turn in fiction, other voices pipe up to decry the trend. The following excerpts from a dialogue between 'Matt' and 'Nicholas' defend the precepts of a group of young, mostly British, fiction writers who pledge to set their works in the present day and avoid all 'improbable or unknowable speculation about the past or the future' (Blincoe and Thorne *All Hail the New Puritans* xiv–xv). In support of the promise to employ present-day settings, Nicholas explains that British 'historical fiction has become so common that, if it was possible to speak of the judgment of posterity, the assumption would be that nothing of interest happened in the late twentieth and early twenty-first century. That is insane – if anything, we live in too exciting times.' The charge here is that the emphasis on the past directly results in failures to represent the present. Matt replies that the situation is worse than Nicholas imagines: '[T]he biggest problem with the predominance of historical fiction throughout the 1980s and 1990s (at least as far as reviews, prizes, and best-selling literary fiction) is that new, exciting voices have been marginalized. At the same time, readers have lost faith in literature.' Far from serving the revisionist aims of a lively, marginalized minority, feminist, or postcolonial subculture, historical fiction now squats in the camps of the literary establishment. Predictable, dull, and unfairly lauded by reviewers and prize committees, historical fiction even deprives readers of the faith they evidently once had in literature (to do what, Matt does not specify). When Nicholas answers, his attack on historical fiction completes Matt's turn in a theological direction: 'Current historical fiction seems to be written with the sole purpose of denying life. These novelists believe that literature belongs in a heritage theme park or, better, the grave. Anywhere but the here and now' (*All Hail* xv). It would be all too easy to dismiss these comments, or to dwell on their incoherent moments, but they represent a spirited attack from the first generation of twenty-first-century writers on the preoccupations of the contemporary period.

Will the vogue for romances of the archive continue into the next decades? It is difficult to imagine the wholesale disappearance of so prevalent and so successful a form. It will certainly live on in formula fiction: recently I heard that television's Inspector Morse has done Josephine Tey's bedridden detective, once again. Even if traditional historical fiction comes to seem stodgy and life-denying, as the New Puritans would have it, the romance of the archive always has one foot firmly located in the present, where most archival questers live and conduct their research. This leaves plenty of opportunity for examination of the present through contrasts or comparisons with paradigmatic pasts. Particular periods of the past will certainly begin to appear over-visited – the well-worn pathways through the Victorian period may for a time discourage serious writing, while the tourists and the film crews crowd the avenues. Yet periods and places scarcely touched will suggest new routes. The histories attached to these destinations in the past will themselves provoke new historiographical arguments and fresh revisions of traditional understandings. Possibly, extraordinary performances of historical pastiche, like Byatt's in *Possession*, may inhibit the choices of another generation of writers. It will become increasingly difficult to produce an entirely fresh archival romance, but the narrative possibilities of the new technologies have hardly been exhausted. (Jeanette Winterson's *Power Book* [2000] just begins the task of representing the possibilities of our on-line lives.)

But for every fictional world not created, another one comes into being instead. The current fad of 'reality' TV may seem to work against fiction and history altogether, but I can envision a writer saturated by *Survivor* and *Temptation Island* rediscovering the meddlesome 'what ifs' set in motion in Shakespeare's forests, or the moral experiments painstakingly imagined and observed by Iris Murdoch. As for history, it is too early to read the entrails. Generations of novelists have demonstrated that the historical period of 'thirty years back' exerts a magnetic attraction. Whether they conjure up recent history or a more deeply sedimented time, novelists will continue to find fresh uses of the past, and to create new versions of imagined archives in which material traces of actions and intentions collect. What quests are undertaken in tomorrow's archives, or what 'truths' fictive researchers recover, will depend on the certainties and the anxieties of times we have not yet lived.

Notes

1: Contemporary Fiction, Postimperial Conditions

1 On the 'documentarist' impulse in traditional history, see Dominick LaCapra, *History and Criticism* 18.

2 Throughout this study I employ 'history' and 'heritage' to mean different things, following the examples of Raphael Samuel, Robert Hewison, and David Lowenthal. See Samuel's *Theatres of Memory* (1994), Hewison's *The Heritage Industry: Britain in a Climate of Decline* (1987), and Lowenthal's *Possessed by the Past: The Heritage Crusade and the Spoils of History* (1996).

3 Andrzej Gasiorek's *Post-War British Fiction* (1995) is exceptional in its attention to the diversity of the British novel during a time of critical preoccupation with postmodernism.

4 Hutcheon defines this characteristically postmodern sub-genre and analyses key examples in *A Poetics of Postmodernism* (1988) and *The Politics of Postmodernism* (1989). See my discussion in chapter 2 for the contrasts between historiographic metafictions and more conventional (though generically diverse) romances of the archive. In her applications of Hutcheon's terminology, Amy Elias makes the point that historiographic metafictions themselves arise out of an array of sub-genres. See Elias's 'Defining Spatial History' and 'Meta-*mimesis*?' The best general introduction to postmodernism is Steven Connor, *Postmodernist Culture: An Introduction to Theories of the Contemporary*, 2nd ed. (1997).

5 Raymond Williams, *Marxism and Literature* 132–4. Fredric Jameson has influentially adopted Williams's terms for his study of postmodernism (*Cultural Turn* 43–4). As should become clear shortly, I do not use postmodernism as Jameson does, to define the whole contemporary culture and time within which dominant, emergent, and residual forms operate. (In

later formulations, Jameson suggests that postmodernism is merely the dominant with which the residual and emergent must contend [*Postmodernism* xix];
this revision of his original statements brings him closer to Brian McHale on
postmodernist fiction.)

6 For Diane Elam, 'postmodernism ... is the rethinking of history as an ironic
coexistence of temporalities'; the excesses and anachronisms of romance
make it postmodern 'all along.' *Romancing the Postmodern* (1992) 3.

7 Nathaniel Hawthorne, *The House of the Seven Gables* 1–2.

8 See David Leon Higdon, *Shadows of the Past in Contemporary British
Fiction* (1984); Steven Connor, *The English Novel in History, 1950 to the
Present* (1996); Margaret Scanlan, *Traces of Another Time: History and
Politics in Postwar British Fiction* (1990); and Frederick M. Holmes, *The
Historical Imagination: Postmodernism and the Treatment of the Past in
Contemporary British Fiction* (1997).

9 Here again I must distinguish my use of a term from Fredric Jameson's. For
Jameson, pastiche is 'the imitation of a peculiar or unique style,' but 'blank
parody, parody that has lost its sense of humour' (*Cultural Turn* 5). Jameson
laments the loss of the satirical intention of a motivated ridiculing of style
and suspects that the postmodern habit of pastiche supports its nostalgic
attitude towards the past. I use pastiche neutrally, preferring not to judge the
successes or failures of any narrative device *en masse*.

10 See, for instance, Jean-François Lyotard, *The Postmodern Condition* xxiv.

11 M.H. Abrams, 'Periods of English Literature,' in *A Glossary of Literary
Terms* 217.

12 F. Jameson, *Postmodernism, or, The Cultural Logic of Late Capitalism* (1991).

13 Linda Hutcheon, *Poetics of Postmodernism*; Brian McHale, *Postmodernist
Fiction* (1987). For a useful introduction to the history of the term 'post-
modernism,' see Groden and Kreiswirth, eds, *The Johns Hopkins Guide to
Literary Theory and Criticism* 585–7.

14 George Landow, ed., 'Contemporary Postcolonial and Postimperial Literature,' at <http://www.stg.brown.edu/projects/hypertext/landow/post/misc/
postov.html> (2 August 1999).

15 Not all accounts of the postcolonial limit it to the times of twentieth-century
decolonization; indeed, studies of the Victorian and modern periods have
also been enlivened by postcolonialists. Dennis Walder is typical in dating
postcolonial writing as 'primarily postwar' (*Post-Colonial Literatures in
English* 60).

16 It could be observed with some justice that 'British' fiction as I use it almost
always refers to texts by English authors. Under vigorous assault in the

contiguous fields of history and politics, the category of twentieth-century 'Britishness' still has meaning in literary circles, perhaps only as a designation meaning 'not American.' I do not intend it to include contemporary Irish writing. Scottish and Welsh writers make brief appearances.

17 I am indebted to Alan Sinfield's treatment of many of the topics mentioned in this paragraph. Sinfield usefully surveys the writing of the postwar period. See his *Literature, Politics, and Culture in Postwar Britain* (1989).

18 For two fictional treatments of the Suez crisis, see P.H. Newby's Booker Prize–winning *Something to Answer For* (1968) and Ian McEwan's screenplay for Richard Eyre's 1985 film, *Ploughman's Lunch*. The standard historical account is Keith Kyle's *Suez* (1991).

19 Greene's *The Honorary Consul* (1973); Anthony Powell's *A Dance to the Music of Time* (1951–75); Bowen's *Eva Trout* (1968), shortlisted for the 1970 Booker Prize.

20 The *Granta* lists of 1983 and 1993 have exaggerated the difference between the Rushdie/Amis/McEwan generation and a slightly younger 'new' group of young novelists.

21 For Booker Prize short lists, winners, judges, and commentary, see my Booker Prize website at <http://home.wlu.edu/~keens/booker.htm>.

22 The title of an influential and controversial 1989 study of postcolonial literature by Bill Ashcroft, Gareth Griffiths, and Helen Tiffin, the phrase 'the Empire writes back' originates with Salman Rushdie.

23 For an extended reading of the Thatcherite hero as cynical opportunist in *The Ploughman's Lunch*, see David Monaghan, *The Falklands War: Myth and Countermyth* 86–100.

24 See Alan Sinfield, *Literature, Politics, and Culture* 136–7, 139 and D.J. Taylor's response to Margaret Scanlan's 1990 *Traces of Another Time* in *After the War* (52–62).

25 Martin Green's works on the subject include *Dreams of Adventure and Deeds of Empire* (1979), *The Adventurous Male: Chapters in the History of the White Male Mind* (1993), and *The English Novel in the Twentieth Century: [The Doom of Empire]* (1984).

26 For a brief account of the Indian mutiny, see Lawrence James, *The Rise and Fall of the British Empire* 226–30.

2: Romances of the Archive: Identifying Characteristics

1 During the postwar period, American romances of the archive, such as Thomas Pynchon's *The Crying of Lot 49* (1966), James Hall Roberts's *The Q*

Document (1964), and Saul Bellows's 'The Gonzaga Manuscripts' (1954) emphasize the Cold War, conspiracy, and the atom bomb. The prototypical example is Walter M. Miller, Jr's *A Canticle for Leibowitz* (1960).

2 According to Martin Green, the self-regarding nerdiness of the literary establishment accounts in part for the critical neglect of adventure fiction (*Seven Types of Adventure* 1, 3).

3 See David Leon Higdon, *Shadows of the Past* (19–38) for a discussion of the conventions of retrospective fiction, focused on L.P. Hartley's *The Go-Between* (1953).

4 For recent American examples of this sub-genre, see Richard Russo, *Straight Man* (1997) and Jane Smiley, *Moo* (1995).

5 Anita Brookner proves an exception to the rule here. Her depiction of teaching in *Providence* (1982) is both sympathetic and recognizable. However, her researcher Kitty Maule performs no research in the pages of the novel; typically, Brookner's characters go to libraries and think about the novels that they are reading, prepare and deliver lectures, and teach. They do not undertake archival quests.

6 For a view of *Possession* as postmodern, see Frederick Holmes, 'The Historical Imagination and the Victorian Past' 319–24. Questioning *Possession's* postmodernism are Jackie Buxton, 'What's Love Got to Do with It' 212–17 and Ivana Djordjevic, 'In the Footsteps of Giambattista Vico' 46ff. I agree with the views articulated by Buxton and Djordjevic.

7 I employ terms for the representation of fictional consciousness as described by Dorrit Cohn in *Transparent Minds* (1978).

8 Thelma J. Shinn writes well about the blend of romance and realism in *Possession* in '"What's in a Word?" Possessing A.S. Byatt's Meronymic Novel,' esp. 164–75.

9 Louise Yelin's 'Cultural Cartography: A.S. Byatt's *Possession* and the Politics of Victorian Studies' represents an early reaction invigorated by a healthy scepticism about Byatt's picture of the discipline.

10 Jean-Louis Chevalier writes beautifully of *Possession* as a work fraught with conclusions, with six 'crowning' moments plus the epilogue: 'In *Possession* the art of resolution is glorious in all of its numerous meanings, including the dramatic sense of unravelling complications and reaching a final solution, the musical sense of making discord pass into concord, and the psychological sense of boldness and firmness of purpose' ('Conclusion in *Possession*' 126).

11 Anita Brookner, 'Eminent Victorians and Others,' *Spectator*, 3 Mar. 1990: 35.

12 Kermode comments, 'The taboo sacralizes closure; it suggests that to give away the solution that comes at the end is to give away all' ('Novel and Narrative' 180). See also Kermode's *The Sense of an Ending* (1966), still a standard work on narrative closure.

13 Altick's book used to put a little glamour and excitement into graduate courses on research methods, when those courses were still taught. It is hard to imagine that Byatt did not have passages of it in mind as she composed *Possession*.

14 Mark Samuels Lasner. Re: literary discoveries. VICTORIA listserv. <victoria@listserv.indiana.edu> (18 Sept. 1996).

15 Lesley Hall. Re: Acquisition of British Manuscripts. VICTORIA listserv. <victoria@listserv.indiana.edu> (23 June 1999).

16 A related variation is Nancy Armstrong's concept of the 'shadow archive,' which she conceives as a visual order of things (*Fiction* 19), 'composed of image-objects, neither image nor object, yet the ultimate source of meaning for both' (27).

17 See Roberto González Echevarría's *Myth and Archive: A Theory of Latin American Narrative* (1990) for a powerful extension of Foucault's archive into narrative theory.

18 Jackie Buxton persuasively employs Walter Benjamin to explore the views on history embedded in Julian Barnes's later novel, *The History of the World in 10½ Chapters*. Buxton argues that Barnes proffers an 'apocalyptic philosophy of history rooted in a vehement disavowal of the concept of historical progress' ('Julian Barnes's Theses' 58). Not a romance of the archive but an important historiographical narrative, *The History of the World* offers (among other things) a stowaway woodworm's corrective account of the Flood, countering 'an official history of self-congratulation with an history of accusation' ('Julian Barnes's Theses' 64). Denying historicism's cause and effect, continuity, and progress, Barnes's mixed account of doomed voyages instead emphasizes decline, ruin, and what Buxton characterizes as 'a parodic apprehension of redemption' (74). This scantily sketched dream of happiness advocates a 'belief in love and truth' that would provide a 'theoretical alternative to a despairing descent into postmodern historical relativity,' according to Buxton (85).

19 For a thorough reading of *Flaubert's Parrot*'s postmodernism, see James B. Scott's 'Parrots as Paradigms' (1990).

20 See, for example, Keith Windschuttle's entertaining diatribe in *The Killing of History: How a Discipline Is Being Murdered by Literary Critics and Social Theorists* (1994, rev. ed. 1996).

21 For a capable, if old-fashioned, survey of nineteenth- and early-twentieth-century novels with university settings, see Mortimer R. Proctor, *The English University Novel* (1957). Ian Carter's *Ancient Cultures of Conceit: British University Fiction in the Post-War Years* (1990) should be consulted for more recent authors, such as David Lodge.

22 For an account of a recent flap along these lines, see Matthew Sweet's article

on the acquisition of British manuscripts by American institutions, 'Goodbye to All These,' *Independent*, Sunday, 27 June 1999: Culture, 3.

23 Where *Possession* is celebratory, Graham Swift's *Waterland* (1983) reveals seamy family histories paralleling the rise and fall of the British Empire. *Waterland* is not an archival romance, but it is among the most important contemporary historiographic metafictions. Here the past bequeaths trauma, deceptions, and the consequences of incest to the present-day history teacher Tom Crick. Swift's vision coincides with a 'broadly tragic' view of history, which, as Frederick Holmes observes, is one of two contradictory attitudes available in British fiction – the other side of the coin is *Possession*'s nurturing, curative past (*Historical* 48–50). *Waterland*'s treatment of history and historiography has stimulated a great deal of critical commentary. Its intertextuality, denial of closure, and meditations on the uses and role of histories and History are all delivered by a manifestly unreliable narrator, who claims to have undertaken a great deal of archival research into family histories. The revelations afforded by the research include the incestuous relations between the narrator's mother and grandfather, the gothic reasons for the decline of the doomed brewing dynasty of the maternal line, and the family role in the natural history of the fens (drainage, siltage, murder, and abortion). The novel offers through its history teacher's grandstanding a critique of grand narratives, of linear histories, and of causal explanations, but it also shows the substitute, Crick's decentred, cyclical, and seemingly random storytelling, as an evasion of more straightforward narratives of cause and effect that would entail the admission of his guilt and culpability. See especially Ernst van Alphen, 'The Performativity of Histories: Graham Swift's *Waterland* as a Theory of History'; Pamela Cooper's 'Imperial Topographies: The Spaces of History in *Waterland*'; George Landow's 'History, His Story, and Stories in Graham Swift's *Waterland*'; John Schad's 'The End of the End of History: Graham Swift's *Waterland*'; and Richard Todd's 'Narrative Trickery and Performative Historiography.'

3: Wellsprings

1 In order of publication, these works include (but are not limited to) Julian Barnes, *Flaubert's Parrot* (1984), Robert Goddard, *Past Caring* (1986), Peter Ackroyd, *Chatterton* (1987), Nigel Williams, *Witchcraft* (1987), Barry Unsworth, *Sugar and Rum* (1988), Alan Hollinghurst, *The Swimming-Pool Library* (1988), A.S. Byatt, *Possession* (1989), Lindsay Clarke, *The Chymical Wedding* (1989), Lawrence Norfolk, *Lemprière's Dictionary* (1991), Margaret Drabble, *The Gates of Ivory* (1991), Robert Harris, *Fatherland* (1992) (fol-

lowed by *Enigma* [1995] and *Archangel* [1998]), Adam Mars-Jones, *The Waters of Thirst* (1993), Bharati Mukherjee, *The Holder of the World* (1993), P.D. James, *Original Sin* (1994), Margaret Drabble, *The Witch of Exmoor* (1996), Alan Wall, *Bless the Thief* (1997), Peter Dickinson, *Some Deaths before Dying* (1999), and Vikram Seth, *An Equal Music* (1999).

2 Separate cultural, historical, and literary contexts would have to be studied in order to account for the popularity of recent romances of the archive in other national traditions. This study does not attempt that task, though the 'wellsprings' described in this chapter would certainly be relevant to contemporary American writers.

3 See 'Canon Alberic's Scrapbook' (9–23), 'Number 13' (*Ghost* 69–87), 'Count Magnus' (89–105), and 'The Treasure of Abbot Thomas' (131–53).

4 For representatives of these alternative views, see Mary Poovey, 'Ideology and *The Mysteries of Udolpho*,' *Criticism* 21 (1979): 307–30, and Patrick Brantlinger on 'imperial gothic' in *Rule of Darkness: British Literature and Imperialism, 1830–1914* (1988), 227–53.

5 Homosocial relations between men include bonds of feeling and desire not exclusively sexual in nature. See Eve Kosovsky Sedgewick, *Between Men*.

6 E.M. Forster, *Aspects of the Novel* 78.

7 Though thieves have pillaged the archive for issues with stories by famous writers, the Library of Congress's pulp-fiction collection remains a rich resource; that is, until it flakes away, for the pulps (as their name suggests) were printed on highly acidic and fugitive paper stock.

8 This is not to suggest that thrillers originate in the cold war period. As Michael Holquist observes, the 'pattern of spy thrillers changes quite markedly after Hiroshima. Instead of the elegant, patriotic heroes of E. Phillips Oppenheim ... we now have amoral supermen who save the entire planet from atomic destruction – the suggestion being that while the world may be full of mad scientists and bumbling statesmen, a lone hero can still keep us all from being blown up' ('Whodunit' 153).

9 Both sorts appear, revised and updated to rich comic effect, in Tom Stoppard's drama *Arcadia* (1993), a critically acclaimed play that brings the contemporary vogue for the romance of the archive to the stage. In dramatizing research, Stoppard takes on one of the basic problems of a story that depends primarily on events such as learning, discovering, and interpreting. Using intellectual conversation and the juxtaposition of past and present times, Stoppard manages to make a play about research into a suspenseful and poignant experience.

10 *Postmodernist* 9. In contrast, 'ontological fictions' such as fantasy, gothic horror, and postmodernist novels ask instead questions about worlds and

states of being (10). McHale acknowledges that the two modes may be blended in a single work, but he argues that earlier twentieth-century modernist fiction tends to be epistemological, while later twentieth-century postmodernist fiction can be recognized by its tilt towards ontological moves of self-conscious world-making.

11 *The Name of the Rose* (1986), directed by Jean-Jacques Annaud, garnered honours from the British Academy of Film and Television Arts.

12 Eco ruminates on the generic-historical compulsion he felt to burn the Aedificium at the end: '[I]n the Middle Ages, cathedrals and convents burned like tinder; imagining a medieval story without a fire is like imagining a World War II movie in the Pacific without a fighter plane shot down in flames' ('Postscript' 515).

13 On Eco's allusions to Borges, see Joel Black, '(De)feats of Detection: The Spurious Key Text from Poe to Eco' 84–6. On Borges's 'Tlön, Uqbar, Orbis Tertius' as the *ur*-archival fiction in the Latin American tradition, see Roberto González Echevarría, *Myth and Archive* 161–5, 172–86.

14 Byatt told interviewer Eleanor Wachtel that she originally conceived the idea for *Possession* in 1972, but that she didn't come to write the novel until after leaving university teaching in 1984. Byatt remarks, 'I think one should acknowledge one's debts: I was inspired by Umberto Eco's *The Name of the Rose*. I saw that one could be at once both very serious and quite funny, and write a detective story into the bargain' (Wachtel *Writers and Company* 80). Byatt does not mention Penelope Lively's *According to Mark* (1984), but the closeness of some of the passages to Lively's novel suggests a more than incidental influence. Although it is considerably less well known than *Possession* now, in 1984 *According to Mark* made the Booker Prize short list.

15 A good account of these phenomena can be found in Richard Todd, *Consuming Fictions* (1996).

16 Nigel Jones, 'Oh Yes, This Man Is Most Definitely John Major's Favourite Author,' *Guardian*, 9 Dec. 1996: T10.

4: History or Heritage?

1 Carl Becker, *Everyman His Own Historian* (1935) 253. The essay was first presented as a presidential address to the American Historical Association, 29 December 1931.

2 The term is Robert Hewison's. He glosses it as a new force made up of cultural insitutions absorbing considerable public and private resources and replacing real industry in Great Britain (*Heritage Industry* 9).

3 *The Road to Lichfield* is Lively's first novel written for adults; many of the themes she rehearses here she revisits in greater depth in the Booker short-

listed novel *According to Mark* (1984) and in her Booker Prize–winning novel, *Moon Tiger* (1987). *According to Mark*, a full-scale romance of the archive featuring a literary biographer, is treated in chapter 1. In *Moon Tiger*, the memories of a dying historian reveal her life story as she fantasizes writing a history of the world. Although she recalls her adventures as a war correspondent, no research takes place. The conclusive document – her dead lover's diary – revealed at the end of the novel arrives not as a result of searching in archives, but by accident.

4 For the case against this perceived decline, see Peter Clarke, *Hope and Glory: Britain 1900–1990* (1996).

5 Throughout this discussion I draw on David Lowenthal's books, *The Past Is a Foreign Country* (1985) and *Possessed by the Past: The Heritage Crusade and the Spoils of History* (1996), and on Robert Hewison's *The Heritage Industry: Britain in a Climate of Decline* (1987) and *Culture and Consensus: England, Art and Politics since 1940* (1995). For a hearty defence of heritage from the left, see Raphael Samuel's enjoyable volumes, *Theatres of Memory*, Volume 1: *Past and Present in Contemporary Culture* (1994) and Volume 2: *Island Stories: Unravelling Britain* (1998).

6 On the varieties of New History, see Ignacio Olábarri, '"New" New History: A *Longue Durée* Structure' 2, 4–8.

7 On the influence of Piaget's ideas and the aims of New History, see Vivienne Little, 'A National Curriculum in History' (1990) 320–2.

8 See Raphael Samuel, 'History's Battle for a New Past,' originally published in the *Guardian* (21 January 1989), in *Island Stories* (197–202).

9 DES and Welsh Office, *National Curriculum History Working Group Final Report* (1990).

10 VTC Conferencing: <http://vtc.ngfl.gov.uk/vtc/meeting/meeting.html> 17 Nov. 1999.

11 The revised National Curriculum for History: <http://www.dfee.gov.uk/nc/hisindex.html>. 17 Nov. 1999. Scotland and Wales have their own curricula.

12 Real teaching is of course not necessarily limited to the topics listed in the National Curriculum History. The resourceful responses of teachers to the interests and gaps of the National Curriculum can be inferred from the wide array of materials and topics available on the excellent internet resource, the Spartacus Educational web site for teaching history online. <http://www.spartacus.schoolnet.co.uk/welcome.html> (accessed 18 Dec. 2000).

13 J.H. Plumb is a notable exception. See *The Making of an Historian: The Collected Essays of J.H. Plumb* (1988) 155–7.

14 See Robert Phillips, 'National Curriculum History and Teacher Autonomy' (1991).

15 See, e.g., David Kerr, 'History and Economic Awareness in the National

Curriculum' (1990) and Philip Rubenstein and Warren Taylor, 'Teaching about the Holocaust in the National Curriculum' (1992).

16 A.N. Wilson, 'The Spaniards Couldn't Sink Drake ... but 399 Years Later the British Are Arranging to Do It for Them,' *Daily Mail*, 18 Sept. 1987; quoted in Crawford, 'History of the Right' 441.

17 J. Keegan, 'History Meets Its Waterloo When Lunacy Is in Command,' *Daily Telegraph*, 5 May 1994; quoted in Crawford, 'History of the Right' 443.

18 Unsworth shared the prize with Michael Ondaatje, whose novel *The English Patient* (1992) was a co-winner with *Sacred Hunger*.

19 Robert Winder, 'Unsworth before and after Hannibal' 3.

20 Amy Gamerman, 'Fiction's Time Traveler Goes Medieval' A16.

21 Dina Rabinovitch and Anthony Quinn, 'The Booker: Two for the Price of One' 17.

22 Between 1938 and 1945, like the American USO, ENSA (Entertainments National Service Association) produced entertainments such as variety shows and concerts, mainly for troops.

23 British readers will recognize Unsworth's version of the July 1981 rioting in Toxteth, Liverpool.

24 See Hewison, *Culture and Consensus* 61.

25 Small correspondences underline the parallels between these novels. Like Miss Kenton, Lily Butler also brings flowers to brighten up the bachelor's digs (133–5). A dead father still oppresses the narrator; like Ishiguro, Unsworth narrates the deathbed encounter between son and father (166–70).

26 'Interview: A Conversation with Barry Unsworth,' <*boldtype*>, 22 Dec. 1999. <http://www.randomhouse.com/boldtype/1099/unsworth/interview.html>.

27 Peter Ackroyd's work diaries 1981–92, box 7, Uncat. Ms. Vault 706.

28 For Eliot materials in the Peter Ackroyd papers, see boxes 3 and 12, Uncat. Ms. Vault 706 and boxes 6 and 7, Uncat. Ms. Vault 789.

29 Letter, Julian Symons to Peter Ackroyd, 5 Jan. 1984, box 3, Uncat. Ms. Vault 706.

30 Letter, Dannie to Peter Ackroyd, 4 Oct. 1985, box 2, Uncat. Ms. Vault 706.

31 Letter, Colin and O-Lan Style to Peter Ackroyd, 13 July 1992, box 16, Uncat. Ms. Vault 706.

32 Photocopy of map of London with Ackroyd's marking, box 16, Uncat. Ms. Vault 706. See also John Clute, 'Conjurors of Clerkenwell' 39.

33 Claude Rawson, Review of *First Light*, *TLS* 4491 (28 April–4 May 1989): 453.

34 Two notebooks with Wilde witticisms in quotation marks; Ackroyd's imitations in quotation marks: box 18, Uncat. Ms. Vault 706.

35 Typed interview with unknown interlocuter, box 7, Uncat. Ms. Vault 706.

36 Typed interview, box 7, Uncat. Ms. Vault 706, 3–4.

37 Here I am in agreement with Susana Onega, who writes that Ackroyd's 'attempt to recuperate the (unreal and fictional) texts of the past' becomes in his novels 'a way of conferring meaning on the present and of achieving self-identity' (*Peter Ackroyd* 23). I differ from her in reading this strategy as romantic, rather than characteristically postmodern.

38 See Susana Onega, 'British Historiographic Metafiction' 208. Onega employs the term invented by Linda Hutcheon; see also Frederick Holmes, *Historical Imagination* 55ff.

39 For a useful discussion of presentism and related historiographical issues in postmodern fiction, see Frederick Holmes *Historical* 54–5, 74–86.

40 Ackroyd's mother's reminiscences, box 17, Uncat. Ms. Vault 706, unnumbered pages 5–6.

41 His recent book *London: The Biography* (2000) explores these in detail.

42 Ackroyd gives a version of this insight to his narrator Matthew Palmer in *The House of Doctor Dee* 39.

43 Letter from Patrick Cormack to Peter Ackroyd, 28 May 1988, box 3, Uncat. Ms. Vault 706. Letter from Peter Ackroyd to the author, 9 Nov. 1999.

44 *Albion* filmscript, 21: box 1, Uncat. Ms. Vault 789.

45 1994 lecture typescript, 17–18: box 8, Uncat. Ms. Vault 789.

5: Time Magic and the Counterfactual Imagination

1 Jules Michelet, 'Prefatory Note,' *History of France*. To Michelet the archive was a catacomb or necropolis of lives.

2 See Valerie Krips's superb study, *The Presence of the Past: Memory, Heritage, and Childhood in Postwar Britain* (2000). Her chapter 'The Memory of Objects' is especially fine.

3 For a treatment of H.P. Lovecraft's Cthulhu, see chapter 3, 'Wellsprings.'

4 For a detailed reading of Norfolk's response to Pynchon, see Amy J. Elias, 'The Pynchon Intertext of *Lemprière's Dictionary*' (1997). Elias relies on the American edition of the novel.

5 Steven Poole, 'The Horn of Plenty,' *Guardian*, 26 April 1996: 17.

6 *The Chymical Wedding* did not find a taker in Hollywood. John Boorman, 'Bright Dreams, Hard Knocks' 14.

7 See Colin Manlove, *The Fantasy Literature of England*, for a good discussion of the differences between English and Scottish fantasy.

8 This is in fact the view of some influential theorists of fictional worlds (Thomas Pavel, Nelson Goodman). For my present purposes, the counterfactuality of fantasy and related ontological genres must be distinguished

from the difference between narrative history and narrative fiction. For an influential account of the evolution of the distinction between history and fiction, see Michael McKeon, *The Origins of the English Novel 1600–1740* (1987); on the effects of narrativity in historical writing, Hayden White is the most prominent guide.

9 See John Robison, 'Proofs of a Conspiracy Against All the Religions and Governments of Europe, carried on in the Secret Meetings of Free Masons, Illuminati, and Reading Societies' (1797), excerpted in David Brion Davis, ed. *The Fear of Conspiracy* 37–42.

10 Steven Poole, 'The Horn of Plenty' T17.

11 Richard Hofstadter notes in *The Paranoid Style in American Politics* that the response to a putative conspiracy often takes the form (at least rhetorically) of an all-out crusade to defend the universe against annihilation (29–30).

12 See, e.g., Marita Sturken, 'Reenactment, Fantasy, and the Paranoia of History: Oliver Stone's Docudramas,' *History and Theory* 36.4 (1997): 64–79; William D. Romanowski, 'Oliver Stone's *JFK*: Commercial Filmmaking, Cultural History, and Conflict,' *Journal of Popular Film and Television* 21.2 (1993): 63–71; Roy M. Anker, 'The Kingdom of Wish: Oliver Stone's Problem with History,' *Fides et Historia* 25.2 (1993): 89–118; and Richard Grenier, 'On the Trail of America's Paranoid Class: Oliver Stone's *JFK*,' *National Interest* 27 (1992): 76–84.

13 See Edward Shils, *The Torment of Secrecy*, for a good discussion of the differences between American and British attitudes towards secrecy (36–57).

14 David Streitfeld, 'Book Report' *Washington Post Book World*, 20 Sept. 1992: 15.

6: Custody of the Truth

1 See Peter Brooks, *Reading for the Plot* 23; on narrative form see, e.g., Umberto Eco, 'Narrative Structures in Fleming' 144–72 and Susan Elizabeth Sweeney, 'Locked Rooms: Detective Fiction, Narrative Theory, and Self-Reflexivity' 1–14. Both of Heta Pyrhönen's books, *Mayhem and Murder: Narrative and Moral Problems in the Detective Story* (1999) and the survey of criticism *Murder from an Academic Angle* (1994), are indispensable guides for the student of detective fiction.

2 See also Marjorie Nicolson, 'The Professor and the Detective' (1946).

3 For treatments of scientific inquiry as a model for detection, see Umberto Eco and Thomas Sebeok, eds, *The Sign of Three: Dupin, Holmes, Peirce* (1983).

4 By far the most subtle investigation of the morality and ethics of detective fiction is Heta Pyrhönen's *Mayhem and Murder* (1999).

5 Peverell Press bears little resemblance to P.D. James's own publishers, Faber and Faber (est. 1925), who have Georgian offices in Bloomsbury at 24 Russell Square. Nonetheless, readers familiar with Faber's list will notice the fun that James has characterizing the rivalries of poetry, popular mysteries, and 'Booker short-list' fiction in *Original Sin*.

6 For a classic description of the detective genre as a substitute for religion, see W.H. Auden, 'The Guilty Vicarage.' Auden writes, 'I suspect that the typical reader of detective stories is, like myself, a person who suffers from a sense of sin ... To have a sense of sin means to feel guilty at there being an ethical choice to make, a guilt which, however "good" I may become, remains unchanged' (*The Dyer's Hand* 157). Heta Pyhrönen surveys moral interpretations of detective fiction in *Murder from an Academic Angle* 53–64.

7 Harris's *Enigma* (1995) celebrates the work of the British code-breakers who figured out the German Enigma machines. Tom Stoppard authored the screenplay.

8 Raul Hilberg complains of discovering, in a glitzy best-seller, an 'amalgam of history and fantasy,' 'more than a whole page containing [his] translation of a German document that the author ... had lifted from a document book I had compiled' (*Politics of Memory* 139). I speculate that Hilberg had spotted Harris's *Fatherland*. Novels do not usually contain footnotes, and it is unfair of Hilberg to suggest that a reader would not be able to tell the difference between the real document and the invented documents of Harris's counterfactual novel.

9 For example, the overt postmodernism of the historical thinking and the form of Graham Swift's 1983 novel *Waterland* makes the interpretation of this acclaimed historiographic metafiction a matter of vigorous debate among critics. I do not discuss *Waterland* in detail because its protagonist/narrator Tom Crick does no research in the novel, reporting only the existence of his grandfather's notebooks, and referring to his work in old newspapers and other archival materials just in passing.

10 Paul Mansfield, 'Interview: Passage to Cambodia,' *Independent*, 4 Oct. 1991: Arts, 15.

7: Envisioning the Past

1 'This Be the Verse,' *Collected Poems* 180.

2 See Barthes's *Camera Lucida: Reflections on Photography* (1981) and his essay 'The Reality Effect' in *The Rustle of Language* (1986) 141–8.

3 A.S. Byatt's *The Biographer's Tale* (2000) makes an interesting exception to this rule of thumb, which is not so surprising in a theoretically knowing text that invokes Barthes explicitly.

4 For more of a cultural historian's thinking on photographs, see Samuel's *Theatres of Memory*, vol. 1, 'The Discovery of Old Photographs' 337–49, 'Dreamscapes' 350–63, and 'Scopophilia' 364–77.

5 The fact that Lloyd George does not come through with full female suffrage Goddard explains away as a broken campaign promise, and he does not explore the problem of Pankhurst's failure to pressure George for reneging on the deal.

6 For a recent influential example of a historian treating archival materials as deliberately shaped stories, see Natalie Zemon Davis's account of pardon narratives. As vehicles of fact, these documents must be treated with finely adjusted scepticism; Davis is concerned with the pre-existing structures that influence the form of the telling, 'possible story lines determined by the constraints of the law and approaches to narrative learned in past listening to and telling of stories or derived from other cultural constructions' (*Fiction in the Archive* [1987] 4).

7 See the new edition of *The Oxford Companion to English Literature* (2000), ed. Margaret Drabble, which draws on Davies's expertise in its new inclusion of seventeenth-century women (Drabble, 'A Woman's Place Is in the Reference Books' 5); see also the Brown University Women Writer's Project at <http://www.wwp.brown.edu/wwp_home.html> (accessed 15 May 2000).

8 Stevie Davies acknowledges her reliance upon John Prag and Richard Neave's volume, *Making Faces: Using Forensic and Archaeological Evidence* (1997). On the Manchester protocol, see 21ff.; for the pages on actual forensic cases, with reconstructions compared to photographs, 34–9.

9 Margaret Drabble explores maternal heritage in a novel that begins with scientists mapping the genes in a contemporary village to match a prehistoric ancestor. See *The Peppered Moth* (2001).

Epilogue: Postcolonial Rejoinders

1 After Rushdie's success, print runs, advances, and sales of serious literary fiction all increased. Publishers became more receptive to postcolonial writers, but English novelists such as Martin Amis also benefited. I rely here on Karen McGuinness's unpublished senior essay on Salman Rushdie and the revitalization of the market for literary fiction in Britain (written under my direction at Yale University, 1994).

2 For the short lists, judges, chairs, winners, and commentary, see my Booker Prize website at <http://home.wlu.edu/~keens/booker.htm>.

3 See my analysis and commentary at <http://home.wlu.edu/~keens/commentary.htm>.

4 This term comes from two influential issues of the literary magazine *Granta*. See *Granta* 7 (1983) for the novelists singled out by Bill Buford, and 43 (1993) for those chosen by a committee chaired by Salman Rushdie.

5 For a historical account emphasizing multiple cultural, ethnic, and linguistic identities, see Norman Davies, *The Isles: A History* (1999); among the many literary historians rewriting the story of English literature, Robert Crawford stands out. See his *Devolving English Literature* (1992) and his edited volume, *The Scottish Invention of English Literature* (1998).

6 As Robert D. Hamner observes, Walcott also suggests that Maud and Plunkett are versions of his own father and mother. The poet also acknowledges a parallel between Plunkett's use of Helen and Walcott's own intentions in adapting local materials to his literary ends (*Epic* 143–6).

Bibliography

Abrams, M.H. *A Glossary of Literary Terms.* 7th ed. Fort Worth: Harcourt Brace College Publishers, 1999.

Ackroyd, Peter. *Blake.* London: Sinclair-Stevenson, 1995.

– *Chatterton.* London: Hamish Hamilton, 1987.

– *Dickens.* London: Sinclair-Stevenson, 1990.

– *Diversions of Purley.* London: Abacus, 1987.

– *English Music.* London: Hamish Hamilton, 1992.

– *First Light.* London: Hamish Hamilton, 1989.

– *The Great Fire of London.* London: Hamish Hamilton, 1982.

– *Hawksmoor.* London: Hamish Hamilton, 1985.

– *The House of Doctor Dee.* London: Hamish Hamilton, 1993.

– *The Last Testament of Oscar Wilde.* London: Hamish Hamilton, 1983.

– *London: The Biography.* London: Chatto and Windus, 2000.

– *Notes for a New Culture: An Essay on Modernism.* London: Vision, 1976.

– Peter Ackroyd Papers. Uncat. Ms. Vault 706 and Uncat. Ms. Vault 789. Beinecke Library, Yale University, New Haven, CT.

– 'The Same Old Haunts.' *Independent* 20 July 1994: 7.

– *T.S. Eliot.* London: Hamish Hamilton, 1984.

Ahmad, Aijaz. *In Theory: Nations, Classes, Literatures.* London: Verso, 1992.

Alexander, Marguerite. *Flights from Realism: Themes and Strategies in Postmodernist British and American Fiction.* London: Edward Arnold, 1990.

Alphen, Ernest van. 'The Performativity of Histories: Graham Swift's *Waterland* as a Theory of History.' *The Point of Theory: Practices of Cultural Analysis.* Ed. Mieke Bal and Inge E. Boer. New York: Continuum, 1994. 202–10.

Altick, Richard D. *The Scholar Adventurers.* New York: Macmillan, 1950.

Ambler, Eric. *The Schirmer Inheritance.* New York: Knopf, 1953.

Amis, Kingsley. *The Green Man.* London: Jonathan Cape, 1969.

– *Lucky Jim.* London: Victor Gollancz, 1953.

Amis, Martin. *London Fields.* London: Jonathan Cape, 1989.

Anderson, Benedict. *Imagined Communities: Reflections on the Origin and Spread of Nationalism.* Rev. ed. London: Verso, 1991.

Anderson, Linda. 'The Re-Imagining of History in Contemporary Women's Fiction.' *Plotting Change.* Ed. Linda Anderson. London: Arnold, 1990. 129–41.

Anderson, Perry. *English Questions.* London: Verso, 1992.

Anker, Roy M. 'The Kingdom of Wish: Oliver Stone's Problem with History.' *Fides et Historia* 25.2 (1993): 89–118.

Appleby, Joyce, Lynn Hunt, and Margaret Jacob. *Telling the Truth about History.* New York: W.W. Norton, 1994.

Armstrong, Nancy. *Fiction in the Age of Photography: The Legacy of British Realism.* Cambridge, MA: Harvard UP, 1999.

Ashcroft, Bill, Gareth Griffiths, and Helen Tiffin, ed. *The Empire Writes Back: Theory and Practice in Post-Colonial Literatures.* New York: Routledge, 1989.

– *The Post-Colonial Studies Reader.* London: Routledge, 1995.

Auden, W.H. 'The Guilty Vicarage.' *The Dyer's Hand* (1948). Rpt. New York: Random House, 1962. 146–58.

Ball, Michael, Fred Gray, and Linda McDowell. *The Transformation of Britain: Contemporary Social and Economic Change.* London: Fontana, 1989.

Banta, Martha. 'Editor's Column: Mental Work, Metal Work.' *PMLA* 113.2 (March 1998): 199–211.

Banville, John. *The Newton Letter: An Interlude.* London: Secker and Warburg, 1982.

Barker, Pat. *The Eye in the Door.* London and New York: Viking Penguin, 1993.

– *The Ghost Road.* London: Viking, 1995.

– *Regeneration.* London and New York: Viking Penguin, 1991.

Barnes, Julian. *England, England.* London: Jonathan Cape, 1998.

– *Flaubert's Parrot.* London: Jonathan Cape, 1984.

– *A History of the World in 10½ Chapters.* London: Jonathan Cape, 1989.

Barnhardt, Wilton. *Gospel.* New York: St Martin's P, 1993.

Barthes, Roland. *Camera Lucida: Reflections on Photography.* 1980. Trans. Richard Howard. New York: Hill and Wang, 1981.

– *The Rustle of Language.* 1984. Trans. Richard Howard. New York: Hill and Wang, 1986.

Barzun, Jacques, and Henry F. Graff. *The Modern Researcher.* 3rd ed. New York: Harcourt, Brace, and Co., 1977.

Bass, Randy. 'Story and Archive in the Twenty-First Century.' Symposium: English 1999. *College English* 61.6 (July 1999): 659–70.

Becker, Carl. *Detachment and the Writing of History: Essays and Letters of Carl L. Becker.* Ed. Phil L. Snyder. Ithaca: Cornell UP, 1958.

– *Everyman His Own Historian: Essays on History and Politics.* New York: F.S. Crofts, 1935.

Beer, Gillian. *Arguing with the Past: Essays in Narrative from Woolf to Sidney.* London: Routledge, 1989.

Bellow, Saul. 'The Gonzaga Manuscripts.' 1954. *Mosby's Memoirs and Other Stories.* New York: Viking, 1968. 111–42.

Benjamin, Walter. 'Theses on the Philosophy of History.' *Illuminations* (1968). Trans. Harry Zohn. New York: Schocken, 1969. 253–64.

Bergonzi, Bernard. 'Fictions of History.' *The Contemporary English Novel.* Ed. Malcolm Bradbury and David Palmer. London: Edward Arnold, 1979. 42–65.

Berube, Michael. 'Teaching Postmodern Fiction without Being Sure That the Genre Exists.' *Chronicle of Higher Education* 19 May 2000: B4–5.

Bhabha, Homi K. *The Location of Culture.* London: Routledge, 1994.

Bhabha, Homi, K. ed. *Nation and Narration.* New York: Routledge, 1990.

Black, Joel. '(De)feats of Detection: The Spurious Key Text from Poe to Eco.' *Detecting Texts: The Metaphysical Detective Story from Poe to Postmodernism.* Ed. Patricia Merivale and Susan Elizabeth Sweeney. Philadelphia: U of Pennsylvania P, 1999. 75–98.

Blincoe, Nicholas, and Matt Thorne, ed. *All Hail the New Puritans.* London: Fourth Estate, 2000.

Bloch, Marc. *The Historian's Craft.* Trans. Peter Putnam. New York: Alfred A. Knopf, 1953.

Boorman, John. 'Bright Dreams, Hard Knocks.' *Independent* 5 Apr. 1992: 14.

Borges, Jorge Luis. *Labyrinths: Selected Stories and Other Writings.* 1962. Ed. Donald A. Yates and James E. Irby. New York: New Directions, 1964.

Boston, Lucy M. *The Children of Green Knowe.* New York: Harcourt, Brace & Co., 1954.

– *The River at Greene Knowe.* New York: Harcourt, Brace & Co., 1959.

Bowen, Roger. 'Investing in Conrad, Investing in the Orient: Margaret Drabble's *The Gates of Ivory.*' *Twentieth-Century Literature* 45.3 (Fall 1999): 278–98.

Bradbury, Malcolm. *The History Man.* London: Secker and Warburg, 1975.

– *Rates of Exchange.* London: Secker and Warburg, 1983.

Brantlinger, Patrick. *Rule of Darkness: British Literature and Imperialism, 1830–1914.* Ithaca: Cornell UP, 1988.

Breisach, Ernst. *Historiography: Ancient, Medieval, and Modern.* 2nd ed. Chicago and London: U of Chicago P, 1994.

Brisbane, Mark, and John Wood. *A Future for Our Past? An Introduction to Heritage Studies.* n.p.: English Heritage, 1996.

Bronfen, Elisabeth. 'Romancing Difference, Courting Coherence: A.S. Byatt's *Possession* as Postmodern Moral Fiction.' *Why Literature Matters: Theories and Functions of Literature*. Ed. Rüdiger Ahrens and Laurenz Volkmann. Anglistische Forschungen 241. Heidelberg: Universitätsverlag, 1996, 117–34.

Brookner, Anita. 'Eminent Victorians and Others.' Rev. of *Possession*, by A.S. Byatt. *Spectator*, 3 Mar. 1990: 35.

– *Providence*. London: Jonathan Cape, 1982.

– *A Start in Life*. London: Jonathan Cape, 1981.

Brooks, Peter. *Reading for the Plot: Design and Intention in Narrative*. New York: Alfred A. Knopf, 1984.

Bryant, Marsha, ed. *Photo-Textualities: Reading Photographs and Literature*. Newark: U of Delaware P; London: Associated UP, 1996.

Burgess, Anthony. *99 Novels: The Best in English since 1939: A Personal Choice*. New York: Summit Books, 1984.

Burt, E.S., and Janie Vanpée. 'Editors' Preface.' *Reading the Archive: On Texts and Institutions*. Ed. E.S. Burt and Janie Vanpée. *Yale French Studies* 77 (1990): 1–4.

Bush, Julia. 'Moving On – and Looking Back.' *History Workshop Journal* 36 (1993): 183–94.

Butterfield, Herbert. *The Whig Interpretation of History*. London: G. Bell and Sons, 1931.

Buxton, Jackie. 'Julian Barnes's Theses on History (in 10½ Chapters).' *Contemporary Literature* 41.1 (Spring 2000): 56–86.

– 'What's Love Got to Do with It? Postmodernism and *Possession*.' *English Studies in Canada* 22 (1996): 199–219.

Byatt, A.S. *Angels and Insects*. London: Chatto and Windus, 1992.

– *The Biographer's Tale*. London: Chatto and Windus, 2000.

– *On Histories and Stories: Selected Essays*. London: Chatto and Windus, 2000.

– *Possession: A Romance*. London: Chatto and Windus, 1989.

– *Still Life*. London: Hogarth P, 1985.

– *The Virgin in the Garden*. London: Chatto and Windus, 1978.

Carter, Ian. *Ancient Cultures of Conceit: British University Fiction in the Post-War Years*. London: Routledge, 1990.

Cawelti, John G. *Adventure, Mystery, and Romance: Formula Stories as Art and Popular Culture*. Chicago: U of Chicago P, 1976.

Chatman, Seymour. *Story and Discourse: Narrative Structure in Fiction and Film*. Ithaca: Cornell UP, 1990.

Chevalier, Jean-Louis. 'Conclusion in *Possession* by Antonia Byatt.' *Fins de Romans: Aspects de la conclusion dans la littérature anglaise*. Caen: UP de Caen, 1993. 109–31.

Clarke, Lindsay. *The Chymical Wedding.* London: Jonathan Cape, 1989.

Clarke, Peter. *Hope and Glory: Britain 1900–1990.* London: Penguin, 1996.

Clute, John. 'Conjurors of Clerkenwell.' Rev. of Peter Ackroyd, *The House of Doctor Dee. New Statesman and Society* (1992): 39.

Cohn, Dorrit. *Transparent Minds: The Representation of Fictional Consciousness.* Princeton UP, 1978.

Collini, Stefan. *English Pasts: Essays in History and Culture.* Oxford: Oxford UP, 1999.

Collins, Wilkie. *The Moonstone.* London: Tinsley Brothers, 1868.

Connor, Steven. *The English Novel in History, 1950 to the Present.* London: Routledge, 1996.

– *Postmodernist Culture: An Introduction to Theories of the Contemporary,* 2nd ed. Oxford: Blackwell, 1997.

– 'Rewriting Wrong: On the Ethics of Literary Reversion.' *Liminal Postmodernisms.* Ed. Theo D'haen and Hans Bertens. Amsterdam and Atlanta: Rodopi, 1994. 79–97.

– *Theory and Cultural Value.* Oxford: Basil Blackwell, 1992.

Cooley, Martha. *The Archivist.* Boston: Little Brown, 1998.

Cooper, Pamela. 'Imperial Topographies: The Spaces of History in *Waterland.*' *Modern Fiction Studies* 42.2 (1996): 371–96.

Cormack, Patrick. *Heritage in Danger.* London: New English Library, 1976.

Cowart, David. *History and the Contemporary Novel.* Carbondale: U of Southern Illinois P, 1989.

Cox, Michael, and Jack Adrian, editors. *The Oxford Book of Historical Stories.* Oxford: Oxford UP, 1994.

Crawford, Keith. 'A History of the Right: The Battle for Control of National Curriculum History 1989–1994.' *British Journal of Educational Studies* 43.4 (December 1995): 433–56.

Crawford, Robert. *Devolving English Literature.* Oxford: Clarendon P, 1992.

Crawford, Robert, ed. *The Scottish Invention of English Literature.* Cambridge: Cambridge UP, 1998.

Crowley, John. *Ægypt.* New York: Bantam, 1987.

– *Love and Sleep.* New York: Bantam, 1994.

Darwin, John. *Britain and Decolonisation: The Retreat from Empire in the Postwar World.* Basingstoke: Macmillan, 1988.

– *The End of the British Empire: The Historical Debate.* Oxford: Blackwell, 1991.

Davies, Alistair, and Alan Sinfield. Ed. *British Culture of the Postwar: An Introduction to Literature and Society 1945–1999.* London: Routledge, 2000.

Davies, Norman. *The Isles: A History.* Oxford: Oxford UP, 1999.

Davies, Stevie. *Four Dreamers and Emily*. London: Women's P, 1996.
- *Impassioned Clay*. London: Women's P, 1999.
- *Unbridled Spirits: Women of the English Revolution, 1640–1660*. London: Women's P, 1998.
Davis, David Brion, ed. *The Fear of Conspiracy: Images of Un-American Subversion from the Revolution to the Present*. Ithaca and London: Cornell UP, 1971.
Davis, Fred. *Yearning for Yesterday: A Sociology of Nostalgia*. London and New York: Free P, 1979.
Davis, Natalie Zemon. *Fiction in the Archives: Pardon Tales and Their Tellers in Sixteenth-Century France*. Stanford: Stanford UP, 1987.
Deane, Seamus. 'Imperialism/Nationalism.' *Critical Terms for Literary Study*. 2nd ed. Ed. Frank Lentricchia and Thomas McLaughlin. Chicago: U of Chicago P, 1995. 354–68.
Derrida, Jacques. *Archive Fever: A Freudian Impression*. 1995. Trans. Eric Prenowitz. Chicago: U of Chicago P, 1996.
- 'The Law of Genre.' *Glyph* 7 (1980).
- 'Sendoffs.' *Reading the Archive: On Texts and Institutions*. Ed. E.S. Burt and Janie Vanpée. *Yale French Studies* 77 (1990): 7–43.
DES and Welsh Office. *National Curriculum History Working Group Final Report*. HMSO: 1990.
D'haen, Theo, and Hans Bertens, ed. *British Postmodern Fiction*. Postmodern Studies 7. Amsterdam and Atlanta: Rodopi, 1993.
- *Liminal Postmodernisms: The Postmodern, the (Post-)Colonial, and the (Post-)Feminist*. Postmodern Studies 8. Amsterdam and Atlanta: Rodopi, 1994.
Dickinson, A.K., and P.J. Lee, ed. *History Teaching and Historical Understanding*. London: Heinemann, 1978.
Dickinson, Peter. *Some Deaths before Dying*. Mysterious P, 1999.
Dirda, Michael. 'The Secret History of the World.' *Washington Post Book World* 29.44 (29 Oct. 1989): 1–2.
- 'The Secret Masters of the World.' *Washington Post Book World* 22.38 (20 Sept. 1992): 1, 14.
Djordjevic, Ivana. 'In the Footsteps of Giambattista Vico: Patterns of Signification in A. S. Byatt's *Possession*.' *Anglia* 115.1 (1997): 44–83.
Doyle, Sir Arthur Conan. 'The Adventure of the Musgrave Ritual.' *Strand Magazine* 5 (May 1893): 479–89. Rpt. *The Complete Original Illustrated Sherlock Holmes. Reproduced from the original publication in the Strand Magazine with the classic illustrations by Sidney Paget*. Secaucus, NJ: Castle Books, 1976. 248–58.
Drabble, Margaret. *The Gates of Ivory*. London and New York: Viking, 1991.
- *A Natural Curiosity*. London and New York: Viking, 1989.

- *The Peppered Moth*. London: Viking, 2001.
- *The Radiant Way*. London: Weidenfeld and Nicholson, 1987.
- *The Witch of Exmoor*. London: Viking, 1996.
- 'A Woman's Place Is in the Reference Books.' *Daily Telegraph* 12 Feb. 2000: 5.

DuMaurier, Daphne. *The House on the Strand*. New York: Doubleday, 1969.

Duncker, Patricia. *Hallucinating Foucault*. Hopewell, NJ: Ecco P, 1996.

Eagleton, Terry, Fredric Jameson, and Edward W. Said. *Nationalism, Colonialism, and Literature*. Minneapolis: U of Minnesota P, 1990.

Eco, Umberto. *Foucault's Pendulum*. London: Secker and Warburg, 1989.
- *The Name of the Rose (Il nome della rosa* [1980]). Trans. William Weaver. London: Secker and Warburg, 1983.
- 'Narrative Structures in Fleming.' 1966. Rpt. *The Role of the the Reader: Explorations in the Semiotics of Texts*. Bloomington: Indiana UP, 1979. 144–79.
- *Postscript to the Name of the Rose*. 1983. *The Name of the Rose*. San Diego: Harcourt, Brace, Jovanovich, 1984. 503–36.
- 'Travels in Hyper-Reality.' *Faith in Fakes: Essays*. London: Secker and Warburg, 1986. 1–58.

Eco, Umberto, and Thomas Sebeok, ed. *The Sign of Three: Dupin, Holmes, Peirce*. Bloomington: Indiana UP, 1983.

Elam, Diane. *Romancing the Postmodern*. London: Routledge, 1992.

Elias, Amy J. 'Defining Spatial History in Postmodernist Historical Novels.' *Narrative Turns and Minor Genres in Postmodernism*. Ed. Theo D'haen and Hans Bertens. Postmodern Studies 11. Amsterdam: Rodopi, 1995. 105–14.
- 'Meta-*mimesis*? The Problem of British Postmodern Realism.' *British Postmodern Fiction*. Ed. Theo D'haen and Hans Bertens. Postmodern Studies 7. Amsterdam: Rodopi, 1993. 9–31.
- 'The Pynchon Intertext of *Lemprière's Dictionary*.' *Pynchon Notes* 40–1 (1997): 28–40.

Eliot, George. *Middlemarch: A Study of Provincial Life*. 1871–2. Ed. Rosemary Ashton. Penguin Classics. Harmondsworth: Penguin Books, 1994.

Ellis, Alice Thomas. *Fairy Tale*. London: Viking Penguin, 1996.

Ermarth, Elizabeth Deeds. *Sequel to History: Postmodernism and the Crisis of Representational Time*. Princeton: Princeton UP, 1992.

Farrell, J.G. *The Seige of Krishnapur*. London: Weidenfeld and Nicolson, 1973.

Felski, Rita. *The Gender of Modernity*. Cambridge, MA: Harvard UP, 1995.

Ferguson, Niall. *The Pity of War*. New York: Basic Books, 1999.

Ferguson, Niall, ed. *Virtual History: Alternatives and Counterfactuals*. New York: Basic Books, 1999.

Finney, Brian. 'Peter Ackroyd, Postmodernist Play, and *Chatterton*.' *Twentieth-Century Literature* 38 (1992): 240–61.

Fleishman, Avrom. *The English Historical Novel.* Baltimore: Johns Hopkins UP, 1971.

Forster, E.M. *Aspects of the Novel.* New York: Harcourt, Brace and World, 1927.

Foucault, Michel. *The Archaeology of Knowledge.* 1971. Trans. A.M. Sheridan Smith. New York: Pantheon Books, 1985.

– *Power/Knowledge: Selected Interviews and Other Writings 1972–1977.* New York: Pantheon Books, 1977.

Fowles, John. *The Magus.* Boston: Little Brown, 1965.

Fraser, George MacDonald. *Flashman: from the Flashman Papers 1839–1842.* Edited and arranged by George MacDonald Fraser. London: Herbert Jenkins, 1969.

Frayn, Michael. *Head-long.* London: Faber and Faber, 1999.

Gamerman, Amy. 'Fiction's Time Traveler Goes Medieval.' *Wall Street Journal* 5 Dec. 1995: A16.

Gasiorek, Andrzej. *Post-War British Fiction: Realism and After.* London: Edward Arnold, 1995.

Ghosh, Amitav. *The Calcutta Chromosome: A Novel of Fevers, Delirium, and Discovery.* New York: Avon Books, 1995.

– *In an Antique Land.* London: Granta Books, 1992.

– *The Shadow Lines.* Delhi: Ravi Dayal, 1988.

Gibson, Jeremy, and Julian Wolfreys. *Peter Ackroyd: The Ludic and Labyrinthine Text.* London: Macmillan: 2000.

Goddard, Robert. *Caught in the Light.* London: Bantam, 1998.

– *Past Caring.* London: Robert Hale, 1986.

González Echevarría, Roberto. *Myth and Archive: A Theory of Latin American Narrative.* Cambridge: Cambridge UP, 1990.

Gorra, Michael. *After Empire: Scott, Naipaul, Rushdie.* U of Chicago P, 1997.

– 'Introductions for Julian Barnes and A.S. Byatt.' 92nd St. Y, New York City, 20 May 1997.

Grady, James. *Six Days of the Condor.* New York: Norton, 1974.

Grafton, Anthony. *The Footnote: A Curious History.* 1997. Cambridge: Harvard UP, 1999.

Gray, Alasdair. *Poor Things.* London: Bloomsbury, 1992.

Green, Martin. *The Adventurous Male: Chapters in the History of the White Male Mind.* University Park, PA: Pennsylvania State UP, 1993.

– *Dreams of Adventure and Deeds of Empire.* New York: Basic Books, 1979.

– *The English Novel in the Twentieth Century: [The Doom of Empire].* London: Routledge & Kegan Paul, 1984.

– *Seven Types of Adventure Tale: An Etiology of a Major Genre.* University Park: Pennsylvania State UP, 1991.

Greetham, D.C. *Textual Scholarship: An Introduction*. New York: Garland, 1992.

Grenier, Richard. 'On the Trail of America's Paranoid Class: Oliver Stone's *JFK*.' *National Interest* 27 (1992): 76–84.

Groden, Michael, and Martin Kreiswirth, ed. *The Johns Hopkins Guide to Literary Theory and Criticism*. Baltimore: Johns Hopkins UP, 1994.

Haggard, Rider. *She*. 1887. The World's Classics. Ed. Daniel Karlin. Oxford UP, 1991.

Hall, Adam. *The Berlin Memorandum*. London: Collins, 1965.

Hamilton, Ian. *Keepers of the Flame: Literary Estates and the Rise of Biography from Shakespeare to Plath*. London and Boston: Faber, 1994.

Hamner, Robert D. *Epic of the Dispossessed: Derk Walcott's* Omeros. Columbia: U of Missouri P, 1997.

Harris, Robert. *Archangel*. London: Hutchinson, 1998.

– *Enigma*. London: Hutchinson, 1995.

– *Fatherland*. London: Century Hutchinson, 1992.

– *Selling Hitler*. New York: Pantheon Books, 1986.

Hartley, L.P. *The Go-Between*. London: Hamish Hamilton, 1953.

Harvey, David. *The Condition of Postmodernity: An Enquiry into the Origins of Social Change*. Oxford: Basil Blackwell, 1989.

Hassan, Ihab. *The Dismemberment of Orpheus: Towards a Post-Modern Literature*. 2nd ed. Madison: U of Wisconsin P, 1982.

– *The Postmodern Turn*. Columbus: Ohio UP, 1987.

Hawthorne, Nathaniel. *The House of the Seven Gables*. 1851. Ed. Milton R. Stern. Harmondsworth: Penguin Books, 1965; rpt. 1981.

– *The Scarlet Letter*. 1850. Norton Critical Edition. Ed. Scully Bradley, Richard Croom Beatty, and E. Hudson Long. New York: W.W. Norton, 1962.

Hellenga, Robert. *The Sixteen Pleasures*. New York: Soho P, 1994.

Hewison, Robert. *Culture and Consensus: England, Art and Politics since 1940*. London: Methuen, 1995.

– *The Heritage Industry: Britain in a Climate of Decline*. London: Methuen, 1987.

Higdon, David Leon. *Shadows of the Past in Contemporary British Fiction*. London: Macmillan, 1984.

Hilberg, Raul. *The Politics of Memory: The Journey of a Holocaust Historian*. Chicago: Ivan R. Dee, 1996.

Hill, Susan. *The Mist in the Mirror*. London: Sinclair-Stevenson, 1992.

Himmelfarb, Gertrude. 'Telling It As You Like It: Postmodernist History and the Flight from Fact.' *The Postmodern History Reader*. Ed. Keith Jenkins. London: Routledge, 1997. 158–74.

Hobsbawm, Eric and Terence Ranger, ed. *The Invention of Tradition*. Cambridge: Cambridge UP, 1983.

Hofstadter, Richard. *The Paranoid Style in American Politics, and Other Essays*. New York: Knopf, 1965.

Hollinghurst, Alan. *The Swimming-Pool Library*. London: Chatto and Windus, 1988.

Holmes, Frederick M. 'The Historical Imagination and the Victorian Past: A.S. Byatt's *Possession*.' *English Studies in Canada* 20.3 (September 1994): 319–34.

– *The Historical Imagination: Postmodernism and the Treatment of the Past in Contemporary British Fiction*. English Literary Studies 73. Victoria, BC: U of Victoria Dept. of English, 1997.

Holquist, Michael. 'Whodunit and Other Questions: Metaphysical Detective Stories in Postwar Fiction.' 1972. Rpt. *The Poetics of Murder: Detective Fiction and Literary Theory*. Ed. Glenn W. Most and William W. Stowe. San Diego: Harcourt Brace Jovanovich, 1983. 149–74.

Hopkirk, Peter. *Quest for Kim: In Search of Kipling's Great Game*. London: John Murray, 1996.

Hosmer, Robert E., Jr, ed. *Contemporary British Women Writers: Narrative Strategies*. New York: St Martin's P, 1993.

Hotho-Jackson, Sabine. 'Literary History in Literature: An Aspect of the Contemporary Novel.' *Moderna Språk* 86.2 (1992): 113–19.

Hulbert, Ann. 'The Great Ventriloquist: A.S. Byatt's *Possession: A Romance*.' *Contemporary British Women Writers: Narrative Strategies*. Ed. Robert E. Hosmer, Jr. New York: St Martin's P, 1993. 55–65.

Hulme, Keri. *the bone people*. 1984. Baton Rouge: Louisiana State UP, 1985.

Hutcheon, Linda. *Narcissistic Narrative: The Metafictional Paradox*. Waterloo, ON: Wilfrid Laurier UP, 1980.

– *A Poetics of Postmodernism: History, Theory, Fiction*. London: Routledge, 1988.

– *The Politics of Postmodernism*. London: Routledge, 1989.

Huyssen, Andreas. *After the Great Divide: Modernism, Mass Culture, Postmodernism*. Bloomington: Indiana UP, 1986.

Irwin, John T. *The Mystery to a Solution: Poe, Borges, and the Analytic Detective Story*. Baltimore: Johns Hopkins UP, 1994.

Ishiguro, Kazuo. *The Remains of the Day*. London: Faber and Faber, 1989.

James, Henry. *The Aspern Papers*. *The New York Edition of the Novels and Tales of Henry James*, vol. 12. 1908. Rpt. New York: Augustus M. Kelley, 1971.

James, Lawrence. *The Rise and Fall of the British Empire*. New York: St Martin's P, 1994.

James, M.R. *Ghost Stories of an Antiquary*. 1904. Ed. E.F. Bleiler. New York: Dover, 1971.

James, P.D. *Devices and Desires*. London: Faber and Faber, 1989.

– *Original Sin*. London: Faber and Faber, 1994.

– *The Skull beneath the Skin*. London: Faber and Faber, 1982.

– *An Unsuitable Job for a Woman*. London: Faber and Faber, 1972.

Jameson, Fredric. *The Cultural Turn: Selected Writings on the Postmodern, 1983–1998*. London: Verso, 1998.

– *The Political Unconscious*. Ithaca: Cornell UP, 1981.

– *Postmodernism, or, The Cultural Logic of Late Capitalism*. Durham: Duke UP, 1991.

JanMohamed, Abdul, and David Lloyd. 'Introduction: Toward a Theory of Minority Discourse.' *Cultural Critique* 6 (Spring 1987): 5–12.

Jones, Nicolette. 'No Bridles for a Heretic: Stevie Davies Digs into the Passions of the Past, and Comes up with Fiction to Treasure.' *Independent* 15 May 1999: 11.

Jones, Nigel. 'Oh Yes, This Man Is Most Definitely John Major's Favourite Author.' *Guardian* 9 Dec. 1996: T10.

Kaplan, Alice. 'Working in the Archives.' *Reading the Archive: On Texts and Institutions*. Ed. E.S. Burt and Janie Vanpée. *Yale French Studies* 77 (1990): 103–16.

Keneally, Thomas. *Schindler's Ark*. London: Hodder and Stoughton, 1982.

Kermode, Frank. 'Novel and Narrative.' 1974. Rpt. *The Poetics of Murder: Detective Fiction and Literary Theory*. Ed. Glenn W. Most and William W. Stowe. San Diego: Harcourt Brace Jovanovich, 1983. 175–96.

– *The Sense of an Ending: Studies in the Theory Fiction*. Oxford: Oxford UP, 1966.

Kerr, David. 'History and Economic Awareness in the National Curriculum: Exploring the Issues.' *Teaching History* 59 (April 1990): 9–15.

Kipling, Rudyard. *Kim*. 1901. Ed. Edward Said. Harmondsworth: Penguin, 1987.

Kitson Clark, G. *Guide for Research Students Working on Historical Subjects*. Cambridge: Cambridge UP, 1958.

Kolbert, Elizabeth. 'Wandering through History: Interview with Peter Ackroyd.' *New York Times Book Review* 19 Jan. 1986: 3.

Krieger, Leonard. *Ranke and the Meaning of History*. Chicago: U of Chicago P, 1977.

Krips, Valerie. *The Presence of the Past: Memory, Heritage, and Childhood in Postwar Britain*. New York: Garland, 2000.

Kyle, Keith. *Suez*. New York: St Martin's P, 1991.

LaCapra, Dominick. *History and Criticism*. Ithaca: Cornell UP, 1985.

Landow, George. 'History, His Story, and Stories in Graham Swift's *Waterland*.' *Studies in the Literary Imagination* 23.2 (Fall 1990): 197–211.

Lane, Christopher. *The Ruling Passion: British Colonial Allegory and the Paradox of Homosexual Desire.* Durham, NC: Duke UP, 1995.

Lang, Andrew. 'The Supernatural in Fiction.' *Adventures among Books.* London: Longmans, 1905. 273–80.

Larkin, Philip. *Collected Poems.* 1988. Ed Anthony Thwaite. New York: Farrar, Straus, Giroux, 1989.

Le Carré, John. *The Spy Who Came in from the Cold.* London: Victor Gollancz, 1963.

– *Tinker, Tailor, Soldier, Spy.* London: Hodder and Stoughton, 1974.

Lee, Alison. *Realism and Power: Postmodern British Fiction.* London: Routledge, 1990.

Lee, Peter, John Slater, Paddy Walsh, John Smith, and Denis Shemilt. *The Aims of School History: The National Curriculum and Beyond.* The London File. Papers from the Institute of Education, the University of London. London: Tufnell P, 1992.

Leivick, Laura. 'Following the Ghost of Dickens.' *New York Times* 22 Dec. 1991: sect. 6, 27.

Lemprière, John. *Classical Dictionary of Proper Names Mentioned in Ancient Authors, with a Chronological Table.* 1788. Ed. F.A. Wright. London: Routledge and Kegan Paul, 1949.

Lessing, Doris. *Canopus in Argo: Archives. Documents Relating to the Sentimental Agents in the Volyen Empire.* London: Cape, 1983.

– *Canopus in Argo: Archives. The Making of the Representative for Planet 8.* London: Cape, 1982.

– *Canopus in Argo: Archives. The Marriages between Zones Three, Four, and Five (as narrated by the chroniclers of zone three).* London: Cape, 1980.

– *Canopus in Argo: Archives. Shikasta: re, colonised planet 5: personal, psychological, historical documents relating to visit by Johor (George Sherban) emissary (grade 9) 87th of the period of the last days.* London: Cape, 1979.

– *Canopus in Argo: Archives. The Sirian Experiments: the report by Ambien II, of the five.* London: Cape, 1981.

– *The Golden Notebook.* London: Michael Joseph, 1962.

Little, Vivienne. 'A National Curriculum in History: A Very Contentious Issue.' *British Journal of Educational Studies* 38.4 (November 1990): 319–34.

Lively, Penelope. *According to Mark.* London: Heinemann, 1984.

– *The Ghost of Thomas Kempe.* London: Heinemann, 1973.

– *Moon Tiger.* London: Andre Deutsch, 1987.

– *The Road to Lichfield.* London: Heinemann, 1977.

Lodge, David. *The British Museum Is Falling Down.* London: MacGibbon and Keo, 1965.

– *Changing Places: A Tale of Two Campuses*. London: Secker and Warburg, 1975.
– *Nice Work*. London: Secker and Warburg, 1988.
– *Small World: An Academic Romance*. London: Secker and Warburg, 1984.
Lovecraft, H.P. 'The Call of Cthulhu.' 1928. *Best Supernatural Stories of H.P. Lovecraft*. Ed. August Derleth. Cleveland and New York: World Publishing Co., 1945. 130–59.
– 'The Dunwich Horror.' 1929. *Best Supernatural Stories of H.P. Lovecraft*. Ed. A. Derleth. 160–202.
– 'The Haunter of the Dark.' 1936. *Best Supernatural Stories of H.P. Lovecraft*. Ed. A. Derleth. 98–120.
– *Supernatural Horror in Literature*. Intro. August Derleth. New York: Ben Abramson, 1945.
Lowenthal, David. *The Past Is a Foreign Country*. Cambridge: Cambridge UP, 1985.
– *Possessed by the Past: The Heritage Crusade and the Spoils of History*. New York: Free P, 1996.
Lukács, Georg. *The Historical Novel*. 1962. Trans. Hannah and Stanley Mitchell. Lincoln: U of Nebraska P, 1983.
Lyotard, Jean-François. *The Postmodern Condition: A Report on Knowledge*. Trans. Geoff Bennington and Brian Massumi. Minneapolis: U of Minnesota P, 1984.
– 'Re-writing Modernity.' *Sub-Stance* 54 (1987): 3–9.
Magee, David. *Infinite Riches: The Adventures of a Rare Book Dealer*. Paul S. Eriksson, 1973.
Malamud, Bernard. 'The Last Mohican.' 1958. *The Complete Stories*. Ed. Robert Giroux. New York: Farrar, Straus and Giroux, 1997. 200–20.
Malone, Michael. *Foolscap*. Boston: Little Brown, 1991.
Manlove, Colin. *The Fantasy Literature of England*. London: Macmillan; New York: St Martin's P, 1999.
Mansfield, Paul. 'Interview: Passage to Cambodia.' *Independent* 4 Oct. 1991: Arts, 15.
Marius, Richard. *A Short Guide to Writing about History*. Glenview, IL: Scott, Forsman, 1989.
Mars-Jones, Adam. *The Waters of Thirst*. London: Faber and Faber, 1993.
Martin, Raymond. 'Forum: Raymond Martin, Joan W. Scott, and Ushing Strout on Telling the Truth about History.' *History and Theory* 34 (1995): 320–9.
Massie, Alan. *The Novel Today: A Critical Guide to the British Novel 1970–1989*. London: Longman, 1990.
McEwan, Ian. *The Ploughman's Lunch*. London: Methuen, 1985.

McEwan, Neil. *Perspective in British Historical Fiction Today.* London: Macmillan, 1987.

McHale, Brian. *Constructing Postmodernism.* London: Routledge, 1992.

– *Postmodernist Fiction.* NY and London: Methuen, 1987.

McKeon, Michael. *The Origins of the English Novel 1600–1740.* Baltimore: Johns Hopkins UP, 1987.

Merivale, Patricia, and Susan Elizabeth Sweeney. 'The Game's Afoot: On the Trail of the Metaphysical Detective Story.' *Detecting Texts: The Metaphysical Detective Story from Poe to Postmodernism.* Ed. Patricia Merivale and Susan Elizabeth Sweeney. Philadelphia: U of Pennsylvania P, 1999: 1–24.

Merriman, Nick. 'Understanding Heritage.' *Journal of Material Culture* 1 (1996): 377–85.

Miller, J. Hillis. 'Narrative and History.' *English Literary History* 41 (1974): 455–73.

Miller, Walter M., Jr. *A Canticle for Leibowitz.* 1960. Intro. Norman Spinrad. Boston: Gregg P, 1975.

Monaghan, David. *The Falklands War: Myth and Countermyth.* London: Macmillan, 1998; New York: St Martin's, 1998.

Morgan, Kenneth O. *The People's Peace: British History 1945–1989.* New York: Oxford UP, 1990.

Morley, Christopher. 'Preface.' *Boswell's London Journal.* Ed. F.A. Pottle. New York: McGraw-Hill, 1950.

Morris, Steve. Interview with Peter Ackroyd. 'Word Up.' *The Buzz Magazine* (1987): 74–5. Peter Ackroyd papers, box 7, Uncat. Ms. Vault 706, Beinecke Library, Yale University.

Morrison, Toni. *Beloved.* New York: Alfred A. Knopf, 1987.

Moseley, Merritt. *Understanding Kingsley Amis.* Columbia: U of South Carolina P, 1993.

Motion, Andrew. *Philip Larkin: A Writer's Life.* New York: Farrar, Straus and Giroux, 1993.

Mukherjee, Bharati. *The Holder of the World.* London: Chatto and Windus, 1993.

Namier, Lewis Bernstein. *Personalities and Powers.* London: Hamish Hamilton, 1955.

Nash, Gary B., Charlotte Crabtree, and Ross E. Dunn. *History on Trial: Culture Wars and the Teaching of the Past.* New York: Knopf, 1998.

Neville, Katherine. *The Eight.* New York: Ballantine, 1988.

– *The Magic Circle.* New York: Ballantine, 1998.

Newby, P.H. *Something to Answer For.* London: Faber and Faber, 1968.

Nicolson, Marjorie. 'The Professor and the Detective.' 1946. Rpt. *The Art of the*

Mystery Story: A Collection of Critical Essays. Ed. Howard Haycraft. New York: Simon and Schuster, 1946: 110–27.

Nora, Pierre. 'General Introduction: Between Memory and History.' In *Realms of Memory: Rethinking the French Past.* Under the direction of Pierre Nora; ed. Lawrence D. Kritzman; trans. Arthur Goldhammer. Vol. 1. New York: Columbia UP, 1996–8: 1–20.

Norfolk, Lawrence. 'The Honesty of Pagemonsters.' *TLS* 2 Sept. 1994: 6.

– *Lemprière's Dictionary.* London: Sinclair-Stevenson, 1991.

– *Lemprière's Dictionary.* Rev. New York: Harmony Books, 1992.

O'Brien, Flann. *The Dalkey Archive.* London: MacGibbon & Kee, 1964.

Olábarri, Ignacio. '"New" New History: A *Longue Durée* Structure.' Trans. Ruth Breeze and Karen Sanders. *History and Theory* 34.4 (1995): 1–29.

Oman, Sir Charles William Chadwick. *On the Writing of History.* London: Methuen, 1939.

Onega, Susana. 'British Historiographic Metafiction.' *Metafiction.* Ed. Mark Currie. London: Longman, 1995. 92–103.

– 'Interview with Peter Ackroyd.' *Twentieth Century Literature* 42.2 (1996): 208–20.

– *Metafiction and Myth in the Novels of Peter Ackroyd.* European Studies in the Humanities. Columbia, SC: Camden House, 1999.

– *Peter Ackroyd.* Writers and Their Work. Plymouth: Northcote House in association with the British Council, 1998.

Orr, Linda. 'The Revenge of Literature: A History of History.' *Studies in Historical Change.* Ed. Ralph Cohen. Charlottesville: UP of Virginia, 1992. 84–108.

Orwell, George. *Nineteen Eighty-Four.* 1949. Ed. Bernard Crick. Oxford: Clarendon P, 1984.

Osborne, John. *The Entertainer: A Play.* New York: Criterion Books, 1958.

Palliser, Charles. *The Quincunx.* London: Canongate Publishing, 1989.

– *The Unburied.* London: Phoenix House, 1999.

Palmer, Jerry. *Potboilers: Methods, Concepts, and Case Studies in Popular Fiction.* London: Routledge, 1991.

– *Thrillers: Genesis and Structure of a Popular Genre.* London: Edward Arnold, 1978.

Parks, Tim. 'Sentimental Education.' Rev. of Vikram Seth, *An Equal Music. New York Review of Books* 46.12 (15 July 1999): 20–3.

Pearce, Philippa. *Tom's Midnight Garden.* Philadelphia: J.B. Lippincott, 1958.

Pears, Iain. *An Instance of the Fingerpost.* London: Jonathan Cape, 1997.

Perkins, David. *Is Literary History Possible?* Baltimore: Johns Hopkins UP, 1992.

Phillips, Robert. 'National Curriculum History and Teacher Autonomy: The Major Challenge.' *Teaching History* 65 (October 1991): 21–4.

Plumb, J.H. *The Making of an Historian: The Collected Essays of J.H. Plumb.* London: Harvester-Wheatsheaf, 1988.

Poole, Steven. 'The Horn of Plenty.' *Guardian* 26 April 1996: 17.

Poovey, Mary. 'Ideology and *The Mysteries of Udolpho*.' *Criticism* 21 (1979): 307–30.

– *Making a Social Body: British Cultural Formation 1830–1864.* Chicago: U of Chicago P, 1995.

Porter, Dennis. *The Pursuit of Crime: Art and Ideology in Detective Fiction.* New Haven: Yale UP, 1981.

Prag, John, and Richard Neave. *Making Faces: Using Forensic and Archaeological Evidence.* London: British Museum P, 1997.

Proctor, Mortimer R. *The English University Novel.* Berkeley: U of California P, 1957.

Pullman, Philip. *The Amber Spyglass.* New York: Knopf, 2000.

– *Northern Lights.* 1995. Rpt. *The Golden Compass.* New York: Knopf, 1996.

– *The Subtle Knife.* New York: Knopf, 1997.

Punter, David. *The Literature of Terror: A History of Gothic Fictions from 1765 to the Present Day.* London: Longman, 1980.

Pynchon, Thomas. *The Crying of Lot 49.* Philadelphia: Lippincott, 1966.

Pyrhönen, Heta. *Mayhem and Murder: Narrative and Moral Problems in the Detective Story.* Toronto: U of Toronto P, 1999.

– *Murder from an Academic Angle: An Introduction to the Study of the Detective Narrative.* Columbia, SC: Camden House, 1994.

Quayson, Ato. *Postcolonialism: Theory, Practice or Process?* Oxford: Polity P, 2000.

Raban, Jonathan. *God, Man, and Mrs. Thatcher.* Counterblasts. London: Chatto and Windus, 1989.

Rabinovitch, Dina, and Anthony Quinn. 'The Booker: Two for the Price of One.' *Independent* 15 Oct. 1992: Arts, 17.

Rabinovitz, Rubin. *The Reaction against Experiment in the English Novel, 1950–1960.* New York: Columbia UP, 1967.

Raine, Craig. *History: The Home Movie.* Harmondsworth: Penguin, 1994.

Ramazani, Jahan. 'The Wound of History: Walcott's *Omeros* and the Postcolonial Poetics of Affliction.' *PMLA* 112.3 (May 1997): 405–17.

Rawson, Claude. Rev. of *First Light. TLS* 4491 (28 April–4 May 1989): 453.

Reiman, Donald H. *The Study of Modern Manuscripts: Public, Confidential, and Private.* Baltimore: Johns Hopkins UP, 1993.

Reynolds, L.D., and N.G. Wilson. *Scribes and Scholars: A Guide to the Trans-*

mission of Greek and Latin Literature. 1968. 3rd edition. London: Oxford UP, 1991.

Rhys, Jean. *The Wide Sargasso Sea.* 1966. Norton Critical Edition. Ed. Judith L. Raiskin. New York: W.W. Norton, 1999.

Richards, Thomas. *The Imperial Archive: Knowledge and the Fantasy of Empire.* London: Verso, 1993.

Ricoeur, Paul. *Time and Narrative.* Trans. Kathleen McLaughlin and David Pellauer. Chicago: U of Chicago P, 1984.

Roberts, James Hall. *The Q Document.* New York: William Morrow, 1964.

Roberts, Keith. *Pavane.* 1966. Rpt. Ace, 1968.

Robinson, Sally. *Engendering the Subject: Gender and Self-Representation in Contemporary Women's Fiction.* Albany: SUNY P, 1991.

Rolfe, Frederick [Fr. Rolfe, Baron Corvo]. *Nicholas Crabbe, or the One and the Many.* Intro. Cecil Woolf. London: Chatto and Windus, 1958.

Romanowski, William D. 'Oliver Stone's *JFK*: Commercial Filmmaking, Cultural History, and Conflict.' *Journal of Popular Film and Television* 21.2 (1993): 63–71.

Rostron, Tim. 'A Clever Plot to Delight the PM: The Intricate Mysteries of Robbert Goddard.' *Daily Telegraph* 10 Apr. 1995: 21.

Rubenstein, Philip, and Warren Taylor. 'Teaching about the Holocaust in the National Curriculum.' *British Journal of Holocaust Education* 1.1 (1992): 47–54.

Rushdie, Salman. *Haroun and the Sea of Stories.* London: Granta Books, 1990.

– *Midnight's Children.* London: Jonathan Cape, 1980.

– 'Outside the Whale.' 1984. *Imaginary Homelands: Essays and Criticism 1981–1991.* London: Granta Books, in association with Penguin Books, 1991. 87–101.

Russo, Richard. *Straight Man.* New York: Random House, 1997.

Said, Edward W. *Culture and Imperialism.* New York: Alfred A. Knopf, 1993.

– *Orientalism.* New York: Pantheon Books, 1978.

Samuel, Raphael. *Theatres of Memory.* Vol. 1. *Past and Present in Contemporary Culture.* London: Verso, 1994.

– *Island Stories: Unravelling Britain. Theatres of Memory.* Vol. 2. Ed. Alison Light with Sally Alexander and Gareth Stedman Jones. London: Verso, 1998.

Scanlan, Margaret. *Traces of Another Time: History and Politics in Postwar British Fiction.* Princeton: Princeton UP, 1990.

Schad, John. 'The End of the End of History: Graham Swift's *Waterland*.' *Modern Fiction Studies* 38.4 (Winter 1992): 911–25.

Schmitt, Cannon. *Alien Nation: Nineteenth-Century Gothic Fictions and English Nationality.* Philadelphia: U of Pennsylvania P, 1997.

Scholes, Robert. *Fabulation and Metafiction*. Urbana: U of Illinois P, 1979.

Scott, James B. 'Parrots as Paradigms: Infinite Deferral of Meaning in "Flaubert's Parrot."' *Ariel* 21.3 (July 1990): 57–68.

Scott, Sir Walter. *Waverly; or 'Tis Sixty Years Since*. 1814, 1830. Ed. Claire Lamont. The World's Classics. Oxford: Oxford UP, 1986.

Sedgwick, Eve Kosofsky. *Between Men: English Literature and Male Homosocial Desire*. New York: Columbia UP, 1985.

– *The Coherence of Gothic Conventions*. 1980. Rpt. London and New York: Methuen, 1986.

Seth, Vikram. *An Equal Music*. New York: Broadway Books, 1999.

– *A Suitable Boy*. London: Orion, 1993.

Shields, Carol. *Swann*. Toronto. Stoddard Publishing Co., 1987.

Shiller, Dana. 'The Redemptive Past in the Neo-Victorian Novel.' *Studies in the Novel* 29.4 (Winter 1997): 538–60.

Shils, Edward. 'The Intellectuals. I. Great Britain.' *Encounter* 4.4 (April 1955): 5–16.

– *The Torment of Secrecy: The Background and Consequences of American Security Policies*. Glencoe, IL: Free P, 1956.

Shinn, Thelma J. '"What's in a Word?" Possessing A.S. Byatt's Meronymic Novel.' *Papers on Language and Literature* 31.2 (Spring 1995): 164–83.

Sidney, Philip. *An Apology for Poetry*. c. 1579. Ed. Forrest G. Robinson. New York: Macmillan / Library of Liberal Arts, 1970. Rpt. 1987.

Sinfield, Alan. *Literature, Politics, and Culture in Postwar Britain*. Berkeley: U of California P, 1989.

Skinner, Quentin, ed. *The Return of Grand Theory in the Human Sciences*. Cambridge: Cambridge UP, 1985.

Smiley, Jane. *Moo*. New York: Alfred A. Knopf, 1995.

Smith, Zadie. *White Teeth*. London: Hamish Hamilton, 2000.

Sollers, Werner, ed. *The Return of Thematic Criticism*. Cambridge, MA: Harvard UP, 1993.

Spark, Muriel. *The Ballad of Peckham Rye*. London: Macmillan, 1960.

Spenser, Edmund. *The Faerie Queene*. 1596. Ed. A.C. Hamilton. London: Longman, 1977.

Spilka, Mark, and Caroline McCracken-Flesher, ed. *Why the Novel Matters: A Postmodern Perplex*. Bloomington: Indiana UP, 1990.

Spivak, Gayatri Chakravorty. *A Critique of Postcolonial Reason: Toward a History of the Vanishing Present*. Cambridge, MA: Harvard UP, 1999.

– *In Other Worlds: Essays in Cultural Politics*. New York: Methuen, 1987.

Stoppard, Tom. *Arcadia*. London: Faber and Faber, 1993.

– *Indian Ink*. London: Faber and Faber, 1995.

Stratton, Jon. *Writing Sites: A Genealogy of the Postmodern World.* London: Harvester/Wheatsheaf, 1990.

Streitfeld, David. 'Book Report.' *Washington Post Book World* 20 Sept. 1992: 15.

Sturken, Marita. 'Reenactment, Fantasy, and the Paranoia of History: Oliver Stone's Docudramas.' *History and Theory* 36.4 (1997): 64–79.

Suleri, Sara. *The Rhetoric of English India.* U of Chicago P, 1992.

Sutherland, John. *Fiction and the Fiction Industry.* London: Athlone, 1978.

Sweeney, Susan Elizabeth. 'Locked Rooms: Detective Fiction, Narrative Theory, and Self-Reflexivity.' *The Cunning Craft.* Ed. Ronald G. Walker and June M. Frazer. Macomb: Western Illinois P, 1990. 1–14.

– '"Subject-Cases" and "Book-Cases": Impostures and Forgeries from Poe to Auster.' *Detecting Texts: The Metaphysical Detective Story from Poe to Postmodernism.* Ed. Patricia Merivale and Susan Elizabeth Sweeney. Philadelphia: U of Pennsylvania P, 1999. 247–69.

Sweet, Matthew. 'Goodbye to All These.' *Independent* 27 June 1999: Culture, 3.

Swift, Graham. *Ever After.* London: Picador, 1992.

– *Waterland.* London: Heinemann, 1983.

Swinden, Patrick. *The English Novel of History and Society, 1940–80: Richard Hughes, Henry Green, Anthony Powell, Angus Wilson, Kingsley Amis, V.S. Naipaul.* London: Macmillan, 1984.

Taylor, D.J. *After the War: The Novel and English Society since 1945.* London: Chatto and Windus, 1993.

Tey, Josephine [Elizabeth MacKintosh]. *The Daughter of Time.* 1951. New York: Macmillan, 1952.

Theroux, Paul. *The Kingdom by the Sea: A Journey around Great Britain.* Boston: Houghton Mifflin, 1983.

Thompson, Jon. *Fiction, Crime, and Empire: Clues to Modernity and Postmodernism.* Urbana and Chicago: U of Illinois P, 1993.

Todd, Richard. *Consuming Fictions: The Booker Prize and Fiction in Britain Today.* London: Bloomsbury, 1996.

– 'Narrative Trickery and Performative Historiography: Fictional Representation of National Identity in Graham Swift, Peter Carey, and Mordecai Richler.' *Magical Realism: Theory, History, Community.* Ed. Lois Parkinson Zamora and Wendy B. Faris. Durham: Duke UP, 1995. 305–28.

Tracy, Ann B. *The Gothic Novel 1790–1830: Plot Summaries and Index to Motifs.* Lexington: UP of Kentucky, 1981.

Trevor-Roper, Hugh. 'History: Professional and Lay.' Rpt. in *History and Imagination: Essays in Honor of H.R. Trevor-Roper.* Ed. Hugh Lloyd-Jones, Valerie Pearl, and Blair Worden. New York: Holmes and Meier Publishers, 1982. 1–14.

- 'History and Imagination.' Rpt. in *History and Imagination*. Ed. Lloyd-Jones, Pearl, and Worden. 356–69.
Unsworth, Barry. *The Hide*. London: Gollancz, 1970.
- *Losing Nelson*. London: Hamish Hamilton, 1999.
- *Mooncrankers Gift*. London: Allen Lane, 1973.
- *Morality Play*. London: Doubleday, 1995.
- *The Rage of the Vulture*. London: Granada, 1982.
- *Sacred Hunger*. London: Hamish Hamilton, 1992.
- *The Stone Virgin*. London: Hamish Hamilton, 1985.
- *Sugar and Rum*. London: Hamish Hamilton, 1988.
Voss, Paul J., and Marta L. Werner. 'Toward a Poetics of the Archive: Introduction.' In Voss and Werner, ed., *The Poetics of the Archive*. *Studies in the Literary Imagination* 32.1 (Spring 1999): i–viii.
- Ed. *Studies in the Literary Imagination* 32. 1 (Spring 1999).
Wachtel, Eleanor. *Writers and Company*. Toronto: Alfred A. Knopf Canada, 1993.
Walcott, Derek. *Omeros*. New York: Farrar, Straus and Giroux, 1990.
- 'Reflections on Omeros.' *The Poetics of Derek Walcott: Intertextual Perspectives*. Ed. Gregson Davis. *South Atlantic Quarterly* 96.2 (Spring 1997): 227–46.
Walder, Dennis. *Post-Colonial Literatures in English: History, Langage, Theory*. Oxford: Blackwell, 1998.
Wall, Alan. *Bless the Thief*. London: Secker and Warburg, 1997.
Warhol, Robyn R. *Gendered Interventions: Narrative Discourse in the Victorian Novel*. New Brunswick, NJ: Rutgers UP, 1989.
- 'Guilty Cravings: What Feminist Narratology Can Do for Cultural Studies.' *Narratologies: New Perspectives on Narrative Analysis*. Ed. David Herman. Columbus: Ohio State UP, 1999.
Warren, Robert Penn. *All the King's Men*. New York: Harcourt Brace, 1946.
Waterman, David F. *Disordered Bodies and Disrupted Borders: Representations of Resistance in Modern British Literature*. Lanham, MD: UP of America, 1999.
Watt, Stephen. 'Photographs in Biographies: Joyce, Voyeurism, and the "Real" Nora Barnacle.' *Photo-Textualities*. Ed. Marsha Bryant. Cranbury, NJ, and London: Associated UP, 1996. 57–72.
Waugh, Patricia. *Feminine Fictions: Revisiting the Postmodern*. New York: Routledge, 1989.
- *Metafiction: The Theory and Practice of Self-Conscious Fiction*. New York: Methuen, 1984.
- *Practicing Postmodernism, Reading Modernism*. London: Arnold, 1992.

Weiner, Martin J. *The Decline of the English Industrial Spirit, 1850–1980*. Cambridge: Cambridge UP, 1981.

White, Hayden. *The Content of the Form: Narrative Discourse and Historical Representation*. Baltimore: Johns Hopkins UP, 1987.

– *Figural Realism: Studies in the Mimesis Effect*. Baltimore: Johns Hopkins UP, 1999.

– '"Figuring the Nature of the Times Deceased": Literary Theory and Historical Writing.' *The Future of Literary Theory*. Ed. Ralph Cohen. London: Routledge, 1989. 19–43.

– *Metahistory: The Historical Imagination in Nineteenth-Century Europe*. Baltimore: Johns Hopkins UP, 1973.

– 'The Question of Narrative in Contemporary Historical Theory.' *History and Theory* 23.1 (1984): 1–33.

– *Tropics of Discourse: Essays in Cultural Criticism*. Baltimore: Johns Hopkins UP, 1978.

– 'The Value of Narrativity in the Representation of Reality.' *Critical Inquiry* 7 (1980): 5–27.

Whitney, Craig R. 'Inventing a World in Which Hitler Won.' *New York Times* 3 June 1992: C17.

Widdowson, Peter. 'The Anti-History Men: Malcolm Bradbury and David Lodge.' *Critical Quarterly* 26.4 (1984): 5–32.

Williams, Nigel. *Witchcraft*. London: Faber and Faber, 1987.

Williams, Patrick, and Laura Chrisman, ed. *Colonial Discourse and Post-Colonial Theory: A Reader*. New York: Columbia UP, 1994.

Williams, Raymond. *Marxism and Literature*. New York: Oxford UP, 1977.

Wilson, A.N. *Hearing Voices*. London: Sinclair Stevenson, 1995.

Winder, Robert. 'Unsworth before and after Hannibal.' *Independent* 7 Sept. 1996: Living, 3.

Windschuttle, Keith. *The Killing of History: How a Discipline Is Being Murdered by Literary Critics and Social Theorists*. 1994. Rev. ed. Paddington, Australia: Macleay P, 1996.

Winks, Robin W. 'Foreword.' *The Sleuth and the Scholar: Origins, Evolution, and Current Trends in Detective Fiction*. Ed. Barbara A. Rader and Howard G. Zettler. Westport, CT: Greenwood P, 1988. ix–xiii.

– *Modus Operandi: An Excursion into Detective Fiction*. Boston: David R. Godine, 1982.

Winks, Robin, ed. *The Historian as Detective: Essays on Evidence*. New York: Harper and Row, 1968.

Winterson, Jeanette. *The Power Book*. London: Jonathan Cape, 2000.

Wood, Michael. *Children of Silence: On Contemporary Fiction.* New York: Columbia UP, 1998.

– 'The Contemporary Novel.' *The Columbia History of the British Novel.* Ed. John Richetti. New York: Columbia UP, 1994. 966–87.

Woodward, C. Vann. *American Attitudes toward History.* Oxford: Clarendon P, 1955.

Woolf, Virginia. *Between the Acts.* New York: Harcourt Brace Jovanovich, 1941.

Worpole, Ken. *Reading by Numbers: Contemporary Publishing and Popular Fiction.* London: Comedia, 1984.

Wright, F.A. 'A Memoir of the Rev. John Lemprière, D.D.' *Lemprière's Classical Dictionary of Proper Names mentioned in Ancient Authors.* Ed. F.A. Wright. London: Routledge & Kegan Paul, 1949. vii–xi.

Wright, Patrick. *On Living in an Old Country: The National Past in Contemporary Britain.* London: Verso, 1985.

Yelin, Louise. 'Cultural Cartography: A.S. Byatt's *Possession* and the Politics of Victorian Studies.' *Victorian Newsletter* 81 (1992): 38–41.

Young, Robert C. *Colonial Desire: Hybridity in Theory, Culture, and Race.* New York: Routledge, 1995.

Index